D0147574

CAMBRIDGE STUDIES IN EARLY MODERN HISTORY

Editors

J. H. ELLIOTT OLWEN HUFTON

H. G. KOENIGSBERGER

Absolutism and Society in Seventeenth-Century France

CAMBRIDGE STUDIES IN EARLY MODERN HISTORY

Edited by Professor J. H. Elliott, The Institute for Advanced Study, Princeton, Professor Olwen Hufton, University of Reading, and Professor H. G. Koenigsberger, King's College, London

The idea of an 'early modern' period of European history from the fifteenth to the late eighteenth century is now widely accepted among historians. The purpose of the Cambridge Studies in Early Modern History is to publish monographs and studies which will illuminate the character of the period as a whole, and in particular focus attention on a dominant theme within it, the interplay of continuity and change as they are represented by the continuity of medieval ideas, political and social organisation, and by the impact of new ideas, new methods and new demands on the traditional structures.

The Old World and the New, 1492–1650
J. H. ELLIOTT

The Army of Flanders and the Spanish Road, 1567–1659: The Logistics of Spanish Victory and Defeat in the Low Countries Wars
GEOFFREY PARKER

Gunpowder and Galleys: Changing Technology and Mediterranean Warfare at Sea in the Sixteenth Century
JOHN FRANCIS GUILMARTIN JR

The State, War and Peace: Spanish Political Thought in the Renaissance 1516–1559
J. A. FERNANDEZ-SANTAMARIA

Calvinist Preaching and Iconoclasm in the Netherlands 1544–1569
PHYLLIS MACK CREW

Altopascio: A Study in Tuscan Society 1587–1784
FRANK McARDLE

The Kingdom of Valencia in the Seventeenth Century
JAMES CASEY

Filippo Strozzi and the Medici: Favor and Finance in Sixteenth-Century Florence and Rome
MELISSA MERIAM BULLARD

Rouen during the Wars of Religion
PHILIP BENEDICT

Neostoicism and the Early Modern State
GERHARD OESTREICH

The Emperor and his Chancellor: A Study of the Imperial Chancellery under Gattinara
JOHN M. HEADLEY

The Military Organization of a Renaissance State: Venice c. 1400 to 1617
M. E. MALLETT AND J. R. HALE

Prussian Society and the German Order: An Aristocratic Corporation in Crisis c. 1410 to 1466
MICHAEL BURLEIGH

Richelieu and Olivares
J. H. ELLIOTT

Society and Religious Toleration in Hamburg 1529–1819
JOACHIM WHALEY

Absolutism and Society in Seventeenth-Century France: State Power and Provincial Aristocracy in Languedoc
WILLIAM BEIK

Turning Swiss: Cities and Empire 1450–1550
THOMAS A. BRADY JR

The Duke of Anjou and the Politique Struggle during the Wars of Religion
MACK P. HOLT

Neighbourhood and Community in Paris 1740–1790
DAVID GARRIOCH

Renaissance and Revolt: Essays in the Intellectual and Social History of Early Modern France
J. H. M. SALMON

Louis XIV and the Origins of the Dutch War
PAUL SONNINO

The Princes of Orange: The Stadholders in the Dutch Republic
HERBERT H. ROWEN

The Changing Face of Empire: Charles V, Philip II and Habsburg Authority, 1551–1559
M. J. RODRIGUEZ-SALGADO

Absolutism and Society in Seventeenth-Century France

State Power and Provincial Aristocracy in Languedoc

WILLIAM BEIK
Northern Illinois University

CAMBRIDGE UNIVERSITY PRESS
Cambridge
New York New Rochelle
Melbourne Sydney

Published by the Press Syndicate of the University of Cambridge
The Pitt Building, Trumpington Street, Cambridge CB2 1RP
32 East 57th Street, New York, NY 10022, USA
10 Stamford Road, Oakleigh, Melbourne 3166, Australia

First published 1985
Reprinted 1987
First paperback edition 1988

Printed in Great Britain by the
University Press, Cambridge

Library of Congress catalogue card number: 84–9561

British Library cataloguing in publication data

Beik, William
Absolutism and society in seventeenth-century
France. – (Cambridge studies in early
modern history)
1. Despotism 2. Languedoc (France) –
Politics and government 3. France – Politics
and government – 17th century
I. Title
321.6′0944′8 DC611.L319

ISBN 0 521 26309 3 hard covers
ISBN 0 521 36782 4 paperback

UP

To P.H.B. and D.H.B.
who started it all on the rue d'Assas

Contents

Tables

Figures

Preface

This book is the product of many years' effort to grasp the special quality of government in seventeenth-century France and its relationship to the social system. The seventeenth century saw fascinating shifts away from a France of particularist dissidence towards a more centralized monarchy, but the essence of the change has not yet been successfully captured by historians. Standard generalizations like the decline of provincial liberties, the rise of personal government, the domestication of the nobility, and the use of a regime of *commissaires* to supplant one of *officiers* are abstractions based on a certain conception of the modern state which fail to come to grips with the special nature of authority in the seventeenth century. More important, they fail to deal with the question of class interest.

I set out, therefore, to explore the anatomy of absolutism by studying the system in action in one manageable region, Languedoc. I discovered rapidly that I was pursuing two distinct and somewhat contradictory purposes. The first was descriptive: to recreate the atmosphere of the various governing institutions, whose distinctiveness would be an essential part of any understanding of the nature of the system. The second was analytical: to explore the collective rule of these individuals and agencies as part of a system with social implications. But description requires attention to specific cases, while analysis calls for comparative treatment and interaction. Doing both requires jumping back and forth from the actors to the action. It risks repetition and enforces selectivity at the expense of comprehensiveness. Trying to do 'too much' has been a problem from the start. No one is more aware than I of the history that might have been written of each corporate body, each town, each conflict; of the narrative and legal precision which has been sacrificed to the analysis; and especially of the second-hand nature of my presentation of the economic realities which underlay the political action. But I am confident that a suggestive attack on the whole will be more useful than an exhaustive survey of some of the parts, and hopeful that my suggestions can lead to a better understanding of the system of absolutism, which, to my knowledge, has not been studied as a whole in any province.

I also have the advantage of relying on two magnificent syntheses which continue to amaze me: the old-fashioned and absolutely authoritative political history of Ernest Roschach, the nineteenth-century archivist of Toulouse who based his work in turn on the notes of Dom Devic and Dom Vaissete, eighteenth-century Benedictine friars; and Emmanuel Le Roy Ladurie's massive *Paysans de Languedoc*, without which my ruling class would be living in a vacuum. The more I have learned, the more I have realized that these two men knew it all already.

This study began as a doctoral thesis directed by Franklin L. Ford at Harvard University. It was supported by a Woodrow Wilson Dissertation Fellowship which enabled me to spend the year 1966–7 in France, where I learned to appreciate the warmth of the people and landscape of the Midi and the riches of their archives. The thesis which was completed in 1969 concentrated on the Estates and the intendants. But it was already apparent that a full treatment of the subject would require more extensive investigation of the sovereign courts, the municipal governments, and the ministerial archives in Paris. This work was carried out over a number of later visits in the midst of other preoccupations. I am grateful to Northern Illinois University for support in purchasing microfilms in 1970, to the American Philosophical Society for a travel grant in the summer of 1971, and to the American Council of Learned Societies for a Grant-in-Aid in 1977 to complete the documentation. Northern Illinois University accorded me a sabbatical leave in the fall of 1977. In addition, I had a leave of absence in 1974–5 during which I was working on another project with the aid of a fellowship from the National Endowment for the Humanities and a fellowship from the Shelby Cullom Davis Center for Historical Studies at Princeton University. These last occasions were devoted to the study of popular revolts and popular culture, but they nevertheless afforded me the opportunity to tend to a number of details concerning Languedoc.

Like all historical writing, this study bears the mark of its time. The original project was conceived amidst outrage and protest against the Vietnam War; its research was carried out in a France seething with discontent on the eve of Mai 68. The critical stance of Boris Porchnev was especially welcome under these conditions, even as the diffusion of the magnificent *thèses* of Goubert and Le Roy Ladurie made us conscious of the 'Annales' approach. At the time the two schools – Marxist and Annales – seemed somehow allied in an effort to unmask the tyrannies of history 'from above'. I was too much of a novice then to be aware of the debates over 'orders', 'classes' and 'feudalism' which were raging at that very moment in the French academy. But this study matured in the aftermath of those debates as waves of Marxism, structuralism, and regional 'conjunctional' history washed over the Anglo-Saxon intellectual world. Like many of the heirs of the sixties, I moved from critical iconoclasm towards assimilation of these various traditions and from anti-war alienation to analysis of social systems, while in the meantime falling under the sway of the striking 'cultural' approaches associated with E. P. Thompson, Natalie Zemon Davis, and Maurice Agulhon. All of these influences lie behind the present work, and I like to think that some of the anger of its inception has been translated into critical analysis, borrowing some of the strengths of these schools without abandoning its original critical momentum.

In a project begun so long ago the list of those who have helped along the way is enormous. When I was just beginning, Irene Brown shared her expertise on Toulouse with me; and when I arrived there Janine Estèbe took the time to introduce me to the departmental archives. She probably does not remember that without her prodding I might still be sitting in the Bibliothèque Municipale. Professors at the University of Toulouse were hospitable far beyond the call of duty, notably Nicole Castan, Yves Castan, Henri Gilles, Frédéric Mauro, and Philippe Wolff. Jacques Sennelier and Jean-Luc Schreiner initiated a long, productive friendship by showing me the countryside south of Toulouse, and Robin Briggs shared his archival knowledge with me.

Through the years I have benefited from the attention of innumerable archivists and library personnel, many of them nameless. I am grateful to them all, and especially to Henri Blaquière, conservateur-en-chef, Robert Nadal, and Anne de Font-Reaulx in the Archives Départementales de la Haute-Garonne; to Odon de Saint-Blanquat, archiviste, and the indomitable Madame Maillard in the Archives Municipales de Toulouse; and to Jean Sablou, directeur, in the Archives Départementales du Gard. A number of experts read all or parts of this study, including Paul H. Beik, C. H. George, David Hunt, Sharon Kettering, J. Russell Major, Richard Price, Marvin Rosen, Harvey Smith, Gerald L. Soliday, and Charles Tilly. My colleagues in the history department at Northern Illinois were consistently supportive, especially Emory G. Evans, Stephen Kern, J. Carroll Moody, and Otto Olsen. I want to thank Cheryl Fuller, Elaine Kittelson, and Jean Schiller for so cheerfully and expertly coping with the typing, and Joseph Parot and Myrtie Podschwit whose help in Founders Library was indispensable. I also want to thank two of the editors of this series, Olwen Hufton and J. H. Elliott, whose comments have greatly improved the text. I am grateful to Mark and Marion Cummings, Claude Jego and Michel Thomas, Dolores Portis, and Terry Murphy for special kinds of encouragement, and to Nancy L. Roelker whose warm support through the years has meant a great deal to me.

Then there are those whose influence has been so pervasive that no simple thanks are adequate. My powers of analysis and my understanding of the real world have been immeasurably enriched by ongoing dialogue with three friends and historians: David Hunt, Larry Portis, and Paul Robinson. My sons Eric Kauffman and Carl Kauffman, who have had to grow up living with a Languedoc they have never seen, contributed endless patience, encouragement and good cheer. Finally there is Millie Beik who has taught me more than words can acknowledge and whose influence is alive on every page.

Abbreviations

A.A.E. France	Archives des Affaires Étrangères, Paris. Fonds France
A.D. Gard	Archives Départementales du Gard
A.D. Hér.	Archives Départementales de l'Hérault
A.D. H-G.	Archives Départementales de la Haute-Garonne
A.D. Lozère	Archives Départementales de la Lozère
A.M. Albi	Archives Municipales d'Albi
A.M. Mende	Archives Municipales de Mende
A.M. Mp	Archives Municipales de Montpellier
A.M. Nm	Archives Municipales de Nîmes
A.M. Tse	Archives Municipales de Toulouse
A.N.	Archives Nationales, Paris
Aubéry	Antoine Aubéry, ed., *Mémoires pour l'histoire du Cardinal duc de Richelieu*, 2 vols. Paris, 1660
B.M. Tse	Bibliothèque Municipale de Toulouse
B.N.	Bibliothèque Nationale, Paris
Clément	Jean-Baptiste Colbert, *Lettres, instructions et mémoires*, ed. Pierre Clément, 7 vols. Paris, 1861–73
Depping	Georges-Bernard Depping, ed., *Correspondance administrative sous le règne de Louis XIV*, 4 vols. Paris, 1850–5
Dubédat	Jean-Baptiste Dubédat, *Histoire du Parlement de Toulouse*, 2 vols. (Paris, 1885)
Le Pesant	Michel Le Pesant, *Arrêts du conseil du roi: règne de Louis XIV*. Paris, 1976
Lubl.	A. D. Lublinskaya, ed., *Lettres et mémoires adressés au Chancelier P. Séguier*. Moscow–Leningrad, 1966
Malenfant	Étienne de Malenfant, 'Mémoires, collections et remarques du palais', A.D. H-G. mss. 147–9
Mel. Col.	Bibliothèque Nationale, Paris, Cabinet des Manuscrits, Mélanges Colbert
ms. fr.	Bibliothèque Nationale, Paris, manuscrits français

Narbonne, Inventaire	Ville de Narbonne, *Inventaire des archives communales antérieures à 1790*, série BB, vol. I. Narbonne, 1872
nouv. acq.	Bibliothèque Nationale, Paris, manuscrits français, nouvelles acquisitions
Porchnev	Boris Porchnev, *Les Soulèvements populaires en France de 1623 à 1648*. Paris, 1963
P-V	Procès-verbaux of Estates of Languedoc
Roschach, vol. XIII	Dom Claude Devic and Dom J. Vaissete, *Histoire générale de Languedoc*, vol. XIII by Ernest Roschach. Toulouse, 1876
Roschach, vol. XIV	Dom Claude Devic and Dom J. Vaissete, *Histoire générale de Languedoc*, vol. XIV (documents) ed. Ernest Roschach. Toulouse, 1876
Rozoi	Barnabé Farmian de Rozoi, *Annales de la ville de Toulouse*, 4 vols. Paris, 1771–6

Languedoc in the seventeenth century

PART ONE

Introduction

I

Absolutism and class

This is a study of the exercise of power in one French province under absolutism. Two questions need answering. The first concerns Louis XIV's dramatic success in ruling France more effectively than his immediate predecessors. In the days when historians regarded the Fronde as a frivolous detour in the inexorable progress of royal power, it was possible to see the Sun King's effectiveness as simply an act of will – a crackdown or 'restoration of order'. But now that there is general agreement on the depth and seriousness of the social discontent which filled the period 1610 to 1661 with noble revolts, popular insurrections, and sporadic civil wars, it is much harder to see how the situation could have been righted by the initial actions of a twenty-three-year-old monarch.

All the textbooks report that Louis XIV subjugated the aristocracy by luring them to Versailles and tantalizing them with status shorn of power, while transferring their authority to bureaucratic agents. But could such deep-seated dissatisfaction really have turned so rapidly to placid indifference? And what about all the aristocrats out in the provinces? It almost seems as if a cast of turbulent frondeurs was swept from the stage around 1661 and replaced with a company of obsequious courtiers, yet the courtiers and the frondeurs were the same individuals.[1] If the sequel to the story is that after 1715 the aristocrats once again refused to be dominated and set about reviving claims for power and status similar to those which they had been making before 1661, the matter becomes doubly perplexing. Given the longer history of aristocratic rebellion before and aristocratic reaction after, the Louisquatorzian phase of order and obedience needs explanation.

The second question concerns the relationship between state and society or, more precisely, the meaning of absolutism as a stage in the evolution of French society from feudalism to capitalism. The absolute monarchy is usually placed at an advanced point on the road leading from a decentralized 'feudal' monarchy to a 'modern' state. Absolute monarchs are seen as

[1] This paradox has been pointed out by Theodore K. Rabb, *The Struggle for Stability in Early Modern Europe* (New York, 1975), pp. 64–5, who notes that the prince de Condé, 'still treasonous during the Fronde, ended his days rowing ladies on the lake at Versailles'.

progressive figures whose organizing, unifying, and levelling impulses developed a state which was above traditional vested interests and which acted as stalking horse for a future bourgeois order. In this scenario France and England are treated as directly comparable, and their respective governments are viewed as interesting variations on the common theme of the rise of the Western industrial nation-state. We have the English developing constitutional forms more precociously while the French invent a more powerful central state and lag a bit in economic development. Both are nevertheless seen as undergoing the same changes in more or less the same way, making French absolutism a stage in a wider European process of modernization.

This orthodoxy continues to be repeated despite the findings of a generation of social historians that French society was structurally very different from English society in the sixteenth to eighteenth centuries. In France a mass of peasants continued to subsist on small plots subjected to onerous taxes which transferred their surplus product to an elite with claims based on privilege. Neither they nor their landlords had much incentive to consolidate plots or modernize farming techniques through capital investment. The nobility held its own or revived instead of withering away; its privileged situation was confirmed, not abandoned. Merchants and manufacturers remained low in esteem and weak in political influence. All these circumstances contrast dramatically with those in England.

But if French absolutism presided over such a different social environment just at the moment of its greatest triumphs, might we not expect that its nature would be related to the needs of that society and not to a standard of progress which was better represented elsewhere? This hypothesis is confirmed by the fragility of English absolutism relative to French and by the outbreak of the English Revolution in 1640, so long before the French Revolution of 1789. How then did the nature of Louis XIII and Louis XIV's government relate to the nature of their societies? A vast polemic has long revolved around the 'bourgeois', 'feudal', 'aristocratic', 'transitional', 'arbitrating', 'exploiting', 'levelling' monarchy which has important implications for all interpretations of the rise of modernity in Europe but which has never been thoroughly examined.

These central questions can best be answered by dissecting the workings of a single region in order to capture the interplay of interests, attitudes, and jurisdictions which cannot be discovered in the history of one institution and which is too complex to tackle on the level of the entire system. This is one such study: an exploration of political action in one unit of the system, Languedoc. The aim is to understand absolutism better by finding out why it worked first so badly and then so well in the seventeenth century and what its relationship was to the changing social situation in the provinces.

Such an analysis can never be value-neutral. The salient lines of power and interest are not self-evident in the multitude of issues, conflicts, and actions which left their mark in the documents of the era, and a principle of selection must be adopted. Questions have to be posed which, in turn, derive from ideological assumptions needing careful examination. Studies of seventeenth-century France are full of conscious or unconscious points of view, although this fact is not sufficiently discussed or acknowledged. I must therefore begin with a critical look at these implications, as a way of clarifying how we are to proceed and what assumptions will be used as the foundations of this study.

It is a curious historiographical phenomenon that the two questions of the institutional effectiveness and of the social underpinnings of absolutism have been treated by three separate schools in virtual isolation from each other. The first question has generally been discussed by political and institutional historians who approached the state as a beneficial, more or less autonomous, organism. This venerable tradition has been greatly modified by the invasion of influences from social history, but it retains its original pedigree in that its proponents still focus on statebuilding as something outside of, and distinct from, society. Meanwhile Marxist historians who should have been the leading advocates of a sophisticated class analysis capable of shedding light on the second question concerning social underpinnings have, until recently, relegated the early modern state, and in particular French seventeenth-century society, to a dim corner of their historical tableau. Yet their class analysis offers sophisticated ways of relating power to society and raises the sorts of questions which a study like this must answer. A third – and probably dominant – school which might be called the 'social history tradition' has arisen in reaction to the first two. It dismisses political history as superficial, but also implicitly rejects or deemphasizes the Marxist focus on class relations as the key to a more fundamental evolution of society. At their most theoretical level social historians, like the famous 'Annalistes' in France, single out long-term movements of measurable factors like prices, population, wages, or land distribution patterns as the basic indicators of historical change. On a less schematic plane others trace the history of social phenomena like the family, disease, literacy, or charity as historical forces with their own intrinsic interest. In either case the result is a deepened understanding of social context without relating it back to politics.

All three of these schools contribute important insights; yet each could use the ideas of the others to better advantage. In order to see the issues clearly, we must disassemble and then reconstruct their elements, stressing points of parallel or complementary content. First we must look at the analytical foundations of the analysis of seventeenth-century society; then we must examine the developments in institutional history which relate to the evolution of society, and finally the developments in social or Marxist history which relate to the state.

ANALYTICAL FOUNDATIONS: CLASSES AND ORDERS

Any examination of seventeenth-century society comes square up against the great debate over early modern social stratification. Are we dealing with a society of traditional interest groups vying over status and position, or do we have a society of socio-economic classes struggling to maintain their control over resources and production processes – in short, was it a 'society of orders' or a 'society of classes'? This issue may appear rather tired after a generation of polemical debate, and the jaded reader may well wonder 'why not both orders and classes, or neither'? But the matter is crucial because it determines the kinds of questions to be asked and the kinds of results that will be obtained. It is also important because the most eminent scholar of French absolutism, Roland Mousnier, has dramatized the issue to the point where it threatens to distort the whole study of French social relations and leave important questions unanswered.[2]

The concept of a 'society of orders' (or of 'estates'), which Mousnier has developed for seventeenth-century France in his long evolution away from a 'class' approach to social history, is a variant on a kind of sociological analysis which is appearing with increasing frequency as an assumed frame of reference in historical works.[3] The argument goes something like this:

[2] Mousnier's work is voluminous. A good starting point might be the essays in Roland Mousnier, *La Plume, la faucille et le marteau* (Paris, 1970) or his grand synthesis, *Les Institutions de la France sous la monarchie absolue*, 2 vols. (Paris, 1974–80), the first volume of which has been translated as *The Institutions of France under the Absolute Monarchy 1598–1789: Society and State* by Brian Pearce (Chicago, 1979). His theoretical essay on stratification is *Les Hiérarchies sociales de 1450 à nos jours* (Paris, 1969), which is translated as *Social Hierarchies, 1450 to the Present* by Peter Evans (New York, 1973). A perceptive study of Mousnier's views is Ettore Rotelli, 'La Structure sociale dans l'itinéraire historiographique de Roland Mousnier', *Revue d'histoire économique et sociale*, 51 (1973), 145–82.

[3] On Mousnier's change of position, see the note in Roland Mousnier, *Les XVIe et XVIIe siècles*, 4th edn (Paris, 1965), p. 159. For sociological expressions of this approach see Max Weber, *The Theory of Social and Economic Organization*. tr. A. M. Henderson and Talcott Parsons (New York, 1964); Talcott Parsons, 'An Analytical Approach to the Theory of Social Stratification', *American Journal of Sociology*, 40 (1939–40), 841–62; and T. B. Bottomore, *Classes in Modern Society* (New York, 1970), pp. 3–35. A textbook version of the same doctrine which looks almost like a caricature is Kurt B. Mayer and Walter Buckley, *Class and Society*, 3rd edn (New York, 1970), pp. 18–41. The sources of Mousnier's concepts in American sociology are discussed in Armand Ariazza, 'Mousnier and Barber: the Theoretical Underpinning of the "Society of Orders" in Early Modern Europe', *Past and Present*, 89 (1980), 39–57. A useful survey of theories of stratification is James Littlejohn, *Social Stratification* (London, 1972). Examples of historical applications are Jerome Blum, *The End of the Old Order in Rural Europe* (Princeton, 1978), pp. 3–7; and Franklin L. Ford, 'The Revolutionary–Napoleonic Era: How Much of a Watershed?', *American Historical Review*, 69 (1963–4), 24–8. Important historical discussion of these issues by some of the principals examined here appears in *L'Histoire sociale, sources et méthodes: colloque de l'École Normale Supérieure de*

in a society of orders social groups are arranged hierarchically in a descending scale of status and privilege. The organizing principle is the social esteem accorded to the mystical or real function which each group performs and which has no necessary connection to the group's economic role. Orders (or estates) are subdivided into 'strata' or 'corps' or 'états', also arranged according to social esteem, each of which is a group with a legal identity and a sense of common purpose. This system is commonly presented as fundamentally different from a 'society of classes' in which individuals are legally equal, formal privileges do not exist, and social classification follows one's function in the economy. In a society of classes wealth is the central factor determining social position, for although status is influenced by occupation, education, lifestyle, and patterns of consumption, all of these derive directly from wealth or ownership of sources of wealth.

This contrast of 'orders' and 'classes' is seductive for early modernists because it speaks to an aspect of historical reality with which we are especially familiar. Privilege and status were inordinately important in seventeenth- and eighteenth-century France, and many conflicts followed corporate lines. At the same time society was obviously not governed by the laws of the marketplace in the manner of later capitalist societies, and it is only by the most extreme stretching of categories that one can transpose nineteenth-century 'classes' or 'class struggles' into an early modern setting. Consequently when early modernists speak of the 'society of orders' they are opting for distinctiveness. What they really mean is that in their pre-modern world classes did not exist and class analysis cannot be applied.

However understandable this usage may be, it is unfortunate. It confuses the issue of whether modern categories can be transposed back to the seventeenth century (obviously not) with the issue of whether there were classes of any kind in the seventeenth century (clearly so). By 'classes' I mean groups whose social and economic interests are necessarily antagonistic to one another because of their differing relationships to resources, power, and the fruits of labor. Class analysis implies the existence of fundamental conflicts in society, ruling out the possibility of absolute social solidarity or uniform social outlook. It means that different segments of the population produced and consumed in vastly different ways and that their thoughts and actions were correspondingly different. Seventeenth-century classes took different forms and played different roles from those of today, and there is room for debate over how to interpret them. It is undeniable,

Saint-Cloud, Mai 1965 (Paris, 1967), pp. 9–33, 97–114; Roland Mousnier, ed., *Problèmes de stratification sociale: actes du colloque international (1966)* (Paris, 1968); and Daniel Roche and C. E. Labrousse, eds., *Ordres et classes: colloque d'histoire sociale; Saint-Cloud 24–25 mai 1967* (Paris, 1973).

however, that groups with profoundly unequal and mutually antagonistic relationships to production existed in early modern France.

A system built upon the principle of social esteem cannot cope properly with these class relationships; first, because it plots its definition from a single vantage point at the top of society; second, because focusing on solidarity groups arranged according to a single principle of stratification makes it difficult to analyze the interdependence and interaction among groups; third, because this approach sidesteps the essential issue of how and why a particular kind of society came to have a particular kind of social stratification. Orders and estates did exist as an important part of the seventeenth-century French experience, but they did not determine the structure of society itself, which is what the term 'society of orders' usually implies.

It is essential to bring out the implications of Mousnier's philosophical position, since too often the importance of his scholarly contribution has caused his less scholarly assumptions to be accepted uncritically. Mousnier is implicitly an apologist for seventeenth-century society who accepts the justifications for its social structure and institutions put forth by the very persons who dominated it. His theory of orders is an attempt to sidestep the issue of conflicts deriving from unequal social relations by providing alternative categories. Thus in a study which purports to demonstrate empirically the existence of the society of orders by delving into Parisian notarial archives, he uses a large sample of marriage contracts and property settlements representing a cross-section of the population to derive nine 'social strata'.[4] Each of these consists of certain social types who are found to have associated with each other extensively to the exclusion of other social types. These strata do not coincide with degrees of wealth or occupational categories (which do not, of course, necessarily reflect 'classes' anyway), but rather represent shades of social esteem. The individuals in the top echelons were, among others, 'men performing military, judicial, or police activities resulting in the power of command, who acted in the service of the king and thereby personified the common good, that is to say, the state'.[5] This double assumption – that these individuals were on top because of their service and that the state personified the common good – is staggering. To claim that such people owed their position to 'the principle of the superiority of service to the king' is to take a mere rationalization as a cause. Persons like gentlemen of the king's bedchamber, minor country nobles, bourgeois of Paris, or various superfluous venal officers who are listed in this stratum were clearly not on top because society esteemed their

[4] Roland Mousnier, *Recherches sur la stratification sociale à Paris aux XVIIe et XVIIIe siècles: l'échantillon de 1634, 1635, 1636* (Paris, 1976).

[5] Ibid., p. 126.

service to the king so highly. Nor is it possible to maintain, as Mousnier does, that they 'had no relationship with activities producing material goods'.[6]

This example is not unusual. Mousnier believes that institutions are created to promote ideals: 'an institution is first of all a guiding idea, the idea of a set goal of public welfare', and that 'all social stratification is dependent on a group of value judgments which constitutes the fundamental principle of society'.[7] But the guiding principles of a society reflect the biases and interests of an intellectual elite which formulated them and not those of society as a whole. Indeed, the very assumption of the existence of a single set of values for a whole society presumes a fundamental social solidarity which is belied by vast amounts of historical evidence.

These assumptions underlie a central interpretation of seventeenth-century conflict. For Mousnier the turbulence before and during the Fronde was a manifestation of the rebellions of orders and communities against the centralizing, modernizing policies of the crown. In other words, organized solidarity groups of heterogeneous class composition such as provinces, corps of officers, towns, and villages provided the impetus for rebellion, and classes or class conflicts were not an issue.[8] Since we will be studying the relations of a province with the crown, we will have occasion to test the validity of this assumption.

As my remarks have already suggested, this study is based on different hypotheses: that societies are organized around the production and distribution of the essentials and luxuries of life; that these activities result in classes with antagonistic relations to each other; that consequently social conflicts are more fundamental than social solidarity in explaining the functioning of a given society. The central premise of this book is that the absolutist state can best be understood by looking at the class interests it served and the social functions it performed – in short, by developing some sort of class analysis in the Marxist tradition. This approach requires a thorough examination of the elements of provincial political society capable of revealing points of conflict and points of common interest.

[6] Ibid., pp. 126, 127, 25–30.

[7] Mousnier, *Institutions*, vol. I, p. 5; *Hiérarchies*, p. 8. Mousnier's position is deliberate and is clearly set forth twice virtually word for word in *Plume*, pp. 7–11; and *Institutions*, vol. 1, pp. 5–8.

[8] These views were originally developed in the critique of Porchnev's work, first in Roland Mousnier, 'Recherches sur les soulèvements populaires en France avant la Fronde', *Revue d'histoire moderne et contemporaine*, 4 (1958), 81–113; then in the same author's *Fureurs paysannes: les paysans dans les révoltes du XVIIe siècle* (Paris, 1967), pp. 13–62, translated as *Peasant Uprisings in Seventeenth-Century France, Russia, and China* by Brian Pearce (New York, 1970). Another overview is Roland Mousnier, 'The Fronde', in Robert Forster and Jack P. Greene, eds., *Preconditions of Revolution in Early Modern Europe* (Baltimore, 1970), pp. 131–59.

INSTITUTIONS IN SOCIETY

The reasons for the dramatic effectiveness of Louis XIV have traditionally been treated by the 'institutional school' in the context of the rise of the modern state. For professorial functionaries of the Second Empire and the Third Republic like Chéruel, Depping, or Lavisse, the state was the central bearer of progress, and its gradual articulation out of the irrational confusion of royal whim and feudal reaction was an end in itself.[9] In this context the reasons for Louis XIV's success were self-evident, and thus the question of how he really ruled was hardly posed at all. Rebellions like the Fronde had been irresponsible or (for constitutionalists) premature. The monarchy might not yet be ready, as Ernest Lavisse put it, to undertake the 'novel project' proposed by Colbert which was 'to *organize* for labor, *enrich oneself* by labor, *dominate the world* by the power of these riches', but it could certainly continue the 'ancient project which was to establish stronger authority and total, prompt obedience, and *to complete the state which was still so imperfect*'. Louis XIV's secret was simply 'the reduction to obedience' of those who had been unruly by means of a 'struggle against all sorts of autonomy'.[10] Lavisse describes one 'subjugation' after another without ever asking why the powerful subjects of a vast kingdom allowed their power to be so rudely expropriated or what they might have gained in return.

More recent institutional historians have modified this traditional view. Consciousness of the uneven development of institutions, the slowness and incompleteness of the evolution of effective royal power, and especially the resistance of the rest of society to what the monarchy was trying to do has led to a nuanced, less triumphant version of the story, as we can see from Pierre Goubert's more cautious summary:

> In the sixteenth century the kingdom seemed to have very little homogeneous about it, with morsels and shreds maintaining semi-independence; or – to go even further – it was a monarchy which 'rested', as Roger Doucet forcefully put it, 'on a collection of contracts concluded with the groups which constituted the nation: provinces, towns, economic groupings, ecclesiastical establishments, classes of society'. In the following centuries this monarchy, which remained juridically contractual, had worked to empty its contracts of most of their substance. To do this, it was necessary to reduce four forces which frequently had reciprocal links

[9] For example, P. A. Chéruel, *Histoire de l'administration monarchique en France depuis l'avènement de Philippe-Auguste jusqu'à la mort de Louis XIV*, 2 vols. (Paris, 1855); Ernest Lavisse, *Histoire de France depuis les origines jusqu'à la Révolution*, 9 vols. (Paris, 1903–11); or the monumental compilations like Georges, vicomte d'Avenel, *Lettres, instructions diplomatiques et papiers d'état du Cardinal de Richelieu*, 8 vols. (1853–77); and G. B. Depping, *Correspondance administrative sous le règne de Louis XIV*, 4 vols. (Paris, 1850–55).

[10] Lavisse, *Histoire*, vol. VII, part 1, p. 267 and titles to book 4, chapter 1, section 2. My italics.

among themselves: the ambition of the great noble lineages, the profound autonomism of the great peripheral provinces (even the near ones), the repeated and annoying frondes of the great corps and companies of royal officers, including the parlementaires (who relapsed, however, in the eighteenth century, especially after 1750), and the violent rebellions of a more or less popular character which broke out especially in the half century 1620–75, to reemerge inopportunely at the end of the Old Regime.[11]

Whereas the original 'institutional' account showed a state steadily increasing its power by promoting its sources of strength (towns, trade, bourgeoisie) and undermining ancient rivals whose day had passed (nobility, international church, autonomous provinces), the new 'institutional' account here provides *two* worthy antagonists, the state and society, and a long struggle between them, even in the seventeenth century.[12]

New research has further underlined the difficulties of effective local rule even in the state's most ancient tasks of rendering justice and collecting taxes. Studies of communities show how distant the state was for the vast majority of people, most of whom literally never saw a royal agent.[13] Kings and ministers received one-sided information, and their edicts were likely to be evaded.[14] A vast literature on popular rebellions has underlined the massive resistance which filled the annals of every province. Enforcement agents were run out of town, tax collectors ambushed, rival authorities murdered. Sharon Kettering portrays street confrontations between factions of Aix parlementaires which look more like Renaissance clan battles than assemblages of royal judges.[15]

Problems like these only emphasize the need to understand Louis XIV's success, for despite some historians' skepticism about even that monarch's ability to impose his will, there seems little doubt that he did much better than his predecessors.[16] Take the popular revolts. In two massive regional

11 Pierre Goubert, *L'Ancien régime*, 2 vols. (Paris, 1969–73), vol. II, pp. 12–13.

12 Early versions of this reevaluation appear in the works of Georges Pagès, Roger Doucet, Gaston Zeller, and Edmond Esmonin. Mousnier's own work follows in their footsteps, crowned by his general synthesis, *Les XVIe et XVIIe siècles*, 4th edn (Paris, 1965) which conceives of seventeenth-century absolutism as an attempt to resolve a series of crises. A more recent collection of revisionist institutional essays is Ragnhild Hatton, ed., *Louis XIV and Absolutism* (London, 1976).

13 Yves Castan, *Honnêteté et relations sociales en Languedoc* (*1715–1780*) (Paris, 1974), pp. 467–73.

14 Eugene L. Asher, *The Resistance to the Maritime Classes: Survival of Feudalism in the France of Colbert* (Berkeley, 1960).

15 Sharon Kettering, *Judicial Politics and Urban Revolt in Seventeenth-Century France: the Parlement of Aix, 1629–1659* (Princeton, 1978). Mousnier, *Fureurs*; Boris Porchnev, *Les Soulèvements populaires en France de 1623 à 1648* (Paris, 1963); Madeleine Foisil, *La Révolte des Nu-Pieds et les révoltes normandes de 1639* (Paris, 1970); Yves-Marie Bercé, *Histoire des Croquants: étude des soulèvements populaires au XVIIe siècle dans le sud-ouest de la France*, 2 vols. (Geneva, 1974); René Pillorget, *Les Mouvements insurrectionnels de Provence entre 1596 et 1715* (Paris, 1975); Sal Alexander Westrich, *The Ormée of Bordeaux: a Revolution during the Fronde* (Baltimore, 1972); Yvon Garlan and Claude Nières, *Les Révoltes bretonnes de 1675: papier timbré et bonnets rouges* (Paris, 1975), and a vast literature.

16 On the doubting side, Roger Mettam, *Government and Society in Louis XIV's France* (London, 1977).

studies René Pillorget, for Provence, and Yves-Marie Bercé, for the southwest, each find that uprisings multiplied between 1630 and 1660 and that there was a dramatic decline in them after 1660.[17] The rebellions, they argue, were the regional rejection of the state's attempt to assert its authority in matters which had previously been the domain of provincial society. The local response was the mobilization of whole communities to reject the 'foreigner' and reassert a traditional, integrated local culture. After 1660, by contrast, the atmosphere changed completely. Why? Pillorget attributes the change to the fact that after 1660 the *menu peuple* were forced to riot without the leadership of the notables, whose support was suddenly withdrawn, and argues that without leaders more riots were inconsequential. But he has no satisfactory explanation for such a striking defection of the elite. Bercé, on the other hand, concludes that the fight was knocked out of the southwest by systematic terrorism. The use of vicious fusiliers to collect 'totalitarian taxes' after 1635, deliberate brutality by intendants, constant passages of troops disrupted the very fabric of local society until military occupation and heavy taxation became accepted realities.[18]

What is important here is what is left out of all these accounts, whether seen close up in studies by Lavisse or from afar in monographs on regional rebellion. Whether the leaders of French society were 'reduced to obedience' after a hiatus, overcome by a 'contagion of obedience', as Pillorget puts it, or subjected to a grinding repression, the categories are the same: state versus society, royal against provincial, modern versus backward – always a dichotomy of forces. As long as 'institutionalists' persist in thinking of the state as 'above' society, acting as an autonomous entity with independent goals and programs, the state's activity will be conceptualized at least implicitly in terms of repression: a progressive government *imposes* uniformity, *quashes* rivals, *buys off* enemies, plays opposition forces *off* against one another. This 'repression model' rules out any notion of interaction between the state and the various classes in society, making it impossible to detect common interests or class alliances. If the leading authorities of Provence or Guyenne rebelled, then collaborated, was it only because of repression, fear, or bedazzlement? Did they receive nothing in return?[19]

[17] Pillorget, *Mouvements*, p. 988; Bercé, *Croquants*, pp. 680–82.

[18] Pillorget, *Mouvements*, pp. 863–4, 1007–8; Bercé, *Croquants*, pp. 100–12, 254.

[19] The same criticism can be made of J. Russell Major's formulation of the rise of absolutism in terms of a shift from the consultative 'Renaissance monarchy' to the more dictatorial absolutism of Louis XIV. Major's work has much to recommend it, not least of which is the fact that he does allow for a dialogue between the king and his society. But he invokes almost the same repressive model as Lavisse to explain the end of consultation under Louis XIV. J. Russell Major, *Representative Government in Early Modern France* (New Haven, 1980).

The newer institutional historians have nonetheless launched a major reevaluation of the nature of the early modern state; in fact, they are faced with the paradox of having been so successful in their revisionism that they have undermined their own view of the state as the *mobilizer* of society by demonstrating with increasing clarity the many ways that the state was infiltrated *by* society, was even a creation *of* society. This reevaluation has affected at least four aspects of politics and government.

A. *Venality of office.* Much of the institutionalists' reevaluation has been inspired by the work of Roland Mousnier. A starting point was his discussion of venality of office, the practice of selling posts in the government to royal officers for life, and then guaranteeing them the right to bequeath or sell the office at any time in return for payment of the annual paulette tax.[20] A full realization of the implications of venality has had the effect of 'demodernizing' seventeenth-century government. Venality tied absolutism to its feudal past by consecrating a new form of private ownership of public authority which enabled rich and influential subjects – noble or bourgeois – to share in the profits and prestige of the state. It was a new expression of the king's inability to control his society without conciliating his most powerful subjects; yet at the same time it was a significant advance over the earlier feudal relationships in that royal authority remained theoretically absolute, not contractual, giving the king direct legal claims over the officers which he had not had over his vassals. In addition, the power that was alienated was not the potent union of economic coercive force and political authority over the peasants which had theoretically characterized the medieval lordship, but rather a segment of political or judicial authority which was distinct from direct economic coercion and shared by any number of competing officers. Venality of office reflected the advances made by the money economy in that offices became marketable commodities which could be bought, sold, transferred, bequeathed, speculated on, and taxed. It thus introduced wealthy, locally-based magnates into the state edifice through the back door just as the traditional noble opposition was being ushered out the front, producing a new potential for collegial, structured resistance to change within the royal system itself.

This multiplication of offices created a new form of political discourse: the king threatened and cajoled his officers, multiplied their numbers, invented rivals for them, taxed and exploited their investments; the officers responded by quarelling endlessly among themselves; delaying, appealing, and refusing royal legislation, reinterpreting the laws or enforcing them selectively, and appropriating the royal prestige to assert their own

[20] Roland Mousnier, *La Vénalité des offices sous Henri IV et Louis XIII*, 2nd edn (Paris, 1971).

magnificence. The existence of venality thus raises the issue of relationships and interests within the system. To what degree were the officers instruments of bureaucratic centralization and to what degree were they infiltrators from the world of particularist demands and class interests? Did they constitute a new officer class, or were they making the state bourgeois or feudalizing it? Where did their interests really lie – with the 'modernizing' crown, with their fellow officers, with their regions, or with their class, and how did they express these interests?[21] Our study of Languedoc must apply these questions to the royal officers, and most specifically to their political function in the province.

B. *Intendants.* A corollary to the existence of venality was the need for the application of large doses of authority to get around it. These became crucial during the Thirty Years War when the needs of the troops and the fisc could not be met because of resistance both inside and outside the regular administration. The solution was the development of *commissaires*, most notably the *maîtres des requêtes* in Paris who served as investigators and reporters for the royal councils and out of whose ranks came most of the intendants in the army and in the provinces. The intendants play a key role in the classic view of absolutism as the agents of effective royal rule. Originally associated with Louis XIV, they were later traced back to the era of Richelieu and even farther. In an influential article Mousnier linked the specific circumstances of their intensified use, starting in 1642, with the need to take the tax collection machinery out of the hands of obstructive financial officers. Richard Bonney has subsequently expanded this picture. The intendants were used in 1630 to reform the taille and to stem the threat of internal subversion. When the war crisis began, the royal council experimented with many kinds of taxes, gradually learning by process of elimination that the only method which worked was to increase the direct tax on the peasantry, install intendants to repartition it, and give them military brigades to collect it. Even so, collections were sabotaged by widespread peasant resistance.[22]

Recent studies have not modified the basic view of commissioners as the active propagators of both effective royal power and the ideology of raison d'état, but intendants can no longer be seen as the triumphant dictators

[21] A. Lloyd Moote, 'The French Crown versus its Judicial and Financial Officials, 1615–83', *Journal of Modern History*, 34 (1962), 146–60; Kettering, *Judicial Politics*; John J. Hurt, 'La politique du Parlement de Bretagne (1661–1675)', *Annales de Bretagne*, 81 (1974), 105–30; Jonathan Dewald, *The Formation of a Provincial Nobility: the Magistrates of the Parlement of Rouen, 1499–1610* (Princeton, 1980).

[22] Roland Mousnier, 'État et commissaire: recherches sur la création des intendants des provinces (1634–1648)', in Mousnier, *Plume*, pp. 179–99; idem, ed., *Lettres et mémoires adressés au Chancelier Séguier (1633–1649)*, 2 vols. (Paris, 1964), pp. 42–192; Richard Bonney, *Political Change in France under Richelieu and Mazarin 1624–1661* (Oxford, 1978); Douglas Baxter, *Servants of the Sword: French Intendants of the Army, 1630–1670* (Urbana, Illinois, 1976).

of centralization, at least not until very late. They appear more frequently in local studies as isolated, beleaguered bearers of unpopular edicts who are threatened with denigration, pillage, and popular insurrection. They act desperately, using military terrorism and political manipulation to achieve their ends. More important, the sharp line between robe *officiers* and royal *commissaires* is dissolving. Socially these two types were indistinguishable, coming from the same milieu of the robe, having similar sources of wealth, marrying into each others' families, and shifting easily from one function to the other. The idea of intendants as independent outsiders who administer a province impartially is also being modified by the discovery of their many ties to local elites, to military commanders, to financial interests, and to each other. In other words, those who served the king most diligently were socially indistinguishable from those who resisted him.[23] We must consider who the royal agents were in Languedoc and how their attitudes, allegiances, and interests fitted into the fabric of local political life.

C. *Clientage.* Another feature of recent scholarship is the renewed emphasis on the importance of personal relationships. Orest Ranum's influential study of the councillors of Louis XIII demonstrated that Richelieu's effectiveness was based not on institutional reorganization but on 'creatures' in key positions who in turn relied on subordinate creatures.[24] This reevaluation is critically important because it calls into question the centrality of institutions *per se.* Whereas institutionalists formerly focused their attention on the articulation of institutional structures, it now became clear that what mattered were the personal ties and loyalties which provided 'substance' to the 'form' of the institutions. Evidence has since been pouring in that *all* political institutions were dominated by networks of clientèles. The maîtres des requêtes had patrons who organized their placement; dynasties of ministers manipulated the royal councils; great nobles protected their provinces and fiefs; sovereign courts took sides along family lines; even Colbert organized the royal manufacturers and the foreign trading companies around carefully placed financial allies.[25] What we are seeing is not widespread corruption, but a system of government in which networks of personal loyalty and institutional lines of authority

23 Denis Richet, *La France moderne: l'esprit des institutions* (Paris, 1973), pp. 84–5.

24 Orest A. Ranum, *Richelieu and the Councillors of Louis XIII* (Oxford, 1963).

25 Goubert, *L'Ancien régime*, vol. II, pp. 54–5; Pierre Lefebvre, 'Aspects de la "fidélité" en France au XVIIe siècle: le cas des agents des princes de Condé', *Revue historique*, 250 (1973), 59–106; Daniel Dessert and Jean-Louis Journet, 'Le Lobby Colbert: un royaume, ou une affaire de famille?', *Annales E.S.C.*, 30 (1975), 1303–36; Robert R. Harding, *Anatomy of a Power Elite: the Provincial Governors of Early Modern France* (New Haven, 1978); Jean-Louis Bourgeon, *Les Colbert avant Colbert: destin d'une famille marchande* (Paris, 1973), pp. 215–37; Jean-Pierre Labatut, *Les Ducs et pairs de France au XVIIe siècle: étude sociale* (Paris, 1972), pp. 98–160.

were interconnected, affecting the very nature of political power and suggesting once again that seventeenth-century institutions were qualitatively different from modern ones.

Mousnier has carried the analysis of clientage one step farther by constructing a 'society of fidelities'. 'From the top to the bottom of society', he writes, 'men were united among themselves by ties of fidelity', and he uses this idea as a principle of social solidarity to link persons of diverse provinces and stations of life in vertical hierarchies joined at the summit by the unifying force of the absolute monarchy.[26] Bercé has applied this analysis to the southwest by demonstrating how certain areas of popular revolt coincided with the territory of great fiefs and by offering many examples of seigneurs protecting their lands from taxes or troops.[27]

The idea of a system of fidelities raises serious questions, however. Mousnier, as usual, glamorizes the *idea* of fidelity by emphasizing the depth of its bond: 'the follower gives himself totally to his master. He espouses all his thoughts, his inclinations, his ambitions, his interests....He serves him by every possible means: he accompanies him, distracts him, speaks, writes, intrigues for him, pleads for him, fights for him, conspires, revolts for him, follows him into exile, aides him...even against the king, even against the state.'[28] But while such loyalties did exist, client ties were more often pragmatic arrangements. Client systems developed and declined; allegiances shifted; ties were broken. There is reason to wonder how much of a universal system such ties formed and what real emotional content there was in the ties between great men and lesser entities like provinces, towns, villages, or petty subordinates.

D. *State finance*. Another major reevaluation has taken place in the area of state finance. Attention has recently been focused on the period of the Thirty Years War as a fiscal turning point which altered the relationship between state and society. The taille was doubled and tripled; extraordinary fiscal measures were manipulated; means were found to cope with the resultant disorders, all at a time when economic growth was slowing down and the population was subject to troop depredations and epidemics. These pressures signalled the advent of a new relationship between financiers and the state. The monarchy was collecting more money in more different ways, borrowing more, and paying out more. The result was a growing interdependence of monarchy and financiers which had lasting effects on the nature of the system. Financiers advanced money in return for contracts

[26] Mousnier, *Institutions*, vol. I, p. 85. His views are best presented in ibid., pp. 85–93 and in 'Les Concepts d'"ordres", d'"états", de "fidélité" et de "monarchie absolue" en France de la fin du XVe siècle à la fin du XVIIIe', *Revue historique*, 247 (1972), 289–312. These themes have been further developed in Yves Durand, ed., *Hommage à Roland Mousnier: clientèles et fidélités en Europe à l'époque moderne* (Paris, 1981).

[27] Bercé, *Croquants*, vol. I, p. 66.

[28] Mousnier, *Institutions*, vol. I, p. 89.

giving them authority to organize tax-collecting ventures or claims on particular sources of revenue. Since the funds available for loans to the state were scattered throughout the country, national tax farms had to decentralize their structures, and networks of financial associates grew up, both to supply the crown with funds and to administer the rights gained in return. Joined together under the name of a Parisian with court connections, these 'cartels' rapidly became 'lobbies', vying for influence in the government to procure lucrative 'treaties', protect their investments, and influence policy. To complicate matters further, the financiers were often themselves royal officers. A parasitic relationship was developing which was new to the seventeenth century and which would last, with modifications, to the days of Necker and Louis XVI.[29]

Far from being a few outsiders called on in times of emergency, the financiers described by Julian Dent functioned at the very heart of the system. Richard Bonney demonstrates the connection between taille collections and financiers, as well as the financial ties of intendants. John Bosher has pointed out that *chambres de justice* were designed to regulate, not punish financiers.[30] Since the collection and rechannelling of state funds was the largest economic enterprise in France, and since Languedoc's system of estates generated especially good financial records, we must explore the role of both taxes and financiers in Languedocian politics.

Thus historians have moved from viewing the state as a triumphant organizer of society to viewing it as a fragile organism struggling against a vast, turbulent society, and finally to the realization that forces in society were influencing, if not defining the very function of the state. The existence of these forces does not necessarily negate the state's progressive role, but it does call for a reassessment of the way distinctive early modern institutions interacted with a distinctive early modern society. The question of the effectiveness of Louis XIV thus leads directly to the issue of the nature of provincial society.

[29] A. D. Lublinskaya, *French Absolutism: the Crucial Phase, 1620–1629* (Cambridge, 1968), pp. 232–43; Pierre Chaunu and Richard Gascon, *Histoire économique et sociale de la France*, vol. 1, part 1 (Paris, 1977), pp. 181–91; Alain Guéry, 'Les Finances de la monarchie française sous l'ancien régime', *Annales E.S.C.*, 33 (1978), 216–39; Richet, *La France moderne*, p. 77; Bonney, *Political Change*, pp. 173–5; Julian Dent, 'The Role of Clientèles in the Financial Elite of France under Cardinal Mazarin', in J. F. Bosher, ed., *French Government and Society 1500–1850* (London, 1973), pp. 41–69; Richard Bonney, *The King's Debts: Finance and Politics in France 1589–1661* (Oxford, 1981).

[30] Julian Dent, *Crisis in Finance: Crown, Financiers and Society in Seventeenth-Century France* (New York, 1973); Bonney, *Political Change*, pp. 52, 184, 189, 209–10; J. F. Bosher, 'Chambres de Justice', in Bosher, *French Government*, pp. 19–40.

SOCIETY AND ABSOLUTISM

Our second question asks how absolutism as a political system was related to the evolution of French society, and where the two stood relative to their past, their future, and their counterparts in other European countries. Social historians and Marxist historians have each provided interpretations of society which open interesting possibilities, but neither has fully pursued the link with politics. Among the social historians the so-called 'Annales School' stands out as the group which comes closest to offering a coherent interpretive picture.[31] There is no single *annaliste* point of view, but key contributors from the early modern group like Fernand Braudel, Emmanuel Le Roy Ladurie, Pierre Goubert, Pierre Chaunu, and Jean Meuvret certainly convey a similar message. Their studies give an overwhelming impression of the backwardness of French society, or perhaps it would be better to say its slowness to change. Underlying their analysis is an awareness of the great demographic cycle stretching from the population collapse of the fourteenth century to the rapid rise of the eighteenth century which preceded, then accompanied, the industrial revolution. Within this period from 1350 to 1750 there were expansions and contractions of population, production, and prices, but European – and especially French – society was nevertheless a unit with continuity, a structure, whose intricate mechanisms and subtle inter-relationships of parts can be uncovered by patient examination of particular regions.

The Annalistes' fascination with the land has had the effect of emphasizing the traditional.[32] Agricultural production was carried out by a mass of small-holding peasants whose numbers and circumstances subordinated them to a small elite of property and power. Profound inequality reigned on all levels of society, intensified but not transformed by population growth. Production and distribution were geographically fragmented.

[31] One critical assessment of the historians surrounding the journal *Annales: Économies, Sociétés, Civilisations* is Traian Stoianovich, *French Historical Method: the Annales Paradigm* (Ithaca, N.Y.,1976); another is 'The Impact of the Annales School on the Social Sciences', a special issue of *Review*, I, no. 3/4 (Winter/Spring, 1978). A narrower discussion concerning Louis XIV is William F. Church, *Louis XIV in Historical Thought* (New York, 1976), pp. 94–110. Of course Marxists and Annalistes disagree very profoundly over the fundamental forces behind historical development, as indicated in the magnificent debate surrounding Robert Brenner's article, 'Agrarian Class Structure and Economic Development in Pre-Industrial Europe', *Past and Present*, 70 (Feb., 1976), 30–75; 78 (Feb., 1978), 24–55; 79 (May, 1978), 55–69; 80 (Aug., 1978), 3–65; 85 (Nov., 1979), 49–67; 97 (Nov., 1982), 16–113.

[32] Succinct summaries of the research described here can be found in Goubert, *Ancien régime*, vol. I, pp. 35–236; and Robert Mandrou, *La France aux XVIIe et XVIIIe siècles* (Paris, 1970), pp. 71–132. More ambitious syntheses are Georges Duby and Armand Wallon, eds., *Histoire de la France rurale* (Paris, 1975), vol. II, *L'Âge classique des paysans 1340–1789* by Hughes Neveux, Jean Jacquart and Emmanuel Le Roy Ladurie; and Fernand Braudel and Ernest Labrousse, eds., *Histoire économique et sociale de la France*, vols. I–II (Paris, 1970–7).

Subsistence crises linked demography directly to climate and disease. Productive investment in land was rare. This picture has so focused attention on the countryside that the traditional historiography of towns, trade, and rising bourgeoisie has been pushed out of the limelight. Most merchants, it turns out, had relatively limited resources and used remarkably primitive credit mechanisms. Manufacture was artisanal; towns were permeated with rural influences. A corollary to this reevaluation is the discovery by other social historians, many of them American, that the nobility was holding its own, even prospering, in the sixteenth and seventeenth centuries, contrary to the traditional stereotype of bankruptcy and obsolescence.[33] Recent work has thus given us a distinctive 'early modern' society to go with the early modern institutions discussed above.

For our purposes the most striking feature of the 'Annales' picture is the relative absence of a political dimension. Traditionally the Annalistes have avoided the elitist, nationalistic orientation of the traditional institutionalists by escaping to the land and looking for the hidden rhythms of social auto-regulation. Recent studies have gone farther in the direction of reintegrating questions of power – hence class – into the analysis, but still without much consideration of the system of power and its relationship to the state. Thus, although he criticizes a Marxist conception of class, Pierre Goubert nevertheless acknowledges the important contrast between a small circle of 'dominant figures' (*dominants*) and the mass of 'dominated' (*dominés*) and stresses the exploitation of the peasantry by absentee rentiers who lived in cities, most notably a tiny political class attached to the state. Denis Richet similarly finds 'a dominant world living directly (by means of seigneurial revenues or the profits of leases) and indirectly (by the redistribution of the receipts of the state) off the revenues of the peasants'. Both, however, shrink from using power as a principle of classification.[34] The most fascinating but exasperating attempt to fit politics into the fabric of long-term structures is provided by Pierre Chaunu, who describes the state as an emanation of the demographically 'filled world' of the late thirteenth century, and then measures its progress in terms of the number

[33] James B. Wood, *The Nobility of the Election of Bayeux 1463–1666: Continuity Through Change* (Princeton, 1980); Dewald, *Formation*, pp. 305–12; J. Russell Major, 'Noble Income, Inflation, and the Wars of Religion in France', *American Historical Review*, 86 (1981), 21–48.

[34] Goubert, *Ancien régime*, vol. I, pp. 69–70, 99–100, 130–3; vol. II, pp. 6, 55; Richet, *La France moderne*, p. 102. On social structure, orders, classes, and power, see also Jean Jacquart, *La Crise rurale en Île-de-France 1550–1670* (Paris, 1974), pp. 445–595 and most specifically pp. 474–6 and pp. 594–5; Guy Cabourdin, *Terre et hommes en Lorraine (1550–1635)* (Nancy, 1977), pp. 331–3; Emmanuel Le Roy Ladurie, *Le Carnaval de Romans: de la chandeleur au mercredi des cendres* (Paris, 1979), pp. 14–23; Marcel Couturier, *Recherches sur les structures sociales de Châteaudun 1525–1789* (Paris, 1969), pp. 274–9; Pierre Goubert, *Clio parmi les hommes* (Paris, 1976), p. 292, see also pp. 281–93; idem. *Ancien régime*, vol. II, p. 204; vol. I, pp. 199–208, especially p. 203; Richet, *La France moderne*, p. 101.

of tons of silver the monarchy extracted in taxes relative to France's aggregate population density and production. The result is a highly deterministic presentation of the institutional dimension as a superstructure required by certain ecological and demographic conditions.[35]

Thus Annalistes have delineated a self-regulating early modern society with distinctive characteristics and identifiable cycles of development, but they do not go very far in explaining the dynamics which produced the inequalities, nor do they help us make sense out of the many political forces and institutions which are discussed in such detail by the institutional historians.

Marxist analysis should do better in this regard.[36] It starts from the premise of fundamental social inequality and implicit conflict which I posited above; it features an analysis of change; and it focuses on issues of power which imply politics. Unfortunately non-Marxist specialists have tended to ignore Marxist approaches, either through lack of familiarity, or in the mistaken belief that they were rejecting determinism or leftist propaganda. It is still not uncommon to read in scholarly monographs of a rejection of *the* Marxist interpretation, as if such a phenomenon existed, or could be quoted. The failure of communication is not all the fault of scholars in the field, however, for there has been a lack of relevant Marxist work available, and what there was seemed to fit the conditions of seventeenth-century France rather badly.

Traditional Marxists have quite naturally concentrated on revolutionary situations, with the result that the French and English Revolutions diverted attention away from the problems of the seventeenth century. Maurice Dobb's work on the rise of capitalism in England and the famous collection of commentaries loosely called the 'Dobb–Sweezy debate' were the Marxist studies most likely to be known by English-speaking readers, along with the works on the French Revolution by Georges Lefebvre and Albert Soboul.[37] But studies of this kind, though masterful in their own proper context, cannot serve as models for analyzing less dynamic, non-revolutionary situations.

[35] Chaunu, 'L'État', in *Histoire économique et sociale de la France*, vol. I, part I, pp. 11–228.

[36] This discussion concerns only Marxist analysis of state and society in early modern Europe. It is difficult to find an easy introduction to this material since elementary texts on Marxism do not deal with this issue, and books that do tend to be difficult reading. The best overall presentation is Eric J. Hobsbawm's introduction to Karl Marx, *Pre-Capitalist Economic Formations* (New York, 1965), pp. 9–65. Another helpful review is Robert S. Du Plessis, 'From Demesne to World-System: a Critical Review of the Literature on the Transition from Feudalism to Capitalism', *Radical History Review*, 4 (1977), 3–41. The most relevant sections of Karl Marx, *Capital: a Critique of Political Economy*, 3 vols. (New York, 1967) are vol. I, part 8 and vol. III, chapters 36, 47, but neither these texts nor those published in *Pre-Capitalist Economic Formations* attack the problem directly.

[37] Maurice Dobb, *Studies in the Development of Capitalism*, rev. edn (New York, 1963); Paul Sweezy et al., *The Transition from Feudalism to Capitalism*, intro. by Rodney Hilton (London, 1976). For the many works of Lefebvre and Soboul, see bibliographies on the French Revolution.

Several problems have plagued traditional Marxist accounts. First was the tendency to focus on relationships between discrete, fully-formed classes and to treat these classes as historical actors. This sort of class analysis can be reductionist if it leads merely to a roster of rising and falling social groups, and there is danger that the role of the state may seem to be limited to supporting or not supporting one class or another. This is as much the problem with Friedrich Engels's often-quoted formulation that the absolute monarchy 'held the balance between the nobility and the class of burghers' as with Mousnier's view of the semi-autonomous monarchy maintaining control by playing one group off against another: 'above these divided orders, the king remained the master'. In each case the reader is encouraged to think of classes like counters on a chessboard, stalemating each other or leaping ahead at one another's expense, and of the state as a manipulator of these distinct social groupings.[38]

A second difficulty was the emphasis on modernity which characterized many earlier works. Partly because most analysts were thinking of England where social change really did come remarkably early, and partly because Marx and his intellectual successors were influenced by the 'whiggish' historiography of the time, there was a tendency to stress the progressive, bourgeois nature of all the 'modern' developments since the Renaissance – national movements, Protestant Reformation, mercantilism, and of course the state. Once serfdom, which was intimately associated with feudalism, disappeared, a new mode of production was called for – if not capitalism directly, then a period of 'petty commodity production' or 'primitive accumulation'. This association of the early modern period with the rise of the bourgeoisie and the rise of capitalism made considerable sense for England, where most attention was directed, but not for France, where the society of lords and dependent peasants persisted for centuries, the aristocracy consistently renewed itself, and absolutism became a powerful force instead of a hollow shell.[39]

Most recent Marxist writers have shifted to a different approach, under the double influence of the revival of Marx's own writings and the vogue of structuralism. Emphasis is now placed more on the functioning of the total system (hence on society and social history) than on the interests of particular classes (which can generate a sort of 'political' history). One identifies the relationships which exist between certain 'givens': on the one

[38] Engels quoted in Perry Anderson, *Lineages of the Absolutist State* (London, 1974), pp. 15–17; Mousnier, *Plume*, p. 221. An example of the 'social roster' approach is Robert Mandrou, *Classes et luttes de classes en France au début du XVIIe siècle* (Messina, 1965). An updated version of the 'noble–bourgeois balance' approach is J. S. Morrill, 'French Absolutism as Limited Monarchy', *Historical Journal*, 21 (1978), 961–72. A fine discussion of the nature of classes and consciousness in earlier periods is E. J. Hobsbawm, 'Class Consciousness in History', in *Aspects of History and Class Consciousness*, ed. István Mészaros (London, 1971), pp. 5–21.

[39] See the essays in Sweezy et al., *Transition*.

hand, the 'forces of production', consisting of the available natural resources and the existing level of technology for exploiting them; on the other hand, the 'relations of production', consisting of the social (or 'class') arrangements governing who controls these resources and the tools for exploiting them, who performs the labor, and who reaps the benefits. The result is a system of relationships, a 'mode of production' in its ideal state, or a 'social formation' in a particular historical manifestation, which ultimately serves the interests of certain classes but which has distinctive characteristics and a momentum of its own. There is room in this schema for a variety of historical particularities: cultural forces, legal traditions, structures of belief.

Although the classification of particular social systems as modes of production is a complicated operation, discussion for our period surrounds two basic possibilities, feudalism and capitalism. The first is an essentially agrarian form of society in which production is done on a small scale, mostly for local consumption, and the basic social contrast is between a class of landed lords and a class of dependent peasants. The second is a society of commodity production and market relationships predicated upon the contrast between the owners of capital and the 'free' labor force they employ. Early modern France corresponded to neither of these stereotypes but contained elements of both. It was part of the famous 'transition from feudalism to capitalism' which can be dated roughly as the period between the fourteenth-century 'crisis of feudalism' and the bourgeois revolution of 1789.

At this point it seems necessary to clarify these definitions. For Marxists feudalism is a broad category referring to the essential characteristics of a certain type of society. For non-Marxist medievalists it refers only to a specific form of relationship between lords and vassals, or, at its broadest, to the societies of the eleventh to fourteenth centuries in which that phenomenon structured other political relationships. There is no excuse for confusing these two usages.[40]

With the term 'capitalism' the problem is reversed. Here Marxists want to use the term narrowly while non-Marxists extend it indiscriminately. Both agree that they are dealing with a broad historical phenomenon, but where non-Marxists often use the term to denote any sort of profit-making enterprise, Marxists mean a system of production in which those who control capital dominate a free labor force of workers who are dependent on selling their labor power in the marketplace for their subsistence. This

[40] See, for example, the uninformed caricature of Marxist analysis in Jacques Heers, 'The "Feudal" Economy and Capitalism: Words, Ideas and Reality', *Journal of European Economic History*, 3 (1974), 609–53; Mousnier's remarks in *Plume*, pp. 362–4; or Pillorget, *Mouvements*, pp. 459–61. On the other hand, there is a very sensible discussion of the definition in David Herlihy, ed., *The History of Feudalism* (New York, 1970), pp. xiii–xx.

distinction is crucial in interpreting the role of many prominent economic forces of the fifteenth to the eighteenth centuries like the rising volume of trade, the colonies, the price revolution. Non-Marxists view these as manifestations of the rise of capitalism pure and simple to the point where capitalism sometimes becomes merely the economic history of the period – the interplay of prices, money supply, trade, production, and credit. For Marxists such activities do not necessarily qualify as capitalistic at all because they did not transform social relations in such a way as to revolutionize production.[41] A Marxist can call these developments 'capitalist' in the loose sense that they were forces helping to transform the old feudal relations based on land, but technically no society was 'capitalist' unless capitalism, narrowly defined, was the dominant form of social relations within that society.

Absolutism has presented just as many interpretive difficulties for Marxists as it has for institutionalists. Marx and Engels made only scattered references to the problem and never developed a sustained analysis of it.[42] For them absolutism represented one of those periods in history when the state became relatively autonomous because of a social equilibrium between two classes, the nobility and the rising bourgeoisie. This view fits with the concept of transition – after all, the society was no longer purely feudal for it was infused with bourgeois activity from top to bottom. But this 'equilibrium' position tended in the direction of calling the state bourgeois, since the rise of the bourgeoisie was the new, dynamic element which would have to be invoked to explain the novelty of absolutism. This position raises two serious difficulties. First, it requires the emergence of a bourgeoisie powerful enough and advanced enough to explain the rise of absolutism. Second, it does not square well with more recent views of the seventeenth-century polity. For if, as we saw above, the state was built upon personal client systems, ownership of office by landed magnates, and parasitic financial arrangements, where are the bourgeois interests which were balancing those of the nobility?

Various creative attempts have been made to cope with these difficulties. The first sustained Marxist analysis of seventeenth-century France was by Boris Porchnev in his celebrated study of absolutism and popular uprisings from 1623 to 1648. This book, published in Russian in 1948, in German in 1954, and in French in 1963, soon evoked a polemical reply from Mousnier which in turn led to such a vast controversy that the original book has tended to be lost in the shuffle.[43] Porchnev elaborates on the

[41] Dobb, *Studies*, pp. 1–32. A good discussion of the problem for England is C. H. George, 'The Making of the English Bourgeoisie, 1500–1750', *Science and Society*, 35 (1971), 385–414.

[42] Anderson, *Lineages*, pp. 15–18.

[43] Porchnev, *Soulèvements*; Mousnier, 'Recherches', reprinted in idem, *Plume*, pp. 335–69.

'equilibrium' approach. The state defended the nobles in two ways, each of which required utilizing the bourgeoisie. Politically, the state was the only force which could coordinate the selfish conflicts of individual nobles in the interests of the noble class as a whole, but, paradoxically, it could only do this by employing bourgeois agents, since the use of any single noble faction would incite the jealousy and rebellion of the other factions. Economically the state aided the nobles by expropriating the surplus wealth of the peasants through royal taxation, or 'centralized feudal rent' and redistributing the proceeds in the form of noble pensions and appointments. The contradiction in this system was that while royal taxes might at first extract that additional portion of the peasant's surplus which the seigneur had not been able to appropriate, they soon grew to the point where the king and the nobles were competing for the same resources, causing serious conflict between the noble state and the noble class. The only solution was a different source of revenue to supplement the traditional one and pacify the nobles – hence mercantilism, which was an attempt to produce taxable bourgeois wealth. If the state thus needed the bourgeoisie to administer noble interests and generate new revenues for the nobility, the bourgeoisie in turn used the state to provide it with the support mechanisms for financial and manufacturing development.[44]

Here Porchnev's view of the bourgeoisie is puzzling. On the one hand, he sees it as an independent force well on the road to becoming a revolutionary class: 'French society in the seventeenth century was already profoundly affected by the new distinction among men based upon the opposition between labor and capitalist property which was breaking down the old feudal and corporative barriers.'[45] On the other, he recognizes that the bourgeois were 'feudalized' by the necessity of accommodating themselves to the existing system instead of transforming it – politically through venality of office, socially by acquiring nobility, and economically through tax farming, state finance, and mercantilistic privilege:

> The bourgeoisie would not have been bourgeois if, to a certain degree, social and political power had not belonged to it. But now, in contrast to the earlier period when the capitalist regime had not yet existed, it was constantly obliged to transform itself by artifice into a 'feudal bourgeoisie' even in order to occupy a portion of social and political power. That is, it had to renounce its class, to renounce itself.... It could not simply believe itself to be bourgeois: to oppose the king and the nobility would have meant uniting with the people in the third estate and opting for revolution, in order to discover beyond the revolution its true class reality. But this moment had not yet come. We have already seen that the French bourgeoisie of the seventeenth century was obliged to confront this dilemma every day, and that it resolved it in the same manner every time.

[44] Porchnev, *Soulèvements*, pp. 563–6.

[45] Ibid., p. 543.

And he adds:

The problem was not limited, however, to the consciousness of the bourgeoisie. Denying itself, renouncing to its very core the revolution, it infallibly lost most of its class character. Reconciliation with the royal power and with the nobility brought about a denying effect on its social existence, changed its economic activity. The very evolution of capitalism took two steps forward and one step backward. This is why we speak of an internal contradiction at the heart of the bourgeoisie in this period.[46]

Such engaging dialectical analysis is really sleight of hand. Porchnev sees his bourgeois as wavering between consciousness of their revolutionary role and subordination to the feudal regime, but only the latter is clearly demonstrated. When he discusses the incorporation of the bourgeois into a feudal state which diverted them from true capitalist enterprises, he is interpreting familiar, documented phenomena like venality of office and state finance. But where is the capitalistic side of his bourgeoisie, the 'capitalist regime' which has now transformed its situation under feudalism to the point where it is teetering on the brink of revolution? The only evidence offered seems to be the seriousness of the Fronde, which is interpreted by analogy with the contemporaneous revolution in England as a bourgeois challenge to the existing order; a challenge which fails, paradoxically, because of the immaturity of the French bourgeoisie. The bourgeois were bourgeois because of a revolution they failed to make.

The real thrust of Porchnev's interpretation lies beyond the triangle of absolutism–nobility–bourgeoisie. He views the many popular revolts of his period as a manifestation of a permanent state of lower-class insubordination so serious that it required the apparatus of the state to keep it in check.

During the middle ages two forces held the working masses in submission: on the one hand the material constraint of the state apparatus (first decentralized in domains and seigneuries, later concentrated under royal authority); on the other hand the influence of respected authorities – first and foremost that of the church which taught subordination, then the force of custom which required unchangeability, and finally the prestige of the royal call for order. The force of the popular masses closely balanced off the pressure which the forces from above exerted on them. Without this pressure [from above] the system for feudal production could not have existed for long. But in the course of time this second constraining force – ideological authority – weakened. An increase in the material force of the state was necessary to assure the maintenance of feudalism. The state finally attained the power of absolutism.[47]

Thus the inner dynamic of history turns out to have been the balance between the resistance of the masses to their oppression and the oppressive

[46] Ibid., p. 545–6.

[47] Ibid., p. 572.

force of the ruling class. Absolutism arose to fill the void caused by the decline of the ideological stranglehold represented by medieval religion and belief. It follows then that 'the principal objective of absolutism was not at all to support the nobility and to find the resources for war.... The principal role of absolutism was to suppress [popular revolts], to hold this turbulent popular mass in submission.' Furthermore the state's cooptation of the bourgeoisie was necessary to keep this class from joining the rebels.[48]

Porchnev's version of the absolutist equilibrium is thus a curious one. He offers interesting ideas about the symbiotic relationship between the bourgeoisie and the nobility in an essentially feudal state, but his emphasis on overt class conflict seems to rely on what can only be called a romantic belief in the revolutionary threat presented by both plebeian rebels and fence-sitting bourgeoisie. The problem is partly one of focus. Porchnev's study highlighted so admirably the seriousness and extensiveness of the dramatic pre-Fronde uprisings that it led to an exaggeration of their overall historical significance. But what did these struggles represent? One of the urgent questions to be addressed in this study of Languedoc in the classic era of popular uprisings and local power struggles concerns social stability itself: what sort of social threat was actually present, how was it perceived, and did it indeed have implications for the nature of the absolutist regime?

Another Soviet scholar, A. D. Lublinskaya, follows the main lines of Porchnev's analysis but rejects some of his most questionable claims and elaborates on other parts of his schema, with the result that her picture of the contending social forces is more evolutionary and less apocalyptic.[49] The core of agreement concerns the essentially feudal nature of absolutism, the state apparatus, and the 'feudalized' robe nobility – on these points she seconds Porchnev and rejects Mousnier. However, she avoids any exaggeration of the revolutionary potential of either the bourgeoisie or the masses. The strife of the Richelieu-Mazarin period 'was not at all a preparation for the appearance of a revolutionary situation alleged to have taken shape in the middle of the century. The development of capitalism, that is, of new relations of production, had not yet encountered within the country obstacles which could be overcome only by a bourgeois revolution.'[50] The lower classes played an important and, in certain respects, progressive role without in any way presenting a threat to the system. The bourgeoisie was central to the rise of absolutism, not as a revolutionary challenge to be coopted, but rather as an independent ally. Here Lublinskaya clears up the confusion about Porchnev's ambivalent

[48] Ibid., p. 567.

[49] This account is based on Lublinskaya, *French Absolutism*; idem, 'Popular Masses and the Social Relations of the Epoch of Absolutism: Methodology of Research', *Economy and Society*, 2 (1973), 343–75; and idem, 'The Contemporary Bourgeois Conception of Absolute Monarchy', *Economy and Society*, 1 (1972), 65–92.

[50] Lublinskaya, *French Absolutism*, p. 330.

bourgeois. The coopted royal officers and financiers *were* feudalized, but there was also a 'trading-industrial bourgeoisie' distinct from them which needed absolutism to protect and develop its potential for capital accumulation, while the absolute monarchy needed the support of this bourgeoisie to defeat the forces of noble revolt and particularism which threatened the strength of the monarchy. This indigenous class of merchants and traders was geographically subdivided, split by religion, and only imperfectly developed, but it *was* rising slowly and steadily, without having reached the point where its interests would be incompatible with the feudal regime. Its influence was, however, great enough to push the state towards developments which prepared the way in the long run for the rise of capitalism. Thus, where Porchnev's equilibrium stresses the state as beleaguered defender of the feudal class, Lublinskaya's stresses its more placid aid to the rising bourgeoisie.

This latter position is much closer to the classic formulation of both Marxist and non-Marxist historians of a traditional France gradually being transformed by a rising bourgeoisie. Its difficulty is twofold. First, the emphasis on the 'progressive' side of absolutism makes it harder to explain the 'feudal' aspects which made sense in Porchnev's view: the diversion of merchant capital into rents and tax farms, the phenomenon of venality, the aristocratic values of the king and his agents. In short, the resilience, rather than atrophy, of aspects acknowledged as feudal becomes an anomaly. The second problem is the very existence of Lublinskaya's 'trading-industrial' bourgeoisie. Her book uses only circumstantial evidence – economic treaties and a few isolated cases – to argue the rising importance of a group which is exceedingly hard to find in the sources.[51]

It is evident from these accounts that any attempt to explain French absolutism must come to grips with the traditional feudal elements of the system, either as a restraining force limiting bourgeois development or as a new, reconstituted – and hence dynamic – version of an older social system. This is exactly the conclusion which emerges from reading the proceedings of the symposium on feudalism held by a group of Marxist and communist historians in Paris in April 1968, and published in 1971.[52] The participants, who provided the first extended discussion of these issues since the publication of Porchnev in France, took pains to reconcile their Marxist approaches with the findings of the latest research and the particularities of the French situation.

[51] An excellent critique of Lublinskaya's suppositions is David Parker, 'The Social Foundation of French Absolutism, 1610–1630', *Past and Present*, 53 (1971), 67–89; and his analysis of the state of the French bourgeoisie is developed further in idem, *La Rochelle and the French Monarchy: Conflict and Order in Seventeenth-Century France* (Royal Historical Society Studies in History Series, no. 19) (London, 1980).

[52] Centre d'Études et de Recherches Marxistes, *Sur le féodalisme* (Paris, 1971).

There was general agreement on three points which demonstrate the direction recent analysis is moving. First, all the commentators presented a definition of the essential characteristics of feudalism which was broad enough to apply to the early modern period, even though this meant deemphasizing the prevalence of serfdom and stressing instead the importance of various forms of feudal property in land and restricted property over persons.[53] Second, they all saw the transition to capitalism as slow and late, with the most significant changes only being felt at the very end of the seventeenth century or, in most cases, not until the second half of the eighteenth.[54] Third, all emphasized the subtle, sometimes imperceptible ways in which the rise of capitalism developed within the still essentially feudal structure.

This emphasis on slow development and fundamental obstacles to change has been carried forward, perhaps inadvertently, by the more recent school of Marxist 'structuralists'. All of them have in common an intellectual debt to Louis Althusser and a fascination with modes of production as structural systems, though they would agree on little else.[55] The change from earlier Marxisms is only one of emphasis. Previous analysts usually focused their attention on one or more dynamic elements in the socio-economic system, stressing a motor of change which generated historical development. Structuralists, by contrast, elaborated on the set of relationships within a given mode of production, and thus on the self-perpetuating nature of the system itself. By concentrating on the links between the various levels – socio-economic, political, and ideological – and within each level on the constituent elements of the system, they devised a tool which cries out for application to the more sedentary conditions of early modern France and suggests parallels to the long-term structures of the Annalistes. This form of reasoning can lead to abstract mystification, as E. P. Thompson has cogently pointed out, but it suggests helpful ways of thinking about the connections between economies, social forms, and politics.[56]

[53] See especially the preliminary dossier by Charles Parain and the comments of Pierre Vilar, *Féodalisme*, pp. 13–48.

[54] This chronological conservatism was so pronounced that it provoked an outburst by Lublinskaya, who was present at the symposium, to the effect that the rise of the bourgeoisie had left feudalism a hollow shell by the eighteenth century. Albert Soboul responded equally insistently that on the contrary it was the *persistence* of feudalism which explained the nature of the Revolution. Ibid., pp. 112–15.

[55] The influential works of Louis Althusser are *For Marx*, tr. Ben Brewster (London, 1969); Louis Althusser and Étienne Balibar, *Reading Capital*, tr. Ben Brewster (London, 1970); and Louis Althusser, *Politics and History: Montesquieu, Rousseau, Hegel and Marx*, tr. Ben Brewster (London, 1972). The analysis relevant to our problem can best be seen in *Reading Capital*, pp. 209–24. Some idea of the ferment which influenced scholarship in the years preceding May 1968 can be obtained by reading the debate in Jean-Marie Auzias et al., *Structuralisme et marxisme* (Paris, 1970) which was held in Paris in February 1968, two months before the Marxist debates discussed above (note 52) and less than a year after the discussion of orders and classes cited in note 3.

[56] E. P. Thompson, *The Poverty of Theory and Other Essays* (London, 1978).

The key to such linkage is the idea that feudalism is based on extra-economic coercion, a concept utilized by such diverse analysts as Barry Hindess and Paul Q. Hirst, Régine Robin, Nicos Poulantzas, and Perry Anderson.[57] This concept is hardly new, and all Marxists have been aware of it, but the structuralists have made it the focal point of their analysis of feudalism. The argument is as follows. Under capitalism workers have to buy their means of subsistence in the marketplace, and consequently they are forced to sell their labor power, giving the capitalists who control the means of production the opportunity to appropriate the surplus produced by the workers. The system is thus impelled forward by invisible economic forces, leaving political and ideological forces to play the secondary role of policing and defending the system. Under feudalism the relative importance of these factors is different. Production is carried out by peasants and artisans who possess most of the resources they need and who produce mostly for local consumption. They are therefore relatively independent and, economically speaking, could manage to live and reproduce quite adequately without supporting a ruling class. The process of surplus extraction must therefore be imposed by extra-economic means: the nobles assert their right to receive labor services or payments in kind or in money, partly by force, but more significantly through political and ideological advantages which are built into the social system. These advantages are therefore of primary, not secondary, importance.

One way of looking at this extra-economic coercion is to identify a type of authority distinctive of feudalism. Because of the nature of production, political authority was amalgamated with economic coercion on all levels, public and private. Feudal landlords combined the power to command and judge with the right to collect dues and dominate the local economy, each power supported by the other. Another way of looking at it is to note a specifically feudal type of legal arrangement: rights over land and over people were expressed in a series of gradations; there was no absolute private property and no absolute freedom for the individual. In each case there was a hierarchy of levels or degrees: in the case of land, this hierarchy was expressed in divided ownership which gave a variety of superiors the right to claim a share of the produce; in the case of persons it resulted in a series of degrees of unfreedom or, put the other way around, in a hierarchy of privileges.

[57] Barry Hindess and Paul Q. Hirst, *Pre-Capitalist Modes of Production* (London, 1975); Régine Robin, *La Société française en 1789: Semur-en-Auxois* (Paris, 1970); Perry Anderson, *Passages from Antiquity to Feudalism* (London, 1974); and *Lineages*. One might have expected Nicos Poulantzas to have made a major contribution, inasmuch as he is one of the leading figures in this school whose concern is especially with the role of the state and political power in the class struggle. However, his discussion of the absolutist state as essentially capitalist is too poorly informed and too dependent on outmoded stereotypes to be useful here: Nicos Poulantzas, *Pouvoir politique et classes sociales*, 2 vols. (Paris, 1968), vol. 1, pp. 166–77.

Here we have a suggestion of central importance for our investigation. Extra-economic coercion is a motif which can be applied both to the fundamental class relationships under feudalism and to the social and legal trappings of absolutist society. If one thinks of feudalism not as the relationship of lord and serf on a twelfth-century manor, but as a whole set of interlocking relationships and cultural themes deriving from this 'core' system of production, then it is easier to imagine the same system continuing in the early modern period, even if aspects of it were modified. It is also easier to explain why fundamental social change was so long in coming. The mere introduction of a new element like bourgeois wealth or partial centralization of political power would not necessarily transform the whole system unless a number of conditions were right.

If feudalism is defined as a society based on the extraction of an agricultural surplus from the peasantry by means of a system of extra-economic coercion which becomes a motif replicated in property relationships and social hierarchies, then it is possible to interpret absolutism as a type of feudalism. Perry Anderson has developed the most comprehensive version of this approach. He notes that 'the end of serfdom did not thereby mean the disappearance of feudal relations from the countryside', for there was still 'private extra-economic coercion, personal dependence, and combination of the immediate producer with the instruments of production'. Consequently 'so long as aristocratic agrarian property blocked a free market in land and factual mobility of manpower – in other words, as long as labour was not separated from the social conditions of its existence to become "labour-power" – rural relations of production remained feudal'. The crisis of the fourteenth century and its aftermath had transformed the circumstances within which this situation prevailed, but not the situation itself. The rise of money rents had weakened the lord's special brand of political and economic control on the local level. The rise of towns and pre-industrial manufacturers (which Anderson sees as integral to feudal society and not as accidental or external) meant that the solution to this problem of the nobility would have to lie in a more centralized, more technological, more exchange-oriented political structure. Absolutism, or the stronger early modern state, was the answer. 'Absolutism was essentially just this: *a redeployed and recharged apparatus of feudal domination*, designed to clamp the peasant masses back into their traditional social position – despite and against the gains they had won by the widespread commutation of dues.'[58]

Anderson, like Porchnev, treats the absolute monarchy as the state apparatus for the defense of the feudal class in a later stage of feudalism.

[58] Anderson, *Lineages*, pp. 17–18.

But, unlike Porchnev, he does not see a dramatic confrontation between rising bourgeoisie and falling nobility, nor does he allow an 'equilibrium' between the two mediated by the state. Rather, he argues that the absolute monarchy was a feudal institution protecting a feudal society, the form of which was influenced by the growth of a mercantile bourgeoisie. This bourgeoisie was able to live with a feudal state, and was even aided by it, because some of the goals of the 'redeployed' nobility and of the merchant bourgeoisie were similar and, more important, because the bourgeoisie was not developed enough to feel itself hampered. Within limits both groups were in favor of centralized police power, mercantilist tariffs, more uniform legal systems, and colonial enterprises. However, Anderson, like our recent institutionalists, is at pains to point out that the typically 'modern' aspects of the early modern state were really only feudal antecedents of their 'modern' successors. In short, there was a 'field of compatibility' between the program of the absolutist state which 'fundamentally represented an apparatus for the protection of aristocratic property or privileges' but simultaneously assured 'the basic interests of the nascent mercantile and manufacturing classes'.[59]

ABSOLUTISM IN LANGUEDOC

All these views suggest that our two questions are closely related and could be answered by utilizing insights already at hand. I propose that Louis XIV's success in ruling France – our first problem – was directly related to the social role of absolutism – our second. The absolute monarchy did defend a traditional social order dominated by a class of privileged landowners, but in the early modern period, and especially the seventeenth century, new conditions made it increasingly necessary for power and authority to be more centralized. This was a lesson which had to be learned the hard way. Faced with popular disorders, noble rebellions, and competition from powerful foreign rivals, the regimes of Louis XIII, Richelieu, and Mazarin took steps which undermined the interests of provincial aristocrats and caused political and social dislocation. This effort failed because it threatened the ruling class too profoundly. Louis XIV's great 'contagion of obedience' was the result, not of repression, but of a more successful defense of ruling class interests, through collaboration and improved direction. The story of seventeenth-century absolutism was consequently the story of a restructured feudal society. Both the king and his landed aristocracy were exploring ways of defending their interests in a changing world without, at the same time, undermining them.

[59] Ibid., pp. 40–1.

The nature of the society they were trying to defend is no longer open to debate, whether one chooses to call it 'feudal' or not, since the definitions of feudalism offered by Marxist experts like Pierre Vilar, Guy Lemarchand, or Guy Bois are not very far removed from the 'neo-Malthusian' analysis of Emmanuel Le Roy Ladurie and Pierre Goubert.[60] This was a society in which most notables based their fortunes on the possession of landed estates. Their income resulted partly from traditional forms of domination over peasant communities and partly from economic advantages relating to the size of their holdings, the power of their connections, and their degree of liquidity of wealth. But it was income deriving from an advantageous social situation dictated by law and custom, not from entrepreneurial investment in the capitalist sense. The same notables derived further advantage from their connections with the monarchy or the church. They inherited, purchased, or had bestowed upon them positions which entitled them to a share of society's income and power – not because of duties performed but because of the status connected to the position. This is another way of saying that most important personages owned a share of public power; that the society was based on a system of privileges which represented differing degrees of ownership over the various social advantages and different claims on the wealth produced by the masses of peasants – an echo on a higher plane of the extra-economic coercion of the lord over his serfs. Many of the 'early modern' characteristics brought out by institutional historians (venality, tax farming, conflicts of authority) make sense, viewed in this context. In this sort of society we might expect the government to have corresponding characteristics – there should be a politics of absolutism relating to the needs and aspirations of the class which benefited. The political system in Languedoc should reflect, reinforce, and perpetuate this 'feudal' society rather than undermine it, and its development should help explain the changes before and after 1660.

These are the themes to seek in Languedoc. I have proposed my hypothesis only as a way of interrogating the material, and the reality will not fall as neatly into place. The chapters which follow will plunge us into a world of historical specifics revolving around local issues, rivalries, and events. As we proceed we must keep in mind the main points of the inquiry. We must ask how public power was exercised in the province – through what agencies, by what groups, with what difficulties. We must consider the rulers collectively to determine what their needs, fears, and interests were, and indeed whether they had enough in common to be viewed

[60] Compare the definitions of Pierre Vilar (in *Féodalisme*, pp. 35–6), Guy Lemarchand (in ibid., p. 87), Guy Bois (in *Crise du féodalisme*, Paris, 1976, pp. 355, 364), Emmanuel Le Roy Ladurie (in *Les Paysans de Languedoc*, 2 vols., Paris, 1966, vol. I, p. 490), Pierre Goubert (*Ancien régime*, vol. I, pp. 128–32), and Robert Mandrou (in *La France aux XVIIe et XVIIIe siècles*, Paris, 1970, pp. 72–8).

collectively. We must ask whether they could cope with the business of government; how they handled the rest of the population; if they were capable of forming a regional alliance against the crown. At the same time we must keep an eye on the bonds that tied them to the monarchy. Did they share interests with the king, and do these interests help to explain the successes of Louis XIV? If clear answers can be found, we will be well on the way to an interpretation which accounts for the existence of orders without forgetting about classes and which relates the peculiarities of seventeenth-century politics to the distinctive society in which they took place.

2

Languedoc and its rulers

In the seventeenth century Languedoc covered slightly less than 10 percent of the territory controlled by the king and held between 7 and 8 percent of the royal subjects.[1] It was the largest province in France except for Guyenne, and its total population was surpassed only by Normandy, Brittany, and Guyenne. It was thus the most extensive province with estates, although not the most densely populated. It usually supplied between 6 and 9 percent of the king's revenues.[2]

Within this large area a tiny elite of powerful individuals – at the most one-tenth of 1 percent of the population – held all the important posts and wielded all significant authority. It is this political class, assumed to belong to a broader ruling class, whose activity will tell us about the nature of absolutism in Languedoc. The sources for their activities are documents in which institutional agents recorded or discussed governmental business. Each institutional point of view has a biased angle of vision, but collectively they provide a multi-dimensional picture in which the distortions of one are corrected by the criticisms of another. Through these sources we get a veritable panorama of issues and controversies from which to determine

[1] These are rough estimates. Pierre Chaunu set the area of effective royal control at 450,000 km² in the early seventeenth century. Léon Dutil calculated the area of Haut- and Bas-Languedoc at 28,588 km², and if we add to this the modern area of the departments of Ardèche, Lozère, and Haute-Loire which Dutil left out, we have a total of 44,325 km². The areas of the eight modern departments approximating the territory of Languedoc add up to 46,331 km². Population is from the estimates for the end of the century by Vauban as cited by Goubert, and the estimates of Georges Frêche. Pierre Chaunu and Richard Gascon, *Histoire économique et sociale de la France*, vol. 1, part 1 (Paris, 1977), pp. 25–6; Léon Dutil, *L'État économique du Languedoc à la fin de l'ancien régime* (Paris, 1911), p. 28; Pierre Goubert, *L'Ancien régime*, 2 vols. (Paris, 1969–73), vol, 1, p. 48; Georges Frêche, *Toulouse et la région Midi-Pyrénées au siècle des lumières (vers 1670–1789)* (Paris, 1974), pp. 25–6.

[2] Such estimates are highly unreliable because they vary according to which sums are counted as revenues. Basville estimates the total revenue from Languedoc between 1689 and 1697 at 124,986,354 livres or 13,887,372 livres per year. In 1696 the gross revenue of the monarchy has been calculated at 156,926,206 livres. This would come to 8.85 percent. In 1647 the 3,426,621 livres which went directly to the king from the taxes granted by the Estates can be compared with a total 'net' revenue of 34,573,436, which comes to 9.9 per cent. A similar calculation for 1677 comes to only 4 percent. See chapter 11 and Nicolas Lamoignon de Basville, *Mémoires pour servir à l'histoire de Languedoc* (Amsterdam, 1736), pp. 226–7; Alain Guéry, 'Les Finances de la monarchie française sous l'ancien régime', *Annales E.S.C.*, 33 (1978), 216–39.

what the most important concerns were and what aristocratic leaders thought about them. But whose concerns were these? A ruling class should include everyone with similar relations to the system of production, and not just prominent individuals who acted politically. I must also assume, therefore, that the issues crucial to the provincial aristocracy made their way into the proceedings of public bodies and that the positions taken by provincial leaders more or less reflected those of their class. This is a rather large proposition, but it seems justified under the circumstances. Provincial aristocrats wielded private influence in many ways, most of them hidden from view. But while in an earlier age such private power might have been the single most important force in the society, by the seventeenth century royal government had clearly become the dominant partner in the fascinating mixture of public and private authority which made up the early modern polity. Disputes of genuine social significance can be expected to have made their way into the records of political institutions because royal influence was needed to resolve them.

It is also reasonably certain that those who made themselves heard represented a significant portion of those who 'mattered'. In a society structured by social prestige the truly powerful were more likely to insist upon public prominence than in a society built on 'invisible' profits. Landed nobles fought to become seneschals or commanders of fortresses; the most influential churchmen became bishops; the richest robe families produced presidents in the sovereign courts; the most successful bourgeois families controlled the consulates of towns. There were, of course, dissaffected factions of individuals who felt betrayed by their hierarchical superiors. But they also had means at their disposal of making themselves heard, either through regular channels or by obstruction and rebellion, and the sources contain many examples of both.

The material under investigation thus represents the tip of an iceberg in the sense that it preselects out of the vast range of activities carried out by many individuals in many different locations only the actions with the greatest political consequences taken by prominent leaders. Moreover, none of the actors were women! But the rulers of Languedoc are the key to the relationship between the province and the national monarchy, therefore we will begin by finding out who they were and examining the province they dominated.

THE PROVINCE

My choice of Languedoc for this investigation may appear curious, given its distinctive customs and unusual history. The reasons are simple. A large province was needed which was far enough from Paris to have an independent existence and which offered good sources on the activities of all the major authorities. Although Languedoc participated in the distinctive culture of the Midi and was especially influenced by the rise of Calvinism, it was one of the most 'French' of the peripheral provinces, having been conquered and assimilated in the thirteenth century long before Provence, Aquitaine, Dauphiné, Brittany or the east of France. A *pays d'états* was preferable over a *pays d'élections* despite its more independent status, because institutions with more freedom of action leave behind more revealing records, and it was necessary to have testimony which did not emanate only from the royal agents.

Of such provinces Languedoc was in many ways the greatest. Its territory stretched from the Garonne at Toulouse on the west to the Rhône on the east; from the foothills of the Pyrenees on the southwest to the beginnings of the Massif Central above Montauban and Albi on the northwest; and from the Mediterranean coastline on the southeast all the way northward across the Cévennes to the valleys near the source of the Loire. It consisted of three main regions: Upper or Haut-Languedoc, with its capital at Toulouse; Lower or Bas-Languedoc with its capital at Montpellier; and the mountainous regions of the Massif Central which were subdivided into Vivarais (around Viviers), Gévaudan (around Mende) and Velay (around Le Puy).

Haut- and Bas-Languedoc are separated by a chain of worn mountains which reach down from the Massif Central (Montagne Noire) and up from the Pyrenees (Corbières) to meet between Carcassonne and Narbonne in the valley of the Aude.[3] Haut-Languedoc is a vast plain around Toulouse, merging on the west with the rolling hills of Guyenne. Bas-Languedoc is the strip of coastline from Narbonne to Nîmes and the Rhône valley which is hemmed in on its north by the rising peaks of the Cévennes. While the area around Toulouse is green and fertile, this region is dry and subtropical. Even today the difference is noticeable as one passes from Toulouse's almost Spanish landscape, highlighted by distinctive red-brick architecture, to the Italianate environment of Montpellier with its vines, olive trees, and cypress groves.

These contrasts had both economic and political implications. Grain (and later corn) thrive on the richer soil and wetter summers of Haut-Languedoc, while grapes need the dry sun of Montpellier. Today each region specializes in its favored crop, but in the seventeenth century the Mediterranean region was impoverished by inefficient grain production instead of specialization in wine exports, while the Toulousain faced an overabundance of grain in good years. The two regions' diversity was thus potentially complementary.[4]

[3] Pierre Vidal de la Blache, *Tableau de la géographie de la France* (Ernest Lavisse, ed., *Histoire de France illustrée*, vol. 1) (Paris, 1911), pp. 351–4.

[4] Ibid., pp. 41–2; Emmanuel Le Roy Ladurie, *Les Paysans de Languedoc*, 2 vols. (Paris, 1966), vol. 1, pp. 33–4, 76–90; Frêche, *Toulouse*, pp. 580–4.

Politically the two capitals, Toulouse and Montpellier, competed for influence, with Toulouse boasting the Parlement and Montpellier the Cour des Comptes.

The third portion of Languedoc, the mountainous northeast arm, presented an obvious political problem. The mountains of the Cévennes, heartland of the Protestant menace and upland supply zone for the merchants of Nîmes, tower over the desert-like *garrigues* between Lodève and Uzès like a solid wall already visible from the Promenade de Peyrou in Montpellier. Behind this barrier lies a maze of valleys and hills comprising the three separate *pays* of Vivarais, Gévaudan, and Velay. The Cévennes were dependent on the lowlands for grain, and the annual summer transhumance of sheep up from the parched garrigues to the mountainsides was an essential feature of the Languedocian economy. In hard times migration of tough mountain people down from the hills was also a fact of life tying the regions together.[5]

The whole south of France belonged to a cultural orbit where the climate, the agriculture, and the style of life were markedly different from the north.[6] Languedoc, the land of the 'oc' instead of the 'oui', was the center of this culture. Its original assimilation into the sphere of the French monarchy had been by military conquest, in the form of the Albigensian crusades of 1209 to 1226. The precise boundaries of the province were set by the Treaty of Calais (1360) after the English had whittled down the royal holdings to their final dimensions. This first annexation was followed by a second. The Hundred Years War undid the work that had been accomplished, as English and French armies took and retook parts of the region. When at last the 'King of Bourges' Charles VII pieced together support in Languedoc as a step in the reconquest of his kingdom, he did so by means of concessions and guarantees. In 1420 he promised Toulouse a parlement; in 1428 he agreed to consult the three estates before levying taxes. Taken by conquest, consolidated by inheritance, defined by foreign treaty, Languedoc was now to be reincorporated into a reorganized monarchy on a 'consultative' basis. Gradually the Estates of Languedoc ceased to be a national body for the southern half of the kingdom and became entrenched as the consultative agency for the province of Languedoc.

In addition to the patriotic advantages provided by these privileges, which afforded the opportunity for eloquent appeals to the inviolability of ancient customs traced sometimes all the way back to the Roman Empire,

5 Le Roy Ladurie, *Paysans*, vol. I, pp. 112–22.

6 The best modern history of the province is Philippe Wolff, ed., *Histoire du Languedoc* (Toulouse, 1967). A shorter survey is Emmanuel Le Roy Ladurie, *Histoire du Languedoc*, 2nd edn (Paris, 1967). The classic multi-volume history is Dom Claude Devic and Dom J. Vaissete, *Histoire générale de Languedoc*, 15 vols. (Toulouse, 1872–92), most of which was originally published in the eighteenth century. A new study from a cultural–regionalist point of view is André Armengaud and Robert Lafont, eds., *Histoire d'Occitanie* (Paris, 1979).

there were practical advantages which made Languedoc the most important of the pays d'états. First, its courts were in the zone of Roman rather than customary law. This distinction had tangible results such as the recognition that allodial lands were exempt from the many taxes that the king imposed as feudal suzerain. Second, the regime of the *taille réelle* applied, under which taxes were collected according to the noble or roturier status of the land involved rather than the status of the individual who paid. Finally Languedoc had its Estates. Other provincial assemblies existed in France, but none had as compact a membership nor as complete a control over their own financial system. All these peculiarities, along with subsidiary claims such as exemption from military lodgings, came to be thought of as a 'package' of rights to be defended by the Estates and the courts. Even in the seventeenth century particularist sentiment and regional pride were operative forces, especially when they could be invoked to defend vested interests.

At the same time there were strong reasons for identification with France and the monarchy. After all, the province owed its very unity and identity to its northern conquerors. Before the events of the thirteenth century, Languedoc had been fragmented, moving in the direction of the separate city-states of Italy. The conquest provided a geographical identity, a common ruler, and all the significant provincial institutions.[7] In the fifteenth century when France was under foreign occupation, Languedoc was one of the first areas to rally to Charles VII, thereby associating itself with the patriotic legends which would become an emotional foundation of the new monarchy. The ties which bound Languedoc to the crown were thus just as fundamental historically as the factors which suggested separatism.

This fundamental ambivalence of loyalties reminds us that the danger of falling into a 'repression' model of royal–provincial relations exists in local as well as national historiography. Too often historians of Languedoc have felt that by measuring the decline of provincial independence and identifying the moment when it was definitively eliminated, they have resolved the most pressing issue concerning the political life of the province. Henri Monin, studying the administration of the intendant Basville in 1884, concluded that Basville's arrival in 1685 had signalled the death of provincial liberties, and that from then on local authorities had become pawns in the hands of an all-powerful Louis XIV. A few years later Paul Gachon revised this view by showing that the change actually came earlier in 1632, when Richelieu imposed the Edict of Béziers on the province.[8]

[7] Le Roy Ladurie, *Histoire*, pp. 40–7.

[8] Henri Monin, *Essai sur l'histoire administrative du Languedoc pendant l'intendance de Basville* (Paris 1884); Paul Gachon, *Les États de Languedoc et l'édit de Béziers* (*1632*) (Paris, 1887).

But Henri Gilles, writing more recently about the Estates in the fifteenth century, tells us that identical dramas were being enacted then and the same battle lines had already been drawn: 'with the coming to power of Louis XI the tutelage begun under Charles VII was completed. The Estates lost definitively the right to discuss the amount of taxes; they lost temporarily that of supervising their assessment.'[9] The Estates were definitively subjugated in 1461, 1632, and 1685; yet they always continued to cause trouble! Clearly there is no point in contrasting 'liberty' with 'subservience', for provincial institutions were never really independent and never definitively 'taken over'. A better approach is to chart the ways that royal–provincial interaction varied with time and circumstances.

Our period from 1620 to 1690 marks not so much a single turning point in Languedocian constitutional history as an era of significant transformation in every area of political life. It moves from Richelieu's strong but disruptive rule through the collapse of the Fronde, the revival under the late years of Mazarin, and the dramatic transformation of Louis XIV's young adulthood. The era began with the great élus crisis of 1628–32 when Richelieu tried to abolish the Estates; it ended with the arrival of the tough Lamoignon de Basville as intendant in 1685 along with the dragonnades which converted the Huguenots, inaugurating the period of greatest royal absolutism. Thus the 1620s saw the last gasp of the semi-autonomous atmosphere of the religious wars. The 1680s saw the advent of a royal regime so strong that the disasters at the end of the reign were borne by local leaders with very little protest. In between lay a fascinating period of change.

Economically the period 1620 to 1690 is well known, thanks to the labors of Emmanuel Le Roy Ladurie.[10] The seventeenth century saw a progressive slowing of the great sixteenth-century expansion of population and land use to a point around 1670 to 1680 when the economy went into a slump. Our limiting dates fall close to two natural disasters which punctuated this period of slow expansion, then retreat. From 1628 to 1632 – the years of the élus crisis – the last great epidemic of plague swept the province, setting back population growth everywhere and sending certain marginal communities into a decline which prefigured the later general recession. We shall see that this round of deaths had its effect even on the political forces of the elite. At the other end of our period, the 1680s were marked by a

9 Henri Gilles, *Les États de Languedoc au XVe siècle* (Toulouse, 1965), pp. 279–80.

10 Le Roy Ladurie, *Paysans*, vol. I pp. 416–508, 511–603. This internationally-renowned classic has been translated as *Peasants of Languedoc* by John Day (Urbana, Ill., 1974), but the translation is from an abridgement which deletes most of the relevant seventeenth-century material. Thus despite the familiarity of the book, this analysis is unfamiliar to many readers. Many of Le Roy Ladurie's broader conclusions have been challenged by Georges Frêche in *Toulouse*; and in 'Compoix, propriété foncière, fiscalité et démographie historique en pays de taille réelle (XVIe-XVIIIe siècles)', *Revue d'histoire moderne et contemporaine*, 18 (1971), 321–53.

series of drought years which consolidated the ruin of farmers already pressed by deteriorating conditions and precipitated a wave of farm abandonments, inaugurating the decline which was to last until the 1730s. Our period thus falls in the last flowering of the expansion begun in the sixteenth century, a sort of Indian summer during which the damages of the religious wars were repaired and a fragile prosperity continued, punctuated by various breakdowns.

Economic life was predominantly agricultural, though manufacturing played a greater role in the eastern districts than in the western grain belt around Toulouse. Relationships to the land were therefore especially important, and Languedoc's 'Indian summer' concealed social changes which directly affected the rulers and their situation. According to Le Roy Ladurie, the sixteenth century had been the great age of agricultural profit, when rising returns from the land, declining real salaries of farm laborers, and stable land rents had given an advantage to the middle-sized farmer who worked his rented farm personally and sold his produce on the market. This age favored the initiative of enterprising middle-to-large-scale farmers. It saw new families push their way into the merchant oligarchies which dominated the towns, and newcomers on the land acquired estates and bought offices for their children.

The period we are studying was very different. From the reign of Henry IV forward, the rural economy began to favor the rentier. Land rents soared as a larger population which had already filled marginal land areas bid with one another for tenures. Former 'gentleman farmers' gave up direct farming and rented out their properties, putting all the risk on the shoulders of their tenants. Meanwhile salaries of farm laborers could go no lower and tax levies of various sorts began to climb rapidly, eroding the profits of the tenant farmers. The church's tithe was collected more assiduously now that the religious wars were over. The royal taille rose considerably, along with the gabelle and indirect excise taxes. Now that the galloping inflation of the sixteenth century had ceased, creditors began to relish their long-term debts while debtors could no longer pay them back.

This 'triumph of rent', which lasted until the 1660s or 1670s, transformed the social climate significantly. The cards were now stacked in favor of absentee landlords whose incomes increased without special effort – a perfect setup for the nobles and officers whose actions concern us here and a fine reinforcement for hierarchy at the expense of bourgeois initiative. Provincial revenues still depended on the sale of grain and wine, but most of the surplus was channelled to the landlords, moving the tenant producers closer to just breaking even and making them vulnerable to even a modest worsening of conditions. The revenues of the church likewise multiplied, showering prelates and cathedral canons with benefits and financing the churches and schools of the Catholic revival. At the same time, finance rather than production became the best place for investment. Tax farming and handling of state revenues offered new opportunities, along with usury in its various forms.

These circumstances help explain the political world of seventeenth-century Languedoc. Its principal actors were no longer active merchants, but, on the one hand, venal officers whose royal authority loomed ever larger as their pedigrees grew longer, and, on the other, fat prelates. Where social newcomers appeared they were invariably connected to finance. A hidden bourgeoisie of dealers in grain and wine, cloth merchants, silk entrepreneurs, and organizers of rural industries made its presence known from time to time, but these were still political small fry whose importance was limited unless they acquired offices in church or state.

The period from 1610 to 1650 saw wealth channelled from the countryside to the urban elite and invested in social ostentation, marks of royal authority, or Catholic reconstruction. At the same time this should not be viewed as a 'time of plenty' even for the aristocracy, since the entire system was riddled with difficulties. The economy was slowing down, expanding at a much slower rate than in the previous century, with signs of impending difficulties. The revenues of rentiers were more directly and obviously exploitative, especially when they were connected to taxes or loans rather than land rents, with the result that popular unrest was a continuing problem. Passages of troops exacerbated the situation, and short-term subsistence crises such as those of 1629–30, 1645–6, and 1651–3 left their mark in the annals of politics as well as economics. Most important, the notables themselves faced increasing pressure. Their rents were subject to the ability of the tenants to pay. The more they invested in offices, the more they became vulnerable to royal decisions about legal jurisdictions and stipends, and the more they were forced into destructive conflicts with rival officers. Finally it should be remembered that under the system of taille réelle even the notables paid taxes on their non-noble lands, and they were thus subject to more of the tax burden than their counterparts in many other provinces.

After 1650 the economic climate gradually changed. Grain prices began to decline from a peak in 1655, and while production on the land seems to have held up for a decade – in fact increased as producers scrambled to sell more at lower prices – by 1665–72 profits from the land had collapsed and farms began to fail. From 1672 to 1680 revenues faltered as farmers abandoned the land or went bankrupt. The bad drought of the early 1680s simply turned a trend into a crisis. The years around 1672, which were a political turning point in royal–provincial relations, thus marked the end of the 'good years' for the rentiers and the beginning of a phase of lower rents which lasted until well into the eighteenth century and which was accompanied by declining agricultural production and rising taxes. The only bright spot for the rich was that, with the price deflation from the 1660s onwards, loans became even more profitable and even harder for debtors to repay. This was the golden age of credit for the aristocracy of the province.

Le Roy Ladurie's slogan 'the land is no longer profitable' is an exaggeration, for the aristocracy continued to live off their properties as they always had, and their prosperity was not dependent only on the level of rents. Nevertheless, our period 1620 to 1690 can be thought of in two phases, an age of shaky prosperity from 1620 to 1660 when the surplus of a slowly expanding agriculture was effectively channelled into the hands of the urban and rural elite, and an age of harder times from 1670 to 1690 when deflation, unsold crops, and shortage of cash were the order of the day. The rulers of Languedoc lived well in either case, but their political options and relations with the monarchy may have been influenced by the changing conditions they experienced.

IDENTIFYING THE RULERS

Who were these rulers? In the largest sense they constituted a ruling class which shared an especially advantageous relationship to the social system and a common interest in perpetuating it. Membership in this group cannot be mechanically defined by legal status, occupation, or level of wealth because their common denominator was a special relationship to power which derived from a varying combination of these qualities. Their position might derive from inherited status, from control of the resources needed to dominate production on the land, or from a privileged relationship to the state machine; usually it involved all three. Most nobles, old and new, were included, though it is possible that some of the poorest were too destitute to derive any advantage from the system, especially if their lands were roturier in status. Most higher political authorities qualified by virtue of the unearned power they derived from their offices and positions, but only to the extent that they exercised real influence as a result of their association with the twin hierarchies of state and church. The same individuals who enjoyed noble status or official power generally also owned country estates which gave them special advantages in the world of traditional rural production. It was also possible for an individual who fitted none of these categories to qualify if he was, for example, a wealthy financier whose fortune was siphoned from tax revenues.

In this broad sense, encompassing the three overlapping circles of privileged nobles, officials, and landlords, the size of the group can only be guessed at. Certainly its outer limit was 10,000 individuals, counting everybody. In 1698 Basville counted 4,486 noble families in the province. An earlier report by Henry de Caux based on the intendant Bezons's 1668 investigation into the nobility listed the 'gentlemen of Languedoc' in 1,561 articles, many of which contained several family members.[11] There were 3,263 fiefs stemming from the crown in the province, according to Basville, including fifty-five marquisates, seventeen counties, and twenty-two viscounty-baronies.[12] But Basville only considered 116 noble families worthy of mention as 'ancient', and hardly any of the dynasties of royal officers listed by Caux qualified for this honor. To these enumerations we would have to add at least the top churchmen who enjoyed special revenues and advantages, though most of them would already have belonged through other connections. There were at least 200 cathedral canons in the province, two universities with a minimum of twenty professors, eleven seminaries, fifteen colleges, and 338 religious houses.[13] If only a few directors of each of these establishments were counted we would still have 500 to 1,000 privileged clerics.

A more precise way of delineating the rulers would be to list the persons holding a significant share of public power. Most of them were already nobles or landed seigneurs, but they were a more select circle in that they had political as well as social influence. This group can be imagined as a series of concentric circles representing diminishing degrees of social advantage and political influence (see tables 1 and 2). At the center are fifty-one 'chief power brokers', the figures who play a central role in this study. They belong to a group of 223 'truly influential powers', who have been arbitrarily ranked on the basis of meeting one or more of three criteria: (a) that they made or directly influenced political decisions of province-wide importance, (b) that they communicated with individuals in the central government in such a way as to serve as a major conduit of influence and information, (c) that their wealth or social status was great enough to influence other provincial leaders, even though they might personally be less involved in public affairs. These standards are hard to apply. In many cases, like the councillors of the Parlement, only a few from a category of individuals were truly influential. In others, like the consuls of towns, political authority was temporary and rotating. The 'influentials' come out of a larger circle of 572 'major officials' and 1,126 'important functionaries'. These figures are only estimates and do not include the myriad petty judges, urban councillors, huissiers, clerks, and other petty agents who would hardly be considered privileged despite their connection with important

[11] Lamoignon de Basville, *Mémoires*, pp. 101–24; Henry de Caux, *Catalogue général des gentils-hommes de la province de Languedoc* (Pézenas, 1676). [12] Lamoignon de Basville, *Mémoires*, pp. 204–5.
[13] Ibid., pp. 65–75.

Table 1. *The 'truly influential powers' (in descending order of importance)*

	Category	Group
1.	Archbishop of Narbonne (1)	fifty-one 'chief power brokers'
2.	Twenty-one other prelates (21)	
3.	Governor (1)	
4.	First president of the Parlement (1)	
5.	First president of the Comptes (1)	
6.	Treasurer of the bourse (1)	
7.	Intendant (1)	
8.	Présidents à mortier of the Parlement (11)	
9.	Presidents of the Comptes (10)	
10.	Three lieutenant-generals of the province (3)	
11.	Twenty most influential councillors from the Parlement and the three royal prosecutors (23)	172 other influential powers (but most of these positions were not held continuously by the same individuals)
12.	Twenty most influential councillors from the Comptes and three royal prosecutors (23)	
13.	Three syndic-generals of the province (3)	
14.	Twenty leading treasurer-generals of finance (20)	
15.	Twenty-two diocesan syndics 'en exercice' (22)	
16.	Nine seneschals and baillis (9)	
17.	Ten barons of the Estates who attend regularly (10)	
18.	Twenty officers from sénéchaussée courts (20)	
19.	Twenty consuls attending Estates (20)	
20.	Twenty-one diocesan receivers 'en exercice' (22)	
Total		223 individuals

agencies. They do include all the major officials of any sort: a group of about 1,000 who ran the province in the interest of up to 10,000 persons like themselves, out of a population of somewhere between 1,000,000 and 1,500,000. From the top to the bottom of the system power was distributed in unequal degrees in a pyramid that was decidedly top-heavy. Even the 'truly influential' were unequal because those at the top of the list had permanent positions with many times as much power as those at the bottom, whose influence was temporary or collective.

This sort of categorization is unorthodox because it classifies the 'agents' of government in terms of their relationship to the 'system' of power, ignoring for the moment the fact that the persons in question held different kinds of power and functioned in different sorts of ways. The idea of a 'circle' of 200 or 1,000 'rulers' is helpful in bringing out one kind of reality. It is also important to recognize that these authorities were not interchangeable and that they operated in particular ways which structured the nature of political life. We need, therefore, an analytical overview of

Table 2. *Governmental functionaries in Languedoc (c. 1678–90)*

	Number	Major officials	'Truly influential'
1. Royal officers – judicial			
A. Parlement of Toulouse	129	114	35
B. Chambre de l'Édit	16	11	
C. Sénéchaussée courts	200	200	20
D. Prévôté (changeable)	15		
2. Royal officers – financial			
A. Cour des Comptes, Aides et Finances	116	67	34
B. Treasurer-generals of finance	57	57	20
C. Gabelle administration	200	1	
D. Receiver-generals of finance	30	10	
E. Royal domaine	20		
F. Cours des monnaies	16		
G. Eaux et forêts (7 maîtrises)	21	2	
3. Royal agents			
A. Governor	1	1	1
B. Lieutenant-generals	3	3	3
C. Seneschals and baillis	9	9	9
D. Commanders of fortresses and towns	11		
E. Intendant	1	1	1
4. Ecclesiastical			
A. Prelates (or vicar-generals)	22	22	22
B. Cathedral chapters, educational and religious houses, etc.			
5. 'Representative' bodies			
A. Capital towns			
(1) Toulouse	8	4	
(2) Montpellier	6	2	20
(3) 20 other towns	40		
B. Diocesan assiettes	154	44	44
C. Estates of Languedoc			
(1) 20 annual barons	20	20	10
(2) 20 rotating barons	20		
(3) Treasurer of the bourse	1	1	1
(4) Syndic generals	3	3	3
(5) Secretary generals	2		
(6) Lesser officers	5		
Totals	1,126	572	223

the parts of the system which will be discussed in later chapters, highlighting the nature of their role and passing over the many other agencies which were of less crucial importance.

A. *Dispersed local units.* The political geography of the province was built around twenty-two towns which were the capitals of twenty-two ecclesiastical and secular dioceses. These included most, but not all, of the important urban centers and several country backwaters which were otherwise undistinguished.[14] Each capital had a consulate, that is a collective governing committee consisting of three to eight consuls chosen annually from among the prominent citizens by a method of indirect election. These municipal committees changed yearly, but the annual consuls were backed up by more permanent councils and appointed officers. In fact, the towns were really dominated by small self-perpetuating oligarchies of wealthy merchants and officers.

The twenty-two capitals were also the seats of the twenty bishops and two archbishops of the province.[15] These prelates, with their vicar-generals, cathedral chapters, and administrations, played a variety of roles from dominant seigneur to local patron. They were national figures who spent considerable time at court, and their decisive role in the Estates made them major power brokers in the province. The towns were also represented in the Estates, with one vote for the capital of each diocese and another for a second town. They took their own demands to the regional assembly, representing the interests of the local oligarchies, but their votes were often controlled by the local bishop. The diocesan assiettes, which met annually to repartition the taxes voted by the Estates among the communities, usually gathered in the same capital towns, where the bishops again presided.

B. *Sovereign and lesser courts.* (1) The Parlement was a company of almost a hundred royal officers distributed in various chambers, who meted out the highest royal justice available outside the king's councils to all of Languedoc and parts of Guyenne. The parlementaires thought of them-

[14] I am presenting the situation as it existed in the early 1670s. The twenty-two dioceses and their idiosyncrasies were: *Haut-Languedoc*: Toulouse (however, the city of Toulouse was independent of the secular diocese), Lavaur, Albi, Castres, Montauban (only included a few parishes, since the city of Montauban and most of the ecclesiastical diocese were outside of Languedoc), Rieux, Carcassonne, Saint-Papoul (which was no more than a rural village), Mirepoix (another backwater), Alet and Limoux (considered one secular diocese), and Comminges (only eleven parishes in Languedoc). *Bas-Languedoc*: Narbonne, Saint-Pons, Béziers, Agde, Lodève, Montpellier, Nîmes, Uzès. *Cévennes*: Viviers, Mende, Le Puy. In 1694 the diocese of Alais was carved out of the diocese of Nîmes, making a total of twenty-three.

[15] The two archbishoprics were Narbonne and Toulouse. In 1678 Albi was raised to an archbishopric. The nineteen other bishoprics were Lavaur, Castres, Montauban, Rieux, Carcassonne, Saint-Papoul, Mirepoix, Alet, Comminges, Saint-Pons, Béziers, Agde, Lodève, Montpellier, Nîmes, Uzès, Viviers, Mende, Le Puy.

selves as defenders of provincial liberties and monitors of local life in the name of the king. For this reason they often took political positions which went beyond the judging of cases, either by delaying and protesting the registration of royal edicts or by asserting a regulatory authority over the activities of rival institutions. The most important parlementaire was the first president, a royal appointee with tremendous influence by virtue of his right to preside over meetings. He corresponded directly with the royal ministers and set the tone for the whole Parlement, while wielding considerable influence in the municipal councils of Toulouse. Next in importance were the presidents of the various chambers, especially the eleven presidents of the grande chambre (*présidents à mortier*). The councillors of the Parlement (*conseillers*) varied greatly in prestige, depending on the size of their fortunes, the extent of their connections, and their age.

(2) The Chambre de l'Édit in Castres was a branch of the Parlement which handled cases involving Protestants, according to the terms of the Edict of Nantes. This small court was one of the few places where Protestant officers could influence events. But although some of them corresponded with royal ministers, they never played a major political role. Nor did the Huguenot Church itself qualify as politically important, despite its urban consistories and regional synods, for the Catholic system simply did not leave room for important Protestant contributions. Calvinist ministers appeared only occasionally on the scene as rebels or petitioners, and Protestant officers in other capacities did their best to play down their religious affiliations.

(3) Under the Parlement was a hierarchy of lower courts and specialized tribunals, most of which need not concern us. There were, however, eight sénéchaussée-présidial courts distributed throughout the province which provided royal justice below the level of the Parlement and served as mini-parlements in towns where no higher court sat.[16] Most of their officers were political non-entities, but certain individuals stood out, either by virtue of their superior titles such as *président-juge mage* or *lieutenant criminel*, or through other connections. Since the sénéchaussée courts were incessantly in conflict with the Parlement, these individuals were natural allies of intendants and royal administrators who needed to keep the Parlement in check.

(4) The second sovereign court was the Cour des Comptes, Aides et Finances in Montpellier. Its structure was similar to that of the Parlement,

[16] A sénéchaussée court was the equivalent of a bailliage court in the north. A présidial was a sénéchaussée with special competence in certain areas, in a sense the highest level of sénéchaussée court. The eight sénéchaussée-présidial courts in Languedoc were in Toulouse, Castelnaudary (for the 'Lauragais'), Carcassonne, Béziers, Limoux (established 1646), Montpellier, Nimes, and Le Puy. There was also a simple sénéchaussée court at Castres.

and its first president, ten presidents, and fifty councillors played very similar roles. The Comptes was a newer and less prestigious court with jurisdiction over questions concerning royal accounts, royal officers, and royal finances. Comptes families dominated Bas-Languedoc the same way the parlementaires dominated the Toulousain, and despite their purely fiscal competence they asserted the same sorts of claims to 'police' the region in ways which exceeded their technical authority.

(5) There were no dispersed lower courts like the sénéchaussée under the jurisdiction of the Comptes. Instead there were two *bureaux des finances* in Toulouse and Montpellier, each of which contained around twenty treasurer-generals of finance (*trésoriers généraux de France*). In other provinces these royal officers handled the repartition of the royal taille for their district (the *généralité*) among the subdistricts (*élections*), where it was then apportioned among the communities by the *élus*. In Languedoc, since the Estates handled the taille through the assiettes, there were no élus and no élections. The treasurer-generals therefore did not play a major role politically despite the fact that they were rich individuals who were usually related to sovereign court judges or financiers. They oversaw the gabelle, aspects of the royal domain, and various tax farms, all of whose cases ended up on appeal in the Comptes.

C. *The royal agents – military and administrative.* The individuals in the previous category were all royal officers, participating in the system of venality with all its ambivalence of loyalties. Logically distinct from them were the royal commanders whose chief role was military. Their function was to exercise the more personal and physical aspects of royal power – not the king's administration of justice and finance, but his capacity to elicit loyalty, express anger or clemency, enforce authority through superiority and physical domination. The royal commanders were invariably military men who were accompanied by troops of some sort. In style they were traditional nobles who imitated the king's manner, moved from town to town, and acted individually, as opposed to the royal officers who stayed in one place and acted collectively.

(1) The most influential royal commander was the governor of the province, a great noble of national stature whose politics and loyalties were attuned to a level which transcended provincial interests. The governor's most important task was to represent the king at the Estates, where he headed a team of 'royal commissioners' empowered to present the monarch's demands and negotiate modifications in them. He also commanded troops in the province, in the absence of a rival commander-in-chief. In addition, the governor served as intermediary between the province and the king, hearing appeals while on the scene, and intervening on the province's behalf when at court. Under him were three

lieutenant-generals who served the same function in his absence, each of whom was assigned a district: Haut-Languedoc, Bas-Languedoc, or the Cévennes.

(2) The other commanders were figures of only local importance. First there were seneschals or baillis who presided over the courts mentioned above.[17] In addition there were twelve to fifteen commanders (or 'governors') of royal fortifications, whose positions conferred local prominence and provided the means to assert a modicum of influence over the areas where their power was situated.

(3) The most important royal agent, however, had administrative rather than military authority – the intendant, or sometimes a team of intendants and other royal experts. The intendancy was a developing institution of crucial importance, but by himself the intendant was just an energetic individual seconded by a secretary or two, and occasionally some 'guards'. Practically speaking, the royal interests were represented not just by one or two such agents but by a 'team' of royal allies comprising the intendant, the top military commanders, and a network of provincial contacts and informers.

D. *The Estates.* The Estates were convoked once a year by the crown in one of the provincial capitals, where they remained in session for a month or more. Represented in the assembly were the two archbishops and twenty bishops, or, in their absence, their vicar-generals; twenty-two noble 'barons'; and the representatives of the towns, who shared forty-four votes. The barons were the owners of the twenty-two estates called baronies which conferred the right to attend. Their number was thus fixed. There was no general assemblage of the nobility as in most other provinces.

The meetings were structured around the negotiations between king and province over taxes. The archbishop of Narbonne always presided over, and spoke for, the Estates, thereby becoming the pivotal figure in the negotiations. In addition, the Estates maintained their own officers who were not of the stature of the deputies themselves but who nevertheless played key roles. Most central was the treasurer of the bourse (*trésorier de la bourse*), an immensely important financier who managed the provincial tax revenues. Three syndic-generals served as provincial administrators whose function was comparable in importance to that of the royal intendants. There were also two secretary-generals of the province. Then on the diocesan level, each assiette had a syndic and a receiver for administration and financial receiving.

[17] The principal seneschals were those of Toulouse, Lauragais (Castelnaudary), Carcassonne, Béziers, Montpellier, Nîmes, and Le Puy. Limoux, as a new court, does not seem to have had one. Castres had a 'seneschal royal', and there were baillis of Gévaudan and Vivarais who seem to have been attached to lesser courts. Thus while there were eight sénéchaussée-présidial courts, there were seven major seneschals, or ten seneschals and baillis if everyone is counted.

These were the key figures in Languedocian politics. They belonged to distinct but overlapping spheres of power which might be categorized as follows: (1) There was a clear separation between the judicial system headed by the Parlement and the Comptes, and the tax administration run by Estates and assiettes. The first was the preserve of royal officers who functioned judicially and had no authority to handle money. The second was dominated by bishops and financiers who had very little judicial competence. (2) There was a logical separation between (a) those who commanded in the name of the crown (military governors) or administered for the king (intendants); (b) those who belonged to corps of royal functionaries (venal officers); and (c) those who 'represented' local entities (town consulates, deputies to assiettes or Estates; urban, diocesan or provincial administrators). (3) Finally none of these categories enables us to predict a third sort of distinction between individuals who would support royal policies and those who would actively oppose them.

LIFESTYLES

This group had much in common despite the levels within it. The great bishops and parlementaires did move in more impressive circles than diocesan syndics or presidial judges. But it is easy to forget that both types shared a similar social preeminence. The bishop of Béziers might enjoy an urban *hôtel* with *cour d'honneur* and more than twenty rooms packed with tapestries, furs, Turkish carpets, carved and upholstered furniture, silver plate, chandeliers, a stable full of horses, and a library filled with 2,500 volumes, in addition to a country chateau which boasted more luxury furnishings and an orangerie with fifty-one orange trees. The bishop of Rieux might enjoy annual revenues of 113,000 livres plus fifty setiers of oats, twelve setiers of wheat, and one hundred pairs of pigeons, to help feed his establishment of thirty-one personal servants. But even Gabriel Le Noir, the far more modest juge mage of Béziers, left behind tapestries from Flanders and Bergamo, thirty paintings of landscapes and religious subjects, and a library of 300 books, most of them in Latin.[18] Although the first two were figures of national prominence and the third was only a local judge, all three would have made a similar impression on an artisan or shopkeeper who ventured into their antechambers to collect a bill or perform a service.

Estimates of wealth can only be impressionistic, but there is no doubting

[18] Louis Noguier, 'Palais épiscopal de Béziers, mobilier des évêques', *Bulletin de la Société Archéologique de Béziers*, 3rd series 1 (1895), 5–36; Jean Contrasty, *Histoire de la cité de Rieux-Volvestre et de ses évêques* (Toulouse, 1936), p. 300; Louis Noguier, *Recherches sur les anciennes judicatures de la ville de Béziers* (Béziers, 1880), pp. 48–9.

the superior resources enjoyed by most of the rulers of Languedoc. Table 3 gives some idea of the incomes and resources of the individuals on my notability list, with comparative figures from other provinces. At their highest ranks the Languedocians had revenues and offices comparable to some of the best in the kingdom, though not equal to those of their counterparts in Paris. At their lowest, they had fortunes similar to prosperous merchants or solid country nobles.

If the rulers of Languedoc were all socially distinguished, some were more so than others. Perhaps the most fundamental factor dividing them was not wealth but the scope of their experiences. On the one hand were prelates, great nobles, intendants, and certain sovereign magistrates whose perspective ranged all over France, and sometimes beyond; on the other were local judges, merchants, lawyers, and petty nobles who seldom left the province. Bishops came to Languedoc from posts elsewhere; they met each other at assemblies of the clergy and had experience preaching in Paris or travelling to Rome. Great nobles understood the antechambers of the Louvre and the chateaux around Paris, the life of garrison towns, and especially the army. The king's intendants knew the idiosyncrasies of many provinces, along with the world of Parisian parlementaires and bureaucrats. The same was true of the greatest officers, who were received in the best robe households of Paris, and who carried on a wide correspondence with other judicial notables. Their lesser counterparts were not nearly as experienced. The bulk of them rarely left the province: they were consuls for whom a deputation to Paris was an adventure, merchants who made the circuit of the fairs of the Midi, venturing perhaps as far as Spain or Italy; mountain nobles still terrorizing the countryside and viewing the royal council only as a distant court of appeal; lawyers for whom the foci of power were the two judicial *palais* in Montpellier and Toulouse.

Military nobles affected a style modelled after the governor. They were gallant and courteous in negotiations, but impatient with bargaining and paper work, preferring to rely on eminence rather than skill. They surrounded themselves with a train of followers, expected brassy welcomes wherever they appeared (or declined them with equally ostentatious modesty), and took special interest in questions of arms or patronage, while cultivating an image of haughty disdain at slights and playing the magnanimous patron to those who were respectfully subordinate. Their statements were usually brief and to the point. Intendants, by contrast, displayed a comprehensive grasp of the complexities of power and a clear sense of reasoned subordination to the common good. Their speeches were crammed with classical and biblical references, rhetorical flourishes and philosophical distinctions.

The bishops were on the whole a learned and distinguished group. They

Table 3. *Wealth of the influential*

These are no more than examples drawn from a variety of sources and from various dates. Prices of offices refer to sums actually paid or offered except those in parentheses, which are official prices. Asterisks indicate revenues of the bishopric alone, not the family fortune. All these figures are subject to many qualifications. Figures in livres.

	Purchase price of office	Annual revenue	Value of fortune
1. National comparisons			
Prince de Condé (1651)		425,012	14,600,794
Capetian ducs et pairs (1625–60)			2,326,000 (av.)
'Gentlemen' ducs et pairs (1625–60)			846,000 (av.)
Secretary of state (1643)	700,000		
La Vrillière (1678)		100,000	2,400,000
Maîtres des requêtes	150,000		
Average dowry (1624–61)			122,000
Charles Pinon (1672)		30,000	815,240
Paris parlementaires			
Office of councillor (1682)	100,000		
Lands owned (1685–90)		to 25,000	10/–500,000
41 dowries (1660–1) (average)			173,000
Parlement of Aix (mid-cent.)			
First President Oppède		50/–60,000	1,700,000
Poor councillors		5/–10,000	100/–200,000
Middling councillors		10/–20,000	200/–400,000
Wealthy councillors		20,000 +	400,000 +
Parlement of Rouen			
Councillor (mid-cent.)	40/–80,000		
President (1632)	186,000		
2. Examples from Languedoc			
Governor: Conti (1666)		400,000	1,100,000
Lieut.-Gen. Grignan (1663–9)		50/–60,000	1,700,000
Archbishop of Narbonne		90,000*	
Bishops:			
Range (1670–90)		16/–80,000*	
Bertier in Rieux (1662)		113,000	
Percin in Saint-Pons (1670s)		110,000	
Parlement of Toulouse			
First president	(150,000)		
Président à mortier (1682)	120,000		
President Donneville (1663)		25,000	
President Caulet (1663)		35/–40,000	

Table 3 (*cont.*)

	Purchase price of office	Annual revenue	Value of fortune
Advocate-general (1682)	100,000		
Maniban family (mid-cent.)		30/–40,000	1,000,000
Councillor (1668)	75,000		
Top families in 1690s:			
4 families			300/–500,000
2 families			200/–300,000
6 families			100/–200,000
Councillor Frezals (1663)		18/–20,000	
Barons and nobles (certain Estates)			
Severac (duc d'Arpajon)		34,000	
La Voulte (Ventadour)		40,000	
Treasurer of the bourse			
From Estates in 1677 (official)		127,000	
Syndic-generals			
Annual stipends (minimum)		5,000	
Retirement gift (1642)		18,000	
Diocesan Receivers	(8/–24,000)		
Diocese/Toulouse (1677) (official)		10,000	
Comptes of Montpellier			
First President Maussac (1642)	150,000		
President (1659)	(100,000)		
President Baudan (1644)	84,000		
Councillor	(50/–60,000)		
Treasurer-generals			
Montpellier, Baudan (1644)	70,000		
Average stipends (1655)		2,223	
Juges mages, presidents of présidial	(10/–20,000)		
Présidial officers	(4/–8,000)		

Principal sources: Mousnier, *Les Institutions de la France*, vol. I, pp. 140–7, vol. II, pp. 327–8; Vialles, *Études historiques sur la Cour des Comptes*, pp. 76–8; ms. fr. 18483, 49; Kettering, *Judicial Politics and Urban Revolt*, pp. 231–46; B.M. Tse ms. 603 ('Description'), 256–61; Mousnier, *La Vénalité des offices*, pp. 358–64; Dewald, *The Formation of a Provincial Nobility*, pp. 335–9; Jean Contrasty, *Histoire de la cité de Rieux-Volvestre et de ses évêques* (Toulouse, 1936), p. 300; Hippolyte Crozes, *Le Diocèse d'Albi, ses évêques et archevêques* (Toulouse, 1878), pp. 124–9; Bonney, *Political Change in France*, pp. 86–7; François Bluche, *Les Magistrats du Parlement de Paris au XVIIIe siècle (1715–1771)* (Paris, 1960), p. 167; Jean-Pierre Charmeil, *Les Trésoriers de France à l'époque de la Fronde* (Paris 1964), pp. 85–91.

were predominantly royal allies, for not only had they been appointed by the king to their posts, but most of them had personally won the nomination through service at court. The few exceptions were either dynasties whose eminence derived from family service, like the Bonzis of Béziers who held the bishopric for six generations after arriving from Italy in the train of Catherine de Medicis (1576–1669); or service families from the robe nobility like the Bertiers of Rieux (1603–1705) and Montauban (1652–74). The Languedocian prelates were notable for their achievements as well as their connections. Marca of Toulouse (1652–62) had been president of the Parlement of Béarn and intendant in Catalonia before being ordained. Plantavit de la Pause (Lodève, 1625–48) knew seventeen languages and travelled as emissary to Venice, Austria, Hungary, Poland and the Netherlands.[19] Because Languedoc was the center of French Protestantism, a real effort was made to name persuasive prelates, and most of them were industrious builders of their spiritual and temporal domains, rebuilding churches, introducing Jesuit collèges and endowing new religious orders.[20]

Below these eminent figures we may imagine several levels of more locally-oriented notables tied to the great by interlocking webs of connections. At the bottom of the scale, barely counting outside their own communities, were the top families of merchants and professionals. Take Étienne Borrelly of Nîmes, for example, who has left an extensive *livre de raison* covering events from 1651 through the rest of our period.[21] He was the son of an avocat in the courts of Nîmes who married the daughter of a notary whose office he later purchased. His brother served as third consul in 1656, and he was a member of the *conseil extraordinaire* in 1670. His most important asset, though, was his connection to the bishopric. Since his father had been legal representative of the bishop d'Ouvrier and the cathedral chapter, Borrelly was no doubt aiming at the same position when he waited fifteen days in Bourg Saint-Andéol, then several more in Beaucaire, to greet the new bishop Cohon when he first set foot on Languedocian soil. The vigil was a success, for Borrelly was granted the post of episcopal secretary-clerk which was obviously central to his career. When the next bishop Séguier was due to arrive in Beaucaire, Borrelly improved on his previous performance by hiring a boat and virtually

[19] M. Bellaud-Dessalles, *Les Évêques italiens du diocèse de Béziers (1547–1669)* (Toulouse, 1901); abbé Cayre, *Histoire des évêques et archevêques de Toulouse depuis la fondation du siège jusqu'à nos jours* (Toulouse, 1873); abbé Constant Blaquière, *Histoire des évêques de Lodève: Plantavit de la Pause* (Montpellier, 1910); Xavier Azema, *Un Prélat janséniste: Louis Foucquet évêque et comte d'Agde (1656–1702)* (Paris, 1963).

[20] Robert Sauzet, *Contre-réforme et réforme catholique en Bas-Languedoc: le diocèse de Nîmes au XVIIe siècle* (Brussels, 1979).

[21] Albert Puech, 'La Vie de nos ancêtres', *Mémoires de l'Académie de Nîmes*, 7th series 8 (1885), 143–298 (includes the *livre de raison* of Étienne Borrelly).

colliding with the bishop's barge in mid-Rhône while delivering a flowery salutation.

Borrelly's experience was strictly limited to Nîmes and the villages nearby. He did have access to information about events which interested him elsewhere, like the restrictions imposed on the Protestants of other towns. But the narrowness of his horizons and the second-hand nature of his information emerge clearly from his jottings. He relates that his father had once travelled to foreign lands with a family benefactor. One of his brothers-in-law had died in Livorno in Italy while dealing in merchandise. Another went to Paris on foot in 1661 to visit an uncle. But Borrelly himself never seems to have gone farther than Montpellier, where he finally went on business in 1678 when he was forty-five. He was humble enough to refer to the local présidial judges, consuls, and other dignitaries attending a pontifical mass as 'ce beau monde', and he seems almost dazzled to have once caught a glimpse of the marquise de Verneuil, the governor's wife, dining at the bishop's palace.

Borrelly's notes give us glimpses of life in the lowest level of our political hierarchy. But, as secretary of the bishop, he already suggests an intermediate level of urban bureaucrats and agents. Every town, corps, and organization had its syndics, clerks, and lawyers who had to deal daily with bishops, governors, and royal officers. They came from local families whose other members were lawyers, notaries, or priests, and whose most successful relatives were in the royal courts. Their jobs led them on missions to other places, creating a network of contacts from center to center and a stack of technical information. Higher up the ladder they became influential intermediaries like the vicar-generals who stood in for the bishops, the syndics of dioceses, or the rich and sophisticated officers of the Estates, who were received in many a Parisian drawing room.

Thus the rulers of Languedoc varied considerably from city fathers and skillful agents through powerful administrators to grandiose judges and magnificent prelates. Their fortunes were proportionate to their relative position, but they were all wealthy and privileged relative to the majority of the population – even Borrelly represented the upper crust of Nîmes – and they all had a connection to that most precious commodity, power.

PART TWO

The distribution of authority

3

Urban setting and local authorities

If economic reality was grounded in the countryside in the seventeenth century, political reality was urban. The towns were, first, the home of the local institutions which provided the grassroots of provincial government – consulates, episcopal sees, assiettes, and sénéchaussée courts. In a society where authority was always passed down from above, these local jurisdictions were not as fundamental as they might have been in another setting, but there was still an interaction between the issues arising 'from below' and the policies of higher authorities. The towns were important, secondly, as an environment within which all authorities functioned. Matters such as the prices of necessities, the intensity of social unrest or religious strife, and the spread of epidemic disease affected all the major authorities for they all lived and worked in the same narrow streets. Thirdly, the proximity of the authorities generated major jurisdictional conflicts which influenced the very nature of political life. The towns were thus important institutionally as the bottom level of various hierarchies, socially as an environment affecting politics, and physically as the geographical battlefield for conflicts of authority. By looking at their situation we set the scene for all the rest of the analysis.

THE ENVIRONMENT

To a visitor from the north, the Languedocian landscape must have seemed to bristle with walled towns, for the high intensity of urban development was one of the features of the Midi.[1] Not that these towns were very large or very distinguished, for most were modest in size and rural in atmosphere. But they had a long tradition of urban pride, consecrated in the high number

1 Among the best travel accounts and contemporary descriptions of Languedoc are Pierre d'Avity, *Description générale de l'Europe*, vol. II (Paris, 1643), pp. 346–72, the Languedocian section of which is by François Ranchin from Uzès, an avocat in Montpellier; 'Description de la province de Languedoc', B. M. Tse ms. 603, written about 1673, probably by the intendant d'Aguesseau; Nicolas Lamoignon de Basville, *Mémoires pour servir à l'histoire de Languedoc* (Amsterdam, 1736); John Locke, *Locke's Travels in France 1675–1679*, ed. John Lough (Cambridge, 1953); Arthur Young, *Young's Travels in France during the Years 1787, 1788, 1789* (London, 1913); Henri, comte de Boulainvilliers, *État de la France*, new edn, vol. VIII (London, 1752); J. B. Tenant de Latour, ed., *Oeuvres de Chapelle et Bachaumont* (Paris, 1854), pp. 47–99.

of 'consulates', or local elected governments, many of them presiding over little more than walled villages, and in the absurd proliferation of bishoprics, more than in any other region of France.[2] Appearances were also different from the Île de France. Seeing the towns' flat, overhanging tile roofs, the cypresses and pines in their gardens, their Italianate public fountains, or the play of bright sunlight and deep shade in their streets and alleys, the visitor would have felt closer to Florence and Rome than to the Gothic landscape of the Beauce. This contrast must have been greater in the seventeenth century, and differences among the sub-regions of the province must have been more marked.

The largest towns were imposing by the standards of the day. Toulouse maintained a fairly stagnant population of around 40,000 throughout the century, while Montpellier grew from 20,000 to maybe 30,000 if we take the more optimistic estimates, and Nîmes came fairly close to Montpellier. A few others hovered around 10,000 (Béziers, Carcassonne, Castres), with totals for the rest dropping off rapidly. Still, only about twenty French cities were larger than 13,000 at the end of the seventeenth century; and in this context Languedoc's showing of three large, two medium-sized and five or six small but fully developed towns was very respectable, not to mention the many other tiny consulates which filled the countryside.[3]

We can still find these towns today, tucked away somewhere in the core of their modern successors, but it is not easy to recreate the feel of the seventeenth century in larger places like Toulouse or Montpellier because even their historic centers have been drastically changed. The claustrophobic feeling which distinguished towns under Louis XIII or Louis XIV is better sensed in small places like the hill town of Sommières whose steep alleys are dank and clammy in the summer or Pézenas where many of the seventeenth-century streets still have trough-like gutters in the middle. But there the bustle which struck peasants entering the gates past municipal sentinels and suspicious tax collectors is long departed, making it hard to recreate the requisite combination of smallness and liveliness.

The remaining seventeenth-century streets still give testimony of a social structure dominated by a group of elite rulers small enough in number for each individual to be known personally in the community. The notables'

[2] By my calculation Languedoc had 22 prelates out of 124 for all of France, or 17.7 percent of the total.

[3] Population figures are very imprecise. For the best estimates, see Jean Coppolani, *Toulouse au XXe siècle* (Toulouse, 1963), pp. 21–4; Paul Gachon, *Histoire de Languedoc* (Paris, 1921), pp. 191–2; Philippe Wolff, ed., *Histoire du Languedoc* (Toulouse, 1967), pp. 380–1; Léon Dutil, *L'État économique du Languedoc à la fin de l'ancien régime* (Paris, 1911), pp. 55–6; Lamoignon de Basville, *Mémoires*, pp. 243–86; Georges Frêche, *Toulouse et la région Midi-Pyrénées au siècle des lumières (vers 1670–1789)* (Paris, 1974), pp. 41–67. For comparison, Pierre Goubert, *Beauvais et le Beauvaisis de 1600 à 1730*, 2 vols. (Paris, 1960), vol. 1, pp. 253–6.

presence is made known through a system of small embellishments on their houses, touches which hint at the elaborate hôtels that only a few had the means to construct. First one perceives the street doors decorated with sculpted molding and pediment: Gothic arches, Renaissance orders, and heavy mannerist columns stand side by side along otherwise drab streets, some rather crude and others quite elegant. These doorways lead to dark, narrow halls and then to tiny courtyards where other elements may be added: windows with sculpture matching the doorway; a second portal on the court: a spectrum of ornamental staircases ranging from tiny spirals in medieval towers to ceremonial entranceways; coats of arms; heads in niches; or small Latin inscriptions.

The few full-scale hôtels belonging to influential notables are correspondingly exalted by comparison. Montpellier's elegant seventeenth-century residences boast courtyards whose modest dimensions are more than overcome by a breathtaking charm worthy of the Marais in Paris. In Toulouse the economic boom of the sixteenth century left behind larger but equally charming palaces in brick, where 'the Toulousain renaissance, rather whimsical and baroque, attempted to discipline itself after the fashion of the great Parisian or Italian models'.[4] These hôtels, along with their rural counterparts, were the scene of most of the parleys, social gatherings, legal strategy sessions, and endless drawing up of papers which underpinned the ruling of a province.

Towns distinguished themselves by public monuments. Like the houses of individuals, these bore the mark of the cumulative efforts of successive regimes, which made their identity known by plaques, carved names, and coats of arms. The town walls symbolized the autonomous jurisdiction of the consulate and delimited an economic as well as legal entity. The best were strategically engineered fortifications requiring guards, like the ones at Narbonne; the worst were merely a circle of connecting backs of houses surrounded by a ditch, as in remote Le Vigan.[5] If the king ordered the walls demolished, their upper levels were usually removed. Conversely if townsmen were preparing for a military threat, they would 'repair the fortifications', which meant filling in the holes or adding height. The size of the wall was roughly proportionate to a town's pride.

Town halls, often called *maisons de ville* or *maisons consulaires*, were the centers of municipal life, repositories of the efforts of many regimes. The Capitole in Toulouse (which, true to form, the Toulousains insisted on baptising with a distinctive name to match the pretensions of their consuls who were called *capitouls*) was a perfect example – a rambling brick pile of chambers, galleries, stairways, and gardens connected by massive

[4] Paul Mesplé, *Toulouse* (Paris, 1961), p. 34.
[5] Pierre Gorlier, *Le Vigan à travers les siècles*, new edn (Montpellier, 1970), pp. 75–6, 123.

decorated portals. The Montpellier equivalent was similar. In 1647 its main assembly room was redecorated with portraits of the consuls of each year, and in 1659 a portrait of the governor Gaston d'Orléans was commissioned to adorn the fireplace in the *salle des états*, with pictures of the lieutenant-generals added to the smaller meeting rooms. Other maisons consulaires were more modest, but they contained the same elements: decorations glorifying the office of consul, facilities for deliberations and rendering of justice, prisons, arsenals, and at least one large room for public elections.[6]

The political climate of each major town was determined by its particular combination of roles. The two capitals, Toulouse and Montpellier, each housed similar collections of agencies, but their atmospheres were markedly different. Toulouse was a haughty, aristocratic city which dominated its region by virtue of its location removed from the centers of military and administrative activity. It was in turn dominated by the parlementaires who saw themselves as monitors of all other governmental activity. The air of superiority emanating from their *palais* at the extreme southern gate of the city was so powerful that the eight capitouls who governed the city from their Capitole on the far northern side of town had to muster all their pomp in order to be able to compete. Toulouse was also a city of religious orders and societies of *pénitents*, with a major university and the semi-autonomous abbey of Saint Sernin within its walls. Its most lofty entertainment was the annual competition of the *académie des Jeux Floriaux* to present the author of the best poem with the golden violet of Clémence Isaure, legendary medieval benefactress of this refined society. Montpellier, by contrast, was a city teeming with Huguenot artisans, royal officers, and flashy military commanders. The councillors of the Cour des Comptes put on airs similar to those of the parlementaires, but they were crowded into a smaller city where they rubbed elbows not only with consuls but also with the intendant and the royal citadel. Here the social tone was more influenced by the gallantry of resident military officers and the social pageantry of the Estates. A characteristic entertainment was the *course de bague* of 1633 in which nobles galloped after rings which would win them jewels put up as prizes by noble ladies, and then held parades, masques, and balls.[7]

While Toulouse was unquestionably dominant in Haut-Languedoc, preeminence on the Mediterranean coast was not as clear-cut. Montpellier,

6 Philippe Wolff, *Histoire de Toulouse*, 2nd edn (Toulouse, 1961), pp. 275–8; Grasset-Morel, 'Les Consuls et l'hôtel de ville de Montpellier', *Mémoires de la Société Archéologique de Montpellier*, 2nd series 1 (1894–99), 17–76; Claude Alberge, Michel Christol, and Jean Nougaret, *Guide de Pézenas* (Pézenas, 1965), pp. 69–72.

7 Robert Mesuret, *Évocation du vieux Toulouse* (Paris, 1960), pp. 575–8; André Delort, *Mémoires inédits sur la ville de Montpellier au XVIIe siècle (1621–1693)*, 2 vols. (Montpellier, 1876–8), vol. 1, pp. 86–90.

the ultimate capital of Bas-Languedoc, had been compromised by a series of Protestant revolts, and until the 1670s governors and intendants spent almost as much time in nearby Pézenas, a quieter town not troubled by major judicial companies, or in Narbonne, the strategic gateway to the Catalonian front. Sometimes they even stayed in Béziers, between Narbonne and Montpellier. Another rival center was Nîmes, but this leading Huguenot stronghold, where Protestant merchants had contacts all over Europe and the consistory maintained close ties with dissidents in the nearby Cévennes, had far too subversive a reputation to be considered seriously as an administrative center.

Militarily it was the towns of the Mediterranean plain – Nîmes, Montpellier, Pézenas, Agde, Béziers, Narbonne – which were most likely to encounter the comings and goings of generals, governors, royal agents, and even the king himself, on the standard route between the Rhône valley and the Spanish frontier. They were the stopping-places where negotiations were carried out, honorific entrances were staged, and the Estates were convoked. The most important link in this chain was the citadel at Montpellier, which had been built after 1622 by Richelieu to survey the town and intimidate the Huguenots of the region.[8] There were *mortes-payes* guarding the ramparts of Narbonne and occasional troops stationed within the medieval cité at Carcassonne. Otherwise the scanty royal garrisons vegetated in crumbling fortresses outside the major towns. Another consideration of military importance was the location of potentially treasonous Huguenot communities like Montauban, scene of so many religious conflicts and gateway to Toulouse; Castres, home of the Chambre de l'Édit until 1671; the sister cities of Montpellier, Nîmes, and Uzès; and the smaller centers in the Cévennes.

In economic terms the list of urban centers would be different. Montpellier and Toulouse would qualify by virtue of their importance as centers of aristocratic consumption, but whereas the former was a rapidly developing center of weaving, drugs, liqueurs, tanning, and trade in wines and wool, the latter was economically stagnant, relying upon the wealth of the better days of the sixteenth century and a certain amount of trade in grain. The power of the wealthy grain and wine exporters in Narbonne, Béziers, and Agde gave those cities a concealed importance not obvious in political documents, and we would have to stress the imposing commercial might of Nîmes where everybody seemed to be engaged in selling wool and silk or buying up sheep and cloths from the hinterland. A number of small but teeming manufacturing towns should be recognized, like Carcassonne with its extensive cloth industry and the smaller centers of crude local cloth

[8] Anne Blanchard, 'De Pézenas à Montpellier: transfert d'une ville de souveraineté (XVIIe siècle)', *Revue d'histoire moderne et contemporaine*, 12 (1965), 35–49.

like Lodève, Mazamet, and Anduze, or of silk weaving like Aubenas and Privas. Pézenas and Beaucaire, known for their international fairs, were not even diocesan capitals.[9]

Finally, religious geography should not be forgotten. Most important were the bishoprics which added to the equation not only a prelate with national influence but a cathedral, an episcopal palace, buildings for the chapter and clergy, courts, granaries – in fact a semi-autonomous complex of buildings which was often fortified and set off from the city proper. Some prelates were particularly powerful in their capital cities. Narbonne enjoyed the reflected glory of its archbishop, the province's richest and most influential churchman, who lived in an imposing complex of palace and church buildings right in the heart of the town. In Albi the magnificence of the bishop (after 1676, archbishop) was signalled by the rose-colored bastions which still overlook the Tarn, embellished with gardens and statuary. Also eminent by virtue of historically prestigious and lucrative sees were the bishop of Mende, nestled in the hills of the secluded Gévaudan, and the bishop of Le Puy, whose great romanesque cathedral had been attracting pilgrims and their money since the days of the crusades. The bishops of Béziers, Agde, and Carcassonne also inhabited fortresses. Each town had a rapidly growing number of religious houses, hospitals, and pious foundations which filled the streets with priests and nuns, and caused conflicts over tax exemptions, representation, or precedence.

All these factors contributed to the chemistry of a town's political environment, which was an important element in the success or failure of governmental maneuvers. Authorities had influence to the degree that they were or were not counteracted by other authorities. In times of stress the configuration of rivalries could influence the ability of local forces to unite. Table 4 gives an idea of how provincial forces were distributed. There is a concentration of functions in the top seven cities, and especially in Toulouse and Montpellier, but more significant is the irregular distribution of the various factors in such a way that no two towns were alike. Especially clear is the inverse relationship between political importance on the one hand and the degree of wealth of the bishops on the other. The richest prelates were seated in otherwise undistinguished towns, making their influence all the more potent.

9 Wolff, *Histoire du Languedoc*, pp. 337–41; Louis-J. Thomas, *Montpellier ville marchande: histoire économique et sociale de Montpellier des origines à 1870* (Montpellier, 1936), pp. 133–55. For other references, see chapter 12.

Table 4. *Importance of towns and dioceses*

Order of votes in Estates[a]	Population: of towns by rank[b]	Population: of dioceses by rank[c]	Dioceses' share of taille[d]	Bishoprics' income by rank[e]	Notable features
1. TOULOUSE	1	3	1	5A	Sen TG
2. MONTPELLIER	2	11	9	8A	Sen TG * P
3. CARCASSONNE	5	12	13	4	Sen *
4. NIMES	3	2	4	15A	Sen P
5. NARBONNE	8	8	7	1	*
6. LE PUY	—	4	8	13A	Sen
7. BÉZIERS	4	10	5	13B	Sen
8. UZÈS	13	7	6	8B	P
9. ALBI	7	5	3	2	
10. VIVIERS	—	1	2	10A	P
11. MENDE	10	6	10	3	P
12. CASTRES	6	9	12	5B	P
13. SAINT-PONS	—	20	17	7	
14. AGDE	9	17	15	10B	
15. MIREPOIX	—	15	19	18A	
16. LODÈVE	12	21	16	18B	
17. LAVAUR	11	13	11	12	P
18. SAINT-PAPOUL	—	18	18	22	
19. ALET/LIMOUX	14	19	14	21	
20. MONTAUBAN	—	16	20	15B	P
21. RIEUX	—	14	21	18C	
22. COMMINGES	—	22	22	17	

[a] B.M. Tse ms. 603, 17v.–23v.

[b] Lamoignon de Basville, *Mémoires*, pp. 243–86 (relative population in 1693. Only the top fourteen towns are ranked – those for which Lamoignon de Basville gives exact figures).

[c] Frêche, *Toulouse*, p. 499: tabulation of figures from Lamoignon de Basville in 1693. The figure for Toulouse includes both the town and the diocese.

[d] Frêche, *Toulouse*, p. 499: tabulation of figures from Lamoignon de Basville and other sources.

[e] Lamoignon de Basville, *Mémoires*, p. 61.

Notable features

Sen: seat of sénéchaussée court TG: seat of treasurer-generals of finance *: important military station

P: known for concentration of Protestants

THE CONSULATES

At the heart of each municipal power system was the consulate which ran the city.[10] These governments were different from many of the communes of northern France in that they had not originated in syndicates of inhabitants banding together to promote group defense or to bargain with a feudal lord. In fact, the first consuls had been appointed by the local seigneur to act as intermediaries between himself and the general assembly of inhabitants. Later the monarchy began interposing its influence by settling disputes in royal courts and sending out *réformateurs* to sell protection when conflicts broke out.

Within each town an election process evolved which was then challenged and modified in the fourteenth century when worsening conditions led to serious revolts by artisans and popular groups. Many times the king was called in as arbitrator, and the result was usually a reform of administrative procedures or a revision of the representation system. The events of the religious wars complicated the situation. After the Edict of Nantes, many towns were given 'mixed' consulates in which half the positions were held by members of each faith (*consulats mi-parti*). This unpopular solution just led to more conflicts and more royal arbitrations, destroying even further any pretext for claiming that the consulates were autonomous institutions. Thus, throughout many phases of greater or lesser participation, the consulates remained an alliance of the urban elite first with the seigneur and later with the monarchy. While consuls made much of their local privileges, these had been ratified and modified so many times by the king on behalf of the more eminent citizens that they can hardly be thought of as more than an expedient compromise between local and royal interests. The consulates had never really been autonomous, and for centuries they had been part of a *royal* system.

Toulouse had an appropriately illustrious government.[11] The eight

[10] For the history of the consulates and the background of local institutions, Paul Dognon, *Les Institutions politiques et administratives du pays de Languedoc du XIIIe siècle aux guerres de religion* (Toulouse, 1896), pp. 57–194; Jean Ramière de Fortanier, *Chartes de Franchises du Lauragais* (Paris, 1939); Pierre-Clément Timbal, 'Les villes de consulat dans le Midi de la France: histoire de leurs institutions administratives et judiciaires', in *Recueil de la Société Jean Bodin*, vol. VI (Brussels, 1954), pp. 343–69; André Gouron, 'Diffusion des consulats méridionaux et expansion du droit romain aux XIIe et XIIIe siècles', *Bibliothèque de l'École des Chartes*, 121 (1963), 26–76; Thomas N. Bisson, *Assemblies and Representation in Languedoc in the Thirteenth Century* (Princeton, 1964).

[11] The most useful studies of the municipal government in this period are Robert Sicard, *L'Administration capitulaire sous l'ancien régime: Toulouse et ses capitouls sous la Régence* (Toulouse, 1953), and Henri Roques, *L'Administration municipale à Toulouse de 1693 à 1699* (Toulouse, 1908). On the Capitole, Henri Ramet, *Le Capitole et le Parlement de Toulouse* (Toulouse, 1926). A classic and very useful chronicle of events is Barnabé Farmian de Rozoi, *Annales de la ville de Toulouse*, 4 vols. (Paris, 1771–6).

capitouls wore special hoods and sumptuous red robes decorated with ermine. They were accompanied wherever they went by a cortège of guards wearing the colors of their *capitoulats* (districts), and announced by the town's trumpets and hautboys. Capitouls acquired legal nobility from their office, which meant that they and their children were exempt from *franc fief* taxes, lodgings of troops, and other annoyances of roturiers.[12]

The electoral system in Toulouse was very narrowly based. Each November the current capitouls met with sixteen former capitouls and drew up a list of twenty-four candidates for the next year. This list was then narrowed down to the eight new capitouls by a group of thirty 'electors' representing almost exclusively the officers in the viguier and sénéchaussée courts. Thus the capitouls named their own successors in conjunction with their predecessors and the chief royal officers below the Parlement. Entrance into this charmed circle was limited to those who were well enough known to be nominated, and eligibility was restricted to écuyers, nobles with higher titles, or procureurs in the Parlement or the présidial. Decisions were made in conjunction with a series of councils. The government of the city was thus run by an aristocracy of the top families in law, finance, and trade. The Parlement posed as a superior regulating influence, for although its members were excluded from everyday affairs, parlementaires presided over the larger municipal council meetings.

Close study of the series of rivalries and conflicts which developed in Toulouse between 1620 and 1660 shows that the power balance was clearly shifting in favor of the royal officers, especially the higher ones.[13] This gradual change, which was obviously related to the rising wealth and security derived from venality of office, did not come about smoothly. There were challenges in meetings, quarrels in the streets, and protracted legal appeals. The capitouls fought with almost every other authority at one time or another: with the viguier whose judicial district was shrinking; with the seneschal and the présidial over election controls; with the treasurer-generals over tax regulations; especially with the Parlement. In the 1640s the sovereign judges took advantage of the confusion of Louis XIV's minority to meddle openly in the city administration, and from 1643 to 1646, a virtual state of war existed between Parlement and capitouls. The only real change came later. Until the age of Colbert the intendant had been a distant figure, but in the 1660s and 1670s he began to monitor the situation more closely, and by the 1680s he was actively regulating every aspect of Toulousain affairs. Then in 1687 the king arbitrarily modified the electoral system. The forms remained, but the choice of eight capitouls from the twenty-four

[12] Sicard, *L'Administration*, pp. 24–34.

[13] Archives of the capitouls in A.M. Tse, especially the BB series.

names was now to be made by the intendant in the name of the crown. In 1688 we even find Basville naming a new city annalist on grounds that the literary quality of the municipal annals had been steadily declining![14]

In Montpellier the consulate was organized by rather different principles.[15] Each year a list of thirty-five *habitants prudhommes* was drawn up by seven *échelles*, or occupational groupings. Each of these named five candidates, from whom one elector was ultimately chosen by the drawing of lots. These seven electors then retired with the six present consuls to draw up a list of eighteen candidates, three each from six échelles. One name from each group was then picked, again by lot, to be consul for the year. The six consuls thus represented six occupational groupings, with the first always being a 'gentleman'; the second a 'bourgeois' or wholesale merchant; the third a notary, procureur, financier or 'bourgeois', the fourth, fifth, and sixth drawn from various trades. This system was more representative than that of Toulouse, for the consuls came from various levels of society down to 'tailors, cobblers, masons, and gardeners' in the sixth slot. The drawing of lots hardly guaranteed impartiality, but it did insure that a particular individual could not be imposed on the community, provided the rules were followed. The system was not as open as it appeared. The most eminent electors obviously influenced the rest when candidates were chosen, and the consuls themselves were unequal since the first and second had far greater authority than the rest. After 1628 the Huguenots, who represented a majority of the population, were excluded from the government, though they must have retained great influence in seeing that congenial Catholics were chosen. Unlike Toulouse, royal officers were eligible to serve, though most of the consuls were either merchants or artisans, with an occasional procureur or notary thrown in. On the other hand, the consuls named their own councils and no magistrates were allowed at elections.

In Montpellier rising tensions reflecting important power shifts converged into general conflict by the 1640s.[16] Three new elements complicated matters: the building of the citadel in the 1620s which strengthened the hand of the royal military commanders; the creation of the united Cour

[14] Ernest Roschach, *Les Douze livres de l'histoire de Toulouse* (Toulouse, 1887), pp. 66–7.

[15] On the municipal government in this period, Ferdinand Pegat, 'Des consuls de Montpellier sous l'autorité des fonctionnaires royaux et notamment pendant les années 1640 à 1657', *Mémoires de l'Académie des Sciences de Montpellier*, 5 (1870–3), 567–608; A. Arnaud, 'Fonctions et juridiction consulaires à Montpellier aux XVIIe et XVIIIe siècles', *Annales du Midi*, 31 (1919), 35–67, 32 (1920), 129–56; Alexandre Germain, 'Les commencements du règne de Louis XIV et la Fronde à Montpellier', *Mémoires de l'Académie des Sciences de Montpellier*, 3 (1859–63), 579–602.

[16] Municipal archives of Montpellier, notably A.M. Mp Joffre 10, 'Élections consulaires', and correspondence with the ministers in Paris. See also William Beik, 'Two Intendants Face a Popular Revolt: Social Unrest and the Structure of Absolutism in 1645', *Canadian Journal of History*, 9 (1974), 243–62.

des Comptes which enhanced the status of the sovereign court; and the rising importance of a resident intendant. In 1643 outcries and blows at the election caused its cancellation, and in the years that followed there was trouble almost every year, culminating in the popular uprising of 1645 and the murder of the first consul by an officer of a cavalry regiment in 1651. Then elections were cancelled until 1657 because of Protestant demands for representation. The intendant who, in the 1640s, was an unwilling participant in all this fracas, by the end of the 1650s was beginning to be able to rise above factional strife and take over the direction of local affairs. In 1662 he audited the municipal debts and oversaw their repayment. In 1683 he bailed the consuls out of imprisonment for debt by commandeering all the fiscal records of the past ten years. Gradually his dominance became unquestioned.

The other consulates presented a multiplicity of variations on the two systems already described, always striving, however, at the same rule from the top by a small elite. In certain out-of-the-way towns power was built around a bishop who was usually correspondingly wealthy. Mende was the most extreme example, where the bishop, with his title of *seigneur et gouverneur de la ville de Mende et comte de Gévaudan*, still dominated in medieval manner. He had officers collecting a *péage* on all goods entering; he could name the consuls; and he could control the 'estates' of Gévaudan, as the diocesan assiette was called. There were no institutions powerful enough to check this predominance, and so opposition to the bishop necessarily took the form of violent factionalism. Conditions were similar in Albi and Lavaur.[17]

During their year in office all consuls bore considerable burdens. Their world was a continuum of daily concerns punctuated by glorious moments and dangerous crises. Each town had its own list of the grand ceremonies which had reaffirmed its identity and which were remembered in terms of who had participated, what sort of finery had been displayed, and where visiting dignitaries had been lodged. These *journées* gave towns direct contact with the great events of their time: the Peace of Alais in 1629 which had ended the Protestant wars; the passage of the king and Richelieu in 1628 and 1632; the dramatic victory at Leucate in 1637 when a Spanish invasion had been repulsed by local forces; the passage of the royal party again in 1642; their triumphal progress in 1659 at the time of the Peace of the Pyrenees; the opening of the Canal des Deux Mers in 1681; the

[17] Charles Porée, *Le Consulat et l'administration municipale de Mende* (*des origines à la Révolution*) (Paris, 1901); Marius Balmelle and Suzanne Pouget, *Histoire de Mende* (Mende, 1947); Émile Jolibois, 'Troubles dans la ville d'Albi pendant l'épiscopat de Gaspard de Daillon du Lude', *Revue du Tarn*, 9 (1892), 49–61, 135–45; Auguste Vidal, 'Un évêque de Lavaur au XVIIe siècle', *Revue du Tarn*, 5 (1884–5), 328–33, 358–64.

Revocation of the Edict of Nantes in 1685. The other pole of collective memory concerned the disasters which periodically struck: sieges, popular revolts, and especially epidemics. These were moments for dignity of a different sort on the part of the consuls, torn between duty and flight. In 1631 three of the eight capitouls died of plague while in office. In Montpellier, when the city clerk Viala died during an epidemic, his family was subjected to the indignity of letting doctors examine his naked body in the middle of the public square in order to reassure the population that he had not died of plague.[18]

These moments of ceremonial grandeur and terrible adversity were common to every town. Even in the normal times, however, the consuls were kept busy. They had to attend innumerable ceremonies, many of which demanded impromptu orations; they worked constantly with complex legal papers and financial accounts; and as personifications of the municipality, they were subject to prosecution and harassment. Thus we can see why most of them were educated merchants and lawyers with considerable wealth.

Consuls had to work hard at maintaining patronage contacts while not antagonizing the great. Much time was therefore devoted to ceremonial greetings. Pierre Sabatier, the greffier of Montpellier, recorded fifteen of these in 1647, an average year, honoring the comte de Bieules, the duc du Plessis Praslin, the comte du Roure, the bishop of Montpellier, the archbishop of Narbonne, the prince de Condé, the comte d'Harcourt, the comte de Grammont, the comtesse de Bieules, and the seneschal of Montpellier.[19] There were many grades of welcomes, classed according to the status of the honored party: meetings so many leagues outside the town, greetings at the gates, processions through temporary triumphal arches, bonfires, firings of rounds of artillery, or lights placed in the windows of every house. Sometimes consuls decided that ceremonies expected by dignitaries were beyond their means, but more often they had to scramble to attract attention. In 1633 the consuls of Narbonne rushed to greet the duc d'Hallwin, their new governor, well beyond Castelnaudary, over fifty miles away. When he told them that they were the first town to have saluted him, they resolved proudly that his arrival in Narbonne should be 'the most magnificent entrance possible, to demonstrate to our lord governor the sincerity of our attachment to his service'. They would carpet the streets 'in imitation of the city of Toulouse', and the first consul would accompany Hallwin as far as Montpellier to gain greater assurance of the favors that would result from their efforts.[20]

[18] Rozoi, *Annales*, vol. IV, p. 412; Pierre Sabatier, 'Mémorial des choses les plus remarquables', 2 vols., A.M. Mp BB 197–198, vol. I, 1–2; Auguste Vidal, 'La Peste en 1630, 1631 et 1632', *Revue du Tarn*, 7 (1890), 151–9, 172–80, 190–6, 205–11, 221–5, 243–54.

[19] Sabatier, vol. II (A.M. Mp BB 198).

[20] Narbonne, *Inventaire*, p. 486 (Aug. 7, 1633).

In between ceremonies, consuls had to administer communal property, exercise the town's rights of justice, 'police' local activities, and see to budgets and debts. Communal property consisted of local taxes and rights which had to be farmed out annually, often after weeks of bidding and negotiating. Justice took the form of special courts. In Montpellier the consuls exercised the office of viguier through an appointed *juge ordinaire* who tried petty royal cases. In Toulouse the capitouls were proud of their 'audiences' which rivaled those of the viguier.[21] Police powers required the maintenance of local standards of morality, surveillance of the price and quality of bread and meat, organization of festival days, regulation of foreigners, beggars, and innkeepers, provision for safety in the streets, putting out of fires, monitoring the storing of powder, policing of crime and prostitution, regulating métiers, and so forth. When an irregularity was discovered, it was the duty of any consul who happened to be on the scene to intervene personally. For example, the capitoul Henri de Montagut rushed single-handed to subdue a riot of 1638 when 'a large number of men and women of base condition' were trying to rescue a condemned prisoner, and commanded them to retire from the scene. Another capitoul, seeing a peasant pass by his house one day with a suspiciously large sack, commanded him to come inside, and after an immediate interrogation discovered that it contained contraband salt from Gascogne. In Mende the third consul had custody of the keys to the city and was literally required to lock the gate each night. The consuls thus represented urban authority in a very personal way and could suffer for it. In 1645 when Jacques Sansus, capitoul, scolded raucous students at the door of the *logis de l'écu*, he was met with an assault of rocks and swords which wounded him severely.[22]

Consuls were aided in their administration by a variety of appointed municipal officers whose number varied with the size of the community. Toulouse had four to six legal agents (*assesseurs*), a highly influential syndic, an equally prestigious greffier–secretary, a company of soldiers comprising the *famille de guet*, a secretary–controller for financial records, a treasurer, and a corps of huissiers, public criers, guards, porters, sweepers of public squares, tasters of wine, and more. In tiny Le Vigan the administration consisted only of a greffier, a *valet de ville* who made public announcements, watched the gates, and supervised the belltowers, a bell ringer, a fountain-keeper, and a few others. Such employees were always reappointed annually by each new administration, but some of the posts stayed in the same families for many generations.[23]

Meetings of the consuls with their councils were formal. The first consul would explain the items of business in an opening speech; each matter

21 B.M. Tse FF 276.

22 A.M. Tse BB 31 (June 30, 1638); FF 68 (Mar. 24, 1638); Porée, *Mende*, pp. cxix–cxxv; A.M. Tse BB 33 (Feb. 16, 1645).

23 Sicard, *L'Administration*, pp. 39–46; Gorlier, *Le Vigan*, pp. 102–4.

would then be discussed, and resolutions would be taken which were recorded in the minutes like a legal document. A single problem would be brought up over and over at successive meetings so that the minutes read like a succession of interwoven plots with many installments, gradually unfolding over time. The specificity of these deliberations is striking. Each item, however inconsequential, had to be discussed in all its particulars each time it arose. There was no thought of establishing general guidelines by which subordinates could act independently. Thus permission for a property owner to cut a window in a wall facing the maison de ville, the need to leave the gates open at night during the harvest season, the distribution of water from a public fountain, the rounding of an awkward street corner, all were subjects for repeated discussion.

The same intricacy prevailed in financial matters. One 'solvent resident' was named each year to underwrite tax collections, and this individual was then held permanently liable for all payments during his fiscal regime. The next year a different party would take on the new contract, but the old books would not be closed until all disputes were resolved and all obligations met. Thus in Toulouse a suit against Devaux, treasurer in 1641, for alleged misuse of 60,000 livres was still at issue in 1645, 1647, 1648, and 1650.[24] At any one time consuls had to juggle the accounts for a number of different years and engage in many distinct operations. Money had to be appropriated each time for each task, and its exact source designated.

The business of the consuls thus revolved around a large number of ongoing practical problems, mostly legal in nature. They kept great registers of arrêts and règlements received from outside authorities – governor, intendants, higher courts, military officers, royal council – each with its proclamation in the name of the municipality duly added; they issued their own regulations in local matters with equal pomp; and they kept an eye on developments in many different locations which had a bearing on local affairs.[25] Despite their pretensions and the éclat of their administration, one senses that much of their work was defensive. They were constantly hoping to fend off a barrage of challenges from without, petty or serious, which compromised their ways of functioning. Privileges, funding, improvements could only be handled item by item as they arose. Responsibilities were personal, temporally limited, and lacking in continuity. There was little room for policy-making or long-range planning. Thus consuls rarely had the initiative, and their greatest pride was usually in defending their particular regime from charges that they had tolerated any encroachments on the rights of the community.

[24] A.M. Tse BB 33, 273; BB 34, 26, 106, 171–4, 306v.
[25] A.M. Tse BB 609/1, AA 22; A.M. Mp BB 284.

OTHER LOCAL AUTHORITIES

Although the consuls were directly responsible for urban government, other local authorities were so intertwined in local affairs and faced such similar problems that their various activities are best thought of together. The consuls always acted in conjunction with councils which included not only the spokesmen of other families like themselves but usually the representatives of other local corps, especially in the larger meetings which dealt with emergencies. Other local authorities confronted similar problems in parallel ways. One of them, the bishop, was influential in too personal a manner to be considered as an institution. Two others, however, should be noted: the sénéchaussées and the diocesan assiettes.

Sénéchaussée-présidial courts increased in importance with their distance from the seat of a sovereign court.[26] The seneschal himself was a noble with only ceremonial functions, but the practicing court was a company of judges determined to assert their influence in municipal affairs as if they were a parlement. At their head were a juge mage (serving also as *lieutenant-général civil*) who convoked the company, presided over its sessions, and administered oaths, and a *lieutenant-général criminel.* Then there were *lieutenants particuliers civil* and *criminel* who served in their absence, and two public prosecutors (the *procureur du roi* and the *avocat du roi*). A body of councillors (*conseillers*) completed the company, along with various clerks and the avocats or procureurs who were authorized to transact business for their clients before the court.

In addition to their legal business, the officers of the sénéchaussée played a role in public affairs. Their job, like that of the Parlement above them, was to register, publicize, and interpret royal edicts. Their arrêts were therefore conspicuous whenever public order was in question or royal ordinances were being announced. They took a special interest in the regulation of inns and taverns, the prices of commodities and the exchange rates of coinage; gave permission to print books, and concerned themselves in general with taxes and public regulations. Their officers usually played an important role in consular elections and participated in or presided over municipal council meetings. In addition, the juge mage, who was sometimes 'president–juge mage', had his own claims to personal authority which set him in conflict with other local dignitaries. In cities like Nîmes he could be a major figure comparable to the first president of the Parlement in Toulouse.

The assiettes met for only a few days each year to carry out the

[26] Lamoignon de Basville, *Mémoires*, pp. 128–32; Albert Puech, *Les Anciennes juridictions de Nîmes* (Nîmes, 1891); Albert Boudon, *La Sénéchaussée présidiale du Puy* (Valence, 1908).

instructions of the Estates on the diocesan level.[27] They were locally important as a deliberative body for the diocese which was dominated by the same forces dominating the towns and which discussed many of the same issues. In addition, the agents of the assiettes were effective administrators who functioned throughout the year even when the assembly was not in session. Each secular diocese had an assiette, but some were perfunctory meetings to administer tax assessments, while others continued to call themselves 'local estates' (*états particuliers*) and to go through the motions of a real consultative assembly. Each had a system of representation reflecting the power structure of the diocese. Sometimes a few towns or nobles dominated their order; sometimes there was a wide membership or a system of rotation.

In the 'Estates of Gévaudan', one of the more developed assemblies, the bishop of Mende or his vicar-general presided. Below him in rank were the commissioner sent from the provincial Estates and the bailli of Gévaudan, who was ordinary commissioner by birth. Then came eight ranked 'barons' of Gévaudan or their envoys, the members of the cathedral chapter of Mende or their envoys, a group of other nobles with a vote, the three consuls of Mende and the three consuls of Marvejols, the consuls of five other towns, and the representatives of various lesser parishes. The bishop, the bailli, and the consuls of Mende and Marvejols dominated the proceedings. During the year a 'steering committee' of the vicar-general, one 'gentleman', and the first consuls of Mende and Marvejols could be summoned by the syndic to approve expenditures and authorize voyages.[28]

In the assiette of Toulouse the archbishop alone represented the clergy and presided 'by birth'; there were only three barons who entered – the three with entrance to the Estates – and the towns consisted of eleven *villes maîtrises*, each sending the first consul plus a second deputy chosen by the community. The meetings had originally been held at each principal town in rotation, and the juge mage of the sénéchaussée in which the meeting took place had entered the assembly. But by the seventeenth century, meetings had settled into the archbishop's palace in Toulouse, and since the city of Toulouse was not in the assiette, its royal judicial officers were excluded.[29] Other dioceses provided variants on these patterns of representation.

[27] Émile Appolis, 'Les Assiettes diocésaines en Languedoc au XVIIIe siècle: essai de synthèse', in *Fédération historique du Languedoc méditerranéen et du Roussillon, XXVIIe et XXVIIIe Congrès* (Perpignan, 1953–4), pp. 115–24; Th. Puntous, *Un Diocèse civil de Languedoc: les états particuliers du diocèse de Toulouse aux XVIIe et XVIIIe siècles* (Toulouse, 1909); Élie A. Rossignol, *Petits États d'Albigeois, ou assemblées du diocèse d'Albi* (Paris, 1875); idem, *Assemblées du diocèse de Castres* (Toulouse, 1878); Ferdinand André, ed., *Procès-verbaux des délibérations des états du Gévaudan*, 6 vols. (vols. VI–XI of *Documents relatifs à l'histoire du Gévaudan*) (Mende, 1876–80).

[28] André, *Procès-verbaux*, vol. I, first documents.

[29] Puntous, *Toulouse*, pp. 76–133.

The assiettes concerned themselves primarily with taxes, an aspect which will be discussed in chapters 6 and 11. They also had a small 'add-on' budget for their own affairs and they played a role in the implementation of measures related to taxes and other local concerns. In Mende, where the issue of highway robbery threatening commerce was repeatedly being discussed, the diocese maintained a prévôt and archers to regulate it. In the diocese of Toulouse there was greater concern for the upkeep of roads and bridges because of the importance of the grain trade. All assiettes faced issues like the handling of troop disorders, the establishment of étape administrations to provide passing soldiers with temporary lodgings, the buying up of vexatious royal offices, and the management of local debts. Their syndics and greffiers worked long and hard during the year monitoring such issues and intervening with the appropriate authorities on behalf of the diocese. Their receivers were central figures in the provincial financial system.

These various local bodies, sénéchaussées, assiettes, episcopal administrations, though distinct in functions, were like interlocking directorates because of their overlapping personnel and close proximity. In Le Puy, for example, rivalries between a dynasty of juges mages, several bishops, and the powerful vicomte de Polignac kept breaking out in parallel fashion at consular elections, in council sessions, in meetings of the 'estates' of Velay, and in the chambers of the sénéchaussée over a period of forty years. The issues and circumstances varied, but the same personalities recurred.[30] Local government, with all its rivalries and compartmentalized functions, can actually be thought of as being managed by a small group of administrative agents who knew each other and who were answerable to various assemblies of notables. When matters of general concern arose like the lodging of troops, the secretary of the bishop or perhaps his vicar-general would contact influential people and make behind-the-scenes arrangements. The consuls or their syndic would issue formal orders, while the syndic of the diocese bustled about trying to enforce the guidelines of the Estates. Meanwhile the sénéchaussée would assemble to issue directives under the leadership of the juge mage and his subordinates. City council meetings in which many of the same individuals or their families were represented would discuss relief measures. In towns with other institutional bodies, there might be additional meetings and more directives. There would certainly be much visiting, consulting and petitioning.

Thus daily concerns were deeply felt and hotly debated by those in the lowest ranks of the 'rulers of Languedoc'. The towns were teeming conglomerations of workshops and warehouses, granaries, markets, gardens,

[30] Boudon, *Puy*, pp. 147–83; Antoine Jacotin, *Preuves de la maison de Polignac: recueil de documents*, vol. III (Paris, 1899), pp. 240–82.

flamboyant hôtels, modestly embellished residences of the merely respectable, churches, monasteries, seats of royal companies of officers, forts and garrisons, Protestant temples, charity hospitals, and slums, as well as all the social types associated with these establishments. They were places of interaction, but in the larger provincial context they did not really allow much initiative to most of their inhabitants. Only their highest leaders – a handful of bourgeois families, clerics, nobles, or administrative agents – could influence events, and even these played a relatively small role.

4

The sovereign courts: a provincial perspective

The sovereign courts were curious institutions whose role is difficult for the modern observer to grasp.[1] As judicial companies with jurisdiction over certain categories of litigation their function is readily comprehensible, but as centers of moral authority, social domination, and political command their importance seems mysterious. Both the Parlement in Toulouse and the Cour des Comptes in Montpellier were concentrations of individuals who combined personal authority, manifested through client ties and the control of seigneuries or investments, with corporate power expressed through their companies' vast influence. In addition to the jurisdictional authority which each exerted over the whole province, the two had more intense spheres of influence around their geographical centers in Haut-Languedoc and Bas-Languedoc respectively. Both were central actors in the drama of provincial affairs.

THE PARLEMENT OF TOULOUSE

The Parlement was the most prestigious center of influence in the province by virtue of its vast jurisdiction, its continuity of tradition, and the aggregate social prestige of its members.[2] These pompous dignitaries

[1] A few of the most useful works on sovereign courts are Roland Mousnier, *La Vénalité des offices sous Henri IV et Louis XIII*, 2nd edn (Paris, 1971); idem, *Les Institutions de la France sous la monarchie absolue, 1598–1789*, vol. II (Paris, 1980), pp. 253–8, 297–305, 318–38; J. H. Shennan, *The Parlement of Paris* (Ithaca, N.Y., 1968); A. Lloyd Moote, *The Revolt of the Judges: the Parlement of Paris and the Fronde 1643–1652* (Princeton, 1971); Albert Hamscher, *The Parlement of Paris after the Fronde, 1653–1673* (Pittsburgh, Pa., 1976); Sharon Kettering, *Judicial Politics and Urban Revolt in Seventeenth-Century France: the Parlement of Aix, 1629–1659* (Princeton, 1978); Jonathan Dewald, *The Formation of a Provincial Nobility: the Magistrates of the Parlement of Rouen, 1499–1610* (Princeton, 1980); John J. Hurt, 'La Politique du parlement de Bretagne (1661–1675)', *Annales de Bretagne*, 81 (1974), 105–30; idem, 'Les Offices au parlement de Bretagne sous le règne de Louis XIV: aspects financiers', *Revue d'histoire moderne et contemporaine*, 23 (1976), 3–31; Maurice Gresset, *Gens de justice à Besançon de la conquête par Louis XIV à la Révolution française 1674–1789*, 2 vols. (Paris, 1980).

[2] On the Parlement of Toulouse the best information can be found in Jean-Baptiste Dubédat, *Histoire du Parlement de Toulouse*, 2 vols. (Paris, 1885); André Viala, *Le Parlement de Toulouse et l'administration royale laïque, 1420–1525 environ*, 2 vols. (Albi, 1953); vicomte de Bastard d'Estang, *Les Parlements de France: essai historique*, 2 vols. (Paris, 1857), vol. I, pp. 124–31, 145–66, 198–203, 206–29, 275–87; Eugène Lapierre, *Le Parlement de Toulouse* (Paris, 1875); Paul Le Blanc, ed.,

presided over a complex of buildings and towers at the southernmost extremity of Toulouse on a site formerly occupied by the château Narbonnais of the medieval counts. They thus occupied the traditional seat of comtal, then royal, authority in a spot as far removed from the Capitole and its rival capitouls as the narrow confines of the city would allow. This palais was an enclosed complex of shabby and elegant buildings entered by three gates, where fancy portals and somber chambers contrasted sharply with crowded rows of dank shops and concession stands, just as the haughty robed parlementaires must have stood out against the throng of hawkers, lackeys, students, and thieves who swarmed about, drawn by the privileged status of the premises.[3] Behind guarded doors the solemnity of the company was enhanced by the decor. In the *grande chambre*, scene of hot debates over resistance to the crown, a morose fifteenth-century crucifixion with a Christ streaming tears and blood looked down upon the company, and it was facing this austere symbol that parlementaires took their annual oath of office.[4] In the *chambre dorée*, where conferences took place, First President Jean de Bertier had commissioned bas-reliefs on the ceiling representing a winged Renown, the three 'theological virtues' (faith, hope, charity), and the 'political and judicial virtues' (religion, justice, force, honor, peace, truth, abundance, victory, immortality). The ceiling of the often tumultuous *chambre des enquêtes* was appropriately decorated with baroque representations of the labors of Hercules.[5] Yet the bustle of valets, coachmen, and brawling students sometimes reached right into these hallowed halls, and little could be done to stop the gaming and quarreling despite repeated arrêts against disorders. In 1662 a murder was actually committed in the Avenue du palais.[6]

This milieu of preeminence and squalor was an appropriate setting for a court whose very considerable theoretical authority was not as effective as the parlementaires would have liked. Their massive district included all of Languedoc and significant portions of Guyenne, Gascogne, Quercy, and Foix. They handled a wide variety of civil and criminal cases, directly for privileged persons with the right of *committimus*, and on appeal for others. Much of their influence stemmed from this private litigation concerning family and property relationships, for these cases could make or break individuals.

Journal de J. Baudouin sur les grands-jours de Languedoc (1666–1667) (Le Puy, 1870); Jules Cambon de Lavalette, *La Chambre de l'édit de Languedoc* (Paris, 1872); Jean-Claude Paulhet, 'Les Parlementaires toulousains à la fin du XVIIe siècle', *Annales du Midi*, 76 (1964), 189–204; Maurice Virieux, 'Une Enquête sur le parlement de Toulouse en 1718', *Annales du Midi*, 87 (1975), 37–51.

[3] C. Barrière-Flavy, 'Les Prisons de la conciergerie du palais à Toulouse aux XVIIe et XVIIIe siècles', *Revue historique de Toulouse*, 10 (1923), 161–71.

[4] Bastard d'Estang, *Parlements*, vol. 1, p. 162. The painting, now in the Musée des Augustins, is reproduced in Robert Mesuret, *Toulouse et le Haut-Languedoc* (Paris, 1961), plate 81.

[5] Robert Mesuret, *Évocation du vieux Toulouse* (Paris, 1960), pp. 74–6.

[6] Barrière-Flavy, 'Prisons', pp. 161–71.

The court consisted of about 100 members who had bought their offices at considerable expense and expected to pass them on to their descendants as an important element of the family fortune. Also attached to the court were a corps of *avocats* (lawyers licensed to plead before it) and *procureurs* (legal consultants and agents), various titled clerks and secretaries, *huissiers* and *sergents* who acted as process-servers, and the clerks, lackeys, messengers, and servants connected to these dignitaries. In all, the court comprised a highly influential segment of many hundreds of Toulouse's inhabitants. In terms of wealth the parlementaires were preeminent in the region, though hardly spectacular. Toulouse was in decline as a commercial center, and merchants presented less competition than they would have in the sixteenth century.[7] The richest families had fortunes ranging from 100,000 to 1,000,000 livres at the end of the century, but less than twenty approached this range, and the majority lived much more modestly. There is evidence that as a group parlementaire fortunes declined in our period, and that, with a few exceptions, their sources of wealth were traditional and conservative.

The company was divided into five chambers: *grande chambre* where the most important cases were tried; *tournelle* for criminal cases; two chambers of *enquêtes* for cases and investigations of secondary importance, especially those conducted in writing; and one *requêtes*, a less prestigious chamber for cases of privileged persons in the first instance.[8] Leaving aside the requêtes, which did not dispense sovereign justice, and the tournelle, which was just a rotating group of councillors from other chambers, the heart of the company was the body of councillors in the two enquêtes and the grande chambre. Each chamber was organized by seniority with presidents (*présidents*) to direct it, and the entire company was directed by the first president (*premier président*). The presidents from the grande chambre, who were the most prestigious, were called *présidents à mortier*. In addition, three *gens du roi* (royal prosecutors) represented the king's interests: a procureur-general and two advocate-generals (*avocats-généraux*). This whole arrangement provided a logical pattern of advancement from avocat to councillor in the enquêtes, then to councillor in the grande chambre, and finally to president.

As a group the company was exceptionally imposing, whether gathered in red robes and square bonnets each twelfth of November after massive pealings of the bells for the public opening ceremonies, or on more whimsical occasions like the day each April when the archbishops of

[7] On fortunes and social place, see Paulhet, 'Parlementaires', and Micheline Thoumas-Schapira, 'La Bourgeoisie toulousaine à la fin du XVIIe siècle', *Annales du Midi*, 67 (1955), 312–29.

[8] On internal organization, Lapierre, *Parlement*, pp. 58–9; Franklin L. Ford, *Robe and Sword: the Regrouping of the French Aristocracy after Louis XIV*, rev. edn (Cambridge, Mass., 1962), pp. 46–9; Henri Gilles, 'Fermat magistrat', in *Actes du XXIe Congrès de la Fédération des Sociétés Académiques et Savantes de Languedoc-Pyrénées-Gascogne* (Toulouse, 1966).

Narbonne, Toulouse, and Auch and the peers of France with Languedocian lands were required to present the entire company with bouquets of roses.[9] But at the same time the company was so factionalized by the hierarchical complexity of their operation that they cannot be categorized as one political force. Procedural sessions were constantly marred by acrimonious debate over intricate points of precedence, bringing confrontations between presidents, gens du roi, and leading councillors.[10] Tempers were often short. When the chambers allowed Councillor Bernard de Segla to imprison one of Procureur-General Saint-Félix's clerks in 1641 because he was withholding necessary papers, Saint-Félix's response was to march straight to the prison with a locksmith and personally release his employee. He then complained maliciously to the court that he had often protected Segla in the past by looking the other way during his gambling bouts and concealing his coinage frauds. Outraged, Segla demanded reparations. Finally, after long negotiations, Saint-Félix was forced to offer a full apology before the court, which he presented begrudgingly in a voice so low that he could hardly be heard.[11]

Such episodes were typical of the intimate alliance between genuine intellectual excellence and motives of spite or private interest which prevailed in the court. The intellectual level of Toulouse's jurisprudence was probably in decline in the seventeenth century, and the leniency with which many applicants for admission were treated suggests that the sharper judges carried along a great many mediocre colleagues. But the judicial process itself lent an air of legitimacy to even second-rate participants. Councillors started work almost at dawn, conferring with procureurs and avocats who were already reading by candlelight at their desks in the *salle des pas perdus*. Hearings were impressive displays of rhetorical skill which required those present to listen attentively as masses of written arguments were debated and summarized. The reputation of the Parlement was also bolstered by the core of luminaries who spent their time in intellectual pursuits: people like Gabriel Barthélemy de Grammont who published a history of Louis XIII in Latin, or Simon d'Olive, 'orator and poet', who plied the chancellor Séguier with his pompous epic poems. Cambolas and Catellan published collections of notable cases. And while Léonard de Secousse was harboring an alchemist who had reportedly created gold and silver before the very eyes of Secousse and his family, his colleague Pierre

[9] Mesuret, *Évocation*, p. 78.

[10] The best source for the internal narrative of the Parlement's operation is the account written by Étienne de Malenfant, greffier of the court, between 1602 and 1647, 'Mémoires, collections et remarques du palais', in three volumes, a copy of which survives as A. D. H-G. mss. 147–9 (hereafter Malenfant, I, II, or III). Examples in Malenfant, II, 132, 293, 73.

[11] Malenfant, II, 268–73.

de Fermat, one of the century's great mathematicians, was corresponding with Descartes, Pascal, and Mersenne.[12] These same men could quarrel, fight bitterly, and even engage in violent private vendettas without any sense of incongruity. The modern assumption that those with 'professional' excellence would be above 'undignified' behavior did not apply to the seventeenth century.

Not only the attitudes of the councillors, but the very legal procedures themselves made the court into a malleable instrument for protecting the interests of parlementaires and people like them. Audiences were conducted in a way which required the judges to match wits and prestige with one another in a situation where sensitivity to precedence and personal dignity was very finely tuned, and private concerns mingled almost indistinguishably with points of legal principle. Even in unimportant cases the odds were good that some of the judges would have prior knowledge of the matter at hand or that their proud tempers would come into play. Clerks and presidents distributed cases to friendly *rapporteurs* who presented them, and plaintiffs could maneuver their business into the right hands if they knew the ropes. The ability of the court to summon witnesses was sometimes used by interested parties to intimidate whole villages.[13] In more flamboyant cases it is frequently obvious that sides were being drawn along factional lines having little to do with the question at hand. It was also considered a merit to show indulgence for 'worthy' individuals.[14] No doubt much of the court's everyday work was carried out impartially, but when it was not, the bias was incorporated into the very fabric of its methods and procedures.

How did the Parlement act politically? First, the court was responsible for publicizing and executing laws, which meant that it would promulgate them in public, issue interpretations of them and orders for carrying them out, investigate violations, and try violators. Second, there was a deep-felt tradition that, as the most distinguished royal authority in the absence of the king, the Parlement should issue commands in emergencies. People expected it to accept declarations of loyalty in times of rebellion, arrange relief during natural disasters, or mobilize resistance to a threatened enemy

[12] Gabriel Barthelemi de Grammont, *Historia prostratae a Ludovico XIII sectariorum in Gallia rebellionis* (Toulouse, 1623); idem, *Historiarum Galliae ab excessu Henrici IV libri XVIII* (Toulouse, 1643); Simon d'Olive, *Questions notables du droit décidées par divers arrests de la cour du Parlement de Toulouse* (Toulouse, 1682); Jean de Cambolas, *Décisions notables sur diverses questions du droit* (Toulouse, 1659); Jean de Catellan, *Arrêts remarkables du Parlement de Toulouse* (Toulouse, 1705); Paul Tannery and Charles Henry, eds., *Oeuvres de Fermat*, vol. II: *Correspondance* (Paris, 1894); on Secousse, Fieubet to Colbert, Oct. 28, 1665: Mel Col. 132 bis, 800.

[13] These problems are described in a memorandum by First President Fieubet in 1662: ms. fr. 17343, 293.

[14] Malenfant, II, 19–21, 38–44; III, 248, 5–6.

invasion. Finally, the court could interpose itself in the legislative process by declining to register royal edicts, suspending all or parts of them, or issuing lengthy remonstrances.

These functions were broad enough to leave room for a wide range of tactics, depending on the mood of various groups within the Parlement and the circumstances of the moment. The possibilities were far more restricted than this enumeration suggests, however, because other provincial authorities had more or less the same responsibilities, and there were confrontations each time parlementaire power was exercised. Another obstacle was the royal will. Councillors were skilled at draping their actions in legal precedents and absolutist statements, provided the king did not counterattack with directly contradictory orders. But the nature of justice and the position of the court made it difficult to oppose the monarch's explicit commands.

There were also strict practical limitations to the court's effectiveness since it lacked the institutional means to enforce its directives. The main contact between the parlementaires and the province was the stream of arrêts they issued on public affairs. Geographically their attention diminished sharply with distance. They had very strong influence within the city of Toulouse, and their archives bristle with directives concerning the area from Foix to Albi and Narbonne to Auch, but farther afield only the most important affairs came to their attention. Inside the city they busied themselves with regulating debauchery at taverns and nocturnal balls, denouncing student disorders, taking note of grain shortages, organizing patrols to protect the city from attack, burning seditious books, regulating the lower courts, and intervening in the university, in elections, in disputes between corps, in popular disturbances and in notable criminal cases. Arrêts also protected the fiscal and professional interests of the members. Farther afield the court intervened in consular disputes all over the province, feuded with the Cour des Comptes, issued regulations unfavorable to Huguenots, and tried to block creation of new offices and companies.

These 'political' matters were what gave the Parlement its intangible influence, which was at the same time both formidable and elusive. In order to fulfill its self-appointed destiny it had to assert political influence all over Languedoc in the name of the crown, while managing to modify or regulate royal policies enough to maintain credibility as a mediating force. Neither task was easy. The parlementaires had no formal monitoring device for watching over Languedoc. Business of a public nature came up in one of two ways. Either a dispute, for example an election conflict, occasioned legal appeals by the interested parties, or the matter was brought up in a chamber audience by one of the members. In the latter case it was the job of the procureur-general to present the problem, after which the court discussed it, ordered investigations, and issued arrêts. The matter at hand could derive from common knowledge ('various inhabitants have been holding gambling bouts day and night'), or it could arrive in the form of a written petition, sometimes anonymous, like the news in 1632 that the bishop of Alet was planning to defect to the rebels.[15] Routine matters were discussed in the grande chambre, but often a plenary session (*chambres assemblées*) of the whole company met to discuss public affairs. These meetings were dangerous because they gave voice and vote to the councillors of the two enquêtes, who were younger and more excitable than their senior colleagues. It was the unfortunate custom in Toulouse that a plenary session had to be held whenever any chamber demanded it; thus in times of rebelliousness the enquêtes could immobilize or galvanize the company.[16]

Once arrêts were issued, the question was whether anyone would obey them. For this reason the necessity of maintaining 'authority' was a constant leit-motif of the Parlement's existence. Being primarily a judicial body, it was best at deciding cases after the fact, upon presentation of written evidence. It had no effective way of directing ongoing enterprises. Short of warrants and legal commands served to individuals, or general regulatory ordinances proclaimed in public squares, the only way the court could influence events in distant places was to send commissioners there to prosecute abuses. If properly managed, these forays into the countryside could be used to rally support or to intimidate the population, but once again success was dependent on the abstract authority surrounding the commissioner, and there were examples of a solitary councillor actually being run out of town. In tense situations authority often proved to be illusory.

Relations with the crown were just as difficult. The period from 1630 to 1660 saw a growing unrest in the company caused by unprecedented fiscal and institutional threats to its well-being, after which conflict declined and a relative equanimity returned under Louis XIV. Some idea of the scope of this unrest is necessary in understanding the internal structure of the company. Faced with the onslaught of special commissions and commissioners which characterized the Richelieu years, the company reacted defensively, protesting edicts, resisting intendants, and taking extreme measures to assert its power over the province. Such issues split the company internally between those who preached delay or resistance to royal commands and those who wanted acquiescence. Among the resisters some thought arrêts alone would suffice, while others wanted to send commis-

[15] A.D. H-G. B 1879, 97, 100.

[16] The technique of using the name of the procureur-general to sanction an arrêt which he had not in fact approved was also used by rebellious councillors. Here again the forms of the court could be stretched without violating the apparent propriety of the proceedings. Ms. fr. 17343, 295.

sioners to intervene directly in the 'execution' of the arrêts. Such choices must have troubled consciences profoundly, since each member had to vote during meetings of the assembled chambers.

Resistance to perceived threats from the crown grew more energetic with time, and royal sanctions became more serious. The company decreed against installation of new officers in présidial courts and began making life legally difficult for *partisans* (tax farmers) by issuing decrees questioning the legitimacy of their contracts. In 1635 it drew up an arrêt suspending unverified *commissions extraordinaires*, and in 1636 it deliberately sabotaged the intendant Miron's handling of the pacification of disturbances in Uzès by ordering the arrest of local magistrates who obeyed him. In 1637 and 1638 it rejected more fiscal edicts.[17]

Such measures were bound to bring reprisals from the monarchy. In August 1636, Miron arrived in Toulouse with edicts creating a president and twelve councillors as well as other officers in the Parlement. The court raised every possible obstruction, tabling, then rejecting the edict and a subsequent *lettre de jussion*, but in the process falling out among themselves. A group within the court wanted to buy the new offices for relatives, and these members, including President Ciron, the *doyen* Maussac, and nine other prestigious individuals, were angrily excluded from the session.[18] In early 1638, after more unpleasant edicts, a distinguished delegation left for Paris to try to soften the blow of royal reprisals, but months of petitioning were unsuccessful. That October the king increased the pressure by announcing the creation of a new Parlement at Nîmes which would cut the old district in half. Finally the negotiators returned in June 1639 with a package settlement: suspension of the Nîmes Parlement in return for registration of a series of other fiscal edicts, and creation of various officers. Even as the angry councillors asked to see the resulting contracts between the king and the Parisian financiers who had underwritten the new edicts, they learned that, although their deputies had settled for a million livres worth of contracts, three million had already been sold. And when the court finally registered the edicts, it found out that the *partisan* in Paris was manipulating the fate of their appeals by pulling strings with the royal council.[19]

After the death of Louis XIII in 1643, pent-up frustrations inevitably burst forth. When rioting against the taille broke out in Rouergue, the more aggressive parlementaires met excitedly and drew up an arrêt denouncing all the abuses of the past ten years and suspending all taxes. The rest of the company toned it down to the point where it suspended only unregistered edicts and illegal collection methods, but it was widely

[17] A.D. H-G. B 1879, 137, 138, 176; Miron to Séguier, Oct. 15, 1636: Lubl., pp. 28–9.

[18] Malenfant, II, 30–7.

[19] Ibid., II, 179–202.

distributed and made a big impression on the region.[20] By 1646 certain 'agitators' in the company were asserting their authority with outrageous arrogance:

The Parlement in unprecedented fashion has named two commissioners from each of the chambers who meet at President Donneville's residence like a *chambre ardente*, summoning the officers of lower courts and giving them commands, or moving about town themselves accompanied by soldiers of the *guet*, and executing the arrest warrants that they have issued.[21]

These sorts of activities continued and expanded during the Fronde while splits within the court deepened. It was only during the 1650s that a relative calm gradually returned to the company. The Parlement had demonstrated both its importance and its weakness. Its vast authority gave it a key role to play in the governing of the province, but its lack of effective enforcement mechanism and its ambivalence about the validity of royal decrees doomed it to posturing and obstruction rather than effective leadership of opposition forces.

THE COUR DES COMPTES, AIDES ET FINANCES OF MONTPELLIER

The Cour des Comptes, Aides et Finances was another sovereign court similar to the Parlement.[22] Its solemn councillors began their work every morning at six in their various chambers, following elaborate rituals which reasserted their relative status. They sat and marched in rank order, saluted each other according to seniority whenever they met, and attended mass after every session unless they were Protestant.[23] Each of these steps was formalized in elaborate regulations. Although the court's competence was different from that of the Parlement, the distinction was not as important politically as it was in the technical realm of jurisprudence. The Comptes was capable of sending deputies to intervene in municipal affairs with all the reckless flamboyance of the Parlement, as it demonstrated in Uzès in 1655 when it supported a local faction which introduced armed men into the town and terrorized the inhabitants in a war against the bishop.[24] But if we shift our attention from Toulousain to Montpellierain society we move also from the isolated, rather smug world of Haut-Languedoc to the bustling tensions of the Mediterranean thoroughfare, and the Cour des

20 Ms. fr. 17296, 63–6; Malenfant, II, 330–8.

21 Bertier to La Vrillière, Mar. 9, 1646: Lubl., p. 179.

22 Studies of Chambres des Comptes and Cours des Aides are rare. The court in Montpellier is described in a contemporary work by Pierre Serres (1649–1725) who was a procureur in the court, *Histoire de la Cour des Comptes, Aides et Finances de Montpellier* (Montpellier, 1878); and in a useful modern analysis, Pierre Vialles, *Études historiques sur la Cour des Comptes, Aides et Finances de Montpellier d'après ses archives privées* (Montpellier, 1921).

23 Vialles, *Études*, pp. 11–29.

24 Bishop of Mirepoix to Mazarin, Jan. 10, 1658: A.A.E. France 1637, 155; Roschach, vol. XIV, p. 586.

Comptes had a somewhat different personality which matched its particular milieu.

First, it was a newer company, having been created in July 1629 by a merger of the old Chambre des Comptes and the old Cour des Aides, both of Montpellier, as part of Richelieu's reformation of the structure of Languedocian government. The idea was to create a new company strong enough to counterbalance the opposition of the Estates and the Parlement to the élus, but when the élus were abandoned, the Comptes remained, an awkward union which tended to become unstuck and a thorn in the sides of local intendants and governors.[25]

Second, the Comptes' particular competence gave its authority a different tone from the Parlement's. Its jurisdiction was over questions concerning taxes: taille, aides, octrois, gabelles, and appeals from lower fiscal courts such as *greniers à sel*. It also audited the accounts of all fiscal agents in the district and had the right to register edicts concerning all of these matters, as well as the power to register letters of nobility and royal grants of privileges to communities. These powers were open to interpretation. It was never clear what rights the court had over the independent tax administration of the Estates, and all the accounts of the day were complicated and ambiguous. Yet they were important because they concerned everybody's taxes and privileges directly, and they made the consuls of every community accountable before the court. Thus the councillors of the Comptes had tremendous influence, especially when town deputies were present in Montpellier during the Estates.[26] While the Parlement could claim general powers of surveillance and thereby intervene anywhere in Languedoc, especially when public order or obedience was at stake, its effectiveness was limited by inability to enforce. The Comptes, with a smaller district and less prestige, nevertheless had a more effective lever of influence in this one area of taxes.

A third difference lay in the nature of the court's membership. There were ten presidents, forty-four councillors (*conseillers-maîtres*), fourteen *correcteurs*, twenty-two *auditeurs*, and three *gens du roi* – two advocate-generals and one procureur-general. The correcteurs and auditeurs were subordinate officers with distinct auditing functions who sat in lesser chambers, rather like the councillors of the requêtes in the Parlement.[27]

[25] Paul Gachon, *Les États de Languedoc et l'édit de Béziers (1632)* (Paris, 1887), pp. 203–6.

[26] Archbishop of Toulouse to Colbert, Aug. 20, 1666: Mel. Col. 139, 286.

[27] The title *conseiller-maître* derived from the fact that the magistrates in the old Comptes had been called *maîtres*, while those in the Aides had been *conseillers et généraux*. The new company retained two chambers, a comptes and an aides, and was divided into two *semestres*, each serving for half the year. But distribution between the chambers was arbitrary and there were no longer two kinds of officers: any conseiller could serve in either chamber. I am therefore using the term *councillor* for all of these individuals, which corresponds to the term used in the Parlement. The *correcteurs*

Whereas the Toulousain dynasties posed as aristocrats and held themselves aloof from capitouls, merchants, and tawdry finance, the Comptes families in Montpellier were more closely tied to municipal affairs and more intimately linked with tax farms and financial enterprises. These councillors often had relatives among the treasurer-generals of finance, in the gabelle administration, or in the Estates' tax administration, and their ranks were more frequently recruited from the lesser officerdom of nearby towns. It would have been unthinkable for the Comptes to express the Parlement's outrage at finding a *partisan* in their midst, since so many of them were themselves involved in financial contracts and speculation. The members were known as the 'richest and greatest holders of taxable land in all of Languedoc' with good reason.[28] A sizeable minority of them were also Huguenots with contacts in the merchant community and ties to the Calvinist church hierarchy. The intendant Baltazar, who exaggerated the threat from the court, nevertheless represented the impression it made very well:

This court is an arrogant company which aims at no less than the destruction of the king's authority and the establishment of an authority of its own to which it has no claim, in order to seem formidable to the people.... Moreover, Monseigneur, it is the richest corps in the province. Join wealth to authority and arrogance, and put all of them at the service of the provincial synod, and I leave you to judge what effect this can have.[29]

Things were not as bleak as all that, but the court did acquire a bad reputation with royal agents. It was newer and less secure than the Parlement, with a less prestigious tradition. It was more immediately interested in local, sometimes Protestant politics, and it had to coexist in closer proximity with the authority of the Estates, the intendants, and the royal garrison in the citadel. The result was wild fluctuation between respectable stolidity and impetuous agitation.

From the moment of its creation in 1629, the Comptes was intimately involved in power rivalries with the other authorities in the close, crowded city of Montpellier. In addition, its merger had caused problems of integration between the two former corps of officers and their two first presidents, not to mention the bitterness caused by the creation of two new offices of president and eight councillors in 1629. These rivalries were superimposed on earlier ones stemming from the religious wars and their aftermath. When the intendants took up residence in the city, they were

and *auditeurs*, by contrast, were distinct, lower-grade officers. The presidents also served indiscriminately in either chamber, as did the first president. Charles d'Aigrefeuille, *Histoire de la ville de Montpellier*, ed. de la Pijardière, 4 vols. (Montpellier, 1875–82), vol. II, pp. 422–4.

28 Archbishop of Toulouse to Colbert, Aug. 20, 1666: Mel. Col. 139, 286.

29 Baltazar to Séguier, Nov. 22, 1644: Lubl., p. 95.

naturally wary of so near and threatening a rival and immediately took the seals of the Comptes' chancery into their own possession so that they would not have to go to the palais to issue legal acts.[30]

These tensions coalesced in 1642 around the choice of a new first president – the first since the two companies had been united. Factionalism nearly tore the company apart as Jacques-Philippe de Maussac, an aggressive newcomer who was noted for his lack of sympathy with Protestant colleagues, battled to buy the post while Protestants and traditional defenders of the status quo tried to stop him by proposing moderate alternatives. This factionalism is hard to evaluate because its religious and political aspects were so intimately intertwined. Both intendants, Bosquet and Baltazar, were convinced that the anti-Maussac faction was a Huguenot conspiracy; yet neither could explain why so many Catholics supported it: 'Catholics are becoming so apathetic and so little concerned about their religion that they are causing a public scandal by allying themselves with the Huguenots through family interests.'[31] In retrospect it appears that the 'Catholic' party was also absolutist, favoring royal over corporate concerns and that the 'Protestant' group was primarily on the side of more local initiative, whatever ulterior motives Huguenots within it may have had. After all in the Parlement, where no Protestants sat, exactly the same 'loyalist' and 'dissident' interests were being played out.

The 1640s saw the more active agitators from the Comptes asserting their influence in the streets of Montpellier, just as their counterparts from the Parlement were doing the same thing in the streets of Toulouse. The Comptes became locked in a power struggle with the intendant Baltazar over municipal finances which led to factional side-taking among the consuls, within their councils, and among the other local authorities. The climax of this struggle was an episode in early December 1644 which had serious consequences. Two councillors, Ranchin and Deydé, led a band of armed retainers through the streets 'announcing that this was for the liberty of the people'; freed their consul-ally Benjamin Carbon from prison where he had been thrown by Baltazar for not letting the latter have the city tax registers; arrested a *trompette* of Baltazar's who had promulgated the ordinance for Carbon's arrest; and dragged one of Baltazar's *archers* through the town, beating and humiliating him. This audacious act was hardly the 'largest, boldest, most dangerous popular uprising which has occurred in Montpellier in thirty years', as Baltazar claimed, for the general population was not involved, the violence was strictly controlled, and there were no arrests. Hatred of Baltazar and frustration at the general situation

30 Trinquere to Séguier, Mar. 8, 1633: ms. fr. 17367, 34.

31 Baltazar to Séguier, Nov. 22, 1644: Lubl., p. 95.

had brought out this aggressive but not atypical reaction which was quickly disowned by the more moderate councillors of the Comptes.[32]

The incident would be forgotten if it had not preceded the major popular revolt of June 29 to July 2, 1645, which will be described further in chapter 9. All accounts suggest that this was a relatively spontaneous popular reaction against taxes, triggered by rumors of terrible levies being prepared by Baltazar and the *partisans*, and nothing seems to implicate the Comptes. Yet some months later Baltazar accused the court unequivocally: 'it was not the people [who started] the sedition in Montpellier of June 30, 1645. It was the Cour des Comptes which took advantage of the presence of Cévenols in town for the harvest and stirred them up by means of servants.'[33] Members of the Comptes had undoubtedly prepared the way for the revolt with their public attacks on Baltazar, though Bosquet, the other intendant, proclaimed their innocence.[34] They could have fomented it, but on the whole their direct intervention seems unlikely. We know that Baltazar was never able to obtain proof he said was forthcoming linking the instigators to the '*gens de condition* of Montpellier' and that only humble people were executed.[35]

These disturbances were nevertheless used as the pretext for the company's disunion, which Baltazar had been advocating from the day he arrived in Languedoc.[36] For him the Comptes was a dangerous center of resistance, tied closely to the Huguenot synod. Disunion would cow the opposition and exile would divide it. Since Baltazar thought that local resistance was caused entirely by the fomentation of officers and Protestants with inflated egos, cutting them down to size would restore order and clear the way for a crackdown on Estates and communities.

In October 1646, after a long delay caused by fear of new unrest, the edict of disunion was issued separating the two companies, exiling the resultant Cour des Aides to Carcassonne, and crippling the resultant Chambre des Comptes which remained in Montpellier by creating a new 'semester' chamber of officers who would serve for half the year. There was reason enough for the disunion even without the uprising. The king stood to make 1,500,000 livres on the sale of the new offices, and semester chambers were being instituted in the Parlements of Aix, Rennes, Rouen,

32 Baltazar's report to Mazarin on Dec. 5, 1644 is in A.A.E. France 1634, 60. The same letter with interesting variations was sent to Séguier, and is reproduced in Porchnev, pp. 639–40 and Lubl., pp. 103–4. Baltazar's explanation, Dec. 28, 1644: ms. fr. 18830, 197; Baltazar to La Vrillière, Jan. 9, 1645: Lubl., pp. 106–7; Bosquet to Séguier, June 27, 1645: Lubl., pp. 148–50.

33 Baltazar to Mazarin, Dec. 19, 1646: A.A.E. France 1634, 262.

34 Bosquet to La Vrillière, Aug. 1, 1645: Porchnev, pp. 650–1.

35 Baltazar to Mazarin, Dec. 19, 1646 and Jan. 16, 1647: A.A.E. France 1634, 262, 267. Pierre Sabatier, 'Mémorial des choses les plus remarquables': A.M. Mp BB 197, 68.

36 Memoir of Aug. 9, 1644: A.A.E. France 1634, 44.

and Metz around this same time.[37] Furthermore, conflicts involving the Comptes had continued to disturb the peace. A confrontation with the présidial in August 1645 had threatened to set off new violence; conflicts with the treasurer-generals had been frequent; and the two treasurers of the bourse had recently been imprisoned by the Comptes for not paying officers' *épices*. In December 1646 there may have been a riot 'when the people were told [by the Comptes] that the king wanted to punish the innocent along with the guilty'.[38]

When the *huissier de la chaîne* arrived from Paris to promulgate the edict of disunion, he encountered a different form of passive resistance which belied the intendant's predictions of successful intimidation. Baltazar assembled a large crowd to hear the edict read and delivered a speech designed, as he saw it, 'to disabuse the inhabitants, reestablish royal authority in a place where it had been so greatly diminished, and humiliate those who had not supported the crown', but which the Comptes in their subsequent appeal to the king claimed had been filled with 'grave insults and atrocities...against our honor, slandering us by making us guilty of the uprising of Montpellier'.[39] When it came to obeying, the councillors simply refused. They were not at home when the consuls arrived to present Baltazar's papers commanding each member to comply, and the doors of their palais were found to be locked when the military commander's troops arrived to take it over. After the building had been occupied by force, the councillors continued their audiences in the home of President Grasset. It was two full months before the Cour des Aides glumly set out for Carcassonne, and then only because their appeals at court had failed and further resistance would be futile.[40]

The disunion made matters worse because it provided an institutional pretext for the rivalries which already existed. Many of the old court's enemies who had thrown in their lot with the king's agents were able to purchase offices in the new chamber, including Jacques-Philippe de Maussac, who now at last was made first president. These unfortunates had chosen a bad moment for their triumph since the government was so distracted by affairs in Paris. The councillors from Carcassonne kept coming back to Montpellier to harass them, claiming that there were no

37 Memoir against the reunion of the Comptes, 1648: ms. fr. 18483, 66. Kettering, *Judicial Politics*, p. 211.

38 Bosquet to Séguier, Aug. 9, 1645: Lubl. p. 152; memoir: ms. fr. 18483, 258; A.M. Mp Joffre 10, 'Élections consulaires', Mar. 1, 1646; Baltazar to La Vrillière, May 29, 1646; Lubl., pp. 192–3; Baltazar to Mazarin, Jan. 16, 1647; A.A.E. France 1634, 267.

39 Baltazar to Séguier, Dec. 26, 1646: Lubl., p. 204. A narrative account is in Sabatier, 'Mémorial', vol. 1, 58v–61; Comptes to Séguier, Dec. 25, 1646; Lubl., p. 203.

40 Sabatier, 'Mémorial', vol. 1, 61v–66; André Delort, *Mémoires inédits sur la ville de Montpellier au XVIIe siècle (1621–1673)*, 2 vols. (Montpellier, 1876–8), vol. 1, pp. 143–5; procès-verbal: ms. fr. 18830, 205.

lodgings or cases in their new location, and the officers in the July (old) semester of the Montpellier Comptes made life difficult for the new First President Maussac by boycotting his joint sessions even when the king ordered a *Te Deum* sung to celebrate his victories.[41] Half the old company seemed to be in Paris lobbying. A list from 1647 included First President Bon, five other presidents, all the gens du roi, and thirteen councillors.[42] In Montpellier fights broke out between the old and new semesters, and an auditeur, Juin, was beaten. In Carcassonne Councillor Clausel claimed he had been suspended by the company for informing the king how few of the members were actually present in Carcassonne and for refusing to acquiesce in an attempt on the life of Dupuy, a new president in Montpellier. His response was to force his way into the palais in Carcassonne brandishing swords and pistols.[43]

The outbreak of the Fronde made things worse. In July 1648 lobbyists obtained an edict returning the Aides to Montpellier, and its officers immediately installed themselves in their old palais along with the old July semester of the Comptes, literally forcing the new January semester out into the streets.[44] In utter despair, Maussac appealed to the Chancellor Séguier for help: 'there is no longer any way to survive with the contemptuous and irreverent acts being committed in this town. After serving courageously for eighteen months it is time I was rescued.'[45] But soon afterwards his son was killed in a duel probably related to these events, and in December the Cour des Comptes, Aides et Finances was reunited by the government.

Having won its reunion, the Comptes could afford to remain relatively placid during the rest of the Fronde period. As Breteuil the new intendant put it, the reunion had calmed the company, and this had a calming effect on the whole region. He might have added that Protestants of Bas-Languedoc were consciously lying low and that the Comptes' basic interest lay on the side of the tax administration. Other episodes in the 1650s and 1660s proved that the Comptes was still an unstable and erratic force. Its agitations lasted longer than the Parlement's and took a more aggressive form, but they declined dramatically in virulence, seeming to become empty gestures more than genuine threats. In 1653 the Comptes imprisoned all the consuls for a brief period, and in 1654, after decreeing against two treasurer-generals, it assembled 500 armed men in the palais to execute its orders, though they were never used because a compromise was arranged.[46] In 1658 the old

41 Maussac to Séguier, Aug. 6, 20, 1647: ms. fr. 17387, pp. 85, 104; procès-verbal by Maussac: Lubl., 207.

42 Ms. fr. 18483, 57.

43 Ms. fr. 18483, 206–7, 213, 215.

44 January semester to Séguier, Apr. 17, July 20, 1648: ms. fr. 17389, 180, ms. fr. 17388, 247; memoir: ms. fr. 18483, 66.

45 Maussac to Séguier, Aug. 4, 1648: ms. fr. 17390, 29.

46 Serres, *Histoire*, pp. 72–6.

spirit was once again displayed when the prince de Conti, representing the king, tried to preside over a joint session of the court called to force registration of an edict for the ennoblement of lands in Languedoc. The preliminary courtesies went smoothly enough, but then some of the councillors began caballing with the rest, and by the time Conti arrived at the appointed hour with the intendant and a train of dignitaries for the formal registration ceremonies, he found the room totally deserted. His response was characteristic of the new era which was beginning: Conti and the intendant registered the edict themselves in the empty room, and two months later the Comptes once again was disbanded, replaced by a substitute chamber of lower officials in Narbonne. Eleven months later it was restored on condition that it register the edict plus a *crue* of eight new offices in the Comptes.[47]

A CHANGING OF THE GUARD?

In the Comptes as in the Parlement, the age of turbulence was largely over by 1660. Conflicts continued to occur, but they were usually lesser affairs without the threatening potential of the earlier episodes. In the Comptes there were conflicts with présidial officers (1663), mutual recriminations among the presidents (1667), agitation over the investigation into false titles of nobility (1668), quarrels with the consuls (1673). In the Parlement there was protest against franc fief edicts in the early 1660s, agitation over taille collection in Guyenne in 1662, and concern over an edict reducing the number of procureurs in the court between 1666 and 1669, to name only a few issues. But the dominant theme in both courts was cooperation with the monarchy, as we will see in greater detail in chapter 13.

The sovereign courts, like the towns, thus crossed a watershed between turbulent dissidence and more orderly government around 1660. Most of the reasons for this important change must be reserved for part 4, but one aspect should be examined here. Lists of the members of the sovereign courts are complete enough to permit a rough analysis of the turnover of the membership at various key dates, raising the question of whether the cooperative generation of Louis XIV's prime years was simply a different group from the 'frondeur' agitators of the 1640s and 1650s. The results are interesting.

Looking at the average term in office of all the presidents of the Comptes in certain key years (table 5), we can see that the turnover of individuals in the offices suggests a cycle of renewal.[48] The average number of years

47 Ibid., pp. 76–83.

48 The best list of councillors and presidents of the Comptes, with their dates of entrance and various genealogical details, is found in Vialles, *Études*, pp. 115–229. Another similar list is in d'Aigrefeuille, *Histoire*, vol. II, pp. 411–33. Many other mentions in the sources help pinpoint the dates when one man replaced another.

Table 5. *Average term in office of Comptes presidents*

Year	Average years as president	Average years as president or councillor
1632	9.5	17.0
1643	11.1	18.9
1646	14.4	21.4
1650	12.6	20.7
1652	5.8	15.3
1660	10.4	21.2
1663	10.8	22.2
1672	14.8	22.6
1678	20.8	29.8
1680	12.6	24.2
1689	17.8	30.8

Figures cover ten presidents, including the first president, through 1663 and eleven presidents thereafter. A new office of president was created in 1659, but in 1663 another office was vacant.

in office in 1632 is relatively low; it rises until around 1646, then declines slightly by 1650 and collapses dramatically in 1652. Then follows a steady rise, with levels still lower than 1650 throughout the 1660s, reaching former levels by 1672 and rising to new heights in 1678, then rapidly decreasing by 1680 to the level of 1650 again, and beginning a new rise in the 1680s. The number of years in office – or roughly the amount of experience – was lowest in 1632 and 1652, both times of plague, and rose steadily thereafter. The most dramatic year was 1652 in the wake of the Fronde. The president who had been in office the longest that year dated from 1624, the next most senior from 1643, and the rest from 1646 to 1652. In other words, the men who dominated the Comptes during the Fronde were relative novices, and four out of the ten had entered during the Fronde! This rapid turnover was not typical, however. In 1660 the venerable 1624 president had died and been replaced, but the other nine presidents were the same individuals, with eight more years' experience. Even in 1678, twenty-six years later, five of the presidents of 1652 were still the same.

Of course presidents often served first as councillors, during which time we might assume that they were already gaining experience in the court. If we look at their years in *either* office we see the same pattern of renewal, somewhat diluted by the differing amounts of prior experience. Both are represented in figure 1-C.

The seniority of all the councillors in the Comptes is harder to determine because no complete lists of the membership at a given date are available. However, information is complete enough to reconstruct these lists for four

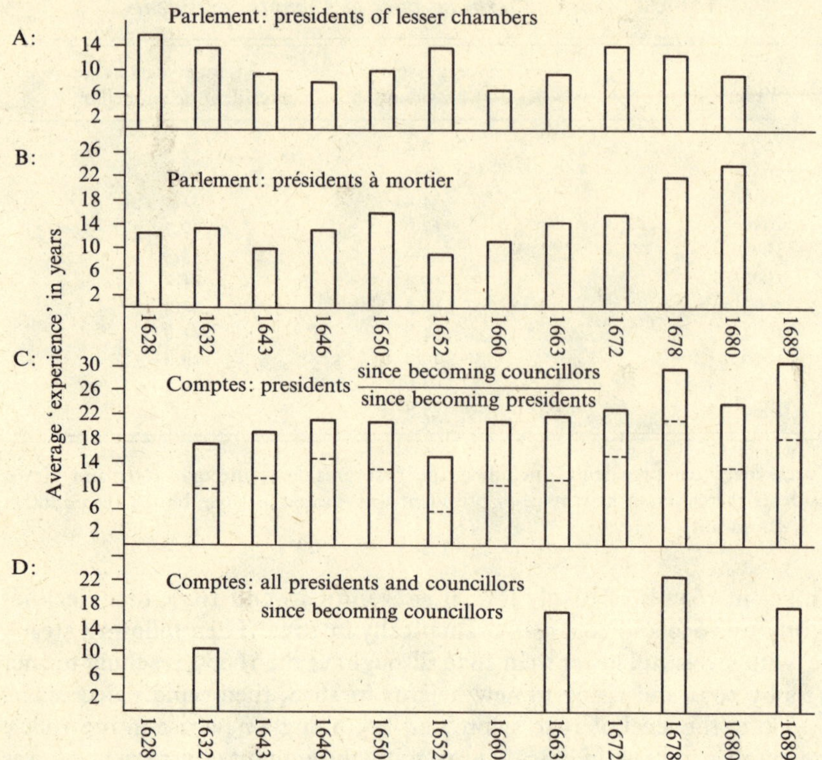

Figure 1. Renewal of membership in the sovereign courts.

key years – 1632, 1663, 1678, and 1689 – and while the absence of a reference point during the Fronde makes analysis more difficult, the same pattern can be discerned for the councillors as for the presidents (figure 1-D).[49] Moving from the lowest to the highest numbers of years in the court, 1678 had cumulatively more in virtually every category, making it the most 'experienced' court. 1632 had the least 'experience'. 1663 and 1689 lay between the two extremes. A breakdown in terms of the era when the

[49] The years 1632, 1663, 1678, and 1689 can be reconstructed because lists of most of the members arranged in order of seniority exist for those years. Without such lists it is impossible to determine who was in the court in a given year because one knows when each member entered but not when he resigned or died. The period between 1632 and 1663 is unfortunately too long to extrapolate the intervening years from existing information. Even the lists used contain some uncertainties. They are found in Vialles, *Études*, pp. 115–20 (for 1632); Depping, vol. II, pp. 131–2 (for 1663, the least complete); Mel. Col. 252, 13v–15r: État de la Gabelle (for 1678); Vialles, *Études*, plate opposite p. 110 (for 1689).

Table 6. *Era when members entered the Comptes*

	% in 1663		% in 1678	
Before union (pre-1631)	9.4		—	
Union and disunion (1631–47)	34.0	'troubled era'	24.5	'troubled era'
Fronde and after (1648–57)	39.6	73.6	28.3	52.8
Young Louis XIV (1658–63)	17.0		13.2	
Colbert's decade (1664–72)	—		18.9	
Dutch War (1673–8)	—		15.1	

members of the 1663 court had entered the company (table 6) indicates that almost 40 percent of them had entered during or immediately after the Fronde and that 73.6 percent dated from the troubled era of 1631 to 1657. Because of the decline in turnover after 1652, the 1678 court still contained 28.3 percent from the 'Fronde generation' and 52.8 percent from the 'troubled era'.

Membership lists for the Parlement are not reliable enough to permit similar breakdowns. However, lists of newly-entering members are reasonably reliable, and when these are tabulated in moving five-year intervals to measure the number of new members entering in particular periods of time, the results correspond to those for the Comptes (figure 2).[50] Here the periods of greatest renewal – hence of lowering of the average 'experience' of the company – came in the periods 1628–36, 1641–7, and 1670–8. The period of *least* renewal, hence greatest continuity of officeholding and collective 'experience' came between 1656 and 1670, the phase which shows up clearly as the longest and deepest 'trough' on the graph. A similar pattern is established by the presidents of the grande chambre in the Parlement (figure 1-B), whose seniority rises from a low in 1652 just like that of the Comptes presidents, although their decline in seniority in 1632 is not as marked. When we look at the presidents of the three lesser chambers in the Parlement (figure 1-A), we see that they too have a marked renewal pattern, but with a chronology that is out of phase with the others, since their 'lows' come in 1646 and 1660, earlier and later than the others we have seen.

[50] The Parlement's membership is harder to reconstruct because the available rosters of members are not well spaced in time. There is a list from 1610 in Rozoi, vol. IV, pp. 21–4; a list of surnames from 1678 in Mel. Col. 252, 10–13; and a list from 1698 in B.N. Languedoc (Bénédictins) 149, 286. The best source is a list of members with entrance dates, and often the names of predecessors or successors, in A.D. H-G. ms. 193, but it is not complete enough to trace the sequence of holders of particular offices.

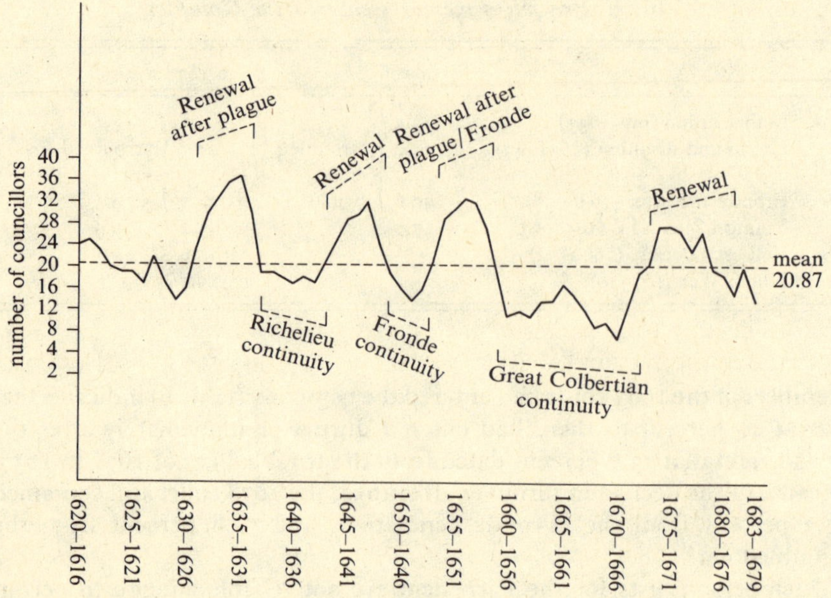

Figure 2. Number of councillors entering the Parlement (in five-year intervals).

These comparisons give only the roughest indication of the 'experience' or 'maturity' of the leaders of the sovereign courts because they measure time in office, not age or function, and they ignore all the other factors which made men leaders or followers, dissidents or loyalists. They do, however, indicate one striking conclusion. Every group studied renewed itself significantly in the period before the 1660s and then remained stable through the 1660s and 1670s. The generation which came to prominence in the age of Colbert – that of the contemporaries of Louis XIV's young adulthood – actually was a different group from the generation of Richelieu and the troubles of the early 1640s, but it was the same group that had come to power on the eve of the Fronde or during and immediately after it. Both Comptes and Parlement had been affected by the plague epidemics of 1628–32 and 1653 which coincided with internal crises – the élus and the union of the Comptes in the first instance, the Fronde and the disunion of the Comptes in the second. These were times when offices changed hands more frequently because of deaths, creations of new positions, and factional squabbling. The result was a sharper break in continuity than usual. In both courts an unusual influx of new members had to confront the crisis of the Fronde. In the Parlement it may be that the renewal of the presidents of the more turbulent lesser chambers in a pattern out of phase with the rest of the company heightened tensions, when younger men from the enquêtes challenged older presidents in the grande chambre, or conversely, when senior enquêtes presidents confronted novice grande chambre presidents.

If there is any value to this 'demography' of the sovereign companies it is in showing that Louis XIV really did preside over a different generation whose formative experiences were not unlike his own, though the sovereign judges were undoubtedly older in years. The judges of the 1660s were not different individuals from the frondeurs; in fact they had grown up professionally during and after the Fronde. But they may have especially appreciated the benefits of orderly government, which they could compare first-hand to the perils of disorder. Unlike their predecessors of an older generation they had not experienced the benefits of the more autonomous 'olden days'. Whereas the judges of the 1630s and 1640s had seen their lot go from bad to worse and had reacted by fighting against evils which they saw as unfortunate innovations, these frondeurs-turned-collaborators fell under the spell of the successful enterprise which Louis was organizing during their early years in power. Their loyalty may have had something to do with this experience, and the fact that the same men ruled so consistently for so long may have contributed to the stability and regularity of Louis XIV's rule.

5

The royal agents: a national linkage

Insinuating themselves among the long-established governing institutions of the province were the royal agents. Their attentions were devoted to enacting the king's program directly and expeditiously, as compared to other authorities who might view themselves as equally loyal to the king and state, but who would nevertheless filter the royal wishes through an interpretive screen of corporate, provincial, and private considerations. There was nothing new about having direct agents of the crown in the province, either in the form of envoys sent out to reside for a time and oversee some particular business, or as resident natives who sought personal advancement by serving the king's interests. Both had existed for centuries. Even in the heyday of royal power the intendant was never the solitary commissar of the textbooks, enacting authoritarian state policy in the midst of a hostile population. Nevertheless, as all commentators have pointed out, the years after 1630 did represent a turning point in that the official *intendants de justice*, *police et finances* did reside longer, do more, and have much greater impact than their predecessors.[1]

They were still supplemented by many other agents. There were temporary royal commissioners who came and went according to the rhythm of business, the military commanders, and various local residents – prelates, robe officers, even merchants – who served the king consistently enough to be considered agents, despite their provincial roots. This heterogeneous group, working separately or jointly, was united only by the royal government's distant coordination, transmitted in the form of a steady stream of letters and instructions. The agents came closest to merging into one body during the annual bargaining session at the Estates, and then dispersed to pursue their separate courses during the rest of the year. As

[1] This argument has been made most comprehensively in Richard Bonney, *Political Change in France under Richelieu and Mazarin 1624–1661* (Oxford, 1978), which provides the definitive discussion of the role of the intendants as seen from the perspective of the central government and includes much information on Languedoc. It is based on the author's dissertation, 'The Intendants of Richelieu and Mazarin' (Ph.D. dissertation, Oxford, 1973), in which Bonney provides additional information not included in the published version.

the century advanced, however, the composite picture of their diverse activities became gradually more coherent, focusing ever more sharply upon the intendancy as an institution.

In watching this process develop, we must keep in mind that the official intendants were only the active center of this coalescing and dispersing 'team' of royal allies. They worked through and not against the local system of authority, for without a network of local contacts they were helpless, and this network could only be developed by sensitivity to local interests. Intendants should be thought of as intermediaries who linked a congeries of local ties to a variety of national ties.

DEALING WITH THE PROVINCE

A proper appreciation of their work begins with a sense of isolation. A royal agent heading for Languedoc faced a distant territory and an awesome governing prospect. As Henri d'Aguesseau, who had served as intendant between 1673 and 1685, advised a new military commander in 1706, it would take him four days to reach Lyons from the capital; then he would take a boat down the Rhône to Pont Saint-Esprit, stopping off at Tain or Valence for the night and arriving on the sixth day. The next morning he could have the choice of continuing down the river to Beaucaire and being met there by a carriage to take him to Nîmes, or of going overland and risking ambush by Camisards in the narrow valley of Valviguières.[2] The seventh day would find our man at Nîmes, and the eighth would get him to Montpellier. Thus the trip was not impossibly long, though making it in eight days would have required determination. John Locke, who passed the same way in 1675 as a tourist, spent five days between Paris and Chalon-sur-Saône, where he took a boat to Lyons; then left on horseback for Saint-Vallier, Valence, Montélimar and Pont Saint-Esprit (eleventh day), whence we may assume he could have reached Montpellier on the thirteenth day if he had not stopped to visit Avignon.[3] Anyone could make the trip, as many of the elderly bishops proved by their annual treks to court, but it was a jolting experience which stood between the world of the court and that of the Mediterranean.

Correspondence suffered the same communication gap. In 1675, when things were running smoothly, Colbert answered the letters of the intendant

[2] Henri d'Aguesseau, *Mémoire secret pour Mr le duc de Roquelaure allant commander en Languedoc*, ed. Gaston Vidal (Montpellier, 1958), pp. 1–27.

[3] John Locke, *Locke's Travels in France 1675–1679*, ed. John Lough (Cambridge, 1953), pp. 2–16. See also Madame de Sévigné, *Lettres*, ed. Gérard-Gailly (Bibliothèque de la Pléiade), vol. I (Paris, 1953), pp. 591–5, vol. III (Paris, 1963), pp. 777–9.

around ten to thirteen days after they had been written in Montpellier, with his fastest answer taking six days. Thus requesting and receiving instructions would take from twelve days to three weeks or more, ruling out immediate responses.[4] Our new intendant would think hard as he rode down the Rhône between the cliffs signalling the beginning of the Midi and the strongholds of the Protestants – first, about his friends at court who would protect his interests while he was away, and second, about the contacts he would be able to rely on locally.

Royal agents knew they were intermediaries. In 1637 Robert Miron told the Estates that intendants could be useful to them: 'they cost you nothing, despite what is sometimes said, and with the aid of the ministers [at court] they provide [services which] might be neglected by provincial officers'. In 1661 the prince de Conti saw the governor's role in the same light: 'if he is the organ of the prince for presenting royal wishes to the people and making them respected, he is also the interpreter of the people, who carries their voices right to the foot of the throne'.[5] These claims were not mere rhetoric. Royal agents did constantly obtain favors for individuals, always at the price of service, and their use as a channel of influence was gradually and begrudgingly discovered by local residents. The same Miron visited Toulouse in 1636 to investigate the city's claims that it was unable to pay its taxes due to depopulation and economic misery. His procès-verbal corroborated the claims of the capitouls, after an extensive on-the-spot investigation.[6]

Intendants functioned by means of a network of personal clients and allies, usually figures from the lesser bodies like municipal councils, présidial courts, or specialized agencies. These clients might serve as simple messengers, or receive authority as temporary 'subdelegates' to carry out a particular mission. 'We judge cases summarily or refer them to subdelegates who are on the scene, for the greater convenience of the litigants', wrote Miron.[7] There are hints of personal contacts throughout the correspondence. Friends would provide information about local politics, speak out in the courts, or protect the 'king's interests' when a riot broke out. In return the intendant got them favors if they had cases before the royal council, spoke for them when they needed royal appointments, named them as his inspectors of royal projects, granted them contracts for supplying the army or building public works. These contacts held a variety of positions: one hears of a treasurer-general of finance, a municipal consul, a councillor in a présidial court or a judge of the admiralty. Some, like

[4] A.N. H 1693.

[5] P-V Nov. 12, 1637; prince de Conti to Estates, Jan. 24, 1661: Roschach, vol. XIV, p. 760.

[6] Roschach, vol. XIV, pp. 1–20.

[7] Miron to Séguier, Oct. 15, 1636: Lubl., p. 29.

Anoul, *juge royal* of Uzès, had a remarkable history of continuous service, having been used by almost every intendant from Miron down to at least 1666, a span of thirty-three years.[8]

When it came to the great companies of officers and the higher provincial dignitaries, intendants had much rougher going. The sovereign courts in particular saw them as interlopers whose judicial functions 'discredit the Parlement and ruin the king's subjects'.[9] Whenever it could, the court snatched cases back from the royal agents, and if it dared, suspended their powers. In return intendants wrote indignantly to the ministers in Paris to demand better support for their activities:

> Will you please make clear that it is no crime to appeal to us to have royal commands executed, and make it known in the Parlement as well as everywhere else that we represent you in this province as executors of the commissions you issue and universal inspectors of everything that happens in this region, and that we must have jurisdiction over whatever is done in executing our commissions.[10]

The hint of desperation which crept into these appeals, especially in the earlier years, was justified, for intendants relied more than anything else on force of personality and the weight of royal authority to get things done. One's influence had to be deployed in the right way at the right time in order to neutralize the opposition. As Jean Baltazar put it in 1644, 'it is sometimes necessary to strike all the right chords of royal authority at the same time in order to maintain a proper balance and transcend many obstacles in advancing the service of their majesties....'[11] The job also required constant physical exertion, with frequent journeys on horseback from town to town, and at each stopping-place visits to dignitaries, conferences, judicial proceedings, and piles of paper work.

The itinerary of the intendants shows them staying in one spot for a month or two – usually Montpellier or Narbonne – then moving to a secondary center (Nîmes or Béziers) for a few weeks, with side trips along the way, and returning to the Mediterranean axis. Their appearance in Haut-Languedoc was infrequent, and they only went into the Cévennes on special assignments. After 1653 the intendants slowed down a bit, but they still followed a similar pattern of circulation. Although Montpellier gradually became the seat of the intendancy, Bezons (1653–73) spent considerable time in Pézenas because it was the residence of the prince de

[8] Examples of subdelegations: Miron to Séguier, Oct. 15, 1636: Lubl., p. 29; Baltazar to La Vrillière, May 31, 1645: Lubl., p. 139; Bezons to Séguier, Mar. 10, 1664: ms. fr. 17404, 87; Tubeuf to Colbert, Sept. 14, 1666: Mel. Col. 140, 386; Froidour to Colbert, Nov. 20, 1669: Mel. Col. 154, 349.

[9] Bertier to Séguier, Aug. 1, 1635: ms. fr. 17369, 93.

[10] Miron to Séguier, Oct. 15, 1636: Lubl., p. 29.

[11] Baltazar to Séguier, Oct. 4, 1644: Lubl., p. 80.

Conti, and it was only after twelve years on the job that he saw Vivarais for the first time![12] There was still no substitute for on-the-scene direction, but intendants increasingly held court in one place, expecting the province to come to them.

The residences of intendants were quite modest, to judge by those which are still standing in Pézenas and Montpellier, and they were not lavishly furnished. It was the noble governor, not the intendant, who was expected to wine and dine the prestigious during sessions of the Estates. Personal staffs were not very large either. Normally they consisted of a clerk or two, though as the work load got heavier these secretaries could be very influential. Foucault, intendant of Montauban, fired his man Gendron in 1676 for taking too many bribes from eager petitioners.[13] Military enforcement was also minimal. The most intendants could claim was a few sergeants for process-serving, and they probably only had these some of the time. Bezons used two *hoquetons du roi* to examine forests in 1665. Baltazar had a personal 'prévôt' named Vernole to serve warrants for him, whose legal authority was somewhat questionable. In major confrontations the agents always relied on the governor and his guards or on *huissiers de la chaîne* sent from Paris to announce the royal will with appropriate solemnity.[14]

Just as important as local ties for the intendant were his relations in Paris. It is sometimes forgotten that, coming as they did out of the milieu of the Parisian maîtres des requêtes, most intendants had experience sitting on or reporting to the royal councils and had known each other as collaborators, sometimes for many years. Thus an ordinance from Languedoc of December 27, 1633 is signed by Miron and Le Camus, the two intendants, and by Jean Baltazar, who was there as secretary of the governor Hallwin and would become intendant of Languedoc ten years later. François Bosquet (1642–6) had worked with François de Verthamont (who attended the Estates in 1653) in Normandy. Baltazar, Le Camus, Breteuil, Boucherat, Bezons, and d'Aguesseau, all royal agents in Languedoc, became important advisors to the central government after their provincial service, and thus continued to influence Languedocian affairs. Boucherat became chancellor of France in 1685. Thus agents, however beleaguered, were able to visualize their reports being received in Paris, and the Parisian councillors in turn could picture the situation in the province when they discussed policy in the royal councils.

[12] Bezons to Colbert, May 26, 1665: Mel. Col. 129 bis, 728.

[13] Nicolas-Joseph Foucault, *Mémoires*, ed. F. Baudry (Paris, 1862), p. 42.

[14] Bezons to Colbert, July 29, 1665: Mel. Col. 130 bis, 1029; Barbier to Séguier, June 22, 1644: ms. fr. 17379, 133; Pierre Serres, *Histoire de la Cour des Comptes, Aides et Finances de Montpellier* (Montpellier, 1878), p. 59. In this respect Languedocian intendants were significantly different from those in pays d'élections who had to be supplied with troops to collect the taille.

Relations within this dispersed, yet interlocking, group of administrators were not always harmonious. Intendants, like other notables, had to lobby to get their stipends paid and had to fight for favors for friends and relatives. Like true courtiers, they made a point of participating in projects that would please the ministers.[15] More important, courtly pull was necessary to see that the royal council backed up the intendant's decisions; otherwise his authority would have little effect. Before 1661 this problem of coordination of authority was especially common. Typical was the dilemma of Baltazar in 1643 when he was trying to import grain from Marseilles to reduce the shortage in Languedoc. Although royal orders had already been issued requiring the consuls of Marseilles to permit the export, it was necessary to use his influence with Séguier and Letellier to obtain additional letters reinforcing a decision already made because the Marseillais adamantly refused to obey.[16] If this Parisian influence failed, the intendant would be left helpless. An intendant would sometimes learn from Parisian friends that his enemies were threatening to discredit him in the royal council unless he changed his policies.[17]

Always insecure, intendants naturally reacted defensively against any rebuke: 'those who are not on the scene...cannot comprehend all the circumstances involved', they lamented, or 'nothing destroys authority as much as allowing the least pretext for doubting it'. Their calls for support against corporate rivals poured out of the province: 'if our competence were dependent upon the chambres de l'édit and the parlements, our function in the provinces would be useless'.[18] The dependence of intendants on the situation at court made them especially vulnerable during the royal minority of the 1640s when support in the royal council was changeable. As we will see below, the insecurity of patronage and authority could also turn the intendants against each other.

Intendants were jacks-of-all-trades who functioned as general agents of the Parisian government. Their commissions granted wide powers of investigation, intrusion, and reform; but at the same time they were held to very specific reporting of their activities, item by item, and their assignments arrived in similar form, instructing a particular man to investigate a particular problem. There was little effort to keep systematic files, though, under Colbert, massive questionnaires and streams of specific

[15] On Feb. 28, 1665, Bezons asks for protection of his private investment in alienated *aides* contracts; on Mar. 10, 1665, he ostentatiously subscribes to Colbert's East India Company and notes that help in the *aides* affair would supply him the necessary funds. Mel. Col. 127 bis, 1121; Mel. Col. 128, 298.

[16] Baltazar to Séguier and Letellier, Dec. 22, 1643; Lubl., pp. 56–7.

[17] Bosquet to Séguier, July 10, 1644: ms. fr. 17379, 201; Baltazar to Mazarin, Jan. 2, 1647: A.A.E. France 1634, 265.

[18] Baltazar to Séguier, Nov. 16, 1643: Lubl., p. 46; Baltazar to La Vrillière, Jan. 9, 1645: Lubl., p. 106; Baltazar to Séguier, Dec. 6, 1643: Lubl., p. 51.

queries began pouring in which led to the exchange of unprecedented volumes of information. It was in the 1680s or 1690s that the intendancy began to have permanent files of information which stayed with the office and have come down to us in the C series of the various departmental archives. Before that time whatever files there were were personal, and disappeared with the intendant.

Instructions arrived from the royal council in a packet containing arrêts calling for investigation of a particular matter, along with letters from the various ministers involved, lettres de cachet providing the specific orders requiring individuals to act, and sometimes personal letters from notables indicating their special interest in the matter. Armed with these, the intendant would set out on his mission, or if the matter could wait, he would hold it until an opportune moment arose. Such assignments were eagerly solicited, for they indicated favor, and when they stopped coming an intendant was left in an embarrassing state of underemployment implying suspension of patronage.

Missions usually involved a combination of investigation, legal prosecution, and simple persuasion. For example, an arrêt of 1644 instructed Baltazar to look into the case of a parlementaire of Aix whose family had concealed his death to avoid losing his office for non-payment of the *droit annuel.* Baltazar arrested an accomplice, then found that the family had sworn to secrecy the augustins déchaussés who knew the story, and forced many of these monks to leave for Avignon where they could not be pursued by royal officers. Extradition proceedings had to be undertaken with the papal legate; the superiors of the order had to be convinced of their duty; and public opinion had to be pacified through the influence of the first president of Aix. The whole affair took over a month of conferences to resolve, which was not unusual.[19] Often, in the course of such assignments, parties could be brought around with promises to resolve difficulties they were having in the royal council. Then the intendant would draw up a proposed arrêt du conseil and send it off to be approved and issued. He was therefore dependent on the ministers for the proper decisions and arrêts which would constitute his bargaining points as well as his ultimate authority.[20]

Once embarked on a particular journey, the intendant would take advantage of his location to investigate local governments, hear complaints, catch up on small items of business in the vicinity, and make contacts. His letters described each such matter specifically. Whereas before the 1660s intendants seemed more isolated from the king and thus in the short run more independent, afterwards their letters became more frequent, more technical, and in addition more inconclusive, for it was assumed that the

[19] Lubl., pp. 71–5. [20] For example, Tubeuf to Colbert, Apr. 10, 1666: Mel. Col. 137, 166.

ministers would advise them on each item, often using independent sources of information. But business was still reported with that sense of concreteness and specificity which was the trademark of intendants. In a single letter of 1669 Bezons reported in detail to the controller general about financial arrangements for building the port of Sète; about a case being sent to the royal council concerning payment of back taxes in Privas; about obstacles created by the treasurers-general of Grenoble to the repair of the bridge at Pont Saint-Esprit; about a complaint against someone's monopoly for the transport of coal for which the intendant had no information; and about the intervention of the marquise de Malause in the drawing up of a *papier terrier*.[21] When we consider that Bezons and Colbert would probably exchange views several times on each item and imagine the preliminary work each response would require, we can get some idea of the extent of an intendant's rudimentary but spectacularly energetic administration.

THE INTENDANCY DEVELOPS

A. *Before 1633*.[22] During the 1620s Languedoc was still under the sway of its famous governor, Henri II, duc de Montmorency, or in his absence of Henri de Lévis, duc de Ventadour, the governor's brother-in-law. These men set a gallant tone for provincial social life, gathering the lesser nobles around them, and personifying for the Estates and many of the towns the particularist glories of the past. The pattern of intendants in the 1620s reflects the Montmorency hegemony and the military concerns of the day.[23] A variety of them passed through, usually with special assignments related to pacification of Protestants or support of royal armies. The two most often seen were François du Faure, who served as intendant 'in the service of Montmorency', and François-Théodore de Nesmond, who appeared when the prince de Condé arrived with his army.[24] These men divided their loyalties between the military commanders and the crown, but there was no open rivalry until 1629 when Richelieu's plan to abolish the Estates and

[21] July 9, 1669: Mel. Col. 154, 92.

[22] The only general survey of Languedoc's intendants is Florentin Astre, 'Les Indendants du Languedoc', *Mémoires de l'Académie des Sciences, Inscriptions et Belles-Lettres de Toulouse*, 5th series 3 (1859), 7–36, 5th series 4 (1860), 421–43, 5th series 5 (1861), 102–24, 6th series 6 (1868), 20–55, 7th series 3 (1871), 31–54.

[23] Sources for this early period include David Buisseret, 'Les Précurseurs des intendants du Languedoc', *Annales du Midi*, 80 (1968), 80–8; Paul Gachon, *Les États de Languedoc et l'Édit de Béziers (1632)*, (Paris, 1887), pp. 93–103; the list in B. N. Languedoc (Bénédictins) 71; attendance at sessions of the Estates mentioned in *Inventaire Haute-Garonne*, série C, II; and Bonney, 'Intendants', which lists all the known intendants in a series of appendices.

[24] On Nesmond see also Pierre Lefebvre, 'Aspects de la "fidélité" en France au XVIIe siècle: le cas des agents du prince de Condé', *Revue Historique*, 250 (1973), 66–7, 93–5; and Nesmond's commission in Gabriel Hanotaux, *Origines de l'institution des intendants des provinces, d'après les documents inédits* (Paris, 1884), p. 251.

establish the élus in their place thrust Montmorency into the unfortunate role of having to preside over the suppression of his province's privileges. While he was wavering in loyalty, the province was already being flooded by agents strictly loyal to Richelieu, who kept an eye on conditions in the various regions and on the loyalty of the governor and his followers. When Montmorency was drawn into open rebellion, these men were already on the scene where they remained until well into 1633, especially Charles de Machault who toured the mountains with a company of troops directing the demolition of rebel fortifications.

B. *1633 to 1642.* The new regime imposed after the disgrace of the province's traditional leaders was part of the network of Louis XIII and Richelieu, but it was not at all divorced from provincial sympathies, and it continued with modifications the traditions of the past. The new governor was Charles, duc d'Hallwin, a gallant thirty-three-year-old officer whose father, the maréchal de Schomberg, had died shortly after commanding the royal army which defeated Montmorency. Hallwin himself became maréchal de Schomberg in 1637; therefore his usual title is Schomberg, not Hallwin. He was a royal creature without local ties. Belonging to a German family which had come to France under Charles IX and risen through royal favor, he himself had grown up at court as *enfant d'honneur* of Louis XIII. Yet he was popular enough to fill the void in Languedocian affections left by the removal of Montmorency and sympathetic enough to be accused of being soft on the rioters in 1645. André Delort, a priest in Montpellier, wrote admiringly in his annals that Schomberg not only spoke four or five languages, knew Vergil almost by heart, and had learned Languedocian in order to be able to speak to the common people, but that he charmed the natives as well with his 'touching manner of speaking and pleasant voice; and although he had a martial spirit he never failed to be sweet, honest, courteous, affectionate, tender, and a loyal friend'.[25]

Schomberg was served by a changing pair of intendants, first Robert Miron (1631–6) and Antoine Le Camus (1633–6); then Miron and Barthélemy Dupré (1636–40); then Hercule de Vauquelin and André Rancé (1640–2).[26] The distinguishing characteristic of this sequence of teams was

[25] André Delort, *Mémoires inédits sur la ville de Montpellier au XVIIe siècle (1621–1673)*, 2 vols. (Montpellier, 1876–8), vol. I, pp. 82–3.

[26] General biographical information on the intendants comes from various sources. There is genealogical information on intendants in ms. fr. 32785–32786, some of which is printed in Roland Mousnier ed., *Lettres et mémoires adressés au chancelier Séguier (1633–1649)*, 2 vols. (Paris, 1964), vol. II, pp. 1183–227. Richard Bonney has compiled additional material in 'Intendants', pp. 252–8, 269–85, 309–15, 317–28, 337–49. Dates cited do not always agree, depending on whether one uses the date on a commission or the date when an intendant was known to be on duty in the province. There is also difficulty deciding which men were full-fledged intendants. For example, some of the intendants listed by Bonney were apparently commissioners to the Estates rather than resident administrators. Here I am using the pragmatic test of who was 'on duty' regardless of the niceties of title and date of appointment.

the close rapport all of them had with Richelieu and their ability to work with Schomberg. As long as the latter was in command and had the support of the cardinal, there were only minor signs of friction. The intendants of these years were still teams with changing membership rather like those of the 1620s, but they stayed longer in place and made more of an impact on local government. Schomberg, too, acted like an intendant, travelling about and settling disputes while his subordinate agents made trips to other areas and rejoined him periodically to judge cases or confer on tactics.[27]

Robert Miron, the mainstay of the group, was an aged and eminent bourgeois of Paris who had been president of the third estate at the Estates-General of 1614 and ambassador to Switzerland.[28] His younger colleague, Antoine Le Camus, fitted better the stereotype of an aggressive man on the rise. His father had been born in Reims and made a fortune in Paris under the auspices of Henry IV. He himself entered the Parlement of Paris in 1624 and became maître des requêtes in 1631. His appearance in Languedoc was part of the social ascension of his whole family to prominence through Parisian financial connections. His brother was intendant of the armies of Italy and Languedoc in the 1630s. He himself later became controller-general of finances (1648–57), succeeding his more notorious brother-in-law Michel Particelli d'Hémery.[29] The other intendants were less prominent. Dupré was the son and the brother of a secrétaire du roi. Vauquelin rose from the présidial of Caen to the conseil d'état. Rancé is hardly known. A 'third' intendant, Charles Machault, sieur d'Arnouville, served as intendant 'near' the prince de Condé from 1639 to 1641. Known as 'coupe-tête' for his tough stance in a number of Richelieu's criminal prosecutions, he had already served in Languedoc in 1622 and 1629–31.

The tradition of having two intendants serving simultaneously, which had roots in the assignments of the 1620s, became regular practice in the 1630s. There were technical justifications for it in that Languedoc comprised two généralités, Toulouse and Montpellier, each of which might have had its own agent. But the commissions of the intendants never

27 Roland Mousnier, 'Note sur les rapports entre les gouverneurs de provinces et les intendants dans la première moitié du XVIIe siècle', *Revue historique*, 228 (1962), pp. 339–50; and Miron to Séguier, Oct. 15, 1636: Lubl., p. 28.

28 On Miron, Astre, 'Intendants', *Mémoires de l'Académie de Toulouse*, 5th series 3 (1859), 7–36; and A. Miron de l'Espinay, *Robert Miron et l'administration municipale de Paris de 1614 à 1616* (Paris, 1922); ms. fr. 32785, 174–5.

29 On Le Camus, Mousnier, *Lettres*, vol. II, pp. 1208–9; Julian Dent, *Crisis in Finance: Crown Financiers and Society in Seventeenth-Century France* (New York, 1973), pp. 95–9, 117–18; Gachon, *États*, pp. 225–7. Difficulties remain as to the identity of the various Le Camus and d'Hémerys. Bonney believes that Antoine Le Camus, sieur d'Hémery, only served in 1635–6; but another Le Camus, possibly Antoine's brother Nicolas, was corresponding in Languedoc in 1633. Apparently neither was Michel Particelli, sieur d'Hémery, who was in Languedoc in 1631–2 and who was the brother-in-law of the other two.

reflected any distinction between districts, and in reality the two men nearly always stayed close together.[30] The Estates exerted their taxing power province-wide from a single center, and military considerations kept the royal agents in the eastern end of the province. The 'team' spirit of the joint intendancy emerges clearly in a letter Schomberg wrote in 1643 giving reasons why one of the intendants should not be sent to reside in Toulouse:

> the delay which the king's service would suffer, the length of time required for transmitting business, and the eternal conflict of jurisdiction [which would arise] between [the intendants] or with the Parlement, not to mention the fact that if the intendant who was in Bas-Languedoc was sent towards Pont Saint-Esprit or towards the frontier, as often happens, I would be left without intendants, and thus my ordinances could not be countersigned. And since individuals or envoys of communities who have business with me frequently have business before them as well, these people would consume twice as much time and money if we were separated. Besides, there are a hundred occasions when we have to work together between ordinances, and I leave you to imagine, Monsieur, what disorder would then ensue.[31]

However, there were also factional reasons for having two intendants in a province so far from Paris. The dual intendancy was an expression of the complexities of a political situation where nuances of command within the province had to be expressed, as well as shades of difference in patronage groupings at court. The correspondence of Charpentier, Richelieu's personal secretary, reveals that there were constant pressures at court for particular appointments to be made in Languedoc.[32] Intendants were still thought of as adjuncts to military commanders, and after 1635 Languedoc was almost in a war zone. Miron and the others were expected to serve as Schomberg's secretaries and legal consultants, even while carrying out commissions for the government and keeping an independent eye on the local situation. The governor in turn had to lobby to impose his own viewpoint at court and fight for congenial men with whom he could work.

The two resident intendants fitted into different circles of contacts and loyalties which seemed to be transmitted with the office, either by conscious briefing or through the play of circumstances. Miron and his successors were more congenial to Schomberg, whereas Le Camus and his successors quarreled with the governor. In the 1640s the successor to the 'friendly' Miron was Jean Baltazar, who had previously been Schomberg's Parisian agent, and who denounced the allegiances of his colleague Bosquet in terms

[30] See, for example, Baltazar's commission in Mousnier, *Lettres*, vol. II, pp. 1068–71. Richard Bonney has a different emphasis in his discussion of double intendancies: *Political Change*, pp. 45–8.

[31] Schomberg to Séguier, Dec. 21, 1643: Lubl., p. 55.

[32] Schomberg writes to Charpentier (in 1640?) asking for monsieur de Miraumont as intendant, 'not having had anyone for almost ten years in Languedoc who aided me and understood the financing of troops as well as he did'. B.N. Baluze 340, 82.

almost identical to those he had formerly used in Paris against Bosquet's predecessor Le Camus.[33] At court it was a matter of gossip among the influential whether a governor like Schomberg had gotten his own man as intendant or had been saddled with the clients of someone else.

C. *1643 to 1653*. In the next decade the rivalry and hesitation resulting from the royal minority caused a steady deterioration of the governmental 'team', even though its basic characteristics remained unchanged. First came the appointment of François Bosquet as intendant, which occurred before the death of Louis XIII in November 1642. Bosquet was unusual in that he was a native of Languedoc whose father had been a notary and consul in Narbonne, and who had first attracted the attention of local prelates through his erudition. He was editing eleventh-century Greek texts at age seventeen and corresponding with leading humanists like Peiresc in Aix and Pierre de Marca while still studying at the University of Toulouse. These intellectuals put him in touch with the chancellor Séguier, himself a book-lover, who seems to have patronized Bosquet primarily as a scholar. Even when the Chancellor took him on his famous mission to pacify Normandy in 1639 after the revolt of the Nu-Pieds, Bosquet was assigned primarily to making inventories of rare manuscripts for Séguier's library. Shortly afterwards he was named intendant of Guyenne and then transferred to Languedoc. He was not unqualified for the job, having achieved the status of conseiller d'état, worked with many of the leading maîtres des requêtes in Normandy, and weathered a serious popular revolt in Montauban. But his interests were primarily ecclesiastical, his ties were local, and his patronage came from Séguier and the clergy. Such talent was not of a sort to complement the martial courtier Schomberg, and it seems probable that his appointment was primarily a sign of the rising power of Séguier himself. Bosquet was a reluctant intendant who complained to his mentor continually about his fate – his lack of support, the dangers of excessive taxes, or the aggressiveness of others. He kept angling for a more congenial post, first as bishop of Pamiers, then as president in the Parlement of Aix.[34]

In July 1643 Jean Baltazar, seigneur de Malherbe, was appointed intendant to accompany Bosquet. Baltazar was an older man, son of a councillor in the présidial of Sens with family connections in the Paris

[33] Letters of Baltazar to Charpentier of May 20, 1636, and those between folios 21 and 25 of B. N. Baluze 339. The logic of having double intendancies to smooth over clientage clashes is illustrated in 1657 when lieutenant-general Bieules asks Mazarin to send a second intendant 'like before' because Bieules does not get along with the intendant Bezons: Bieules to Mazarin, Dec. 3, 1657; A. A. E. France 1637, 123.

[34] On Bosquet, abbé Paul-Émile Henry, *François Bosquet intendant de Guyenne et de Languedoc, évêque de Lodève et de Montpellier* (Paris, 1889); Alexandre Germain, ed., 'Une vie inédite de François Bosquet, publiée avec une notice', *Mémoires de l'Académie des Sciences de Montpellier*, 3 (1859–63), 71–80; on Bosquet and Baltazar, William Beik, 'Two Intendants Face a Popular Revolt: Social Unrest and the Structure of Absolutism in 1645', *Canadian Journal of History*, 9 (1974), 243–62.

Parlement and considerable experience in the central government.[35] He had been in the Valtelline in the 1620s, and he had accompanied the old maréchal de Schomberg to Languedoc in 1632. In 1635 he had become a councillor in the Paris Parlement, all the while serving as agent of the Schomberg family, and he had made money in royal tax deals. One description of him as 'man of fortune, devoted to the great powers, dangerous, and capable of doing anything for the court or for his own interests' seems particularly apt.[36] Whereas Bosquet was a reluctant intendant, always trying to soften the blows he had to deliver to the province, Baltazar was an eager military administrator, quick to give orders, hard-headed, and arrogant. He was sarcastic in dealing with rivals, and he saw conspiracies against himself in every move of his opponents. From the moment of his arrival he and Bosquet quarreled over precedence, then began accusing each other of ineptitude, with Bosquet charging that Baltazar was causing unnecessary friction and exaggerating his successes in letters to court, while Baltazar saw Bosquet as naive, overly conciliatory towards local interests, and completely ineffective.

The 'team' continued to function, but Baltazar and Schomberg gradually turned against Bosquet, monopolizing royal commissions and leaving him isolated. As conflicts at court became more heated during the minority, things went from bad to worse. Bosquet and Baltazar evaded each other and sent in contradictory reports. The frustrated Bosquet resorted to vilification: 'the spirit of that little viper is so envenomed that he turns good meat into poison'; and began counterattacking: 'at least I don't preach about myself, send out great reports of what I have done and haven't done filled with truths and lies, or attribute to myself all the praise that belongs to other people'.[37]

Meanwhile Baltazar took Bosquet's share of the Estates' stipend, withheld information from him, and antagonized most of the local authorities with tough, arbitrary decisions. But more serious was the public impact of their quarreling. The province naturally discovered that the two enemies could be played off against one another, as a letter to the first consul of Montpellier in 1645 clearly proposes.[38] In Béziers contradictory settlements by the two intendants of an election crisis in 1646 helped bring on an uprising in which several persons were killed.[39] None of these problems were totally new, but the personality conflicts of the two men,

[35] On Baltazar, B. N. Pièces originales 180; ms. fr. 32785, 557–8; Bonney, *Political Change*, pp. 92, 128–9, 302, 396.

[36] Quoted in Bonney, *Political Change*, p. 128.

[37] Bosquet to Séguier, July 25, 1644: Lubl., p. 69; Jan. 10, 1645: Henry, *François Bosquet*, pp. 188–9.

[38] A.M. Mp BB 284 (Soubeyran to Belleval, Nov. 17, 1645).

[39] Procès-verbal and memoir of Bosquet, ms. fr. 18830, 230, 240.

heightened by the fact that they represented different patrons at court, greatly exacerbated a difficult situation.

Matters were further complicated in early 1644 when, amidst complicated court intrigues, Mazarin was forced to transfer the governorship to Gaston d'Orléans to keep him loyal to the crown. Since Schomberg was kept on as lieutenant-general and Gaston never entered the province, there was no immediately visible change. But it was symptomatic of the instability at court that the old conspirator of 1632 could reappear as the leader of the province he had led astray. Soon Orléans's allies, most of them fellow conspirators with local origins, were appointed to local positions of command.

From 1643 to 1647 the Schomberg–Bosquet–Baltazar team continued to manage the province, but there was now a third pole of influence. Bosquet was Séguier's appointment, while Baltazar had been appointed by Cardinal Mazarin and the queen, upon the strong insistence of Schomberg. Now Orléans's friends worked at cross-purposes to Schomberg and built up a following in the various provincial agencies. Even the prince de Condé, who still wanted Orléans's governorship, continued to meddle. As competitive intrigues became more dangerous amidst the rising social tensions of 1645 and 1646, each agent reacted in characteristic fashion. Bosquet renewed his pleas for transfer, which were finally granted in March 1646. He ultimately returned to the province as bishop of Lodève and later became bishop of Montpellier. Baltazar stayed on until he was transferred in January 1647, but his reports became increasingly conspiratorial, and he even began denouncing the ineptitude of Schomberg as he shifted his allegiances more and more to Mazarin himself.[40] Schomberg resigned his position in disgust in early 1647, leaving Orléans and his three lieutenant-generals in military command of the province.

Louis Le Tonnelier de Breteuil (1647–53), the man who replaced Baltazar, faced a difficult situation. He was another intelligent administrator from a Parisian robe family whose father had been procureur-general of the Paris Cour des Aides and who had held offices in the Parlements of Rennes and Paris.[41] He succeeded Le Camus as controller-general in 1657 and was one of the financiers who later paid indemnities after Colbert's prosecution of François Fouquet. Breteuil was really the first solo intendant, but his stay in Montpellier was far from triumphant because he was forced to move gingerly during the Fronde. He was isolated, first by the questionable loyalty of all three lieutenant-generals, and second by the rampage of the Toulouse parlementaires, who drove Mazarin's agent

[40] Baltazar to Mazarin, Oct. 16, 1646: A.A.E. France 1634, 251.

[41] On Breteuil, ms. fr. 32785, pp. 582–5; Dent, *Crisis in Finance*, p. 97.

Thomas Morant out of the province in 1650 with their threats and gave the old veteran Machault similar trouble when he arrived in Montauban in 1653.[42] Meanwhile Mazarin kept a tenuous control over events by maintaining Breteuil in relative safety in Montpellier and by sending a high-level bargaining team to reinforce his authority every time he had to meet with the Estates.

D. *1653 to 1661*. Breteuil's successor was Claude Bazin de Bezons, who arrived in late 1653.[43] Bezons fitted into the same mold as his predecessors, but he was the first unequivocal disciple of Mazarin, and he was one of the most experienced intendants yet. After becoming advocate-general in the Grand Conseil in 1639, he had served as intendant in Soissons and Bourges and as inspector-general in Catalonia during the critical years of the Fronde, where he worked with Pierre de Marca, Bosquet's friend who would later become archbishop of Toulouse and archbishop of Paris. Bezons was also known in Parisian literary circles, and by the end of his life he had become *doyen* of the Académie Française. In his early years he still sounded like one of the original royal commissioners as he fussed about his unpaid salary or tried to defend his 'mediocre fortune'.[44] But he ended his life in a position of great eminence, and one of his sons became intendant of Limoges, Orléans, Lyons and Bordeaux, while another became archbishop of Bordeaux in 1698. Thus Bezons represented a transition from the subordinate status of the early intendants to the high aristocracy of the later ones.

Bezons has been called the first full-fledged intendant of Languedoc, and, with his twenty years in office during the formative period of Colbert's reforms, he certainly deserves the title. But the contrast with earlier regimes should not be exaggerated, and a distinction should be made between the troublesome 1650s, when Bezons was only marginally better off than Breteuil, and the very different period after 1660. In this first phase the province was still turbulent, and local agencies were still relatively hostile. Until 1660 the governor was a distant and now less consequential Orléans, while locally the three resident lieutenant-generals, who were shifting with the times back into a loyalist stance, gradually proved themselves to be reliable, if minor, collaborators in combatting urban disruptions and troop disorders. A team was beginning to function again, but gradually: Bezons and lieutenant-general Bieules were fired on and narrowly missed by an angry mob while executing royal orders in Nîmes in 1658.

42 Edmond Esmonin, 'Un Épisode du rétablissement des intendants: la mission de Morant en Guyenne', *Revue d'histoire moderne et contemporaine*, 1 (1954), 85–101; letters of Morant in ms. fr. nouv. acq. 1081; Fieubet to Mazarin, Oct. 12, 1653: A. A. E. France 1636, 214.

43 On Bezons, Astre, 'Intendants', *Mémoires de l'Académie de Toulouse*, 6th series 6 (1868), 21–35; ms. fr. 32786, 777–9; Roschach, vol. XIII, pp. 297, 357; Bonney, *Political Change*, pp. 129–30.

44 Mel. Col. 107, 437; Mel. Col. 131 bis, 1194; Mel. Col. 132, 218.

E. *1661 to 1673*. When Mazarin died there was a brief period of uncertainty and then a marked change in the intendancy. In October 1661 Bezons wrote sycophantically to Colbert in the old manner of the devoted servant:

I don't know why you take the precaution of saying that there was no time to send a more authentic authorization than the letter you took the trouble of writing. This [style] is useful for acts that must appear in public, but in [private] orders I beg you to believe that I will act so punctually that you will be entirely satisfied.[45]

He had missed the point that orders now had to be legitimized by the king in person, and that such private commands were no longer considered appropriate. Compare these remarks with the protestations of Bosquet to Séguier in 1645: 'since I belong to your person more than to your post, please honor me with your orders...which will always be inviolable laws that I will keep faithfully'.[46] Such language, which Bezons was echoing at first, would have led to arrest or disgrace under Louis XIV.

Bezons gradually became a full-scale administrator, engaging in vast investigations and directing massive financial and economic projects as no previous intendant had done. But his rule was still not solitary. For one thing, the new governor after 1660 was Armand de Bourbon, prince de Conti, whose impeccable family connections included his father, the prince de Condé, who had often commanded in the province; his mother, the sister of Montmorency; his godfather Richelieu; and his wife, the niece of Mazarin. Since Conti held properties in Languedoc, he frequented the province, came to the Estates, and exerted considerable influence. His presence in Pézenas and elsewhere meant a last flurry of courtly attention, including the performances of Molière's young troop of comedians before Conti and at the Estates. Until his death in 1666 he played an active role, but he was the last governor to do so. His successor, Henry de Bourbon, duc de Verneuil, bastard of Henry IV, was no more than a courtier who showed up for the Estates.

The fact that a second intendant was appointed between 1665 and 1668 also indicates that the dual intendancy had not been definitively abandoned. Charles de Tubeuf, son of one of Mazarin's surintendants des finances, was a man in his early thirties whose eager, redundant letters betrayed his inexperience.[47] He was named to participate in the Grands Jours of Puy and to help Bezons with his heavy work load. He was more of an apprentice than an equal, and there were no signs of the old-style rivalry. It should also be noted that Colbert's 'team' included a widening group of other

[45] Bezons to Colbert, Oct. 3, 1661: Mel. Col. 103, 731.
[46] Bosquet to Séguier, Mar. 31, 1645: Lubl., p. 130.
[47] For example, May 1, 1666: Mel. Col. 137 bis, 529.

correspondants, many of whom were resident dignitaries rather than lesser officials.

F. *1673 to 1685*. Bezons's considerable success at directing provincial affairs and getting money out of the Estates would have brought laurels to an earlier intendant, but times had changed and a great deal was expected. More important, Bezons had difficulty getting along with Verneuil, the governor, and Colbert gradually came to distrust him. The mismatching of the 'team' became acute when Cardinal Bonzi, who will be discussed elsewhere, became president of the Estates. In return for his considerable services Bonzi demanded great authority in the province, and his pretensions brought him into conflict with Bezons, who made the mistake of taking too defensive a stand on the indemnification of notables for lands taken in the construction of the Canal du Midi.

He was replaced in 1673 by Henri d'Aguesseau, son of a first president of the Parlement of Bordeaux, president in the Grand Conseil, then intendant in Limoges and Bordeaux.[48] D'Aguesseau was a man who combined immense stature already achieved with great experience and talent. He was a close ally of Verneuil before coming to Languedoc, and he managed very rapidly to establish a working relationship with Bonzi. As the first intendant to inherit a well-established intendancy and to bring with him the status to match it, he knew how to surround himself with an aura of authority befitting the new prestige of Louis XIV. His first act was a triumphal journey through the province, something no previous intendant had attempted, in which he was welcomed at the gates of each town like a major power. To the compliments of the capitouls he replied 'that Toulouse is the only town in the kingdom which knows and practices the appropriate manner of receiving persons invested by the king with a proper authority for making his orders observed'.[49] It is hard to imagine Baltazar in such a role. But at the same time d'Aguesseau cultivated an image of austerity and moderation, dressing like a magistrate and staying away from the brilliant society around Bonzi.

Under d'Aguesseau the preoccupations and methods of Bezons continued – after all, it was still Colbert directing the show. The difference was that whereas Bezons was still essentially a technician, gathering data and executing policy, d'Aguesseau was a creative intellect who grasped the totality of situations and thought a great deal about general policy – more a satellite of Colbert than a mere facilitator. Not only did he expand the provincial projects already under way, but he held conferences with other

[48] On d'Aguesseau, Ernest Roschach, 'Henri d'Aguesseau, intendant de Languedoc', *Mémoires de l'Académie des Sciences, Inscriptions et Belles-Lettres de Toulouse*, 7th series 7 (1875), 576–92; ms. fr. 32785, 379–82, 678–9, 682–5.

[49] Astre, 'Intendants', *Mémoires de l'Académie de Toulouse*, 7th series 3 (1871), pp. 35–6.

intendants concerning tax reform and drew up general programs for Colbert to study. He was a hard-headed, but constructive administrator whose resignation in 1685 at the time of the revocation of the Edict of Nantes has led historians, following the lead of his son, the chancellor d'Aguesseau, to exaggerate his compassionate nature.[50] What no doubt discouraged him was not so much the forced conversion of Protestants, which he had encouraged in the past, but the advent of a new regime of military hardness which he found uncongenial. After all, Colbert his mentor was gone, and he must have realized that the age of Louvois was not going to be favorable to his administrative and economic projects. Despite the account of his family virtually fleeing the province in 1685, as news of forced conversions by royal dragonnades followed close behind them, d'Aguesseau was able to return to Paris where he continued to advise the government placidly as a prestigious councillor of state.

With Nicolas Lamoignon de Basville, who arrived in August 1685 accompanied by the troops which had already terrorized Poitou, the development of the intendancy was complete.[51] Basville was a man of his age, similar in family background to d'Aguesseau but more eminent and more powerful, with connections befitting the atmosphere of Louis XIV's last thirty years. Where d'Aguesseau had been the son of the first president from Bordeaux, Basville was son of First President Lamoignon of the Paris Parlement and grandson of a président à mortier from the same body. His brother was advocate-general in the Paris Parlement; one sister became the wife of First President Harlay; and another became comtesse de Broglie. Basville himself had been intendant of Pau, Montauban, and Poitiers. His allies at court were Louvois, Madame de Maintenon, and Père La Chaise, and his sympathies lay with the Jesuits.

Basville's long 'reign' in Languedoc, which lasted until 1719, is beyond the scope of this study. It is worth noting, though, that his authority was the culmination of what had come before. Like d'Aguesseau, he was a Parisian aristocrat with fully-formed ties in the central government, and he was a brilliant administrator whose memoirs on the province are still used as a basic source for its economic life. There was a little of Baltazar in him too, for he took the last steps towards gaining unchallenged control of the province by gradually discrediting Cardinal Bonzi and inaugurating a tough, effective regime.[52] But whereas Baltazar was unjustifiably arrogant

50 For example, ibid., p. 44; or Georges Frêche, *Un Chancelier Gallican: Daguesseau* (Paris, 1969), p. 12. The origin of this exaggerated sympathy is Henri-François Daguesseau, *Discours sur la vie et la mort...de M. d'Aguesseau, conseiller d'état* (Paris, 1812).

51 On Basville, Henri Monin, *Essai sur l'histoire administrative du Languedoc pendant l'intendance de Basville (1685–1719)* (Paris, 1884), pp. 1–17; Roschach, vol XIII, pp. 540–2; ms. fr. 32785, 592–4; ms. fr. 32786, 749–51, 888.

52 C. Joret, 'Basville et l'épiscopat de Languedoc', *Annales du Midi*, 6 (1894), 420–64, 7 (1895), 5–50.

and authoritarian, yet powerless, Basville was both more powerful and more realistic. He may even have been more humanitarian, for recent historians have found a reluctance to harm the province and a distaste at overly-rigorous orders which is more reminiscent of Bosquet.[53] Basville was in a sense trapped in the province. In 1709 he had not been back to Paris since 1685, despite the death of his mother and brother and repeated requests for leaves of absence. Like previous intendants he was an intermediary of sorts, and some of the same problems of distance and influence still prevailed.

Between 1620 and 1690 the intendancy developed from an occasional institution attached to special missions and adjuncts of military commanders, to a full-fledged agency which had become the command center for directing and coordinating royal projects in the province. In its growing function of mediating between a monarchy wanting various things done in the province and a collection of rulers wanting various measures enacted by the monarchy, it was probably not unlike the intendancies in other provinces. But its evolution was special in that intendants in Languedoc had to deal primarily with the Estates, whereas in other provinces they had to take over and run the taille administration in the 1640s, often by force. Languedocian intendants, therefore, had to work especially closely with governors and other negotiators, and their success was especially embroiled in political factionalism because the Estates had to be won over by negotiation and influence.

[53] Jean-Robert Armogathe and Philippe Joutaud, 'Bâville et la guerre des Camisards', *Revue d'histoire moderne et contemporaine*, 19 (1972), 45–72.

6

The Estates: central bargaining place

The sessions of the Estates were a major event in the yearly life of Languedoc.[1] For those involved they were a high point in the social season in which the leading members of the three orders could act out to full advantage their subtle differences in rank, status, and personal prerogatives; and even for those too low in the scale to participate, the processions and ceremonies provided large-scale diversion. This pageantry, so seemingly superficial, was deadly serious, for the Estates were the place where political bargains were realized, relative influence was tested, and contacts were made or reinforced with individuals close to the king. Moreover, unlike the other agencies we have examined, the Estates transacted business of a genuinely political nature – business in which the conflicting interests of various groups had to be negotiated. They provided a central bargaining place, but not for all dominant groups equally – much less the entire population since they viewed issues from a particular social perspective.

The meetings were held once a year, usually in the autumn or winter, for a period of about three to six weeks, or sometimes longer if unresolved difficulties kept the royal agents from realizing their manipulative schedule. The king convoked the Estates regularly every year because the alternative was to do without taxes or to find another collection method. He also designated the site, which was usually one of the centrally-located bishoprics of Bas-Languedoc: Montpellier, Nîmes, Béziers, or Narbonne. Once the sessions were under way, the archbishop of Narbonne, permanent president

[1] There is no modern study of the Estates in the seventeenth century. The best accounts of what went on in each session can be found in the narrative volumes of the *Histoire générale de Languedoc* (Toulouse, 1872–92): Devic, vol. XI, which covers 1443 to 1643, and Roschach, vol. XIII, which covers 1643 to 1789. Roschach vol. XIV contains invaluable documents. Detailed analytical accounts of the situation at the two ends of our period are in Paul Gachon, *Les États de Languedoc et l'édit de Béziers (1632)* (Paris, 1887); and Henri Monin, *Essai sur l'histoire administrative du Languedoc pendant l'intendance de Basville* (Paris, 1884). An early survey is Baron Trouvé, *Essai historique sur les états-généraux de la province de Languedoc*, 2 vols. (Paris, 1818). Studies of earlier periods are Henri Gilles, *Les États de Languedoc au XVe siècle* (Toulouse, 1965); and James Eastgate Brink, 'The Estates of Languedoc: 1515–1560' (Ph.D diss., University of Washington, 1974). In addition there are good sections on Languedoc in Richard Bonney, *Political Change in France under Richelieu and Mazarin 1624–1661* (Oxford, 1981), pp. 344–83, and J. Russell Major, *Representative Government in Early Modern France* (New Haven, 1980), pp. 470–6, 549–57.

by virtue of his episcopal rank, scheduled the order of business, led debates, and called for votes.

The Estates were the manifestation of the privilege, granted by various monarchs and repeatedly renewed, of not being subject to any taxes which the province had not approved. But that which had been granted and confirmed could also be revoked, and, in a practical sense, the Estates were simply a convenience consecrated by long-standing custom. The right of the assembly to refuse grants was long-established, but so was the power of the king to command them to obey. Both sides were really engaged in a perpetual dialogue which pulled them closer to true negotiations or closer to dominance and subservience, depending on the strengths of each side in a given era.

An essential corollary to taxation by consent was the right to collect and administer the funds granted. To meet this need a separate administration had grown up, directed entirely by the assembly and administered by its own officers. The machinery for collection was a relatively efficient organization parallel to the hierarchy of royal officers in other parts of France. Approved taxes were repartitioned by the Estates among the twenty-two secular dioceses, each of which had its own assembly, the assiette, which we have already encountered in chapter 3. The assiettes repartitioned their sum among the individual towns and villages, where local collectors were responsible for extracting the money from local taxpayers according to the *compoix*, or local tax rolls. The diocesan receivers, who were responsible to the assiettes, sent the money on to the treasurer of the bourse, who was an officer of the Estates. The assembly also had its own permanent agents: three syndic-generals and two secretary-generals who took care of administrative business during the year.[2]

The king's interest lay in obtaining from the assembly the financial support he needed – a *don gratuit* or 'free grant' of uncommitted funds, plus approval of special fiscal edicts and other fiscal measures – without undue resistance or delay. The royal demands were presented by a delegation of commissioners who arrived bearing royal commissions and secret instructions specifying what they were to obtain and where they might compromise. In the seventeenth century the delegation always consisted of a military noble (the governor, a lieutenant-general, or an important army commander), a royal agent (the intendant or a maître des requêtes sent from Paris) and two local treasurer-generals of finance whose presence was purely ceremonial. Sometimes two military nobles or two royal agents were sent together. The commissioners' job was to 'manage' the Estates, but they could not attend the sessions, which were supposed

[2] A laudatory description of the Estates' officers is vicomte de Carrière, *Les Officiers des états de la province de Languedoc* (Paris, 1865).

to be secret. So they made periodic formal visits to announce the royal wishes in a series of elegant speeches and spent the rest of the time negotiating with deputations sent to them by the assembly and trying to manipulate the members behind the scenes.

This whole process was a complex mixture of ritual, social interaction, and hard bargaining. If all went smoothly it could be over in a matter of weeks, but matters could go seriously awry. Success was dependent on the proper combination of environment and circumstances, which in the context of the time meant that a certain group of notables had to be placated to the extent that they heeded the royal interests (or their own) more than any expressions of concern which might reach them from their provincial constituencies. If the province was in misery to the extent that the good will of its leaders was being called into question; if important notables felt slighted and became obstreperous; or if the rulers felt their direct interests threatened, then a subtle combination of bribery, appeasement, and concession was all that could win the day for the crown. The Estates were one of the most important consultative assemblies in Europe, but because their function was built upon personal client ties, the principle of social inequality, and an ideology of favoritism and deference, their workings cannot be analyzed in modern 'representative' or 'parliamentary' terms.

SESSIONS AND MEMBERS

The ritual of the sessions was carefully organized to facilitate the bargaining process.[3] After the king had convoked the Estates, *affiches* would be posted assigning lodgings to the deputies in the houses of local nobles and officers, according to rank and the elegance of the accommodations. As the crowds trickled into town, the two 'bargaining teams' would begin to gather for the ritual confrontation in the assembly. The royal intendants or special envoys were required to call on their military partners immediately upon arrival; and as the bishops and barons arrived they too had to make the rounds of the royal commissioners. These calls were 'only visits of civility, not obligation', but they must have been the occasions for renewing personal ties and making the promises which underlay most of the bargaining.

This was only the first round of visits. On the day of the opening, the newest of the two treasurer-generals serving as royal commissioners would

[3] An entire manuscript by a certain Descudier, written in 1665, 'Memoires servants au ceremonial des Estats generaux de la province de Languedoc' (A.N. H 748[120]) details these matters. There are also discussions of ceremonial in d'Aguesseau's 'Description de la province de Languedoc' (B.M. Tse ms. 603) and of procedures in Nicolas Lamoignon de Basville, *Mémoires pour servir à l'histoire de Languedoc* (Amsterdam, 1736), pp. 158–201. A collection of 'controlles des logements de nosseigneurs des états de la province de Languedoc' from 1698 to 1789 is in B. N. Imprimés Lk[14] 81.

fetch the other at his residence. Then they would go together to pick up in turn the intendant, the lieutenant-general and the governor at their residences. This complete delegation would be received at the outer door of the Estates' assembly hall by ten of the deputies of the third estate, who would escort them to the inner door, where a group of bishops and barons would lead them to their seats in the places of honor. The speeches which followed would reiterate the basic framework of the dialogue to follow. The governor would make a short speech followed by a longer, more detailed harangue by the intendant, both emphasizing the king's supremacy, but also his mercy and consideration for the well-being of his subjects and his unfortunate yet urgent needs for the current year. The president of the Estates would then reply by praising the king and his commissioners and emphasizing the assembly's total submission to their sovereign's wishes, while reluctantly feeling constrained to remind everyone of the province's privileges, their abject misery, and their total inability to do all that they would like in aiding His Majesty. After this florid display of rhetoric, the entire group would range itself hierarchically in the choir of the local church to hear mass. Later in the week, after the assembly had checked credentials and seated all its members, the company would join the royal commissioners in church again, this time to hear a pontifical mass and sermon by one of the bishops, after which they would march through the carpeted streets of the town, in a public display of the rank and ceremony of the representatives of God, king, and province. The people were allowed to observe these ceremonial functions, but the working sessions of the Estates were held behind closed doors.

The deliberations were also structured hierarchically. The meeting chamber was the largest hall in town, usually the chapel of a religious establishment or a room in the hôtel de ville. It was richly hung with tapestries and decorated with the arms of the province, the royal agents, and the king by the *tapissier des états*. The president sat on a raised platform, surrounded on three sides by raised benches. To his right were the bishops in order of precedence, and to his left the barons. Opposite him on benches at floor level were the deputies of the five leading towns, and around the sides at the feet of the bishops and barons were the rest of the third estate. In the middle was a table for the officers of the Estates.

The president controlled the order of business and recognized each speaker, who would then give a harangue introducing a particular item of business. Discussion and voting followed in order of precedence, with the oldest bishop, the leading baron, and then the consuls of the leading town (one vote between them) and the 'diocesans' of that diocese starting off. The vote proceeded in rounds, each consisting of a bishop, a baron, and two votes from the third, in keeping with the ratio in the Estates. Each man who voted made a speech explaining his position.[4] The advantage of this method was that the most eminent members could influence the rest because they spoke first. Oral voting made it easy to reward collaborators and punish defections.

The most striking factor in the assembly was the complete predominance of the first estate. The prelates not only ran the assembly, but controlled the subordinate assiettes. Thus they were becoming year-round managers of affairs totally distinct from their official functions as churchmen or their positions as local lords. This role had not always existed, and it was still being asserted. It may have reflected social shifts within the province: the merchant oligarchies were less dominant in the seventeenth century or were being absorbed into the corps of venal officeholders which were excluded from the Estates, while bishops and other rentiers were enjoying a relative revival of land rents. It may also have resulted from the rising prestige of the bishops chosen by the crown as agents of the Catholic revival and from the fact that bishops were the allies of the crown in the political maneuverings necessitated by increasing royal demands on the Estates. In any event, the prelates as a group had greater names, more experience, and more continuity than any other group in the company.[5]

The bishops were a diverse group whose role in various client networks will be discussed in chapter 10. They can loosely be divided into those with local roots and those from outside the province, although it did not necessarily follow that local potentates would be protective of regional interest or that outside nominees would be loyal servants of the crown.[6] In the first category were certain bishops whose sees remained under the influence of powerful local families through much of the century: Carcassonne under the Maynard de Lestangs (1603–52) and Rieux under the Bertiers (1602–1705), both families from Toulouse; Viviers under Louis-François de la Baume de Suze, member of a powerful family in Vivarais (1621–90), and others. Some bishops had other ties to dignitaries of the region. Jean-François Percin de Montgaillard, bishop of Saint-Pons (1664–1713), for example, was an aristocratic trouble-maker who was related to the Bassabats de Pardiac, barons in the Estates, the duc d'Épernon, and the Fieubets of Toulouse. In the second category, and vastly more important, were the many bishops who were royal favorites, named because they had attracted attention at court or because of their families' long tradition of royal service. Such were the Bonzis of Béziers (1576–1669), Claude de Rebé

[4] Descudier, 'Memoires', 63: 'De la forme d'opiner'.

[5] In the fifteenth century bishops and barons were little interested in the proceedings and often failed to attend: Gilles, *États*, pp. 85, 94.

[6] Lists of bishops and brief histories are available in Pius Bonifacius Gams, ed., *Series episcoporum ecclesiae catholicae quotquot innotuerunt a beato petro apostolo* (Ratisbon, 1873); and *Dictionnaire d'histoire et de géographie ecclésiastique* (Paris, 1912–).

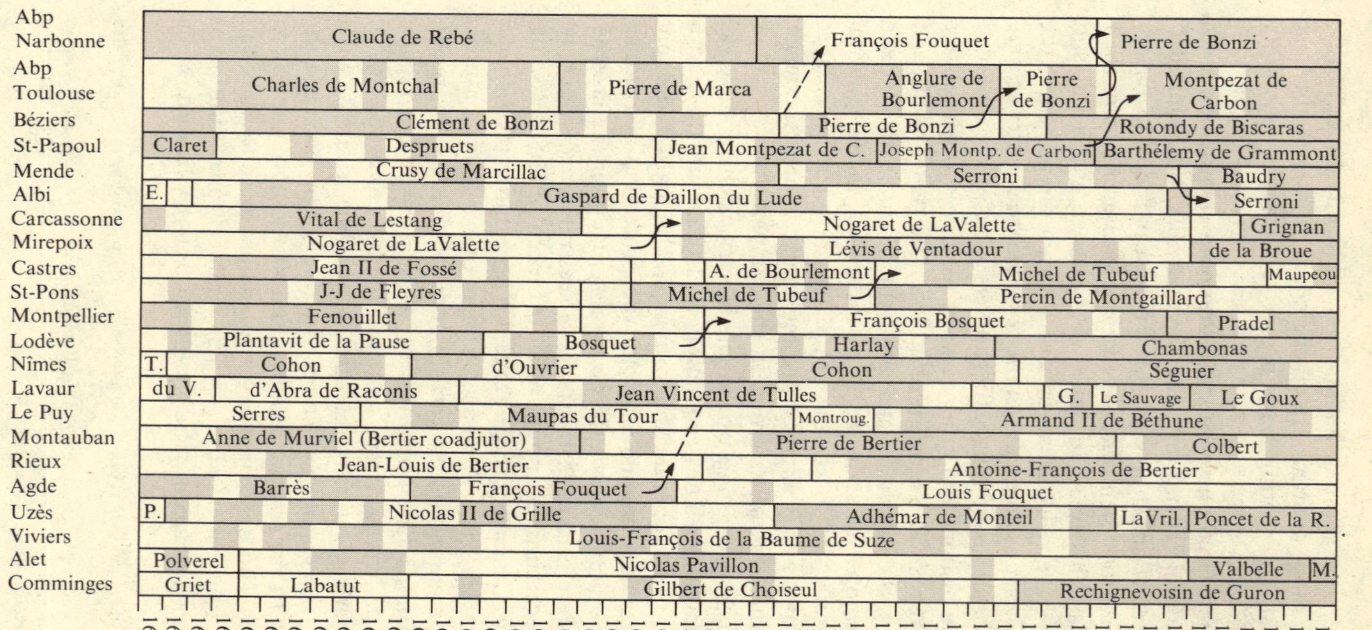

Shading indicates attendance in person.

Note: some dates when bishoprics changed hands are approximate. Three sessions of the Estates (1677–8, 1678–9, 1683) have been omitted for lack of attendance information.

Figure 3. Personal attendance of bishops.

of Narbonne (1628–59), Marcillac in Mende (1628–59), Daillon du Lude of Albi (1635–76), and many others.[7] A look at figure 3, which lists all the bishops for our period, makes evident what one might intuitively expect – that the trend was away from independent, locally-based bishops and toward royal favorites. Even the names of the nominees under Louis XIV suggest this phenomenon: Tubeuf, Grignan, Séguier, Colbert, Poncet de La Rivière, Harlay, Béthune, Phélippeaux de la Vrillière – all courtly nobles or members of administrative families.

In any given session less than half of the twenty-two bishops attended in person, and it made a great deal of difference which bishops they were.[8] Those who did not attend could send their vicar-generals to represent them, and these had the advantage of being experienced agents fully versed in the opinions and interests of their superiors and familiar with the other deputies from their region. On the other hand, vicar-generals could not negotiate with the authority of bishops, and it must have been hard for them to say no to persons more eminent than themselves. Each year three to ten episcopal seats remained empty.

There was no simple pattern to episcopal attendance. Bishops and barons sometimes stayed away to avoid sanctioning unpleasant measures, as in 1633 when only six bishops, five vicar-generals, and four barons were present at the opening. On other occasions they came expressly to voice opposition or to support the crown. Some absences were simply the result of infirmity or indisposition; others were arranged by the royal agents to immobilize the opposition. Several points do emerge from the attendance data, however. First is the fact, evident from the shadings on figure 3, that personal attendance became much more regular under Louis XIV. As table 7 indicates, the average number of bishops in attendance rose from 9.6 under Louis XIII to 14.2 after 1671, and the number of vicar-generals rose as well, so that between 1671 and 1685 almost every seat was filled. Even more interesting is the fact that the notable absences on the chart are almost always connected to prelates identified in other sources as uncooperative, so that the attendance chart appears to the experienced eye almost like a loyalty chart. The very evident difference between the 'spotty' years before 1659 and the 'even' years thereafter – and especially after 1672 – illustrates how much more controversial and turbulent the sessions were in the earlier

[7] On some of these, Jean Contrasty, *Histoire de la cité de Rieux-Volvestre et de ses évêques* (Toulouse, 1936); Joseph Sahuc, *Un ami de Port-Royal: messire Pierre-Jean-François de Percin de Montgaillard* (Paris, 1909); l'abbé Léon Charpentier, *Un Évêque de l'ancien régime: Louis-Joseph de Grignan (1650–1722)* (Arras, 1899); E. Sabatier, *Histoire de la ville et des évêques de Béziers* (Béziers, 1845); Marguerite Sol, *Claude de Rebé, archevêque de Narbonne* (Paris, 1981); Hippolyte Crozes, *Le Diocèse d'Albi: ses évêques et archevêques* (Toulouse, 1878); Léon Ménard, *Histoire des évêques de Nismes*, 2 vols. (The Hague, 1737).

[8] Official attendance lists were placed at the end of the minutes of each session.

Table 7. *Attendance at the Estates*

Sessions	Number of sessions	Average number of bishops	Average number of barons
1633–42	10	9.6	5.0
1643–58/59	15	8.2	5.9
1659–70/71	12	9.8	7.2
1671/72–85	12	14.2	9.8

period and how much better managed they were under Louis XIV. Before, uncooperative prelates came and went unpredictably; after, more of them were cooperative, and they attended more regularly, with fewer appearances from those who were still 'recalcitrant'. It is also noteworthy that transfers of bishops within the province were so much more common under Louis XIV, indicating that loyal supporters were being promoted to better sees without their votes being lost.

The twenty-two barons of the Estates were much less influential.[9] Their titles and entrance were tied to ownership of estates called 'baronies' which could be bought and sold or passed down in families. The reason these particular baronies had entrance to the assembly was lost in the feudal past. They were not the most important fiefs in the province; nor were they held by the greatest nobles. They were not even distributed equally among the dioceses. Toulouse and Nîmes had three apiece; Montpellier and Carcassonne had two; Montauban, Rieux, Saint-Papoul, Comminges, Saint-Pons and Uzès had none at all. As Paul Gachon put it, a baron of the Estates 'sat neither as the elected representative of his peers, nor as the envoy of his vassals, nor as the delegate of the central power'.[10] The Estates themselves had the right to seat the barons or their envoys, and they generally demanded proofs of nobility. There were often extended disputes over entrance when baronies changed hands. Family members of the former entrant were likely to challenge the titles of new purchasers. In addition, the king could modify the representation by excluding old

[9] The identity of the barons has to be pieced together from various sources. The most important of these are Bejard, *Recueil des tiltres, qualites blazons et armes des seigneurs barons des estats generaux de la province de Languedoc*, rev. edn (Lyons, 1657); Jacques Beaudeau, *Armorial des Estats du Languedoc enrichi des elemens de l'art du blason* (Montpellier, 1686); d'Aguesseau, 'Description'; Lamoignon de Basville, *Mémoires*, pp. 102–23; Pierre Louvet, *Remarques sur l'histoire de Languedoc* (Toulouse, 1657); A.D. Hér C 7720, C 7825; plus specific mentions in the administrative correspondence and the minutes of the Estates.

[10] Gachon, *États*, pp. 14–15.

baronies and creating new ones with entrance to the Estates, as he did at various times during our period.[11]

Compared to the bishops, the barons attended in person much less frequently, as indicated in table 7, although they too became more diligent under Louis XIV, no doubt for the same reasons as the bishops. In their absence barons sent 'envoys' who were usually younger sons or minor clients from the lesser nobility. These positions were coveted because they gave entrance to the social world of the sessions, but the envoys were generally men of little experience or continuity, and thus they played much less part in the negotiations than the vicar-generals. Two of the noble seats were even less consistently occupied in that the barons from Vivarais and Gévaudan were represented by a cycle of twelve and eight 'barons de tour' respectively, who attended in rotation.

The families controlling the twenty fixed baronies are listed in figure 4. Thirteen baronies remained in the same hands throughout our period. Three of these were held by families of national prominence (Polignac, Angoulême, Crussol d'Uzès); five were held by local figures who played important roles in the province (Castries, Merinville, Calvisson, Aubijoux, Ambres); the remaining five were owned by local families of little political importance. Four of the other baronies changed hands by sale. Three went to important royal allies and stayed there; the fourth was purchased in 1645 by Pierre Dauteville, a Protestant from the Cour des Comptes whose entrance caused annual controversy until 1671 when Louis XIV intervened by transferring the seat to a different barony which was held by a loyal ally. The remaining three baronies changed hands by inheritance. All three were the object of litigation. In two of the cases the king again took advantage of the situation to transfer entrance to a different barony held by an ally.

We can see, then, why the barons played a minor role in the voting. Few were regular attenders, and virtually all of those who were had a stake in the successful management of the province by the crown. The greatest families never attended. There were no opposition leaders among the barons, although some voted 'badly' on occasion. Still, wherever a disputed succession or a controversial sale left an opening for intervention, Louis XIV, no doubt advised by the intendant, filled the position with a truly reliable follower. The royal success in encouraging these increasingly cooperative barons to attend after 1670–1 is evident in the shading on the right side of figure 4.

[11] Rules about documentation required of nobles: P-V Nov. 13, 1637; entrance of envoys of barons: P-V Nov. 13, 1640; restoration of the baron de Calvisson by royal letters-patent: P-V Nov. 21, 1642; intervention of the king on behalf of an ally, Calvières: Louis XIV to archbishop of Narbonne, Mar. 10, 1647: Depping, vol. 1, p. 11.

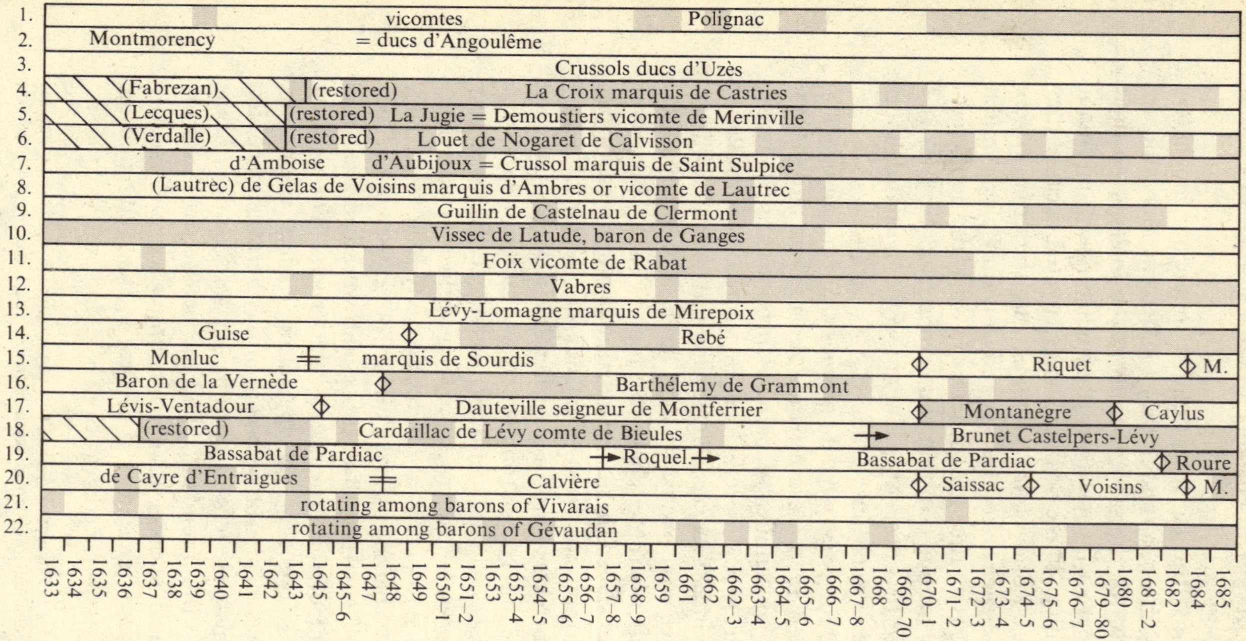

Shading indicates attendance in person. The chart lists names of families, not individual barons.

I. Baronies staying in the same family

1. Polignac
2. Alais
3. Florensac
4. Castries
5. Rieux
6. Calvisson
7. Castelnau-Bonnefous
8. Ambres
9. Clermont
10. Ganges
11. La Gardiole
12. Castelnau-Destretefonds
13. Mirepoix

II. Changing hands by sale

14. Arques
15. Saint-Felix
16. Lanta
17. Vauvert

III. Disputed successions

18. Villeneuve
19. Capendu
20. Couffoulens

IV. Rotating baronies

21. Vivarais
22. Gévaudan

┼► by inheritance

╪ by marriage

◊ by purchase

Figure 4. Personal attendance of barons

The third estate loomed much larger as a group than the bishops or barons because its total number of votes was equal to that of the bishops and barons combined and because its members really represented somebody – the oligarchies of the towns of the province. But this group power was only felt on special occasions when there was a groundswell of opposition to a particularly burdensome demand or when conditions back home were so terrible that the deputies felt they would be disowned if they did not stand up for the needs of the population. Normally the town deputies were divided, not only by the conflicting interests of the different regions, but also by their particular loyalties to local bishops and factions.

Each of the twenty-two dioceses of Languedoc had two votes in the Estates. The first went to the 'capital town', which was always the seat of the bishop; the other went to a 'diocesan' town, that is, some smaller center within the diocese. The rules for entrance were fixed, but they varied by diocese.[12] Usually the capital town sent two men with one vote between them: either the first consul and last year's first consul or the current first and second consul. The diocesan representation varied. In some dioceses a second town always sent a deputy. In others there was a system of rotation among three to ten different towns. As a result, the third was relatively disunited. With the representatives of most towns changing every year, with half of the towns themselves changing in rotation, and with no individual ever attending more than two annual sessions in a row, there was little chance for organized politics beyond that led by the bishops or the syndic-generals of the Estates.[13]

We can see, then, that the Estates were not representative, even of the traditional orders. The bishops did not represent the interests of cathedral chapters, regular clergy, or local priests; the barons stood for their hereditary family rights, not for the body of the nobility; the consuls spoke only for the municipal oligarchies from which they came. Nobody represented the towns with no seat in the assembly, the artisans and laborers of the towns, the vast majority of the direct producers on the land, or even the corps of royal officers whose members were excluded from the Estates.

The work of the assembly fell into three basic categories. First there were the negotiations with the royal commissioners over the *don gratuit*, fiscal edicts, troop lodgings, and related matters involving king and province. These negotiations stretched through the entire session, interspersed among other items of business. The commissioners would enter to present demands; a committee would be named to study these; the committee would report its recommendations back to the assembly which would then

[12] The rules are given in d'Aguesseau, 'Description'.

[13] On this point Bonney has been misled by the alarmist tone of some of the ministerial correspondence: Bonney, *Political Change*, pp. 375–6.

discuss and ratify an offer; this offer would be presented to the commissioners by a special deputation; then the process would begin again. The second category of business was the routine administration of the province, which was carried out by standing committees named early in each session. In 1673–4 these included a committee to audit the accounts of the treasurer of the bourse; a committee to determine whether the commissions of the royal commissioners were in conformity with those of previous years; a committee to hear complaints against powerful individuals who refused to pay their taxes; a committee to audit the repartition of last year's taxes by each assiette; a committee to study and regulate matters involving the legal jurisdiction of the Estates; a committee to draw up the *cahier des doléances*; a committee to hear complaints against the Protestants and to study their violation of royal edicts; a committee to draw up the *ligne d'étape*, or route for the passage of troops; and a committee to draw up the report of military depredations suffered by dioceses, communities, or individuals. All committees consisted of an equal number of deputies from the first and second estates and twice that number from the third. A bishop always presided. When questions of principle or interpretations arose, the committee would refer back to the general assembly, and the decision would be written into the minutes. Often the final report to the assembly would be inserted also.

The third type of business concerned new issues raised by a deputy or a syndic-general, who would address the assembly after being recognized by the president. It is hard to convey an impression of these matters, since they were so diverse, but every session was full of them. They might concern a complaint against the practices of tax farmers in the province, an appeal for the creation of smaller legal districts, or an attack on the fees of the royal officers in the courts. Like the minutes of municipal council meetings, they might also concern very particular matters: an appeal for alms for a local widow, legal aid to an individual being sued for supporting a position taken by the assembly, the repair of a monument, a small grant to a religious house. In each of these affairs the assembly was aiding someone's client and enhancing the authority of that patron in his local dealings, for the Estates were in effect a large patronage machine. Using their collective privileges and contacts the members could achieve more jointly than any one of them could achieve alone, and the rest of the province was provided with a useful pool of influence, provided it could be tapped by maintaining good relations with the influential members.

Managing the Estates effectively was a tricky job, for despite the many safeguards which existed and the essential loyalty of most of the important deputies, there were many things that could go wrong when a unique collection of almost a hundred dignitaries from all over the province got together in one place. Even royal clients might feel responsibility to their compatriots and vote against the king's position. Intendants and other royal agents therefore developed techniques for getting what they wanted. In the first place, location and date were important. The site for the sessions should be small and calm, without sovereign courts to divert the deputies or too many notables to complicate the proceedings, and it should be centrally located near the intendant's friends and contacts. Autumn was the best season because the harvest was in and people were not hungry. Sessions had to be kept short because the third estate was more malleable at the beginning, before the new deputies realized that refusal was a possibility, and before the grain stores began to dwindle. Especially unfortunate was any temporary adjournment, for if the deputies went home, they would be emboldened by their friends or incited to resistance by contact with local conditions, especially lodgings of troops. There were also petty tricks which could be played to get around difficulties. In 1662 the session was opened several days ahead of schedule because it was known that certain difficult bishops had not yet arrived, and a touchy precedence problem could be resolved before they got there.[14]

The first step in conquering a difficult assembly was to convince it swiftly of the royal need and of the king's determination to get what he wanted. Here the speeches were very important. If the proper atmosphere of cooperation could be established, business could be speeded through and the assembly dismissed before anything happened to rock the boat. The second step was influencing individual members. One could start with the bishops and barons who were usually friendly to the royal cause and move on from them to other promising candidates. Outright bribes were often used, as well as pensions for deputies, which were institutionalized under Louis XIV.[15] Key figures were the best targets, since it was well-known that the less important deputies were reluctant to disagree with their superiors who voted first. Conversely, a 'seditious spirit' who voted negatively early in the game could ruin the whole proceedings. In this event the hint of a concession, or a threat carefully handled, or the arrival of a dignitary from Paris might bring a change of mood. But such measures could backfire too. The best way to manage the Estates was to make sure in advance that its leaders were loyal clients. The king's agents were more

[14] Marquis de Castries to Colbert, Sept. 29, 1662: Depping, vol. 1, p. 143.

[15] Bribes are mentioned in Bosquet to Séguier, Jan. 16, 1645; Lubl., p. 109; Bezons to Colbert, Feb. 1, 1664: Depping, vol. 1, p. 142; and Roure to Colbert, Feb. 9, 1665: ibid., p. 181. Basville notes in 1698 that before 1673 up to 10,000 écus were distributed to the deputies in single years: Lamoignon de Basville, *Mémoires*, p. 192. In 1650 the Estates protested against bribes: P-V Dec. 15, 1650.

successful at this after 1600. Before, they often had to try to placate and channel opposition already formed, rather than heading it off before it developed.

THE YEARLY TRANSACTION

The sessions of the Estates, as recorded in their voluminous minutes, provide an ongoing narrative of the interaction between royal demands and provincial concerns. These minutes are formal documents comparable to those kept by the municipal councils.[16] They record in great detail each item of business as it was presented, sent to committee, and voted on, but they do not report the substance of debates or the way members voted. Nevertheless they provide a good sense of the chronology of royal–provincial interaction and the evolving nature of the institution.

A. *The Edict of Béziers.* The balance of power between king and Estates was seriously challenged in the battle over the élus from 1629 to 1632 which culminated in the defeat of Montmorency's rebellion and the imposition of the Edict of Béziers. On November 11, 1632, the deputies of the Estates, along with representatives from the Parlement, the Comptes, and the treasurer-generals of finance were summoned to the church of the Augustins of Béziers to face their aggrieved king.[17] After making them wait for an hour, Louis XIII arrived with his entire court and told the company that he had decided to 'leave behind marks of his paternal affection' by eliminating abuses in the tax system. The edict was read aloud. Then Châteauneuf, garde des sceaux, proclaimed it 'published in the presence of His Majesty with the consent of the members of the Estates and by advice of the deputies of his court of Parlement of Toulouse, Cour des Comptes of Montpellier, and treasurer-generals'.

This document reflected the government's decision to manage the existing Estates better, rather than substitute a new system of venal officers which would be costly and divisive.[18] The idea was to allow the notables their consultation while assuring that the essential fiscal issues could be

[16] Copies of the minutes exist in various departmental archives. The most complete and usable set is in A.D. H-G. C 2301 to C 2339, and is expertly summarized in Archives Départementales de la Haute-Garonne, *Inventaire sommaire des archives départementales*, série C, tome II (Toulouse, 1903). I have cited the procès-verbaux (P-V) by date alone so that any set can be consulted. Sessions were usually held towards the end of the year, and they frequently lasted into the following calendar year. The best way to denote them clearly is by mentioning both years when appropriate, thus 'Estates of 1649' but 'Estates of 1650–1'.

[17] Accounts in Devic, vol. XI, pp. 1080–2; A.D. H-G. C 2301; *Inventaire*, série C, II, pp. 249–50; Antoine Aubéry, *Mémoires pour l'histoire du Cardinal duc de Richelieu*, 2 vols. (Paris, 1660), vol. II, pp. 378–9.

[18] On the Edict of Béziers, Devic, vol. XI, 1083–5; and for a complete analysis, including the idea of a fundamental loss of liberties, Gachon, *États*. The text is in Jean Albisson, *Loix municipales et économiques de Languedoc*, 7 vols. (Montpellier, 1780–7), vol. I, pp. 288–97.

resolved without the delays and equivocation of the past. The key to this new regime was the imposition of a fixed list of taxes which were to be granted each year without discussion. These included not only a modified list of the basic sums which had always been routinely granted, but also a large *don gratuit* of 1,050,000 livres. In addition the Estates were required to buy off the offices of élus at a cost, along with indemnities, of at least 2,300,000 livres; and in order to raise the money for the *élus* they had to alienate their *équivalent* tax farm to a group of Parisian financiers. As a result, the province lost control of a local sales tax the profits of which had traditionally gone to help pay the provincial tax bill.

Other aspects of the fiscal process were also regulated. The king took the office of treasurer of the bourse from the province and sold it to three venal officeholders who would serve in rotation. The province's treasurer, Pennautier, who had been implicated in the rebellion, was deposed. The treasurer-generals, also royal officers, were now to preside over the sessions of the assiettes and audit their accounts. Sessions of the Estates were limited to fifteen days, and their costs to 50,000 livres. Money for repair of roads and bridges and for the prévôté which policed the roads was taken over by the crown. The borrowing and taxing power of the dioceses and communities was strictly limited.

This reform package was certainly a success for the crown in the sense that much more money could be obtained with much less fuss and without any of the expenses of the system of élus – in fact the king turned a profit on the sale of those offices without suffering any of the unpleasant consequences. In a deeper sense, however, the province had been victorious, for it had averted any genuine change and had turned the royal program into just another adjustment of the traditional balance of power. The crucial factor here was the reaffirmation by the king of the province's traditional privileges. Some historians have mistakenly believed that the Estates lost the right to discuss taxes in 1632, but the only taxes they could not debate were those in the fixed royal list. The monarchy had scored a coup by more than doubling the annual tax levy at a single stroke. But like a seigneur commuting tenants' dues, the royal government was too eager to establish a fixed total, for in 1633, the greatest expenses of the Thirty Years War still lay in the future, and any new levies to cover them would still have to be discussed. The paradoxical result was that a desperate monarchy would have to force all sorts of unpleasant measures down the throats of the rulers 'by consent'.

B. *1632 to 1643*. The years up to 1643 were devoted to an exploration of the new balance of power. The king presented additional needs and the Estates tested their ability to put a brake on them. In 1633 they refused an 80,000 livres increase in the taillon and granted only 50,000 of the 200,000 Richelieu wanted for construction of a port at Agde.[19] In 1634 only one of a number of wartime funds and indemnities was granted.[20] In 1635 the government began to strike back by announcing the creation of new royal officers and collecting funds directly which the Estates viewed as illegal. The assembly was astir in 1635 over the imposition by the intendants of 100,000 livres directly on the dioceses and communities for the repair of the fortifications of Narbonne.[21] It was no accident that these were funds previously refused in the assembly.

Royal troops entered the province in 1636, pillaging and exacting funds which the Estates had refused to grant for their upkeep. In 1637 the Spanish invasion and the glorious French victory at Leucate, only about thirty miles from Narbonne, was the occasion for the governor to call a rump session of the Estates at Béziers, where six bishops, two barons, and consuls of seven towns hastily arranged loans to cover the cost of the campaign. In Vivarais 21,000 livres were imposed by order of the governor and levied violently without the participation of the assiette.[22] In 1638 and 1639, as Languedoc became almost a war zone, the cost and management of troops became an overriding issue. The logical solution, proposed repeatedly by the royal agents, was for the Estates to grant and administer funds to support the troops. But such a measure would have violated provincial privileges since the *don gratuit* was supposed to be in lieu of military service, and Languedoc was supposed to be exempt from troop lodgings. As the archbishop of Toulouse put it, any grant would 'entail several dangerous consequences, being directly contrary to the Edict of Béziers and to the most ancient and important rights of the province'.[23] The assembly continued to refuse outright until 1640 when it approved an official *quartier d'hiver* (winter quarters for the troops), after 1,100,000 livres had been illegally levied during the year by the prince de Condé, demonstrating that consent could be evaded. In 1641 an *étape* to pay the lodgings of troops passing through the province was similarly granted.[24]

From 1640 to 1642 the Estates began to give in, a sure sign that the advantages of resistance had reached their limits. The deputies to court in 1640 reported that their efforts at negotiation had been almost totally unsuccessful because the king was angered at the intransigence of the province.[25] By 1642 collaboration – at a higher level of royal demand – was again working. The king allowed the Estates to administer the *subvention*,

[19] P-V Nov. 28, Dec. 9, 1633.
[20] P-V Nov. 13, 21–2, 1634.
[21] P-V Nov. 23, Dec. 1, 6, 1635.
[22] P-V Nov. 19, 24, 1637.
[23] P-V Dec. 7, 1638.
[24] P-V Nov. 13, 17, 1640, Sept. 12, 1641. On the 'illegal' levy by Condé, A.D. H-G. C 988, 'Impositions pour 1640'.
[25] P-V Nov. 16, 1640.

a national sales tax of one sol per livre (8.33 percent), and called a special session in Béziers on May 2, 1642, to negotiate the terms of the agreement. Unlike the meeting of 1637, this was an official session with full representation, called not to grant emergency funds of dubious legality, but rather to arrange a settlement more advantageous to the province of an ongoing affair. The meetings, which lasted until June 1, were efficient and straightforward. Committees were appointed, surveys were undertaken, and a schedule of rates was established for the goods to be taxed.[26] One gets the impression in the regular session of 1642, as well, that the machinery of the Estates was functioning with great efficiency. These sessions might have been the prototype for a new kind of assembly, one looking ahead to the best days of Colbert, if this had been the beginning of a reign. But both Louis XIII and Richelieu were ailing, and their death brought a reversal of the entire situation.

C. *1643 to 1659*. The sudden change in 1643 indicated how fragile the new cooperation was and how dependent on the monarchy being in a position of strength. Where the first item of business in recent years had always been a demand for special funds from the king, the Estates of 1643 opened with a counter-petition addressed *to* 'the king'. It attacked and rejected newly-created offices; suspended the subvention, so recently worked out; criticized étapes; and resolved that no more than 15,000 livres were ever to be granted in one year for the port of Agde.[27] Clearly the royal minority was to be used to regain lost ground by rejecting the compromises forced on the province in recent years. In 1645 the assembly refused to grant a quartier d'hiver at all.[28] Three months after this turbulent session the popular uprising in Montpellier galvanized the province and terrified the authorities.[29] The next session, 1645–6, was viewed by everyone as a real test of authority. Schomberg accused the assembly of having caused the Montpellier riots by their prior refusal, and Étienne d'Aligre, sent especially from Paris for the occasion, outdid himself in his scathing admonition to the assembly:

The king complains of your refusal to continue granting him the aid accorded to his late father in former years, although his number of enemies has not diminished, his needs are no less pressing, his feebleness of age requires no less support. His cause for complaint is increased by the violent acts, if not rebellions, of certain of your people who have pillaged and burned the houses of his officers, killed their fellows, wounded the guards of his lieutenant-general, and finally raised a hand against his very person...I see on your faces that our demand astonishes you...Turn around, messieurs, look the other way! Cast your eyes upon your faults

26 This session is not included in the regular minutes and has often been overlooked. Its minutes are in A.D. H-G. C 3816.

27 P-V Oct. 23, 31, Nov. 5, 11, 16, 17, 20, 1643.

28 P-V Feb. 3, 1645.

29 On the provincial crisis of 1645, see chapter 9.

and reflect on the way you have treated your king in the last Estates without any consideration of the needs of his state...Do not persist in refusals of this sort. Do not force the king to make a third demand. Do not arrive *ad tertiam denuntiationem* ...Do not force an irritated king to approach you and make you feel the effect of his anger.[30]

But instead of granting the 3,100,000 demanded, the assembly offered a meagre 600,000 payable over two years.[31]

In 1647 and 1648 the tables were turned. Now instead of responding to threats from the commissioners, the Estates skillfully bargained them into greater and greater concessions in return for their grants. In 1647 virtually every major edict of recent years was revoked in return for a 3,000,000 livres grant payable over five years. In 1648 the Estates obtained the right to repurchase the *équivalent* tax for 600,000 livres.[32] Then in 1649, during the troubles of the Parisian Fronde, the longest Estates on record (almost six months) negotiated the revocation of the Edict of Béziers itself. The revocation did not change the situation much because, as we have seen, the Edict itself had never stopped negotiation or resistance.[33] The new declaration confirmed all the ancient privileges of the province and supposedly returned the system to that of 1629; yet all regulations about unauthorized impositions, length of sessions, unauthorized debts, and other specifics were restated. The assembly did gain the right to buy back the royal offices of treasurer of the bourse and restore its own treasurer. This change, along with the gradual recovery of the équivalent, returned fiscal management to the province. The other major change was in the amount of taxes imposed. The official list of 1632, including the obligatory *don* of 1,050,000 livres, was abandoned, and the traditional list was reinstated. Hereafter the 'extraordinary tax', or *don gratuit*, would once again be determined by bargaining in each session. The total sum granted automatically in any session was less by 1,253,160 livres than that granted between 1633 and 1649. The province would therefore only gain financially if a *don* lower than this sum were granted and if no additional grants were made in a given session. These circumstances were hardly ever realized, and when they were, it was because of other factors influencing the negotiations, not because the Edict of Béziers was no longer in place.

During the 1650s real bargaining continued. The war in nearby Catalonia was now crucial, and troops were often on hand to influence the discussions. But the Estates had been relatively loyal during the Fronde, as speakers on both sides pointed out, and this fact required a certain tact on the part of the king. The two parties were in a sense equalized: the monarchy needed

30 Roschach, vol. XIV, p. 122.

31 P-V Feb. 3, Feb. 6, Mar. 3–7, 1646.

32 P-V April 13–15, 1647, May 5, 1648.

33 Roschach, vol. XIV, pp. 292–7 for the text of the revocation.

money badly and was insecure enough to have to bargain for it; the Estates were in a good position for bargaining but terribly pressed by the efforts of the nearby war. In 1650–1 the assembly attached to its modest grant of 600,000 livres (instead of the 1,500,000 asked) the condition that Languedoc be free of soldiers and instructed the treasurer of the bourse to hold back enough funds to indemnify the victims of damages caused by troops.[34] In 1653 there were long discussions of the removal of troops already stationed in the province, and when the soldiers were not removed, no *don* was granted.[35] In 1653–4, obviously resenting the trend towards conditions and guarantees, the government tried a more forceful approach. Henry de Malon, seigneur de Bercy, the maître des requêtes sent to bargain with the Estates, asserted a more absolutist position:

> His majesty's first intention...is that there should be no proposition made in this company until the *don gratuit* has been granted, after which all your other demands, which for the most part are nothing but favors, privileges, and liberalities granted by the king, may follow...

but he added that in the event the money was granted,

> I have orders to assure the company that it will be discharged of the present winter quarters of the army of Catalonia and during 1654 it will remain exempt from all lodgings. If any troops stay in the province during the year their expenses, lodging, and damages if they cause any, will be deducted from the sum demanded by His Majesty.[36]

Thus what began as an ultimatum ended as an implied contract. The Estates granted 1,500,000, their largest annual sum since the death of Richelieu.[37] But the problem was only temporarily resolved, and in 1656–7 there was a protracted crisis over troop lodgings and their compensation.

The era of such negotiations was coming to an end by 1659, not only because the war was over, but also because an increasingly intimidating Louis XIV was actually present in Toulouse during the sessions that year. He made it clear that he considered his authority 'wounded' by the revocation of the Edict of Béziers and that he 'would prefer its reinstatement over all other aid that could be desired from the province'.[38] This threat may not have been just rhetoric, for government agents were seriously discussing just such a possibility about this time. However, after considerable debate the assembly resolved that they could not consent to the reestablishment of the Edict since it was against their privileges; and despite

34 P-V Nov. 24, Dec. 23, 1650. Such instructions to the treasurer of the bourse were now possible because he was once again an officer of the Estates.

35 Ms. fr. 18830, 77–83.

36 Roschach, vol. XIV, p. 531.

37 P-V Mar. 23, 1654.

38 Roschach, vol. XIV, pp. 714, 719 (P-V Oct. 16, Oct. 22, 1659); Bezons to Mazarin, Feb. 10, 1654: A.A.E. France 1636, 275.

the boldness of such an assertion in a town where the king was present, the government proved willing to negotiate.[39]

D. *1661 to 1685*. In 1661 the Estates were still taking their bargaining power very seriously. Thereafter, as substantial grants became routine, more and more emphasis was placed on the form of the negotiations. 'Satisfying the king' became a stated goal. Meanwhile Colbert's new economic projects, which will be discussed in chapter 12, were presented one by one to the assembly, each necessitating funds and various sorts of collaboration. Discussions were not always formalities. In the session of 1664–5 some of the bishops were so adamant about the amount of the *don* that they came to blows during the session and had to be physically subdued.[40] In 1665–6 the Estates formally refused to support the construction of the Canal du Midi.[41] Gradually, however, the assembly was diverted from its serious discussion of the *don gratuit*. In 1671–2 the second wave of reform set in, spurred on, no doubt, by the impending Dutch War, but once again involving form and reflecting the style of Louis XIV. We can feel the new ideological tone and see its national orientation in Bezons's speech proposing the new procedure in 1671–2:

> We have informed you, messieurs, that the king was happy with the sums you accorded him but that His Majesty was not satisfied with the way the affair came about. In effect, if you consider the conduct of the clergy, which is the first corps of the state and of which you have such an illustrious portion among you, you will remember that at their last assembly they made such a considerable *don* to the king that he returned part of it. And since they did it in a single deliberation their conduct earned them a relief which they would not have enjoyed if they had granted it in two or three attempts. This year what has been the conduct of Brittany and Burgundy? Their action has produced reductions. And Languedoc, which surpasses these other provinces in all sorts of advantages, will it never resolve to begin where it must end? Why make these offers of 1,200,000 and 1,500,000 livres and then end up afterwards at the sums hoped for, instead of doing in one stroke what the needs of the state and the necessity of affairs require?[42]

This unmistakable hint was rapidly taken up. The grant of 1,700,000 (instead of 2,400,000 demanded) was made in a single deliberation without preliminary offers. Royal letters of satisfaction were promptly forthcoming, and the secretary was told to 'insert the letters in the registers to preserve this glorious memory of having been able to please the king and receiving such advantageous signs of it'.[43] The rest of the desired process soon followed. In 1672–3 the demand of 2,000,000 livres was granted intact, and

[39] Roschach, vol. XIV, pp. 723, 730 (P-V Oct. 15, Dec. 27, 1659).
[40] A colorful account of this episode is in Roschach, vol. XIII, pp. 430–7.
[41] André Maistre, *Le Canal des deux mers: canal royal du Languedoc 1666–1810* (Toulouse, 1968), p. 96.
[42] P-V Dec. 17, 1671.
[43] P-V Jan. 11, 1672; the letter of satisfaction, Roschach, vol. XIV, p. 1092.

in 1673–4 the grant was made immediately after the demand had been presented by the royal commissioners.[44] The system outlined by Bezons had been installed, and the reward he had promised followed, with some delay, in 1680. Then it became common for the king to remit part of the *don* as an act of 'grace'. The age of negotiation of grants was over, at least until the eighteenth century.

Meanwhile wartime demands were piling up again, beginning with the War of Devolution and continuing through the Dutch War and beyond. In addition to the large *dons* and the many expenses connected to Colbert's economic projects, there were increasing numbers of measures reminiscent of the 1640s. In 1671 a tax on tavern-keepers was revoked for a grant of 2,000,000 livres over five years; in 1673 a new group of edicts was bought off for 450,000 livres, including a new *franc fief* investigation, taxes on procureurs, notaires, huissiers and sergeants, and fines connected to the reformation of the *eaux et forêts* administration.[45] There were also expenses related to the military, like the raising of companies of militia and the building of military roads and fortresses. In 1674–5 and in 1685 the province suffered quartiers d'hiver again, and the worst was yet to come. In 1693–4, for example, the Estates granted a *don* of 3,000,000 livres, 45,000 livres for additional funds, 75,000 for the Canal, 220,000 for suppression of an edict, 354,000 for mules to transport troop baggage, and 3,000 for supplies to defend the port at Sète.[46] But, unlike the 1640s, there was very little opposition, and while negotiations and discussions continued in the Estates they were generally about implementation or 'buying off' of edicts, not about rejecting them.

E. *Consultation and redress of grievances.* The changing relationship between the Estates and the king was also reflected in the handling of grievances which was, in a sense, a behind-the-scenes version of the 'public' discussions over grants. The standard vehicle for petitioning was the *cahier des doléances*, drawn up from items discussed during the sessions by a special committee of the Estates, and taken to court by the envoys elected for that purpose.[47] The cahier consisted of about ten to twenty items, most of which were rather specific. Some were requests for abolition of edicts or taxes, and a few were calls for permanent modifications in the structure of institutions like the disunion of the Comptes, Aides et Finances (1635) or the reunion of the Chambre de l'Édit with the Parlement (1669). Most, however, were petitions for rulings in specific situations with broader

[44] P-V Feb. 14, 1673, Nov. 25, 1673.

[45] P-V Jan. 5, 1672, Feb. 14, 1673.

[46] *Inventaire*, C, II, pp. 444–6.

[47] The cahiers are mentioned as separate articles throughout the minutes, and copies of them can be found in the ministerial papers in Paris, as well as in correspondence. There are also collections in A.D. Hér. C 7654 to C 7703.

implications. For example it was requested in 1656 that inhabitants of Haut-Vivarais not be required to pay Lyons prices for salt, even though they were under the gabelle farm of Lyons, and that Protestant artisans in Nîmes be prohibited from refusing to lodge Catholic travelers in their houses.[48] These articles were taken very seriously. The trip to Paris was an occasion for real bargaining with ministers of state, and the result was invariably a series of arrêts de conseil regulating a number of the matters at issue.[49] Some requests received negative replies, of course, and some favorable or non-committal responses were never followed-up, necessitating repetition of the same petition year after year. Nevertheless the annual cahier, which changed relatively little between 1632 and 1685, was an organic part of the proceedings which provided an occasion to take stands before the king on major issues like the religious settlement or the jurisdiction of provincial agencies.

A second form of redress was the direct result of the struggles of the minority. After the tough stands taken by the Estates in 1645 and 1645–6, when bargaining between the royal commissioners and the Estates became more intense, there was inevitably a closer connection made between the granting of special funds and the receipt of favors in return. In 1645–6 the resolution granting 600,000 livres still 'begged His Majesty very humbly' to grant the assembly's demands. In 1647 and 1648 certain sums were directly tied to certain concessions.[50] In 1649 for the first time there was explicit discussion of 'conditions' being attached to a grant, and by the end of the session these had evolved into a specific program: the money was 'on condition' that there be no fixed lodgings of troops during the year, that compensation be paid for grain and wine seized from local merchants by royal galleys, that the king cancel permission for galleys to stop and search local barges, that the king issue an arrêt ordering the gabelle administration to pay local stipends assigned on its funds in accordance with article sixteen of the cahier of 1648, and that the Estates be allowed to decide whether grain could be exported from the province.[51] In 1650–1, noting that royal troops were entering the province and that galleys were still stopping local barges and even 'putting their owners in chains', the assembly instructed the treasurer of the bourse, who was now again their own employee, to withhold part of the *don* money as security, out of which to pay damages for violations of this kind.[52]

Thus evolved the conditions of the *don* which were like a second, more urgent cahier attached directly to the grant and enforced in theory by the

[48] Ms. fr. 23354, 173.

[49] The responses to the cahier often took the form of a series of arrêts issued the same day by the royal council as, for example, on September 16, 1653: A.N. E 1700, 468–513 (cited in Le Pesant, pp. 181–2).

[50] P-V Jan. 4, 1646; May 13, 14, 15, 16, 27, 1647; May 25, 1648.

[51] P-V Oct. 2, Nov. 9, 1649.

[52] P-V Dec. 23, 1650.

withholding of funds. How well this system worked is subject to debate. As the above case illustrates, there was no assurance that the province's conditions, however solemnly accepted by the royal commissioners, would be met by the king, and if they were not, there was really no practical recourse. The withholding of funds did actually take place and was sanctioned by the king, but they were ultimately used to pay for local troop costs, which was what the government wanted anyway. The *don* conditions grew in number and specificity throughout the 1650s and became a regular part of the discussions. At the beginning of each session a committee was named to study whether the previous year's conditions had been met, and, at the end, the new conditions were formally presented to the royal commissioners for acceptance. By 1661 the assembly was drawing up an incredible list of twenty-two conditions, longer than the official cahier and just as specific. But such a proliferation of demands tended to dilute the urgency of the procedure, and articles like the eleventh – that the king transfer cases of communal debts from the Aides of Provence back to the Comptes of Montpellier 'if such is his good pleasure' – indicate that the condition articles were becoming indistinguishable from cahier articles.[53]

It seems curious that the tradition of *don* conditions, which were such a product of the Fronde period, should have survived into the age of Louis XIV, but they were still in force in 1685. The difference was that they had been reduced to routine formalities. In 1671–2 there were still five specific conditions included among the ten which were stipulated. In 1672–3 there was one out of five.[54] By 1675–6 only five routine conditions remained, and shortly after these were reduced to four: (1) that there would be no fixed lodgings of troops until the next Estates, and if there were any they would be at the king's expense, (2) that troops passing through would follow the ligne d'étape, (3) that no taxes would be imposed on the province against its privileges even if they were imposed on the whole kingdom, (4) that as security for these conditions 100,000 livres would be held back from the *don* until the next Estates. What had begun as a real bargaining tool ended up as a repetition of rights the province was supposed to enjoy anyway. The new guarantees, however, would not prove any more effective than the old.

Under Louis XIV the genuine innovation in petitioning was of a different, more characteristic sort. By the 1670s the deputies were taking with them to court, not only the regular cahier of grievances, but also a 'memoir of finance', a sort of 'economic' cahier, which would be presented to Colbert in the form of articles with responses, just like the official cahier.[55] In part this new development may just represent the greater sophistication

[53] P-V Apr. 10, 1661. At the same time the royal commissioners began qualifying some of the conditions and only partially accepting others.

[54] P-V Jan. 11, 1672; Feb. 14, 1673.

[55] For example, A.N. H 748^{205}, 287 (1674).

of the central government's division of labor, for the traditional cahier no longer contained the items which were now presented to Colbert. Nevertheless the trend is interesting, for it illustrates the participation of the Estates in the new age of economic 'management'. The memoirs concentrate on the province as a tax-producing entity and raise issues concerning trade, tariffs, the economic health of the countryside, and the effect of various royal taxes. The pleading is traditional in the sense that it concerns revenue flows and not economic development, but it is increasingly sophisticated. One memorandum of 1680 sounds like a page from Le Roy Ladurie or Goubert: Languedoc has suffered greatly from the recent wars and pays a million livres more in taxes than it did ten years earlier. The best lands produce only five or six times the grain needed for seed, and most of this is sold to pay the taille. Wine doesn't pay the cost of its cultivation. People are abandoning lands and taille collectors are impossible to find. Only hard work and the existence of manufactures enable the province to pay at all. The Estates diminish this burden by borrowing, and the provincial debts are as beneficial to the king as communal debts are detrimental. But now that peacetime has returned measures must be taken to pay off the debts of the recent wars so that credit will be available the next time it is needed.[56]

Advice like this sounds as if it came from d'Aguesseau or Colbert himself, for the Estates – or at least their leaders and officers – were becoming 'intendants' in their own right, and defending their interests by collaborating within the context of royal programs instead of trying to limit them, as in the past. Channels were still available for protest, but they were mostly being used to elaborate policies which served the interests of both sides.

THE BURDEN OF TAXES

The annual debates over grants do not give a complete sense of the direction taxes were moving because the large, controversial grants were not the only sums imposed, and they were not necessarily imposed all in one year. The best indicator is the sum of all taxes imposed on a province-wide basis in a given year, which includes special grants, ongoing projects, 'ordinary' taxes, payments on appropriations made in previous years, and expenses of the Estates. This figure can be worked out by comparing provincial records with the tax 'bills' (*mandes*) sent down to the dioceses, because the latter itemize the categories of expenditures granted by the Estates in such a way that it is possible to determine exactly what was imposed when.[57]

56 A.N. H 748²¹⁰, 129.

57 For this purpose I have used the accounts of the diocese of Toulouse, A.D. H-G. C 988–990, which have been carefully compared to all the financial information available on the Estates. In cases where unauthorized sums were imposed through the system in such a way as to leave accurate records, these have been included in the totals. These figures are analyzed further in chapter 11.

These tax 'bills' were in no sense equally apportioned. The repartitioning of the provincial total was done according to fixed diocesan ratios which had not been changed since 1530, despite considerable shifts in population and economic activities. The city of Toulouse had its own special *abonnement* which freed it from the diocese of Toulouse. Within each diocese the apportionment of individual communities was uneven, and within each community the compoix might be accurate or terribly out of date, depending on when it had been revised and what shifts had occurred in the meantime. Similar taxpayers in nearby villages could pay twice or half as much as their neighbors. Urban properties were not taxed the same as rural ones. Finally, the regime of *taille réelle* meant that lands classified as 'noble' paid no taille at all. Traditional estimates put up to one-third of the land of Languedoc in this category, but Georges Frêche has found that no more than ten percent of the land was noble in the areas he studied. Still, that tenth was mostly held in large estates by the old nobility and the church, shifting more of the burden onto the rest of the population. Although the privileged were not totally exempt as they would have been under the regime of the *taille personnelle*, the burden was still arbitrary, vastly unequal, and skewed against the peasantry.[58]

A look at the provincial tax curve in figure 5 illuminates the fiscal significance of the various episodes we have examined. The most important fact is the dramatic jump in the level of taxation which took place between 1628 and 1633 and which established a new 'cellar' of around 2,250,000 livres, well above the 1,200,000 granted in 1628. In 1633 and 1634 taxes were higher because the province was paying off the expenses of the élus crisis. Then the Estates held the line at the new 'base' level until the pressure of military grants pushed taxes to new highs in 1640 (which shows the effect of 1,210,000 imposed directly by Condé's army), 1641 (with a now-official quartier d'hiver of 1,815,000), 1642 (another 1,815,000 plus 220,000 to buy back new offices), and 1643 (the same, plus 900,000 in étapes). The year 1643, corresponding to the Estates of 1642 and thus to the last session under Louis XIII, had the highest taxes in our whole period, a record not matched even under Louis XIV until 1691. The drop which follows shows the seriousness of the resistance movement between 1644 and 1646 (Estates of 1643, 1645, and 1645–6). However, it is noteworthy that even in the crisis year of 1645 taxes did not fall below the level of 1635–40; thus the loss to the king – or success of the province – did not go beyond the eradication of the highs of the early 1640s. Furthermore, the recovery of 1647 was considerable, and the Fronde years (1649–50) saw no significant collapse

58 Georges Frêche, *Toulouse et la région Midi-Pyrénées au siècle des lumières* (*vers 1670–1789*) (Paris, 1974), pp. 495–501; 'Compoix, propriété foncière, fiscalité et démographie historique en pays de taille réelle (XVIe–XVIIIe siècles)', *Revue d'histoire moderne et contemporaine*, 18 (1971), 337–48. The shares of each diocese are listed in Lamoignon de Basville, *Mémoires*, p. 166.

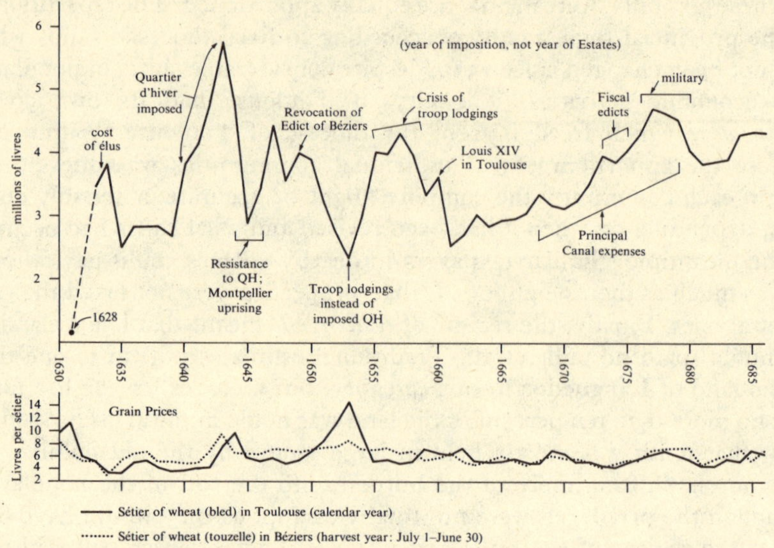

Figure 5. Province-wide taxes.

of royal revenues. The hard bargaining of the Estates was bringing more concessions, but not lower taxes.

Grants did decline after 1650, reaching their nadir in 1653, the lowest year since 1628. This change was a clear indication of the new bargaining power of the Estates, liberated in 1649 from the constraints of the Edict of Béziers's fixed schedule of taxes and left in a strong bargaining position by their relative loyalty during the Fronde. It may also reflect the impetus of the serious grain shortage of the early 1650s. After 1653 grants rapidly regained their former level under the impetus, once again, of troop expenses. The enormous costs of the quartier d'hiver of 1656–7 are evident in the 1657 peak, showing that the national unrest of that time did not affect tax levels. In 1658 and 1659 matters were not much better, and 1660 reflects the grants made in the 1659 Estates of Toulouse, when Louis XIV was present.

The considerable drop of 1661, which precedes Louis XIV's assumption of personal power, and the general low from 1661 to 1670 represent the familiar retrenchment associated with Colbert's best years. This decline reflects the minister's policy of reducing direct taxes all over France. But in Languedoc it also demonstrates the immense importance of military campaigns as a 'bargaining' device, for revenues immediately dropped to the old level of 1635–40, 1645, and 1652–5, which were years when winter quarters were small or non-existent or when *dons* were refused because of troop expenses. The gradual rise of the curve from 1661 to 1677 represents a genuinely new phenomenon since military costs did not account for it. The increase was built instead on grants for public works, notably the Canal du Midi, and, to some extent, on raises in the *don gratuit*. These expenditures were not self-evidently necessary or unavoidable like military expenses, and they required all the persuasive powers of Colbert and his intendants to get them approved. But, for the first time since 1633, they helped to raise the base level of taxes which then became the norm for future expansion.

The Edict of Béziers had permanently raised the tax level in Languedoc, for impositions did not sink back to their former levels when it was revoked in 1649. The assembly had hardly lost its bargaining power, however, for the fluctuations on the chart testify to a great push and pull which established upper and lower limits to the realm of the possible. The crown could achieve great peaks above the 'cellar' of the 1630s, but only by extreme military pressures. There was a limit even to these, for they set off provincial 'rejection mechanisms' which resulted in the lows of 1645 and 1653 – both years when troop pressures were high and when grain prices indicate shortages and hardship. Even in those 'successful' low years, however, the Estates could not lower the 'cellar' established in 1635. Languedoc provided the king with sure, steady revenues *all* the time, even during phases of resistance and social unrest. After 1660 a new form of discourse developed based on collaboration over public works instead of conflict over troops, and only then was it possible to increase expectations permanently so that the 'cellar' of 1635 was gradually raised.

When these tax levels are translated into series for particular dioceses or towns, the results are not identical because local variables like loans, add-on expenses, and particular fiscal manipulations enter the picture. Thus the three examples in figure 6 vary considerably in detail although their proportionate shares of the same provincial totals did not change at all during the period in question.[59] These local series do have the advantage of providing longer time-spans in which to place the episodes discussed here. Looking backwards from 1633, it appears that the great rise was indeed that which accompanied the Edict of Béziers, although it may have begun in the mid-1620s as it did in Montpellier. The general level after 1633 was two to three times higher than it had been between 1600 and 1620. There may have been comparable highs earlier during the religious wars, as in

[59] Town of Nîmes: A.M. Nm NN 11–17; town of Montpellier: Emmanuel Le Roy Ladurie, *Les Paysans de Languedoc*, 2 vols. (Paris, 1966), vol. II, p. 869 and *Archives de la ville de Montpellier, inventaires et documents*, vol. IX (Montpellier, 1939), pp. 149–274; diocese of Castres: Frêche, *Toulouse*, pp. 517–18.

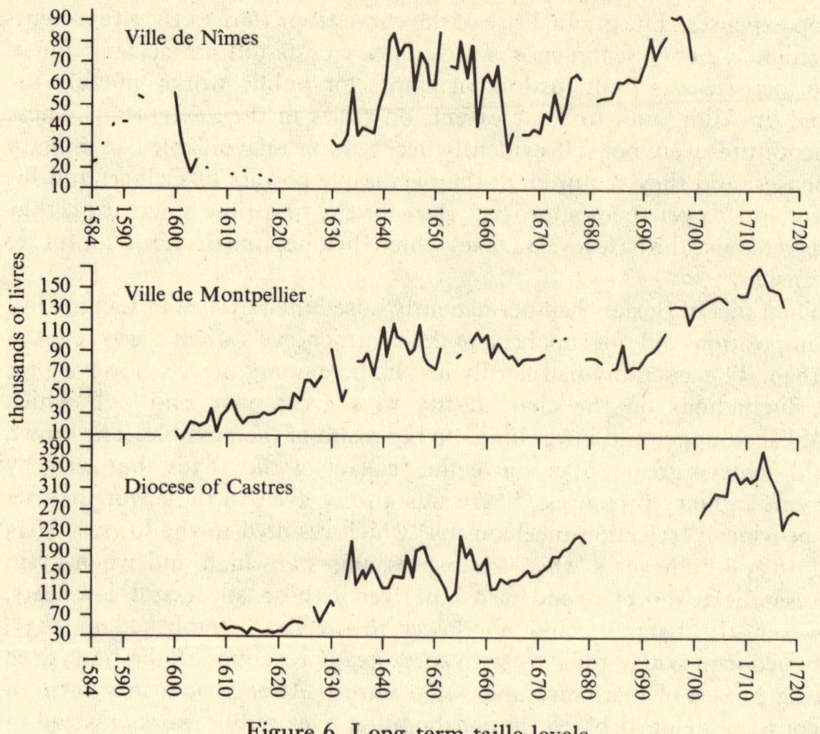

Figure 6. Long-term taille levels.

Nîmes; but there special problems concerning Catholic and Protestant military expenses may be causing exaggerated highs, as they did again during the 1640s and 1650s. Looking forward beyond our period, we can see that a new rise was building which peaked between 1691 and 1697, dipped briefly around 1700, and then rose to even higher levels during the period of 1710–12 before declining back to the level of 1690 or lower. From 1690 on, then, another higher plateau was reached connected to the expenses of the great wars of the end of the reign.

Between the significant increases of 1630 and 1690 lies the period which concerns us. In this longer context its curve appears almost flat, fluctuating widely around a middle point before 1661, then dipping somewhat and rising more regularly back to the higher levels of the same general range before passing on to the higher phase after 1690. The inescapable conclusion is that taxes did not rise that much between 1633 and 1690, although they fluctuated greatly. The rise between 1600 and 1710 was massive, but once the threshold of 1632 was crossed, neither Richelieu, nor

Mazarin, nor Louis XIV made significant gains except during brief emergencies.[60]

According to Paul Gachon, author of the classic work on the Edict of Béziers, the Estates lost all importance after 1632. They had become 'a repartition bureau for taxes they no longer discussed', and 'only one power remained standing in Languedoc – that of the intendants'.[61] Yet Richard Bonney, the most expert contemporary analyst of the workings of the central government, takes the Estates' ability to limit and resist taxes very seriously: 'throughout the ministries of Richelieu and Mazarin the Estates of Languedoc exercised their consent to taxation in an effective way. The Parisian financiers rarely felt sufficiently sure of the size of a forthcoming vote to make loans in anticipation of revenues from Languedoc'. He concludes that 'if all France had been pays d'états the Thirty Years War could not have been won'.[62]

Gachon sees the freedom of the Estates stifled by an authoritarian crackdown from outside. Bonney complains implicitly that the crackdown was not great enough – that the system of using intendants to levy arbitrary tailles on the pays d'élections was what kept the monarchy going through the pressures of the Thirty Years War and that, in protecting itself from this system, Languedoc was hindering the royal program. Gachon's and Bonney's points each have some validity, but Bonney is closer to the truth. Gachon's republican–constitutionalist orientation leads him to think in terms of the loss of a consultative independence which had never really existed. Throughout its history the issue for the Estates had never really been how much 'freedom' it would enjoy, but rather to what extent and in what ways the provincial notables would collaborate with the central government in managing fiscal affairs. This collaboration continued to make an important difference after 1632, although it is true that the terms of the equation were gradually altered. As Bonney says, taxes *were* held down, and Languedoc was not subjected to the extreme demands of the north. On the other hand, Languedoc did pay much higher rates than previously, as Gachon says, and the government did have better control. Throughout the crisis of 1645, the Fronde, and the 1650s, the province kept paying consistently large sums which came in on schedule, which cost the king neither money nor administrative energy to collect, and which provoked no major resistance to collections. In the pays d'élections much greater sums

60 This conclusion is in general agreement with those of Chaunu, Goubert, and Le Roy Ladurie, though it differs in details. Pierre Chaunu and Richard Gascon, *Histoire économique et sociale de la France*, vol. I, part I (Paris, 1977), p. 47; Pierre Goubert, *L'Ancien régime*, 2 vols. (Paris, 1969–73), vol. II, pp. 136–7; Le Roy Ladurie, *Paysans*, vol. I, 426, 481–2.

61 Gachon, *États*, pp. 274, 265. For his analysis of the change, pp. 262–3.

62 Bonney, *Political Change*, pp. 381, 443.

could be extracted, but only at a tremendous cost. It is not entirely clear that the monarchy would not have been better off with Estates everywhere providing regular, negotiable sums instead of having to fight tax rebellions with troops and having to use royal commissioners to counteract royal officers.[63] Languedoc's Estates were not beneficial in the consultative manner meant by Gachon, or by Alexis de Tocqueville, who saw them as precursors of the Estates-General of 1789 or the National Assembly.[64] But they were relatively manageable, and they may have provided a useful compromise between the king, wanting steady funds, and the provincial rulers, wanting a hand in their management.

[63] It is true, as Bonney points out, that intendants with strong-handed authority were less necessary in areas of taille réelle because assessments on land were less controversial and easier to enforce. But the experience of Guyenne shows that taille réelle could also require coercion when Estates were not present. Bonney, *Political Change*, pp. 382–3.

[64] Alexis de Tocqueville, *The Old Régime and the French Revolution*, tr. Stuart Gilbert (Garden City, N.Y., 1955), pp. 212–21.

PART THREE

The province on its own

7

Contradictory aspirations and practical problems

To what extent did the rulers of Languedoc share a common ideological perspective? Viewing the course of political events from their various geographical and institutional vantage points, what did they desire of the king, his government, their society, and what were they afraid of? Information on their attitudes is available in abundance in speeches, letters, and reports, and though most of it is of a highly public nature unlikely to reveal secret antagonisms or seditious inclinations, these stated intentions are nevertheless a good indication of the parameters of their world-view. This diverse body of material reveals both common aspirations and divergences of interest.

COMMON VALUES

The rulers of Languedoc started out with a common frame of reference derived from their social environment. Most of them enjoyed great wealth, belonging to a world of town houses and country estates within which their lives were lived according to familiar patterns of aristocratic courtesy: exchanges of visits and compliments, periodic changes of residence, attendance by 'courts' of servants and followers. All were literate, and all spoke and wrote in French, though one suspects that those of local origin were not free from manners that would have struck Parisians as decidedly meridional. More important, all had some access to a humanist–theological education which offered a common frame of reference for discussion of power and morality, though their facility in using it ranged from certain country nobles' smattering of learning to the vast erudition of some prelates and jurists.

A central experience was the management of property in the form of lists of land parcels, rents, and prerogatives which had to be carefully fostered and protected. While not profit-seekers, these leaders all understood leases, commissions, and interest rates from their experience in handling family patrimonies, and they were used to handling similar matters collectively from their contact with confraternities and religious societies and from the deliberations of judicial companies, assemblies of clergy, municipalities, or

Estates. In these situations certain approaches and procedures were always the same: hierarchically-ordered votes, renderings and auditings of accounts, judicial challenges and counter-challenges, decisions about never-ending sequences of law suits. Such talents were not generalized in the society, for few institutions offered ordinary people the chance to learn them, but they were what made it possible for groups of consuls, intendants, and country squires to work so easily on administrative commissions together.

A first approximation of the scale of values of the rulers of Languedoc might be obtained from the choices made by the capitouls of events significant enough to be painted in their capitular register by specially-commissioned local artists. There were fifteen of these illustrations between 1600 and 1660: the marriage of Henry IV and Marie de Medicis (1610), an allegory of Roman charity (1617), Louis XIII's first entry into Toulouse (1621), the artillery of Toulouse being carried to the siege of the Protestants in Montauban (1621), the second entry of Louis XIII into Toulouse (1622), the entry of Archbishop Montchal (1628), the arrival and departure of Louis XIII in 1632 (thus skirting the issue of the execution in the capitouls' own hôtel de ville of their governor Montmorency in the same year), the victory at Leucate (1637), Louis XIII on horseback trampling under foot the symbols of rebellion and heresy (1640), the conquest of Perpignan (1642), the general procession for the advent of Louis XIV (1643), the elevation of the relics of Saint Edmund (1645), the entrance of Louis XIV (1659), and Louis XIV's marriage (1660).[1] These choices demonstrate well the common denominators of Languedocian values: dynastic interest focusing on the continuity and grandeur of the monarchy; military pride specializing in victory over the nearby Spanish and the indigenous Protestants; pious intolerance combining Catholic ritual with the extirpation of heresy.

The fundamental frame of reference for all authorities was the king, portrayed either as a very personal suzerain to whom unlimited fidelity was owed or as the principle on which the system of authority and hierarchy was based. Never in all their pronouncements did anyone as much as hint at an alternative to this monarchist–absolutist orientation. 'The king is to his kingdom what the first mover is to the heavens or the sun to the stars'; 'the peoples must adore the finger of God which is engraved on the forehead of the prince and which obliges them to blind obedience and inviolable respect'.[2] These sentiments were bound up with a primitive chauvinism which enjoyed the idea of an active, fighting monarch triumphing over

[1] Ernest Roschach, *Les Douze livres de l'histoire de Toulouse* (Toulouse, 1887), pp. 284–90.

[2] *La souveraineté des roys à l'ouverture du parlement de Tolose* (n.p., 1646), p. 4; vicar-general of Mende to the Estates of Mende in 1638, Ferdinand André, ed., *Procès-verbaux des délibérations des états du Gévaudan*, vol. v (Mende, 1878), p. 56.

foreign enemies. In the year of his birth, Louis XIV was already acclaimed for being so closely related to all the leading houses of Europe that he could inherit any one of them. Louis XIII, 'the only power on earth today capable of opposing' the 'pernicious designs' of the Habsburg monarchy, was also portrayed in personal terms as an individual 'suffering under tents and pavillions for your preservation', 'in the perils of war, in air corrupted with pestilence'.[3] These rhetorical expressions were hardly taken literally by the learned and worldly individuals we are studying. It is possible that the most baroque evocations of the 'secrets' of monarchy came from visiting royal agents trying to stir up the awe of the locals. But while the more extreme monarchist flattery might have been distasteful to provincials still charmed by the more gallant style of Henry IV's day, there is no doubt that the rulers of Languedoc accepted and echoed the essentials of the absolutist message.

They had to do so because their own authority was based on the delegation of royal power, and their conception of it was inseparable from these same flattering images. The officers of the parlement associated themselves with the king by glorifying the concept of his justice, expressed in laws and enforced by magistrates:

> All our guidance must descend from God. It descends from Him into the hearts of kings no matter what their age, to be disseminated afterwards to the people by their officers. This guidance takes the form of the justice which the magistrates render you daily. If it were recognized that this is a king rendering you justice through the hands of his ministers and what weight this name of king has and what it stands for, then royal justice would be better received by everyone and would no doubt enjoy greater respect and veneration.[4]

In similar fashion the magistrates of the Comptes considered themselves 'the gods of the earth', receiving from the king the 'rays of his authority', just as the sun 'communicates its light to all the other stars'.[5] Such images, which were the clichés of contemporary political discourse, were infinitely malleable. Governors became 'titulary angels' when their powers of mediation were in demand: 'just as God through his titulary angels communicates with men, and men with God, so kings approach their subjects, and subjects their kings, by means of governors and lieutenants'.[6] And if the capitouls wanted to appeal to Gaston d'Orléans *against* his intervention in their affairs they could invent a more subtle image: 'the goodness of your nature promises that you will act like the sun, which does

[3] Archbishop of Narbonne to Estates, P-V Nov. 26, 1639; Miron to Estates, P-V Nov. 21, 1635; Hallwin to Estates, P-V Nov. 29, 1636.

[4] *Souveraineté*, p. 11.

[5] Charles Grasset, *Remonstrance faicte à l'ouverture des audiences après la S. Martin, en la Cour des Comtes, Aydes et finances de Montpelier* (n.p., 1634), pp. 13, 11.

[6] Joubert, syndic-general, to Estates, P-V June 11, 1649.

not cut through doors and windows in order to enter a house, but is content to flow in gently with the benignity of its favorable rays'.[7] When the procureur-general Marmiesse wanted to assert his own authority, he could claim that 'since the Parlement had been born with the monarchy, it was accustomed to following the king's rules; and just as the king did everything in France, it was up to the procureur-general to say everything [in the Parlement]'.[8] The capitouls could salute the Parlement: 'Messieurs, what the sun is to the world, you are to the state. God, as the prophet says, has placed his tabernacle in the sun, and our very Christian kings who are the images of God have established in you the sacred tribunal of their sovereign justice.'[9]

The trouble with using the monarchy as a buttress to one's influence was the failure of this concept to resolve important questions about the relationships it implied. A particularly troublesome dilemma was the phenomenon of a royal minority, that 'doubtful time when the prince acts and does not act', which was a central experience for the generations we are examining. Many loyalists feared this 'unfortunate period of obscurity [when] the hideous monsters of the state arise, [along with] the ambitions of the great and the licentiousness of all the orders'.[10] First President Bertier argued that it was necessary to reinforce the regency 'to give the state a great, strong, and royal power which relieves the weakness of a minor king'; yet he was wary of the danger of allowing 'the people to taste a certain diversity of government, for they are never fully satisfied with the one they live under'. His published prayer to Louis XIV, then a boy, is striking:

> Grand king, great in power and virtue although still tiny in age and body, grant us peace during your minority. A disheveled Europe soaked in blood demands it of you. If, after your majority, you need to find occasion for warfare worthy of your stature, the East and the Christian religion are calling you, awaiting the end of their captivity; and prophecies of your birth have already caused the mosques to tremble.[11]

The eleven-year-old monarch is used here as a symbol, a necessary buttress against disorder, and at the same time a guarantor of national glory and foreign conquest. It is interesting that this outward thrust of militarism was deflected by Bertier rather archaically onto a crusade against the infidel. Louis XIV was to find more immediate foreign adversaries, and his crusade was to be waged right in the province of Languedoc, to the delight of Bertier's successors. Already in 1650 the age of Louis XIV was being

[7] Roschach, *Douze livres*, p. 185 (in 1644).

[8] Malenfant, III, 24.

[9] Roschach, *Douze livres*, p. 178.

[10] Bosquet to Estates, P-V Oct. 21, 1643.

[11] Jean de Bertier, *La Régence, ou de l'autorité des reynes regentes* (Paris, 1650). Bound in A. A. E. France 1632, 459–74.

created in the aspirations of his provincial leaders a decade before its real beginning.

But meanwhile more opportunistic individuals were ready to exploit the minority's potential for creative readjustment of power. As soon as Louis XIII's death was known, certain parlementaires called for arrêts against all kinds of abuses and taxes, arguing that they could act with impunity because new kings were always required to make concessions, just as Louis XIII had done in 1610. The moderates, not challenging the validity of this commonly-accepted expectation, merely replied that such drastic measures were unacceptable and that the fifty-four edicts revoked in 1610 had been the result of humble remonstrance and royal grace, not unilateral action.[12] The concept of monarchy thus included a belief in an unwritten check against excesses.

But what about more positive limits on the rulers' rather passive view of the monarchy? Did the province not have its own values, its own set of privileges and customs to shield it from those of the king? The best evidence comes from the Estates, especially during the minority when their bargaining position was good. The same feeling was expressed in their sessions that now that a new reign had begun, ancient rights should be restored, and the capitouls, appealing to Orléans for 'freedom' of elections, said almost the same thing.[13] But the freedoms defended so emotionally in these appeals had little identifiable content, being roughly synonymous with 'the right to do things in our accustomed manner'. All of them had been granted or modified many times by the crown, and no one saw any inconsistency in appealing to the king periodically for new interventions or for modifications of these same privileges whenever interest required it.

If we look for expressions of a genuine theory of opposition in the Estates, we find nothing worthy of that label. The closest the president of the Estates came to an argument in favor of inviolable privileges was in his speech of 1647, in the middle of a vehement attack on troop lodgings and royal exactions. After using the usual arguments about total loyalty but inability to pay, he went on:

But after all, even if we did not have the invincible argument of helplessness which God himself bows to, we would have the conditions under which this province was very advantageously for the state and very happily for us joined to the crown; because for all time, without any memory to the contrary, it has lived in the full and complete liberty of our vote. What good would it do us to assemble if we had nothing to decide? What would be the use of consulting us if one could demand

[12] Malenfant, II, 330–6.

[13] Archbishop of Narbonne to Estates, Nov. 28, 1645: Roschach, vol. XIV, p. 90; Roschach, *Douze livres*, p. 184.

violently, by force, and without justice that which we had refused out of helplessness? Donations and liberal gifts are much more free and voluntary than the paying of a debt, and they are consequently more important and must be received at all times and by all sorts of persons – even by sovereign powers – with gratitude and recognition.[14]

This was an attempt to legitimize the Estates' recent refusals. Their claims had weight because (a) their privileges were ancient, (b) it would be ridiculous to call Estates if they were to have nothing to do, (c) a free gift was not to be taken lightly, presumably for motives of honor and courtesy on the part of the superior. But even here there was no hint of an ultimate right to refuse on grounds other than the impossibility of complying.

There was really no viable intellectual alternative to this sort of humble appeal. Groups wanting to protest could use the arsenal of delaying tactics available through the procedures of their corps while they mobilized a series of arguments with which to remonstrate, including the unfortunate effects of the policy, the misconceptions confusing the king, or the undesirability of procedural irregularities resulting from a lack of knowledge about local customs. As a last resort one could rationalize disobedience by appealing to extenuating circumstances or claiming to serve the same ends by different means.

But the most effective tactic was the least constitutional: the appeal to mercy on the basis of abject misery. In the earlier days when such appeals had a chance of succeeding, deputies were in the habit of delivering eloquent soliloquies on the province's inability to satisfy the crown. But by the time of Louis XIV, with his better control of the deputies, such lamentations had become obligatory formalities. In 1665 even routine constitutional procedures had become so embarrassing to prelates loyal to the crown that the bishop of Uzès felt it necessary to apologize to Colbert for going through the motions of deliberating a matter which was really already decided: 'we have to live with certain regulations, and it is not right to overturn the rules which we have always followed'.[15]

But even before 1661 there was no defense against the arrival of a contrary royal command except to try to avoid receiving it or to evade it with new appeals based on new pretexts. As Bertier said when the royal council cracked down on the Parlement in 1646,

I went along with this affair as long as we thought that the commands which gave authority in Toulouse back to the capitouls and damaged the authority of the Parlement were only caused by the pressure of certain individuals. But now that we have come up against the authority of the king and Son Altesse Royale [Orléans] we must stop there, and have only the glory of obedience.

[14] Archbishop of Narbonne to Estates, April 3, 1647: Roschach, vol. XIV, pp. 159–62.
[15] Bishop of Uzès to Colbert, Feb. 14, 1665: Depping, vol. I, p. 189.

The capitouls responded in an almost identical manner. 'Neither the capitouls nor the council ever intended to offer any resistance or obstruction to the execution of the wishes of His Majesty. They only decided to present him with remostrances for the preservation of their privileges and the liberties of the city.'[16]

Did the individuals making these pronouncements really believe their own words, or were they just making tactical retreats from failed resistance efforts? There is no way of knowing their deepest feelings, but a few isolated documents allow us to listen in on situations where defenders of the province talked among themselves about unpleasant royal demands. In letters to the syndic-general Lamotte local colleagues expressed concern about the arbitrary imposition of troop costs on the province in 1641: 'there are blows which come from behind and which the most capable men in the world cannot avoid'; or more explicitly,

I don't doubt that you are as surprised as I am at this new imposition imposed on the region...Personally I am all the more [surprised] in that not a word was heard of it during the Estates, nor was there any way of knowing that this was planned...What I found annoying is that this kind of diversion [of funds] completely ruins the liberty of the province, and it is for a purpose which leads to a thousand kinds of abuses.[17]

The bishop of Viviers wrote to the syndic-general in a similar vein in 1636:

We have had the whole regiment of Roussillon in this diocese and most of the Roure regiment. It is a novelty which we did not foresee and which we tried to avoid at the last Estates, as you know; but which the necessities of war and the large armies which His Majesty is forced to raise have required.[18]

These men believed in their 'liberties'; yet at the same time they were fatalistic about abuses and accepted the king's power as well as his ultimate goals. In a much later exchange between the syndic-general Joubert and Cardinal Bonzi, we can see the contrast between the provincial administrator, still doing his duty in defending usual procedures, and the more cynical cardinal. Joubert wrote to inform Bonzi in Paris that an extra sum not approved by the Estates had been slipped into an assessment for the militia which was 'against the privileges of the province and leads to dangerous consequences'. Bonzi, who was president of the Estates, replied sarcastically, 'I laud your zeal, Monsieur, and thank you for your good advice, but...it seemed to me when I learned of this [abuse] that if it is an evil, it is one without remedy.'[19]

[16] Bertier to Séguier, Mar. 28, 1646: Lubl., p. 182; A.M. Tse BB 33, Mar. 29, 1645.

[17] A.D. Hér. C 8292: De Fayn to Lamotte, Nov. 2, 1641, and Lamotte to Lamotte, Nov. 6, 1641.

[18] Bishop of Viviers to Rochepierre, Mar. 21, 1639: A.N. H 748^{202}, 246.

[19] A.N. H 748^{207}, 11, 93 (in 1675).

These few informal statements suggest that privileges were thought of as desirable procedures or customs which were nevertheless subsumed under the larger concept of royal authority. They were rallying points when opposition was felt necessary, and they provided points of reference in a speech or appeal. It was the duty of provincial agents to uphold them where possible, but in the end the royal will was viewed realistically and accepted begrudgingly, like any other directive of an annoying bureaucracy which could no longer be avoided. Privileges or local 'liberties' could have no autonomous force because they were part of a system defined and regulated by the king.

The rulers of Languedoc also shared a few other fundamental attitudes. One of these was the extreme chauvinism referred to above. 'We are all French by birth and Christian by baptism', intoned Miron in the midst of a long patriotic speech.[20] 'French arms' had delivered the king's 'allies and confederates' from 'the oppressions and insupportable tyrannies of a monstrous and formidable power which had risen in Europe in the last century and made them suffer by means of extraordinary force and violence', rejoiced the archbishop of Narbonne, who was speaking not, as one might assume, of the Turks but of the Habsburgs![21] When the king invaded the Dutch Republic in 1672, the bishop of Uzès exclaimed, rather prematurely,

> Good Lord, Messieurs, what affluence of marvels in this glorious campaign! The most beautiful, most powerful, best disciplined army that has ever been seen has been lacking in nothing, thanks to the vigilance of our great monarch... And these proud people of the United Provinces, who claimed with their usual arrogance to be able to halt the course of the sun of France, have received in their own defeat just punishment for their temerity. They have not been able to save themselves either by the traps they set for us or by the floods they prepared us.[22]

Thus the Languedocians delighted in a sense of dominance which combined might, trumped up moral superiority, and above all glory, to which the later period could add admiration for size and organization ('it is no longer necessary to go among the Ottomans to see an army of two hundred thousand men which arouses fear and panic on sea as well as on land').[23]

This military glory had a special significance for Languedoc because the Spanish frontier was so close and invasion was a real possibility. The glorious battle of Leucate, when Schomberg stopped the Spanish a few

[20] Miron to Estates, P-V Nov. 24, 1636.

[21] Archbishop of Narbonne to Estates, Nov. 28, 1645: Roschach, vol. XIV, p. 115.

[22] Bishop of Uzès to Estates, Nov. 15, 1672: Roschach, vol. XIV, pp. 1108–9.

[23] Ibid. (same speech).

miles south of Narbonne in 1637, was therefore an especially meaningful union of local and national efforts. When news arrived of the invasion, the Estates adjourned in mid-session while the barons, led by the lieutenant-generals and the seneschals and followed by contingents of militia from all the leading cities, rode out to meet the enemy. Towns like Le Vigan recorded proudly in their annals how they had participated in the battle, and the villages around Béziers kept a vigil, preparing to light bonfires to signal approaching danger to those gathered on the roof of the hôtel de ville.[24]

At the same time war meant expense, and since all the most detested taxes of our period were attributed directly to the needs of the army, it is no wonder that there was mounting discontent against the burdens of warfare, despite the general patriotism which animated Languedocian leaders. There were more and more calls for 'peace', as in Bertier's statement cited above. These should not be taken in the modern sense of 'absence of conflict', for it appears that what was usually meant was 'an end to the burdens of war on us', and everyone was delighted to have the king pursue his conquests elsewhere at the expense of the enemy. In some ways patriotism was a trap since a nearby war zone made resistance impossible. Toulouse found this out in 1639 when it had to scramble to keep up with Condé's order for cannons, infantrymen, arms, and cannon-balls, followed by calls for 1,500 pairs of shoes and 900 pairs of stockings for which emergency loans had to be undertaken.[25]

A similar scourge was the reign of the *partisans*. Nothing was more generally unpopular than the prospect of outsiders arriving with bundles of royal edicts saying that the bearer had the right to issue summonses to whole categories of individuals, levy fees on them, or peddle batches of new offices which provided ambitious purchasers with the right to force their way into local corps. As the archbishop of Narbonne told the Estates in 1641, when the cumulative effect of these 'edicts' seemed to have reached crisis proportions:

That which we can tolerate least willingly, which causes us mortal harm and affliction and ruins us irreparably, is to see our compatriots, natural inhabitants, born, nourished, and raised here, who breathe the same air we do... rise up against us, take us by surprise with unworthy acts which would be condemned by anyone with a trace of humanity or legality or desire to do good left in him, and become artisans of our misfortune and titled partisans of so much sorry advice and so many pernicious inventions which devour us pitilessly... May the sinner himself, that

[24] Pierre Gorlier, *Le Vigan à travers les siècles* (Montpellier, 1970), p. 125; Antonin Soucaille, 'Le Consulat de Béziers', *Bulletin de la Société Archéologique de Béziers*, 3rd series 1 (1895–6), ch. 5.

[25] A.M. Tse BB 31, Sept. to Dec., 1639.

is to say in language of state, the publican, the bad compatriot, the author and promoter of *parties* and *partisans*, abandon his pernicious and sacrilegious intentions...[26]

Almost everyone would have agreed. But like troop lodgings, the question of edicts was not so simple, for as Narbonne had himself pointed out, the subcontractors of fiscal expedients were usually local notables, 'compatriots', and for every seller there was a purchaser, who was also an 'artisan of our misfortune'. The general indignation against *partisan* did not necessarily lead to agreement on alternatives.

The most unanimously-felt theme for Languedocians was their absolute bigotry towards the Huguenots. The reports of authorities showed absolutely no appreciation of the motives of their heretical counterparts. For Baltazar the Protestants were 'monkeys [mimics] of the Catholics' whose demands for the maintenance of the Edict of Nantes were 'impertinent' and whose ministers 'for the most part only adhere to their religion because it pays their living'.[27] As early as 1642 the bishop of Nîmes was sending memoranda to Chavigny about how to impose Catholic control of local métiers and force Huguenots to sell their houses so that an episcopal palace, collège, and various convents could be constructed in their midst.[28] In 1653 a brief of the Catholic consuls of Montpellier charged that the Protestants were 'only tolerated in France through the benefits of an edict which could be revoked whenever the king saw fit' and that Protestant protestations of loyalty were hypocritical,

> since they are incapable of tolerating any sovereign authority, having challenged even God by separating themselves from his church in order to set up a separate sect. They do not recognize the authority of the Holy Father, who is the visible head [of the church]. An even better indication is the way the people of their religion acted in Holland towards Philip II King of Spain, their true and natural lord...and [what they did] in England to the person of Charles Stuart, their legitimate king.[29]

The spirit of the Edict of Nantes was so foreign to the rulers of Languedoc that their one-sided interpretations of it seemed perfectly natural. The Estates even asserted in their cahier of 1683 that the Chambre de l'Édit had been created by Henry IV to keep Catholics from being judged by Protestants![30] In Toulouse the 1660 *feu de joie* celebrating the king's marriage featured the ceremonial burning to the ground of a colossal figure representing heresy.[31]

[26] Archbishop of Narbonne to Estates, P-V Sept. 6, 1641.
[27] Ms. fr. 15833, 241–53.
[28] A.A.E. France 1632, 154.
[29] A.M. Mp Joffre 10 (Armoire A, ler rang), 260–2.
[30] A.N. H 748[213], 351–4.
[31] Barnabé Farmian de Rozoi, *Annales de la ville de Toulouse*, 4 vols. (Paris, 1771–6), vol. IV, p. 488.

SEPARATE INTERESTS AND STRATEGIES

These shared values coexisted with more practical concerns which were not unanimously held. In fact, the particular interests of the various ruling agents could be divisive or mutually contradictory, and even where there was general agreement on issues, nuances and differing priorities precluded any simple consensus. A review of the kinds of positions taken by the major governing bodies on public issues reveals a complex web of interlocking interests and conflicts which is important in understanding their role in political events.

As the highest deliberative body, the Estates had the clearest and most prominent positions on public issues, but they were not in any sense the voice of the province as a whole. Two features of their orientation stand out: their vested interest as a tax-collecting administration and their advocacy of the special interests of their own membership. The first was part and parcel of their very existence. Once the year's sums had been approved, the assiettes had to repartition the sums among the communities on schedule, the diocesan receivers had to take in the receipts from the local collectors and transmit them to the treasurer of the bourse by the stipulated deadlines, and he in turn had to make payments to a variety of creditors on designated dates. A lapse in this process threatened the solvency of the province and the credibility of the Estates. Therefore the assembly could not tolerate any failure to pay, whether because of popular resistance, local power struggles, or ambiguity about what was really owed. It was completely unsympathetic to local tax resistance and opposed any institutional change which threatened its monopoly on collections.

The interests best expressed in the Estates were those of the bishops. When assiettes were split by factional rivalries, the Estates invariably sanctioned the faction endorsed by the local bishop, and the same partiality was applied to the bitter municipal struggles in towns like Albi, Mende, and Le Puy. When it came to the towns, the interests which prevailed were similarly those of the consuls who attended the Estates, that is, the interests of the urban oligarchies they represented. In the case of disputed consular elections, the assembly not only took the side of the bishops but issued prohibitions against legal 'syndicates' formed by urban factions to oppose the actions of the clique in power, against 'illicit' assemblies, and against general meetings of the population. It advocated 'freedom' of municipal elections from royal intervention, but smiled on interventions against Protestants or dissident factions. It also defended the regular payment of interest on municipal loans.[32] The problems of artisans, laborers, and even

[32] P-V Dec. 24, 1638, Feb. 11, 1645, Mar. 14, 1648, July 2, 1649, Jan. 13, 1662; ms. fr. 22403, 120 (cahier 1683).

lawyers and officers were rarely considered, and then only in contexts where tax collections or concerns of consulates were at stake.

The interests of the barons, or more generally of the landed nobility, were not strongly expressed in the Estates, partly because their role was a reduced one in the assembly, and partly because the barons had few interests over which the Estates had collective jurisdiction. The Estates did make a point of trying to control the nomination and funding of the posts of governors of garrisons and fortifications in order to reserve them for local nobles. They lobbied against making the posts of seneschal into venal offices so that 'when they fall vacant the king can give them to those nobles who have merited them through their service'. On the other hand, the Estates fought nobles who committed violent acts against bishop and merchants, who oppressed towns from their fortresses, or who refused to pay the taille, and they lobbied against the creation of new governorships of towns.[33] Thus they supported the interests of a small circle of influential barons who held governorships and served the crown, but they had little in common with the traditional feudality.

Where the nobles were supported was in their role as landowners, for the Estates did champion the interests of large estate-owners, and in this sense supported the interests of the ruling class as a whole. The assembly appealed repeatedly for the right to export grain out of the province at moments when demand was high, thus driving prices higher at the expense of the mass of the population, despite the urgent pleas of those whose chief concern was provisioning. They opposed the importation of grain from Marseilles and demanded the right to ship local grain down the Garonne to Bordeaux.[34] They defended the Languedocian principle of *franc alleu* which protected allodial holdings from the king's feudal levies, and they always opposed such levies when they appeared. They defended landed property against royal preemptive efforts. In the midst of their many concerns it is hard to find any issue which showed direct sympathy for the interests of the vast majority of small-holding peasants, except where these interests coincided with other concerns of the Estates.

It goes without saying that the Estates opposed all new taxes and violations of provincial liberties, but their zeal varied considerably with the issue. When it came to new creations of offices, they were especially concerned about the sale of rights or positions which impinged on local administrative business, like controllers of notaries, controllers of tax rolls,

[33] P-V May 8, 1642 (special session, A.D. H-G. C 3816); P-V Oct. 20, 1651; ms. fr. 23354, 173 (cahier 1655–6); ibid., 276 (cahier 1661). The grievances of the unrepresented nobles can be seen in Roschach, vol. XIV, pp. 380–96.

[34] P-V May 8, 1642 (special session, A.D. H-G. C 3816); P-V Jan. 19, 1645 (Estates object to the intendant holding down the price of grain on behalf of the munitioners for Catalonia); ms. fr. 23354, 248 (cahier 1661); A.D. Hér. C 7655 (cahier 1669; asks that Marseilles be forbidden to import grain).

or controllers of the greffiers in judicial bodies. They also denounced creations of new councillors in the sovereign courts, but with less fervor. When it came to the creation of new présidial courts, which were a leading concern of the Parlement, they expressed concern that these courts cost the taxpayers money, charged unnecessary épices, and created a multiplicity of levels of appeal which were ruinous to those pursuing cases. But since they also argued that justice should be close to home, there was qualified approval of a court for Vivarais, provided it did not harm the présidial of Nîmes unduly.[35]

The Estates' usual response to unavoidable new taxes was to assimilate them to traditional ones, thereby maintaining control over their administration. The assembly's undivided indignation was reserved for national tax farms which they could neither control nor make use of. The gabelle was a case in point. Its administration was always provoking irritation with arbitrary purchases of salt, rising rates, patrolling of coasts and borders, house-to-house searches by the guards, and maintenance of courts and jails for offenders. Naturally, then, protests against searches and *crues de sel* were part of the regular diet of the Estates. What is surprising is that they more or less sanctioned riots against the gabelles in Carcassonne in 1656 and in the Vivarais in 1669 or at least took them rather lightly.[36] This stand, which must have been the most universally popular one the Estates could have taken, was possible precisely because they had no stake in gabelle collections. Similar stands could never be taken by the Comptes, which had a jurisdictional interest, or by the Parlement, which was paid out of gabelle funds. On the other hand the Estates would never have thought of opposing the taille the way the Parlement frequently did.

Even more threatening were the purveyors of edicts asserting the king's feudal claims over different kinds of property rights. These had various names and origins: *franc fief*, *amortissements*, *nouveaux acquêts*, *franc alleu*, *ban et arrière ban*, *joyeux avènement*, but they all had in common the fact that they gave investigators the right to look into the status of properties and legal rights which were not only the backbone of the prestige of individuals, but also the core of the identity of collectivities. We can see the concerns of the Estates perfectly in their attempt to get assurances from the farmers of the franc fief in 1636 that

> they did not intend to prejudice the immunities of ecclesiastics, collèges, hospitals, *maladeries*, and other pitiable locations, nor to disturb those who live nobly, whose grandfather and father had also lived nobly, nor communities for their hôtels de ville, squares, public roads, fountains, meadows, ditches of towns which do not mow them, or promenades which collect no rent or revenue; and that the charge

35 A good cross-section of these concerns can be seen in the cahier of 1648: ms. fr. 18830, 51.

36 P-V Dec. 4, 1656, Jan. 2, 1657; Roschach, vol. XIV, p. 1071.

for other communal property will be moderately assessed at the rate of one year's revenue.[37]

These promises to protect the revenues of the very groups best represented in the Estates were never kept, and soon the assembly was desperately fending off many more such edicts and asserting the right to be judged before their 'natural judge', the Parlement. Buying off these 'feudal' edicts became a top priority of the Estates because they hit especially close to home, and the expenses of the 'compensation payments' could then be assessed on the entire population by adding them to the regular taille.

The economic policy of the Estates was protectionist par excellence, favoring any trade and manufacturing which would increase the liquid wealth of the province and facilitate tax collection, but it never transcended very traditional views of the way profit was to be made. They supported the Toulousains' appeal for the banning of indigo imports which were ruining the pastel trade of Haut-Languedoc. They demanded protection for merchant ships on the Mediterranean from attacks by Spanish ships or royal galleys. They asked for a ban on the import of foreign cloth. They tried to protect the coastal sardine and anchovy trade from prosecution by gabelle agents. They complained constantly against the irregular assessments of the border tariffs levied on the eastern boundary of the province. But they were cool to real economic innovation, as we will see in chapter 12.

The positions of the town oligarchies, as expressed in their deliberations and petitions, were much more concrete than those of the Estates.[38] Reading through them, one can see where many of the economic demands of the Estates were coming from, but also how toned down and subsidiary they had become by the time they reached the provincial level. The consuls worried about excessive excise taxes, piracy on the Mediterranean, foreign indigo, and other protectionist concerns. They were angered by the gabelle collectors whose excessive rates, distant places of business, and frequent house-to-house searches disrupted trade. Like the Estates, they abhorred *partisans*, now including small ones like the farmers of the messenger service, the sellers of mirrors, the manufacturers of saltpeter. Unlike the Estates, they were greatly concerned about local grain supplies, now surveying local stocks and requisitioning new supplies, now lobbying for the permission to export 'abroad' in a good year. The same concern was felt for meat supplies, and contracts with local butchers for the local

[37] P-V Dec. 24, 1636.

[38] This synthesis is based on the municipal archives of Toulouse, Montpellier, and the other towns cited in the bibliography. Especially helpful is the series of instructions from the capitouls to the Toulousain deputies to the Estates in the AA series of A.M. Tse.

provisioning monopoly were a source of hot dispute. Particularly delicate was the problem of communal debts. Borrowing was the way municipalities met most emergencies. It was also a means of gaining control over larger sums of money than the restrictive tax mandates permitted. While both towns and Estates favored a responsible policy to protect credit and creditors, there was a potential for conflict between consuls tempted to have excessive recourse to loans and agents of the Estates who were suspicious of exactly this sort of thing.

The difference in emphasis between the wishes of the towns and the pronouncements of the Estates was most noticeable in the municipal attitude towards fiscal considerations. It was the consuls who reacted first against innovations which might lead to heavier burdens on the community and who were even cooler towards potentially expensive public projects. They were cynical about the deals the Estates were always making with the king for the buying up of proposed new offices since 'these frequent reimbursements encourage the creation of all sorts of edicts for the purpose of obtaining money from the province indirectly'; thus, they were more inclined to call for outright refusal.[39] Yet the consuls were loyal to the crown and conscious of the dangers of too much opposition. Toulouse advised its deputies not to speak out openly against fiscal measures but to work against them behind the scenes and reminded them in 1649 never to support their arguments by referring to the privileges of Toulouse 'which are viewed as only too odious in the Estates', but rather to stress the interests of the province.[40]

As the other great pole of provincial influence, the Parlement had rather different concerns and priorities which were expressed in innumerable arrêts, commissions, and particular actions.[41] It was both the proudest and the most threatened institution in the province because it was the only major body to play no official part in the major innovations since 1630 – the regime of the Edict of Béziers, the tax farms, the étapes, the intendancy – yet all of these novelties encroached on its prerogatives. Parlementaires complained that intendants 'assume jurisdictions over all sorts of civil and criminal affairs, introducing great confusion into the system of justice' and, even worse, that 'this completely discredits the Parlement...and ruins the king's subjects, who are torn between a Parlement justly trying to hold onto them and the *commissaires extraordinaires* who try to draw them away'.[42] For the same reason parlementaires detested the contracts of *partisans*, not just

39 A.M. Tse AA 22, 263–8 (Toulouse instructions 1640).

40 A.M. Tse AA 25, 171–3, 70–6 (Toulouse instructions 1666 and 1649).

41 Based primarily on the arrêts of the court, the correspondence of its members, and the memoirs of Malenfant. Certain petitions and appeals are also helpful.

42 Bertier to Séguier, Aug. 1, 1635: ms. fr. 17369, 93.

because they brought new taxes, but especially because they operated under the wing of the intendant by the authority of questionable royal commissions.

A second grievance was the rising number of *évocations générales*, which were transferrals of jurisdiction to a different sovereign court for certain categories of litigants. During the 1650s whole groups of notables were thus sheltered from the Parlement's influence, including the capitoulat of Toulouse, the Cour des Aides of Montauban, the officers of the présidial courts of Béziers, Nîmes, Montpellier, Tarbes, and Rodez, and the entire Cour des Comptes of Montpellier. The result, according to parlementaire gripes, was that the 'whole dioceses' of Montpellier, Nîmes, and Uzès were exempt because the friends, relatives, and servants of these parties all shielded themselves behind the general evocations.[43]

A third problem was the creation of new courts and officers, from the proposed Parlement of Nîmes to the proposed présidial courts of Limoux, Montauban, Privas, Auch, and Foix. The opposition of the councillors towards these dilutions of the power of the Parlement was endless. Their contempt towards présidial courts was expressed in their arguments against the court in Privas. Its judges, who were even more incompetent than those in Nîmes, they asserted, actually aided the Parlement by providing it with more business on appeal. Nevertheless they argued that the court should be abolished because the presence of its judges *increased* the incidence of crime by provoking personal attacks![44]

The parlementaires' position on various public issues differed significantly from that of the Estates. They fought much more vigorously for the full advantages of the paulette tax and the payment of their *gages*. They went much farther than the Estates in moderating and blocking the taille in which they had no stake, thereby currying popular favor. They supported the Estates when they saw fit, defending the provincial constitution and opposing the Edict of Béziers, but they were quite jealous of the Comptes' influence, which rivalled or surpassed their own in the local communities, and if either Estates or Comptes impeded their rather melodramatic assertions of influence through delegated commissioners, they were ready to denounce them with a barrage of negative arrêts. They supported the tax exemption of the city of Toulouse, from which they profited, but otherwise they fought with capitouls and other authority rivals within the city.

All these rivalries and common interests form a pattern. On the highest level, the Estates, the Parlement, and the Cour des Comptes should have represented the three bulwarks of provincial identity and should have stood

[43] Ms. fr. 17340, 265.

[44] Ms. fr. 17483, 275.

together in defense of their constitutional liberties. Occasionally they did so, especially on the broadest issues. But usually the three bodies formed a triangular system of interacting rivalries (see figure 7).

The Estates had very serious differences with the Comptes over their shared financial jurisdiction. A treaty in 1612 had established that the Comptes judged disputes involving tax assessments of individuals or claims of immunity, while the Estates were in charge of auditing the books of their own collection agents and resolving everything to do with the functioning of their administration. This technical and ambiguous distinction did not hold up under the burgeoning complexity of taxes which developed after 1635. In 1645 the Estates declared that the merger of the Chambre des Comptes and the Cour des Aides in 1628 had been 'the source of the greatest misfortunes of this province' and resolved to ask the Parlement to help obtain the Comptes' dissolution.[45]

On this issue the Parlement would have been happy to comply, but its relations with the Estates were also mixed. Because the Toulouse court was farther away from the Estates' center of operations and encroached less on its vital interests, relations between the two bodies were relatively cordial. When the Estates appealed on behalf of the *gages* and paulette of all officers, they seemed more disposed in favor of the officers of the Parlement and, on one occasion, noted that all épices *except* those charged by officers of the Parlement were excessively high.[46] But the Parlement's great flaw, from the Estates' point of view, was its hunger for authority. It was prone to intervene in municipal affairs by sending commissioners into other towns to settle disputes, and although such commissions could be advantageous to the Estates and were even sometimes solicited, they could also encourage factionalism, especially since the Parlement was inclined to oppose the position of the local bishop or the intendant, both of whom were usually supported by the Estates. Even more serious, the Parlement had no stake in tax collections and could generate popularity by stirring up exactly the sort of non-compliance which the Estates feared the most. In this respect, Estates, Comptes, and intendants were all united on the side of maintaining the fiscal system, *against* the Parlement, which was usually followed by the Chambre de l'Édit.

The Estates shared the province's initial animosity towards the intendant, but he was the key negotiator in the Estates, and his function in verifying municipal debts, arranging fiscal expedients, and supporting tax collections was so essential that their collaboration with him necessarily grew closer. On the other hand, the Estates conflicted regularly with the treasurer-

45 P-V Nov. 18, 1643, Feb. 10, 1645. The accord of 1612 in Albisson, *Loix municipales*, vol. 1, pp. 463–7.

46 Ms. fr. 23,354, 321 (cahier 1663).

	Estates	Parlement	Comptes	Consuls	Bishops	Présidial-sénéchaussée	Treasurer-generals
Estates	Work with intendants	✓: Opposition to *partisans*; oppose taxes on privileges; oppose meddling of Comptes; defend 'privileges of the province'	✓: Legitimacy of direct taxes and necessity of collecting them; defense of 'privileges of the province'	✓	✓	×	×
Parlement	×: Attitude to and authority over direct taxes; legitimacy of Estates and assiettes in some areas; influence over consulates	No use for intendants	✓: Defense of paulette and *gages* of officers; oppose new officers, courts or chambers; defend the 'privileges of the province'	✓×	×	×	○
Comptes	×: Jurisdiction over direct taxes, especially new forms of taxes; disagreements over auditing rights and auditing fees	×: Influence over consulates; jurisdiction over taxes, general edicts, public order and 'police' of the province	Local conflicts with intendants	✓×	○	○	✓
			Consuls	–	×	×	×
			Bishops	×	–	×	○
			Présidial-sénéchaussée	×	×	–	○
			Intendants	✓	✓	✓	✓

✓ = concordance of interests
× = conflict of interests
○ = neutrality of interests
✓× = some consulates pro-, some consulates con-

Figure 7. Functional rivalries of major institutions.

generals of finance. These fiscal rivals had taken over taxing powers from the assiettes during the interregnum of 1629–32 and were always waiting in the wings to do so again.

In short, each major issue drew certain authorities together against others, but the alliance was invariably broken by a conflict in some other area of interest. Estates, Comptes, Parlement – each had designs on the same influence within Languedoc even as all tried to fend off unwanted encroachments from outside.

CENTRAL DIFFICULTIES

Several of these deep-felt concerns reflected situations which require further explanation. It was not just that the rulers of Languedoc wanted to regulate taxation, extirpate heresy, and control military lodgings. In each of these areas they faced practical difficulties which illustrate the very nature of their political dilemma.

A. *Tax collection.* A classic case was the collection of taxes which, we have seen, was an essential preoccupation of the Estates and the bane of everyone else. Collection entailed a variety of authority problems. In managing the system of receiver–collectors on various levels the assembly had to enforce two somewhat contradictory imperatives. The first was the coordination of the system in such a way that funds flowed in smoothly so that the king's grants and local expenses could be paid. Collectors and receivers had to be pressured into paying on time instead of passing on their uncollectible receipts or holding liquid funds for their own private advantage. The second was the protection of the taxpayers from excessive intimidation by the very same agents, desperately or cleverly fighting to increase their cash reserves. It was necessary to keep local collectors from seizing plow animals or using illegal means of intimidation like cutting down trees, pulling up vines, or taking away doors, windows, or poultry, and at the same time to keep diocesan receivers from ruining the collectors by excessive use of imprisonments and forced lodgings (*gast et garnison*). Receivers sometimes bypassed collectors in order to foreclose personally on individual taxpayers or even sent their own creditors to molest these unfortunates.[47]

There was also the problem of how to see that subordinates collected all the officially authorized sums and no others. Under the Edict of Béziers special grants made in the Estates had to be approved by the king, which meant that the commissions authorizing their imposition were issued belatedly by the royal council; yet they still had to be accepted as binding by the assiettes and imposed with the other items in the *grande commission* from the Estates.[48] Then when intendants and military commanders began requiring the imposition of similar sums *not* approved in the Estates, it became necessary to instruct the assiettes to reject unauthorized demands. Inevitably the legitimacy of the annual tax 'package' was undermined by these contradictory appropriations, and it became easier for local groups to suspect the authenticity of the sums they were being required to pay.

A more difficult collection problem was presented by the refusal of the independently powerful, or *gens de main forte*, to pay any taxes. This

[47] P-V Dec. 7, 1633, Nov. 17, 1634, Dec. 3, 1636, April 27, 1647.

[48] P-V Dec. 1, 16, 1637.

problem grew as soon as the royal minority made non-compliance more attractive. From the 1640s on, the Estates attempted in vain to find a formula for dealing with the problem of inadequate force. We can see its dimensions, as well as the cumulative effect of the deterioration of authority through the 1650s in the general regulation they issued in 1661:

> In some areas local seigneurs had forced the inhabitants to leave their lands either by guile or by force, and once [the seigneurs] controlled these they resisted paying their tailles. In others the inhabitants refused to pay as a group and led the people into revolt against the receivers or their agents who came to demand payment...In villages and large towns people above the common rank holding offices in the sovereign or lower courts and in the financial offices, and other *personnes de main forte* with noble titles, refuse to pay their share of the taille on principle.[49]

The cumulative difficulties of noble resistance, officer arrogance, and popular resistance were beyond easy solution. The Estates prescribed a new procedure to follow: in the case of non-payment, the collector was first to summon the taxpayer three times; if he still refused to cooperate, the diocesan syndic would call out the prévôt and his archers. If this move failed, the syndic-general was to be notified to lend his support and possibly to appeal 'to those holding royal authority'. All these steps were to be studied in the next Estates where, if necessary, the governor would be asked to use his guards to settle the matter during the session. In addition, rebellious villages were to be held collectively responsible for the debts, and royal officers were to have back taxes taken from their *gages* by the king. If an individual had no office, the magistrates of his town were to deny him municipal offices and forbid him to ship his goods in or out until he paid up. As usual, indirect sanctions and seizure of the tangible were the best hope of success. But most of these measures would have required an improbable collaboration among a variety of individuals, and the most innovative and potentially successful all required the use of royal authority to bolster provincial procedures.

B. *Protestants.* The desire to eliminate Protestantism from Languedoc was more than an idle prejudice for, in the eyes of the Catholic rulers, religious diversity presented a real threat to government, security, and social solidarity. Here, even more than in the case of taxation, the solution had to come from the king, for the status of Protestantism had been established by royal legislation, and no traditional provincial mechanism existed for regulating it. Nevertheless, the religious problem exacerbated other local conflicts and illustrated in many practical ways the weaknesses of local authority.

In order to see the Huguenots as contemporaries did, it is necessary to

[49] P-V Apr. 2, 1661.

realize the political threat which their church as an organism seemed to represent.[50] Although greatly outnumbered in the province as a whole, the Huguenots had concentrated strength in a few main cities, reinforced by clusters of Protestant villages around them. Nîmes was looked to as the center of leadership and wealth, backed up by the Protestant hinterland around Uzès and in the Cévennes. The Chambre de l'Édit in Castres provided a means for legal obstructionism. Montpellier provided a powerful support community bolstered by prestigious members of the Cour des Comptes, though its new role as royal administrative center cramped its Protestant style. Power was organized around the towns where important municipal offices were held by Protestants. Their *consistoires* were organized into *colloques* representing several towns, which were in turn grouped into four provincial *synodes* which met frequently.[51] There was theoretically a national synod over these, but whether it was allowed to assemble depended on the moment.

Huguenots were viewed collectively by Catholics as devious plotters; yet most historians have described them in this period as both fiercely loyal to the crown and declining in religious zeal. Both sides are right. Knowing that their only hope was the king, the Protestants would refuse to join any major rebellion in our period or participate in any major popular disorders. But like modern minority groups, they also understood that a belligerent stance was the only way to protect a declining political influence. Spurred on by faith and motives of self-defense, they had to fight aggressively to retain what they viewed as the rights conferred on them by a series of complex and contradictory edicts of pacification. Much of what Catholics viewed as subversion was simply a tactical battle not unlike those the corps of officers were simultaneously waging to maintain or extend customary privileges. There were some Huguenot activists who pushed their zeal to the point of actual conspiracy, though they were now lesser figures and not the national leaders of the old days. Thus, while hindsight correctly tells us that the Protestants no longer posed a real political threat, authorities of the day were right in watching what seemed to them to be a very real menace.

Listen to Baltazar's arguments against allowing the Huguenot synod to be held in Montpellier in 1643. Such a meeting would allow the Protestants

[50] The basic history of Calvinism in Languedoc is Janine Garrisson-Estèbe, *Protestants du Midi 1559–1598* (Toulouse, 1980). There is nothing comparable for the seventeenth century, although there is a vast array of local studies. Helpful information is available in Samuel Mours, *Le Protestantisme en France au XVIIe siècle* (Paris, 1967); Philippe Corbière, *Histoire de l'Église Réformée de Montpellier depuis son origine jusqu'à nos jours* (Montpellier, 1861); Jacques Boulenger, *Les Protestants à Nîmes au temps de l'édit de Nantes* (Paris, 1903); E. Arnaud, *Histoire des protestants du Vivarais et du Velay, pays de Languedoc, de la réforme à la Révolution* (Paris, 1888); and Élisabeth Labrousse, *Pierre Bayle*, 2 vols. (The Hague, 1958).

[51] Mours, *Protestantisme*, pp. 59–86.

to revive their morale by gathering in the only 'capital city' in the kingdom where public Protestant worship was allowed inside the walls and where the consistory was the best known in France – almost the 'papacy' of Huguenottery, according to Baltazar. This assemblage would gather the colloquies of Montpellier, Nîmes, and Uzès together, thus reuniting what Baltazar considered to be the greatest temporal power the Huguenots had in the kingdom. Such a meeting would be giving them the equivalent of a 'national synod' at the very beginning of a dangerous regency. The presence of royal agents would be useless because conspiracies would be plotted in secret, and the citadel would not help 'because the combat we must engage in against them here will not be bloody...it will be a war of tongues, of pens, of the communication of ideas'.[52]

Baltazar greatly exaggerated the threat. But his emphasis on ideas, morale, and hierarchical organization was right to the point. The battle would be a war of symbolic gestures, small visible gains, and manipulation of a climate of opinion greatly influenced by national events. Ever since 1632 royal agents had been cracking down on the details of Protestant life: limiting worship in illegal spots, fighting excessive appeals to the Chambre de l'Édit, stopping unauthorized ministers from preaching.[53] Now in 1643 the Protestants saw the chance to recoup their losses and took encouragement from the royal declaration confirming their existence. Around Anduze there was talk of ministers trying to raise 2,000 men to reestablish worship at Ribaute by force, and the incident was seen as a test case by both sides.[54] Baltazar reported that the synod of 1644 had secretly decided that the 'present conjuncture' was especially favorable for reestablishment of their influence, that the least internal disturbance would give them the chance to move, and that sixty years of experience had taught them that concessions came only from the raising of arms, not from petitions.[55]

Accounts of synod meetings drawn up by local agents suggest the same themes. The synods met only with royal authorization and only in the presence of a royal commissioner who was a Protestant chosen by the intendant; thus their deliberations, like those of the Estates, were couched in moderate and respectful language. In 1645 the synod of Bas-Languedoc wanted to continue the preaching at Cabiac near Barjac where people were going 'in droves' (Baltazar reminded them that this case was pending in the royal council and that they could not proceed since their religion was

52 Ms. fr. 15833, 239.

53 Le Camus to Séguier, June 14 and June 21, 1633: Lubl., pp. 21, 23; Le Camus to Séguier, Dec. 12, 1633: Mousnier, *Lettres*, vol. 1, p. 278.

54 Bosquet to Séguier, Sept. 21, 28, 1643: Lubl., p. 39; Baltazar to Séguier, Oct. 27, Dec. 6, 1643: Lubl., pp. 44, 49–50.

55 Baltazar to Séguier, Dec. 6, 1644: Lubl., p. 103; Baltazar to Mazarin, Dec. 20, 1644: A.A.E. France 1634, 68.

one 'of edict, of being tolerated, of concession', not of customary right); they wanted to suspend the sacraments for members who allowed their children to be educated by Jesuits (he replied that this 'would eliminate freedom of conscience' and thus was against the royal wishes); they wanted to reestablish their academy at Nîmes (he replied that this was just a pretext to introduce another minister into the city).[56] At another meeting in 1651, the business of the Montpellier consistory included introducing a minister from the Île de France into the community, intervening in the case of certain Nîmois against the bishop, communicating with the Cévennes on various pretexts, and soliciting permission for a national synod in Paris. The synod of Nîmes in 1658 proposed a general fast and tried to admit emissaries from Haut-Languedoc and from other provinces.[57] All of these items were viewed, no doubt correctly, by the royal informants as attempts to keep alive the channels of communication of the national church.

Such sentiments were bound to lead to trouble. There were illegal Protestant assemblies around Aubenas in 1645 on the day the national synod had proclaimed a general fast; by 1646 worship was creeping from village to village; in 1648 Protestants in Uzès attacked the house and valets of the bishop. Bosquet reported that secret meetings in the countryside were supposed to be forming a 'new league'.[58] Protestants had reinfiltrated Privas and the area around it from which they had been expelled in 1629, building a circle of houses to replace the illegal wall, using the ruined church as a prison, and engaging in defiant acts like publicly eating meat on Fridays.[59] Meanwhile a circle of activists in Nîmes, already denounced by Baltazar in 1644 for fomenting trouble in the consulate, surfaced repeatedly in connection with one sort of Huguenot demonstration or another, led by Maurice Baudan, sieur de Vestric, and Jacques de Vignolles. In 1650 Vestric's son, the minister Baudan, wielding a hammer, led a crowd of irate Huguenots into the bishop's palace and kidnapped a converted Protestant boy, thereby creating a *cause célèbre*.[60]

The dramatic peak of Protestant agitation was a near rebellion which took place in 1653 at Vals near Privas, where the synod of Vivarais had been rather flagrantly holding its meeting in the territory of a Catholic seigneur. When the minister Durand, whose illegal installation in 1646 had already preoccupied Baltazar, was forcibly expelled by this seigneur, the consistory of Nîmes organized a large assembly at Uzès which proceeded to raise troops. From 5,000 to 6,000 Protestant troops assembled at Valon led by the Nîmes conspirators Cassaigne, Vestric, and Vignolles and a number of

56 Ms. fr. 15833, 265.

57 A.N. TT 256B, 157; TT 260, 321.

58 Baltazar to Ciron, June 2, 1645: Lubl., p. 140; Baltazar to La Vrillière, Apr. 25, 1646: Lubl., p. 184; bishop of Uzès to Mazarin, July 21, 1648: A.A.E. France 1634, 342; Bosquet to Séguier, Oct. 4, 1648: ms. fr. 17390, 135.

59 Ms. fr. 15833, 337–86.

60 A.N. TT 260, 216, 222; A.D. Gard G 448, G 450; A.M. Nm BB 2, DD 1, OO 58, RR 60.

hesitant Huguenot nobles. Catholic forces were hastily gathered at Aubenas, and it looked for a few months as if the religious wars would recommence. But nobody's heart was in an armed struggle, and the belligerents gradually melted away, while Mazarin hastily made concessions, with an eye to his relations with Cromwell who was watching the situation closely.[61] Meanwhile factional struggles of Protestant and Catholic parties continued in Montpellier as well as Nîmes. The Protestants seized the consulat of Lunel by force, and violent conflicts dominated Uzès from 1656 to 1662.[62]

These examples overemphasize the trouble-making role of Protestants who were on the whole rather passive, but they demonstrate the threat as it appeared to the Catholic population. The point to note is that only intendants and royal agents were qualified to deal with these matters. Only the royal council could resolve serious judicial disputes because appeals to the Chambre de l'Édit crippled the usual judges. Only the king could modify municipal constitutions or authorize Protestant worship or the holding of synods. As deputies of the Parlement told Breteuil in 1649, 'it would be advantageous to the Catholic religion if the intendant would assume his former jurisdiction concerning the affairs of the Protestants, at least in matters concerning the execution of *arrêts de conseil*'.[63] This was during the period when every sovereign court in France was clamoring against the continuation of these royal agents!

C. *Troop lodgings*. Perhaps the most vexing authority problem of all was the regulation of soldiers, *gens de guerre*, during the Habsburg wars.[64] The troops seen by Languedocians were either passing through or stationed in fixed lodgings. For the former a *ligne d'étape* or plan of march would be established, with towns designated as stopping places a day's march apart (*étapes*). For the latter the fixed quarters might be just for a few days or weeks (*logement*), or for the whole winter season (*quartier d'hiver*). In addition, when troops were recruited in the province they were assigned a rendez-vous point (*quartier d'assemblée*) where they would stay while companies were being formed, and the same term applied to regrouping points for troops coming out of winter quarters.

In all these situations the men had to be lodged in private homes and supplied with food, fodder for horses, and necessities of life like wood for the fire, candles, and bed linen. There was always the question of how their

[61] Augustin Cochin, 'Les Églises calvinistes du Midi, le Cardinal Mazarin, et Cromwell', *Revue des questions historiques*, 76 (1904), 109–56.

[62] Ms. fr. 15832, 202.

[63] Breteuil to Séguier, Nov. 9, 1649: ms. fr. 17391, 132.

[64] This subject has been very little treated. For general background, André Corvisier, *L'Armée française de la fin du XVIIe siècle au ministère de Choiseul*, 2 vols. (Paris, 1964); and Louis André, *Michel Le Tellier et l'organisation de l'armée monarchique* (Montpellier, 1906). The best technical treatment is André Eugène Navereau, *Le Logement et les ustensiles des gens de guerre de 1439 à 1789* (Poitiers, 1924).

provisions should be supplied: should the local inhabitants pay cash with which the soldiers could buy their own necessities, or should they supply victuals in kind? It was hard to say which type of lodging was worse – supplying an étape to overnight soldiers or quartering a company for the winter. The latter had the disadvantage of duration, but it allowed for much better regulation because when the troops were stationary they could be counted and their names recorded. An étape was more subject to burning and pillaging since the soldiers knew they were leaving in the morning and would never see the place again. Furthermore, if a whole army passed by the same route, towns on the ligne d'étape were subject to repeated passages, with the whole horror show starting over again every few days.

The presence of troops provided authorities with a real headache. In the best of circumstances there would be masses of paper work to do, orders to send out which might change daily or hourly, and large numbers of claims and disputes to adjust. In the worst cases there could be real atrocities like villages sacked, churches profaned, and women raped. Even lacking these catastrophes, the presence of soldiers always meant trouble and disruption. The consuls of Uzès had trouble restraining a drunken *cornette* who led thirty cavalrymen in a nocturnal attack on their municipal guards after an 'extraordinary debauch'. The consuls were later charged with the murder of the cornette.[65] Extortion was also a serious problem. Soldiers would stray off their route or lodge in towns more to their liking than the ones in their instructions. Once settled, they would demand extra payments as 'protection money' or make deals with the consuls to turn provisions into cash which could be spent on drinking and women. They would demand extra rations from their hosts, charge the town for absentee comrades, requisition horses or mules to transport baggage. All these illegal demands were called *foules*, and they cropped up wherever the troops went. Once the abuses had begun, then intimidation was employed to keep the villagers from reporting them.[66] Finally there was the problem of compensation. Even if the soldiers followed their routes and acted in a relatively docile manner, who should pay their expenses? Would each town 'bear its own foules', and, if not, who would repay them, the diocese, the province, or the king?

Just ascertaining the facts about lodgings was difficult. Consider one example. In early May of 1639 the syndic of the diocese of Toulouse, Faisan, wrote a detailed report of a foray into the countryside to determine first-hand how many companies of the regiment of Montagnac were actually lodged in the diocese. At his initial stop in Grisolles, the first consul could not be located, and the second consul claimed that three companies of seventy-five men each were lodged there, but declined to prove it. There were only nine

[65] P-V June 3, 1647, Oct. 27, 1651. Other examples abound, even under Louis XIV: P-V Jan. 22, 1675.

[66] P-V Nov. 27, 1635.

or ten soldiers present at the moment, he explained, because the rest had been spending the last ten days in the countryside collecting supplies. Out on the road, Faisan's inspectors encountered thirty soldiers marching, but these reported that they were from a variety of different companies. When queried, priests and merchants reported that Grisolles was in collusion with the troops. The next day the inspectors left at dawn for Soulon, where the consuls could not be found at all. Inhabitants reported that the company of Duti had been lodged there, but they were presently out making rounds with Lieutenant Salabert. Soulon was only able to produce one live soldier. The same story was repeated everywhere: in Baridain there was a company in residence, but they could not be assembled 'because there was no drum'. In Fronton the troops had departed for the countryside. In Villefranche the lieutenant-colonel provided proof of three companies, but as he was riding off, the first consul came forth to report that he had signed these fraudulent documents to avoid irritating the captain.[67] This example should be multiplied by the hundreds to convey the aftermath of the winter quarters and the improvised quality of its arrangements.

The existence of extensive troop lodgings after 1635 brought the question of authority to the fore with special urgency. The traditional privileges of the Estates stated that in return for their annual grants they were exempt from all lodgings of troops. If the king wanted to violate this principle, his agents would have to require provincial agencies to provide services which they were not supposed to provide, and the Estates in turn would have to find the authority to obtain redress for military grievances. The syndics of dioceses and the aides of bishops were constantly on the move, gathering evidence, getting troops shifted to more favorable locations, filing appeals with the proper authorities. Their archives contain bundles of petitions and edicts, balance sheets of advances and repayments for hundreds of communities, ledgers of specific lodgings by date, place, and company which continue for many pages.[68] The difficulty was not a lack of channels but rather the poverty of effective remedies. Here, as in so many other areas, formal steps were readily taken, but practical results were hard to come by. On the higher level the files of the syndic-generals are also filled with petitions to intendants or governors which were usually answered favorably.[69] But the ordinances the commanders issued in response merely reiterated the usual injunction that all appropriate authorities should take all necessary steps: royal magistrates should prosecute, prévôts should patrol the roads or force the soldiers to obey, soldiers should obey the rules. When matters reached the sessions of the Estates, their resolutions were similarly formal: the syndic-generals should provide 'all necessary assistance

[67] A.D. H-G. C 716.

[68] A.D. H-G. C 2131, 1640 bundle, for example.

[69] For example those of La Motte, A.N. H 748[202].

at the expense of the province', or delegations of members should be sent to appeal to the intendant, who would then issue an ordinance.

When real sanctions were actually prescribed against soldiers, they were almost impossible to carry out. In 1640 the Parlement issued an arrêt for the arrest of two ensigns at the request of the consuls of Montastruc and sent a *sergent royal* to execute it. He located the men, but when he found one of them shut up in his lodging with 'a large corps of soldiers' blockading the door, he contented himself with having the arrest order announced three times in the streets by the public crier.[70]

In the winter of 1639–40 the crescendo of de facto military burdens reached its peak. The king was sending the entire army of Condé to winter in Languedoc, and although the Estates were repeatedly asked to grant a quartier d'hiver which would cover the cost, they steadfastly refused. Bypassing their consent was a tricky business for the royal agents, requiring individual handling of each step of the process and personal attention to detail. The intendant Machault had to send out the most specific directives from Toulouse to each village:

> In order to feed ten companies of the regiment of Cabreres in the village of Ogerville tonight and for breakfast tomorrow morning without ruining the village, we order the village of Vigoulet to send four quintaux of bread, four sheep, and three setiers of oats, or the sum of fifty livres instead, before four in the afternoon; Saint Ouen is to send two bariques of wine...(etc.).[71]

Meanwhile these immediate measures had to be reinforced by direct commands to important men who would not otherwise have lent their support. The bishop of Viviers received a packet of letters starting with one from Louis XIII himself ('you could render me no service more pleasing or more welcome') and another from the secretary of state Sublet ('His Majesty...is awaiting prompt results'); then one from the intendants.[72] The syndic-generals, who received even more preemptory royal letters, then had to issue legally binding orders to the diocesan syndics, but even this sort of legal notice did not guarantee that the syndics would comply. In Toulouse the syndic Faisan, whom we encountered above, avoided summoning the assiette to grant funds for the troops until he was thrown in prison. Then when the intendant demanded more funds for more troops, he panicked and went into hiding.[73]

Faced with every sort of local subterfuge, the intendants and military commanders had difficulty in making the system of provisioning and lodging work smoothly without the collaboration of local authorities. The

70 A.D. H-G. C 2131.

71 My paraphrase of an ordinance of Machault, Aug. 29, 1640: A.D. H-G. C 716.

72 A.N. H 748[202], 240–6 (letters of Feb. 8, Mar. 7, 1639).

73 A.D. H-G. C 716, 'Estat des dépenses', Dec., 1641.

provincials at the same time had no effective way of licensing the troops, keeping their upkeep within reasonable bounds, and correcting abuses without the help of the royal agents. By the end of 1640 this had become clear to provincial leaders, and the Estates belatedly granted the king a quartier d'hiver, which was followed by a permanent system of étapes in 1641.

A COMMON PROGRAM

Out of the multitude of proclamations, deliberations, acts, petitions, and denunciations issued by all the major authorities of Languedoc emerges a sort of unwritten program, or at least a set of aspirations. Let the king symbolize magnificently the unity of this patriotic, Catholic, hierarchically-ordered polity, by God's will the greatest in Europe; and even more important, let the legitimate provincial authorities participate in this glory, applying it, transmitting it, enjoying it. The king should personify France's virtues of crusading fervor, conquering might, and Christian piety like a medieval suzerain grown more powerful, more internationally conscious, more cultivated, but without abandoning the essential feudal impulses which still motivated the body politic. But he should also keep the peace within, preserving his authorities from each other and from the perils of social disorder, even when he was a minor. Privileges and liberties, in the sense of customary procedures which allowed the traditional authorities to have a respectable, if not dominant, place in the ruling process, should be maintained. Their modification by the king was tolerable and sometimes highly desirable. Their violation would be met with a counterreaction of consternation, appeal, and protest, which usually would be followed, however, by some sort of acquiescence.

Heresy in all its forms should be extirpated. Land rents should be maintained by reasonable tax levels and profitable export regulations, while investments in *rentes* should be guaranteed and the entire financial system stabilized. Traditional trading and manufacturing profits should likewise be maintained by protection and economic privileges, exclusion of competing foreign goods, and regulation of border tariffs to favor the province. The regime of *partisans* and extraordinary taxes should be eliminated; the gabelles strictly regulated; and necessary troops made to follow discipline and pay their own way through the province.

Such a program would have pleased most of the rulers of Languedoc, though hardly the rest of the population. It was a program of landowners and officeholders wedded to procedures which kept fiscal burdens somewhat lower than in many parts of France and gave them considerable say in administering the system. None of the traditional demands of the nobility for the maintenance of the *noblesse de race* against the intrusion of robe nobles, officers, or roturier wealth appeared on the slate because the first estate was so poorly represented among the rulers with real authority. On the other hand, there was no trace of a progressive bourgeois ideology either – no freedom of trade, equality of opportunity, economic modernization – for the rulers were totally immersed in the aristocratic values exemplified by the king and his court, and the townsmen who voiced elements of this progressive message were effectively screened out of the governing process.

This program, though hardly visionary and well within the realm of conceivable possibility, nevertheless contained important contradictions. The rulers of Languedoc wanted a society in which they collaborated closely with a genial but distant king, granting him reasonable funds after appropriate deliberation, policing his province by means of their recognized authority, judging disputes in accordance with their own written law and their distinctive financial procedures. Such a system, suggesting a golden age of semi-autonomy which had never really existed, would perhaps have been possible if this had been the limit of their aspirations. But they wanted much more. They looked beyond Languedoc and associated themselves with a national policy of grandeur and international hegemony. They demanded protection from the Spanish invader and the Mediterranean pirate. They wanted strong measures against the Protestants, yet at the same time an end to religious wars. They needed protection against competition for the produce of their backward and inefficient fields and shops and security against the masses of poor. Their well-being required large infusions of royal authority to make the processes that mattered work smoothly – the collection of taxes, the regulation of troops, the restriction of the Huguenots. In these areas and others, they had increasing recourse to intendants and governors because their own authority was inadequate and because they could not control the sources of the difficulties.

Another contradiction was the disposition of the authorities themselves. Each institution set its sights, first, on the royal authority which it completed or executed and, second, on the provincial groups over which it aspired to impose this sway. None was equipped to coordinate its efforts with other agencies in the region because each held a slightly different kind of power which had been created in relation to particular royal needs, not in relation to the powers of the others in the province. The rulers of Languedoc shared common aspirations, but the modes of operation of their institutions set them against one another in a perpetual equilibrium of adversarial relationships which only the king could arbitrate. Some resolution of these differences was essential if the province was to come together effectively and force the king to accede to its demands. Serious attempts at union were made in the seventeenth century, and we will examine their prospects in chapter 9.

But perhaps the most basic problem of all was the inadequacy of the whole provincial system in solving fundamental problems of 'police' and enforcement. Even within the context of the privileged regional system which every provincial authority paid lip service to defending, it was not possible to assure the smooth functioning of everyday governmental operations because of serious flaws in the local governmental system. This basic dilemma of authority is the subject to which we now turn.

8

The inadequacy of authority

The problem of authority is one of the most fascinating aspects of seventeenth-century political society. Authority, which we may define as the respect attached to a person (or institution) which enabled his directives to prevail, was based more on intangible qualities of prestige than on physical means of coercion. Public officials relied on their delegated royal authority which gave them the right to act officially and lent weight to their actions, but unless they also had the intangible *crédit* based on custom and public approbation, they would not be very successful in making others take notice. For this reason, acts of authority have to be read both as official steps aimed at a certain practical result and at the same time as ritual defenses designed to maintain a certain public image. Quarrels could arise over seemingly petty points of competence or precedence because they had hidden implications for the participants' honor or prestige. By contrast, violent acts were often accepted complacently because they did not have such implications.

THE NATURE OF AUTHORITY

The rulers of Languedoc had at their disposal a slim arsenal of coercive weapons, most of which were subtly indirect. In this society things as they stood (or as they were imagined to stand since many of them were actually changing) had a tremendous force of inertia, and it was easier to make specific exceptions than to modify general rules. The basic tools of governmental action were judicial processes. First among these was the legal command, a written document which varied in form depending on who issued it. Those with a delegated power of command like governors, seneschals, intendants, or military officers issued ordinances (*ordonnances*) commanding that something be done; judicial authorities issued arrêts taking the form of a decision about a matter in dispute or 'police' regulations designed to protect the general welfare. Consuls, Estates, and deliberative bodies had 'deliberations' which recorded their decisions and then were published as 'extracts'. These documents were technically distinct, but the result was similar: an official announcement to be posted, proclaimed at street corners, printed and distributed, discussed, and registered in different courts of law.

Such orders could be very intimidating, replete with coats of arms, counter-signatures, exalted language, and terrible penalties for non-compliance. They directly invoked the prestige of a hierarchy of authorities, always speaking in the name of the king. If they were addressed specifically to individuals whose career depended on a reputation of respectful service, they could be effective. But even then it was possible for the recipient to misconstrue them, to avoid receiving them, to challenge their form, or to appeal that they had been based on false premises. If they were addressed to a group or were general directives, the only enforcement would have to come from local agents who chose to apply them, usually by punishing individual offenders. To make matters worse, these orders were issued by many different agents, often quite casually, so that contradictory commands flew back and forth, sometimes even issued by the same agent on different days. Lawyers and syndics kept sheafs of them which they carried around for ammunition, and spent time petitioning officials to enforce whichever commands suited them. Royal agents saw to their publication or withheld arrêts de conseil until they were needed to bribe recalcitrant parties. Thus the vast majority of these commands were not so much orders as reminders, the constant reiteration of which was a form of publicity, but their effectiveness was entirely dependent on the filter of local authority through which they invariably passed.

If such an order was to be applied, someone would have to present it to the person involved and demand compliance. In the case of petty infractions by common citizens, a consul or other official wearing the appropriate insignia of office and accompanied by guards or *huissiers* would simply command the violators to desist or would arrest them, sometimes literally grabbing them around the waist and calling for help. Some arrests could be the result of chance encounters, but most corrective actions were the result of specific petitions directed against a specific manifestation of the abuse. Enforcement successes were rare enough that the capitouls described each one proudly in their annual 'state of Toulouse' addresses, to the point of citing trivialities like a man caught with a prostitute or persons bearing arms at night.[1] Such petty actions were obviously predicated on the assumption that suspects would respect the authority of the magistrates and that bystanders and neighbors would cooperate. If an arrest was unpopular, if several authorities quarreled in public, or if larger crowds were involved, then the mood of compliance could rapidly deteriorate.

When enforcement concerned more important individuals or more

[1] A.M. Tse BB 36, Dec. 11, 1659.

complex issues the process became a game of legal strategy. The offenders were presented with copies of the appropriate command by huissiers (process-servers) who drew up procès-verbaux to serve as evidence that this dubious event had actually taken place. The subjects then made counter-demands or appealed to alternative authorities, formally insisting that their protestation be recorded by the huissiers. These defensive tactics became increasingly embarrassing as the issuing authority became more eminent or his presence more immediate, for under these circumstances non-compliance began to look like treason. If governors commanded in person, or if royal commands were delivered by *huissiers de la chaîne* from Paris, who wore special insignia and a large medallion portraying the king around their neck, it was best to obey or else arrange to be absent; consequently a large number of such arrêts ended up being handed to wives, servants, or stableboys.

The successful execution of one of these major commands therefore required much plotting and choreographing. Pierre Mosnier, huissier of the royal council, was sent to Toulouse in 1646 to arrest the rather eminent receiver-general d'Aldeguier, along with d'Aldeguier's subordinate Caube. Mosnier went first to Bordeaux, where he engaged seven assistants and sent them ahead to infiltrate Toulouse secretly and take up positions in various inns. A week later he went there in person to determine where the two offenders were actually located, but after ten days of secret inquiries aimed at catching the culprits unawares, he was obliged to come out into the open. He searched their residences, where their wives denied any knowledge of their whereabouts, and after an unsuccessful visit to one of their country estates, he returned empty-handed to Paris.[2] In major enforcement ceremonies like the formal disunion of the Cour des Comptes in 1647, a group of royal agents would have to visit each officer in turn, escort him to the meeting place, and lead the company, command by command, through the motions of registering the royal orders since, while nobody was willing to disobey the king openly, no one would take the initiative to obey either.[3]

Where private parties were well protected and could afford to be defiant, physical coercion became virtually impossible. After a salt riot in Narbonne in 1651 at which the valet of a certain Cazaré had been arrested, Cazaré and a bunch of young friends, brandishing swords and pistols, attacked the director-general of the gabelle in the street and threatened to kill him unless he released the prisoner. Proclaiming that the 'honor' of the king and the town were thereby threatened, the consuls assembled in full regalia and pursued the culprits, but neither they nor the local governor could ever

[2] Ms. fr. 18510, 276.

[3] Ms. fr. 18830, 205; Sabatier's account in A.M. Mp. BB 197, 58v.–66r.

catch them.[4] The arrest of the rapist Saint-Vic in Toulouse in 1643 illustrates other difficulties. The first capitoul d'Espagne grabbed him on a busy street and dragged him into a shop on the ground floor of the nearby Fermat residence because too many carriages were blocking the way to the hôtel de ville. Fermat, also a capitoul, put on his livery to go and fetch the *guet*, but meanwhile a crowd of 'youths from the best families' broke down the door into the shop and tried to free the prisoner, who was 'held in an embrace' by d'Espagne. An angry dispute ensued in which the son of President Puget of the Parlement taunted d'Espagne with the remark that he would be capitoul for only one year and that he would eventually have to give in, while the juge criminel de Loppes of the sénéchaussée and some others tried to seize the prisoner, saying that 'wherever de Loppes stood the authority of the capitouls ceased'. We can see here not only the danger of violent resistance by friends and retainers, but also overtones of the jurisdictional jealousies which obviously lent fuel to the fire.[5]

This physical difficulty of making anyone important do anything out of the ordinary explains why actions were so often directed against the accused's subordinates or his inanimate property. In a society of honor, an insult to one's clerk, one's maid, even to the wall on which one's coat of arms was affixed, could be as damaging to reputation as a face-to-face confrontation. When the consuls of Albi could find no better way to continue their feud with the bishop, they waited until he was away at the Estates and then seized and sold a shipment of his grain. As the prelate told the assembly, he had been compensated for the grain, but he was scandalized that it had been taken while being carried 'on his cart, pulled by his horses, led by his coachmen wearing his livery, for which they had neither respect nor consideration'. His real complaint was that, without cause, these people 'had lost all respect for his person and his character', and his most telling argument was that they had reached the point where 'they see him without saluting him'.[6] If authority was intangible, it was also thereby vulnerable because it required the maintenance of such a variety of signs of deference which had to be observed even in one's absence.

A more practical example of the principle that enforcement could only be achieved by seizing the tangible was the procedure used for collecting debts. What was owed could sometimes be seized in fields or shops, though this method presented the same difficulties as seizures of people. The tactic of sending huissiers to live off a debtor until he paid up was also useful in cases when this was physically possible. And if collectivities owed large sums, there were battles of personal arrests, as when Aymeric and Roquerlan, two bourgeois of Toulouse, each had the other arrested in Paris

[4] Narbonne, *Inventaire*, pp. 538–9.
[5] A.M. Tse BB 33, Apr. 14, 1643.
[6] P-V Nov. 20, 1649.

in a dispute over non-payment of municipal, not personal, debts.[7] The Estates applied this technique collectively by proclaiming *contrainte solidaire* against the merchant community of Toulouse for taxes the city owed the treasurer of the bourse, which meant that any merchant was liable to arrest in Toulouse or elsewhere and to incarceration in a jail in Montpellier for the debts of the city, a form of terrorism which was actually used on several occasions.[8]

These incidents highlight the fundamental lack of physical force available to local rulers. But why was there so little? Let us examine exactly what means of coercion did exist. One thinks first of royal troops, especially since they played a significant role in crushing the nearby communities of Guyenne. But in Languedoc the system of Estates seems to have warded off the worst of these evils. As we know, royal armies, sometimes very considerable ones, passed through the province continually during the frequent periods of war. When they were there en masse, as in 1645 and 1656, their presence was used to intimidate the province although this policy was notably unsuccessful in either year because massive troop lodgings stirred up the belligerence of local leaders without being able to threaten them with a worse fate than they were already experiencing. On a few occasions troops were called out to enforce the royal will, as when Schomberg stationed men on the outskirts of Toulouse to persuade the city to pay its taxes, or when Mende was pacified by a regiment of cavalry in 1660. After the uprising of 1645 there were rumors that Montpellier would be punished by force.[9] At a later date Louvois sometimes threatened to punish towns with lodgings. But within the province there were no intendants leading companies of soldiers, most likely because intendants did not collect the taille. On the whole, large armies were too critically needed on the frontier and too hard to manipulate to be used in any selective fashion.

Another military phenomenon was the use of permanent garrisons. The keystone in this system was the citadel of Montpellier built after 1622, but there were troops elsewhere, usually in older fortifications like the cité at Carcassonne and the fortress of Saint-André across the Rhône from Avignon. Lists of the effective forces in these ancient piles indicate that they were small and suggest that a good many may have been aging *mortes-payes* good only for guard duty.[10] In any event the numbers listed are misleading since Montpellier was supposed to have 400, but only forty

7 A.M. Tse BB 34, June 17–21, 1647.

8 A.M. Tse BB 36, Feb. 18, Aug. 7, 1657.

9 Baltazar to La Vrillière, Dec. 12, 1646: Lubl., p. 201.

10 Lists of garrison forces can be found in A.H. H 748[202], 400, 402 (for 1636); P-V April 7, 1661 (for 1661); Louvois to d'Aguesseau, Jan. 17, 1674: A.N. H 1695 (for 1674); Louvois to d'Aguesseau, Mar. 11, 1769: A.N. H 1700 (for 1679).

were available during the uprising of 1645, and those were very little help.[11] Probably the rest were in Catalonia. The presence of garrisons seems to have made some difference psychologically, especially in Montpellier and Narbonne, but there is hardly any record of their use in enforcement.

A more effective support could be provided by the company of guards of the governor or lieutenant general, for these personal followers could be counted on to reinforce the authority of their master in a disciplined way. Contingents of guards were used, starting in the 1650s, to back up intendants or commanders during particularly threatening missions. The lieutenant-general Bieules took twelve men with him when he went to pacify the city of Nîmes in 1657, though they do not seem to have played a very decisive role. A company of Orléans's light cavalry was financed from the receipts of the gabelle and used by the gabelle administration to enforce its regulations.[12] As a favor, governors sometimes 'lent' a few men to the intendant or the Estates to apply force in cases of difficult arrests or tax collections. They were used, for example, to back up the court of the Grands Jours in 1666.[13] The increasing use of such reinforcements in small affairs was a fact of government after 1660, but still rather specialized, since these soldiers were under the direct auspices of the commander.

In the countryside the *prévôté* provided another kind of police force. The *prévôt-général* was an officer who contracted with the Estates to 'see to the punishment of crimes, especially duels, and protect the security of the roads, the liberty of fairs and commerce, and the levy of the taille'.[14] He supervised the *lieutenants* named in each diocese by the assiette, who in turn commanded a company of *archers*. These road patrols were curious in that, being contractual jobs, they were properly performed only as long as they were profitable. There were even cases of non-residence, absurd in an office of enforcement, but there were also cases of spectacular captures.[15] During the regime of the Edict of Béziers the king made the prévôt and archers into royal officers, with the inevitable result that their wages were not paid and they ceased to function.[16] Afterwards things improved somewhat, but nobody had great faith in the system, least of all the intendants. 'Two guards will have a greater impact than ten archers', complained Bezons, and most others would have agreed. The prévôts were best suited to arrest beggars and protect the roads from bandits, but when it came to preventing

11 Schomberg to Séguier, July 4, 1645; Porchnev, p. 644; Baltazar to La Vrillière, Jan. 9, 1645; Lubl., p. 107.

12 Bezons to Colbert, Sept. 18, 1662; Mel. Col. III, 317.

13 Bezons to Colbert, Oct. 9, 1666: Mel. Col. 141, 220.

14 Contract of 1663: Roschach, vol. XIV, p. 820; P-V June 19, 1649. Little is written on the prévôté, but for general background see Tenaille Champton, *Histoire de la gendarmerie depuis sa création jusqu'en 1790* (Paris, 1829).

15 P-V Nov. 29, 1635, Sept. 23, 1641, Jan. 10, 1674.

16 P-V Mar. 12, 1648. But note the exception of the intendant Baltazar who made a client of the prévôt Bernole and used him against enemies like the second consul of Montpellier: Ms. fr. 17382, 28.

military disorders, arresting important persons, or collecting the taille, they were totally ineffective.[17]

In towns the situation was probably worse. Every major consulate had a *compagnie du guet* or some sort of municipal guard. In Toulouse the guet was a permanent corps of forty professional soldiers who were responsible for containing the crowds at public ceremonies, guarding executions, and patrolling the streets, especially at night. This brutal, negligent force was too small for even routine patrolling, and it was really best suited for providing escorts or breaking up drunken brawls. Like other towns, Toulouse also had a *garde bourgeoise*, but this corps of ten companies, each under a capitoul, seems to have been in decline in the seventeenth century and to have served only to guard the gates.[18] In real disturbances the guet was too incompetent and the militia too fickle to provide effective support. Neither of these forces played a constructive role in any of the many municipal disturbances of our period.

These various armed forces – royal armies, garrisons, guards, archers, guet – were sorely inadequate in numbers and skills to enforce commands or keep the peace. The reasons for this inadequacy were more fundamental than mere lack of manpower: the various forces were geographically dispersed and functionally divided because the authorities they represented were arranged likewise. They could not join together because of poor communications and because they only served under the direct orders of their often preoccupied commanders. Numbers were small partly because of the jealousy and suspicion which each authority felt for the others. How could the capitouls have had an effective police force in a city presided over by the Parlement? How could the Parlement have commanded a force which would have acted against the intendant or the Estates? An effective police would have required a conception of abstract justice and public interest which was totally lacking and would have violated the noble ethic of riding out with one's peers to meet danger. Much as they needed physical coercion individually, it is hard to see how the rulers of Languedoc, viewed collectively, could have tolerated it.

Since judicial processes were complex and ineffective and physical force was in rare supply, we can easily understand the preoccupation of public officials with certain recurrent themes about indirect enforcement. One was an almost metaphysical belief in the value of authority's 'presence', based on the assumption that society was essentially disorderly and that unless authority was regularly and visibly manifested, a sort of creeping debauchery

17 Bezons to Colbert, Oct. 9, 1666: Mel. Col. 141, 220. In 1670 the prévôt of Vivarais not only failed to put down a riot at Largentières, but saw his own house and possessions burned to the ground. Roschach, vol. XIV, p. 1123.

18 Edmond Lamouzèle, *Essai sur l'organisation et les fonctions de la compagnie du guet et de la garde bourgeoise de Toulouse* (Paris, 1906).

would gradually reassert itself. It was essential to restore the présidial to Montpellier from its exile in Lunel, argued Breteuil, because there was no one in Montpellier 'to maintain the people's respect, and many crimes have been committed in the last eight days in hopes of impunity'.[19] We have seen the claims of bishops, sovereign courts, and Estates that their own authority was essential in maintaining provincial social order. The king's support was similarly necessary. First President Maussac of the Comptes pleaded that some disciplinary stroke was needed against his recalcitrant officers 'even if this were only to show the people that the king leaves nothing unpunished when one disregards his orders'. Bertier had the same problem in the Parlement: 'if the heads of Parlements who are immediately dependent on the king and his ministers do not obtain protection when they are forced to oppose their companies, there will no longer be any means of serving well'.[20]

This need led to sensitivity concerning all aspects of symbolic authority. In 1651 the consuls of Narbonne decreed that 'in order to restore the splendor and authority of the consular livery which the current disorders have somewhat tarnished', they would henceforth be accompanied by two halberdiers in livery.[21] Bosquet insisted on appearing publicly in Toulouse in 1643 'to make it known to the people of this province that the intendancy has not been proscribed, since I exercise its functions in the capital city under the very nose of the Parlement, which is supposed to have nullified my commission'.[22] Thus public opinion was seen as highly responsive to nuances detected in public appearances and ceremonies. Tracts could also influence the climate of opinion by reinforcing or diminishing the aura of inviolability of the authorities they discussed. In 1644, learning that the Protestants were circulating a manuscript attacking the papal court of the late Urban VIII, Baltazar introduced an 'antidote' by circulating a printed account of the funeral eulogy of Urban VIII and the consecration of Innocent X. In 1646 he distributed a favorable report about the raising of the siege of Lerida to reinforce the public impression of the royal army's strength and to aid his negotiations with the Estates. Such national news was also a factor in the local mood, and it was unwise to push unpopular measures at moments when the royal armies were suffering setbacks.[23]

Another prominent tactic was exemplary punishment. Example was the best way to deter large groups of people from activities which could not be checked by direct surveillance. It had the merit of making the whole

19 Breteuil to Séguier, Aug. 5, 1647: ms. fr. 17387, 79.

20 Maussac to Séguier, Aug. 20, 1647: ms. fr. 17387, 104; Bertier to Séguier, May 12, 1646: Lubl., p. 187.

21 Narbonne, *Inventaire*, pp. 633–4 (Feb. 26, 1651).

22 Bosquet to Séguier, Aug. 12, 1643: Lubl., p. 38.

23 Baltazar to La Vrillière, Nov. 30, 1644: Lubl., p. 102. Baltazar to Mazarin, Dec. 12, 1646: A.A.E. France 1634, 261. See also Saint-Luc to Mazarin, Sept. 3, 1658: A.A.E. France 1637, 238.

group feel the seriousness and danger of an offense without having to identify or catch all of them. As the archbishop of Toulouse put it, 'the punishment of a squabble makes a dozen people behave, and there was never a region where there was greater need for some little examples from time to time than in Languedoc and Guyenne'.[24] The extravagant and unenforceable sentences issued so often against unreachable enemies performed the same function of making a public, though symbolic, point. Bosquet, speaking of trying the *payeur des gages* of the Parlement for attacking a sergeant, put it this way: 'he did not dare present himself, and I thought that his disobedience raised the penalty; and that setting an example in these times called for imposing the statutory penalty, which is death. When he has repaired his faults he will no doubt have means to diminish his crime.'[25] The death penalty did little more than indicate the seriousness of the offense here. A related tactic was the punishment *par contumace* of offenders who escaped the clutches of the law. Performing a public execution in effigy was almost as useful as the real thing in influencing public opinion and not nearly as embarrassing or irrevocable.

POTENTIAL THREATS: CONFLICT AMONG AUTHORITIES AND POPULAR REBELLION

In this sort of world order was a fragile, elusive quality upset by any number of outside circumstances. 'Order' meant a sort of ideal equilibrium between the different powers and ranks which would keep out the spectre of 'disorder', an evil contagion which reasserted itself the moment the balance of forces was disrupted. But if authority was so fragile, what sort of disorder threatened to upset it? The province had long passed out of its decentralized feudal phase when local nobles ruled directly over the people and supplied the necessary force to control them. Under absolutism the king had established a theoretical monopoly on significant political power which was largely unchallenged. But if territorial magnates no longer posed as rival sources of legitimacy, there was still the problem of private violence when notables took justice into their own hands in defense of honor or prestige. Petty tyrants terrorized backward valleys, and well-known figures perpetrated crimes of honor or passion. These were not only anachronistic feudal bullies like the marquis de Rabat who threatened the life of the bishop of Rieux or the band of nobles who pillaged and burned whole villages in Gévaudan, but also public personalities like Pierre de Crouzet, juge mage of Montpellier who attacked the treasurer-general Greffeuille's house with twelve 'gentlemen' in 1663, tearing up the garden, cutting down trees, and beating the servants half to death, or the various notables who

[24] Archbishop of Toulouse to Colbert, Dec. 10, 1667: Depping, vol. II, p. 181.

[25] Bosquet to Séguier, June 27, 1645: Lubl., p. 149.

tried to assassinate President Dupuy of the Comptes in 1647, Councillor Robin in 1657, and Councillor La Vallette of the présidial in 1680.[26] Such acts cannot be attributed solely to immorality or youth since they had a way of involving respected public figures. They embarrassed the authorities, but the ethic of personal honor was still powerful enough that, when they could, they looked the other way. The system could tolerate personal vengeance as long as it was kept under control, had no public implications (like an attack on someone performing an official act), and concerned only persons whose right to act this way would be understood by the public, thus offering no incitement to imitation among the general population.

A much more serious problem was the endemic outbreak of conflicts *among* authorities. These inevitable clashes were often acted out in public because the stakes involved public esteem, and they revolved around symbolic sanctions because genuine punishments would have been both unenforceable and undesirable. A graphic case was the quarrel of the Parlement with the archbishop of Toulouse in 1639 over whether the latter was obliged to kneel before the former when taking his yearly oath as honorary councillor in the Parlement. Condé, called in to mediate, ruled that Toulouse should take the oath on his knees just once and then appear without kneeling in the future. But this Solomon-like solution did not please the prelate. He appealed to the royal council which ruled that he could remain standing. In horror, the Parlement suspended and appealed this arrêt; but the next Sunday the archbishop mounted the pulpit and formally excommunicated six high-ranking members of the court. Then the Parlement issued a penalty of 6,000 livres if the archbishop would absolve them, and if not, condemned him to a fine of 10,000 livres and seizure of all his temporal goods, while instructing the nearest prelate to excommunicate him in return. The stir that this affair made in Paris caused the matter to be smoothed over, but the issue was not finally settled until 1679.[27] Sentences of this kind were obviously symbolic: nobody expected the archbishop's goods to be confiscated or the leading parlementaires to remain for long in threat of external damnation. What was at stake was the authority of these two powers in Toulouse, as evidenced by simultaneous quarrels over practical matters like the management of the *hôpital général*. The real purpose of these sentences was, on the one hand, to play for public support and, on the other, to lay the groundwork for harassment of subordinates.

The clashes of authorities were not as frivolous as they seem. The quarrel of the dissidents in Mende with their bishop in 1646 led to pro- and anti-episcopal assiettes being held simultaneously; their contradictory tax

[26] On Rabat, Roschach, vol. XIV, pp. 176–180, 191; Dubédat, vol. II, pp. 237–8; on Gévaudan, Roschach, vol. XIV, p. 690; on Crouzet, C. Barrière-Flavy, *La Chronique criminelle d'une grande province sous Louis XIV* (Paris, 1926), pp. 60–2; on Dupuy, ms. fr. 18483, 206–7; on Robin and La Vallette, Barrière-Flavy, *Chronique*, pp. 61–2.

[27] Dubédat, vol. II, pp. 214–18.

rolls jeopardized taille collections in the whole diocese.[28] Public displays could accredit or discredit companies at moments of stress. An absurd conflict in 1645 between the cathedral canons of Montpellier and the councillors of the Comptes over the placement of a bench in the cathedral during a *Te Deum* service led to undignified pushing and shoving only a month after a serious popular uprising. Bosquet, who sided with the Comptes, considered the matter dangerous enough to public order to write to Paris about it:

It is important for you not to expose to everyone's contempt a sovereign company which must be preserved in its prerogatives and advantages in order to retain some authority over the people of this town, who view it as a corps composed of the most important inhabitants.... Agitators are secretly fomenting divisions which can only weaken the respect of the people towards the officers and diminish the authority which these officers could have if their honor were maintained.[29]

In 1649 when a soldier from the citadel of Montpellier insulted the syndic-general of the Estates, such a conflict developed between the Estates and the présidial over the right to punish him that the présidial expelled its *doyen* and several members for having ties to the Estates, and the Estates induced the Comptes to join it in a resolution that the présidial be transferred to Nîmes. Meanwhile the poor soldier was being moved from prison to prison as one side or another claimed the right to hold him and enforced the claim by assaulting the jail or the jailer.[30]

The reason for these incidents was lack of any other means for conflicting corps to get at each other. In any physical confrontation each side would be shut within its palace, unmovable without a military siege. Messengers, huissiers, or prisoners were the only physically accessible targets for insults and symbolic executions. The result was curious wars in which the chief campaigns involved armed attempts to hinder the publication of edicts by the rival's trumpeter, attacks on local prisons to free an arrested agent, and extensive conferences in front of the locked door of enemy companies, all of these accompanied by lengthy procès-verbaux detailing the insults suffered.[31] Such affairs were serious, for however petty the incidents in the streets may have seemed, they demonstrated that local authorities were neutralized in a stand-off fight which would discredit all involved and which could only be resolved by a higher power – the king. Moreover, the accounts often mention crowds gathering to jeer at one side or the other – or both – in a manner that would have given pause to any ruler.

Cases of popular unrest were, in fact, another major source of concern. But what sort of unrest? Petty crimes were rampant in large towns like

[28] Ferdinand André, ed., *Procès-verbaux des délibérations des états du Gévaudan*, 6 vols. (Mende, 1876–80), vol. I, pp. 228–37. [29] Bosquet to La Vrillière, Aug. 1, 1645: Lubl., p. 149.

[30] P-V Aug. 31, Sept. 3, 6, 13, 1649; Breteuil to Séguier, Sept. 3, 1649: Lubl., p. 214.

[31] One example: Roschach, vol. XIV, p. 93.

Toulouse where the streets were unsafe at night; where taverns, balls, and the passage of troops always seemed pregnant with potential brawls and assassinations. Barrière-Flavy, who studied the records of the Parlement's *Tournelle*, notes prostitution rings, student gangs attacking inns and convents for sport, and a genuine crime wave which hit the major hôtels in 1664–5. Beggars also provided a constant menace, distracting worshippers in the churches and molesting people at markets and fairs, or distinguished citizens to the point where periodic steps had to be taken to lock them up.[32] But this undercurrent of disorderliness was not the threat that we would expect because prosperous individuals moved only in environments which they dominated by means of an entourage of loyal servants and retainers. Though popular criminality had to be kept under control and special outrages had to be severely punished, this turbulence only confirmed the rulers' belief in the boorishness and unreliability of the populace when left to its own devices.

The real threat came from the possibility of popular resistance to authority, precisely because the common masses were viewed as irrational and unpredictable. Nobody minded an organized *charivari* against some hated *partisan*, provided that leadership was discreet and the action contained within predictable channels. But the crowd was fickle, and popular indignation was likely to well up at unexpected moments. When times were bad, people muttered in the streets or posted seditious bills on the doors of official buildings, spreading rumors about impending catastrophes which heightened tensions. Then sentiments were heard like the Toulouse merchant whose retort to a capitoul's attempt to collect his tax was 'that if everyone thought as he did there would soon be fire in the houses of all the capitouls'.[33] Women assembled menacingly to challenge the price of grain or to impede its transport out of town; relatives or friends rioted to free prisoners being taken to the gallows or to break open the doors of prisons, in imitation, perhaps, of their magistrates; attacks were perpetrated on gabelle agents and toll collectors.

Since the work of Porchnev, scholars have debated the degree to which these incidents presented a revolutionary threat to the social order. I am not convinced that they constituted the primary class struggle in seventeenth-century France, nor that the chief concern of the rulers of Languedoc was keeping the masses in check. However, popular disturbances of this sort (as distinguished from many other kinds of crowd actions) *could* be spontaneous and *did* present a serious threat to authorities for two other reasons: first, because they undermined the symbolic authority of consuls or officers who had to battle them virtually single-handed; second, because

[32] Barrière-Flavy, *Chronique*, pp. 10–18; A.M. Tse BB 34, 79–83.

[33] Barnabé Farmian de Rozoi, *Annales de la ville de Toulouse*, 4 vols. (Paris, 1771–6), vol. IV, p. 401.

these little riots, though they usually subsided without serious aftereffects, had the potential of becoming major revolts which could paralyze local government. Such spectacles of the populace gone wild, 'these horrible pictures of sedition, these views of men and women massacred without pity, these houses pillaged and burned whose sad remains mingled the richest furnishings with corpses', as the eyewitness Schomberg put it, were always in the minds of contemporaries, as were fears of contagion from neighboring provinces where riots were much worse: 'we have never seen this much disorder in neighboring provinces without experiencing a corresponding effect in this town'.[34]

The social fear of what *could* happen was shared by all authorities, but especially by the most eminent because they had the most authority to lose. It was not so much that they feared personal assassination, deposition, or expropriation of property, for these possibilities were reasonably remote. Few riots lasted more than hours or days, during which time most notables were safe if they stayed out of the way. Rather an uprising was a *governmental* catastrophe for them, an uncontrollable deterioration of prestige and authority. Terrible risks then had to be taken, bad examples were set, and humiliation was ever-present, the aftermath of which was bound to be an investigation, recrimination, and possibly royal punishment.

We can get a good idea of the sort of potential nightmare that was in the mind of officials by looking in on one such outburst in Toulouse in 1635.[35] News of the trouble moving up the Garonne from Bordeaux had led to a state of popular effervescence. On May 31 the capitouls complained that 'there are quantities of mutineers and libertines in town who commit all sorts of excesses every day, beating and attacking soldiers of the guet'. On June 22, when news arrived of the latest riot in Bordeaux, they resolved that although 'the people of Toulouse are full of good will toward the king and are obedient to messieurs of the Parlement and to justice', they should nevertheless undertake the precautions which in Bordeaux 'would have saved the hôtel de ville'. A general assembly was called that afternoon at which the representatives of all the corps were reminded by the capitouls of 'what we owe to our king, the most just and victorious in the whole world', and that 'we must not act like our neighbors'. Then First President Bertier delivered an inspirational oration, asserting that 'enemies of the state' were spreading lies to foment 'abominable seditions', and that Toulouse, 'the second city in the kingdom', must resist by naming captains of each quarter and instituting night patrols. These pronouncements, which

[34] Schomberg to Estates, Nov. 28, 1645: Roschach, vol. XIV, pp. 100–2; Bertier to Séguier, June 3, 1647: Roland Mousnier, ed., *Lettres et mémoires adressés au Chancelier Séguier (1633–1649)*, 2 vols. (Paris, 1964), vol. I, p. 378.

[35] This entire account is contained in A.M. Tse BB 30, 384–411.

betray the real concerns of the officials about order and property and illustrate their attempt to rally local patriotism in defense of authority, were followed by general acclamations of 'Vive le Roy'. But three days later the capitouls arrested their own municipal glazier for uttering 'statements tending to sedition' and planning an attack on the hôtel de ville and on 'many persons of quality'. His case was taken over by the Parlement, which condemned him to public strangulation and instructed the capitouls to carry out the sentence. When the guet was trying to escort him back from the Parlement to the hôtel de ville, a riot broke out which forced a hasty retreat. The victim's mother-in-law suddenly threw herself upon the prisoner, cutting his ropes with a knife and screaming 'that he was going to die for the gabelle', while a large crowd threw rocks at the guards. This was the signal for 'an uprising of the people all over the city, with such alarm ensuing that all the shops were closed in a minute, and the streets barricaded and chained'. The two capitouls on duty had to get on horseback accompanied only by their valets, make their way through a large crowd of porters who were shouting 'long live the king without the gabelle', and ride all alone in different directions through the streets to calm the crowd. One of them rescued a captain of the bourgeois guard from an angry crowd of 500 persons who surged around the capitoul's horse, demanding their prisoner back. Meanwhile the Parlement had closed the Porte Saint-Michel right outside its palais, and inhabitants of the faubourg Saint-Michel were piling carts of straw against the outside of it to burn it down.

All that night chains remained up, and the tocsin rang continuously, but after the execution of the glazier in the yard of the Parlement, the crowds subsided. The powder keg atmosphere continued for several weeks afterwards, however. 'Persons of authority' continued to barricade their own houses, and 'instead of marching as they should', the artisans in the night patrol manifested their insouciance: 'some beat on the doors of the houses they pass and others shout incessantly, make noise, and commit all sorts of insolence'. Meanwhile there were rumours that the présidial had questioned the authority of Parlement and capitouls during the crisis, and there were eyebrows raised when the Parlement added a new gate to its palais – signs of disarray among the authorities.

The 1635 flareup was hardly calamitous in terms of actual damage done, and it was not even one of the major disturbances of our period, but it illustrates well the sort of situation which authorities frequently confronted, their poverty of remedies, and their extremely defensive impulses.[36] Social fear, fed by horror stories from other provinces and frequent near-misses at home, was very real, and played a significant part in the dilemma of authority.

[36] For other accounts, see chapter 13.

A CRISIS OF AUTHORITY

Thus a fragmented, symbolic authority was confronted with a variety of challenges: the need to dominate a poor and dissatisfied population; maintenance of at least the principle of law and order with respect to the independently powerful; regulation of jurisdictional conflicts among the different authorities; exorcism of the threat of social insurrection. These challenges point to the need for a coordinated effort among governmental powers and, consequently, to a royal absolutism which could coordinate the system from above. But, in the first half of our period, events seemed to be conspiring to undermine every one of these governmental imperatives. Problems which could have been handled individually piled up, creating what can only be called a crisis of authority. This was not a general social crisis, but something more diffuse: a crisis of political adjustment which left the door open for isolated manifestations of class struggle and threatened the effective functioning of the entire system. The problem was not as visible or all-encompassing as a civil war or an open confrontation of classes. It was a cumulative deterioration of political relations, the extent of which can only be appreciated by noting the number of distinct, but related conflicts which were taking place concurrently between 1630 and 1660.

In Toulouse, for example, rivalries between the Parlement and the capitouls, revolving formally around authority in the city but harking ultimately back to issues of taxation, reached a peak during these years.[37] Leading parlementaires were not cooperating in paying their taille at a time when the capitouls were under great financial pressure. In 1643 there were signs of a real break in relations. The Parlement refused to prosecute two of its members who had assaulted a capitoul. It denounced two capitouls as grain hoarders and issued other provocative arrêts which created an atmosphere in which several small grain riots occurred. Then, in the spring of 1644, it rejected the novel *joyeux avènement* tax which was being assessed by a traditional authority rival, the juge mage Caulet. These episodes launched a factional struggle within the municipal government. When the conseil de bourgeoisie sent a deputation to Paris to appeal against the Parlement's high-handed maneuvers, these deputies obtained an *évocation générale* transferring all cases concerning the capitouls and bourgeois of Toulouse to the Parlement of Grenoble and engineered a coup whereby Gaston d'Orléans, the new governor of Languedoc, appointed their slate of candidates for the capitoulat of 1645 without allowing a 'free' election. The Parlement and another faction of the bourgeoisie opposed this move

[37] This account is a synthesis of all the sources on the capitouls and the Parlement cited in the bibliography.

vigorously, and a legal war ensued in which the Parlement and the royal council fired arrêts at each other for several months and served them on unwilling representatives of the other faction in church, on the street, or wherever someone could be caught unawares. Once installed, the new nominees retaliated by firing all municipal employees. Then the parlementaires, answering the appeals of the pro-Parlement faction in the city government, started issuing warrants against capitouls who violated their ordinances, until by fall only three of the eight were left at large, the other five having fled to Paris. Another round of feuds and arrests followed in 1646, climaxed by the storming and taking of the maison de ville by dissident parlementaires and excluded capitouls.

In Montpellier developing rivalries converged in a parallel manner into general conflict by the 1640s.[38] In 1641 the work of the bourgeois financial committee which drew up the all-important municipal tax assessments was disrupted by rival claims of regulatory powers asserted by the juge mage Trinquere and the Comptes. In 1644 the seriousness of the issue deepened when the intendant Baltazar entered the fray with his own bid to monitor the tax committee. There were clashes at meetings between the Comptes and the intendant, and by autumn two rival camps had emerged. One group led by Benjamin Carbon, second consul and *clavaire* (tax collector), claimed that the financial committee had been illegally packed with friends of the opposition. This group formed a 'syndicate' of concerned citizens to appeal to the Comptes, which used the opportunity to issue arrêts deposing the 'illegal' committee members and to monitor tax assessments. The other group, led by the first consul Girard and supported by Baltazar, saw these arguments and the 'syndicate' as a power play by the Comptes to seize authority over tax collections. The climax of the controversy was the public humiliation of Baltazar's subordinates by councillors from the Comptes. This incident, along with the disunion and reunion of the Comptes, has been discussed in chapter 4. In 1651 the first consul was murdered. In 1652 the governor of the citadel cancelled the election altogether to avoid 'friction and differences between the seneschal and the juge mage'. Then Protestants began to demand restoration of their representation in the consulate, and nobles of each religion held secret meetings amidst rising threats of violence. No elections were held at all from 1651 to 1657, when only two of the original consuls of 1651 were still alive and functioning.[39]

The climate in other towns was no better. Nîmes was another violent, factionally-divided city where groups took arms in 1645 to free men arrested for billonnage, the illegal traffic in defective coinage; in 1650 to fight over the conversion of a Protestant boy, forcing the bishop who was guarding

[38] This too is a synthesis of all the materials on Montpellier in the bibliography.
[39] A.M. Mp Joffre 10, 'élections consulaires', 222–40, 254–9.

the convert to flee the city; in 1655 to snipe at royal troops which had massacred the Vaudois; and in 1656–7 to form two armed parties, one of which opened fire on the bishop, the intendant, and the lieutenant-general.[40] In Mende the town was in continuous turmoil from 1639 to 1660, as the enemies of the bishop (called 'catarinots') fought for power against his allies (the 'marmeaux').[41] The bishop, Sylvestre de Crusy de Marcillac, surrounded himself with 600 armed men and threw his rival, Charles de Colomb, judge of the bailliage of Gévaudan, into prison. Escaping in 1644, Colomb returned to Mende in March 1645 with a band of eighty followers, invaded the cathedral during a service, and 'almost killed' the bishop at the altar. When Marcillac obtained arrêts de conseil continuing his allies in office for a second year because of this 'disorder', his enemies elected three anticonsuls, seized the keys to the city, and made life so unpleasant for Marcillac and his allies that the bishop had to leave town. In 1650 the city was occupied by men who 'sauntered through town with pistols in their hands and swords at their sides uttering threats against many inhabitants'.[42]

A similar movement against the bishop erupted in Albi.[43] There were secret meetings and assemblies of armed factions, culminating in open intimidation at the election of September 1646. The prelate claimed that his enemies had terrorized the families of eighty supporters and forced them to flee town; meanwhile the consuls vilified him for building a secret gate in the wall of his palace so that soldiers could be sneaked inside. There were fights in the streets, and at one point barricades were thrown up by townsmen in front of the bishopric. Finally, after five years of lawsuits, the Parlement of Grenoble ruled in favor of the bishop, banished a number of citizens, and levied heavy indemnities which only increased the local tax burden.

Angry citizens of Narbonne invaded their council meeting 'tumultuously' in 1635 to demand revision of the *compoix cabaliste*, and at the next election a 'syndicate' of these people began trying to block the usual procedures. In 1640 we learn of a secret meeting of 'artisans' at a mill, from which emerged a new law suit against the current compoix and the clavaire. By 1641 this movement had resulted in another expensive law suit which went to the Cour des Comptes and the royal council. Clearly the problem continued to agitate the public, for we learn of two different goldsmiths and a tinsmith refusing angrily to pay their taxes, and the wives of two 'sieurs' insulting the consuls' deputies while they investigated the

[40] The Nîmes incidents are discussed in the Séguier correspondence and the municipal archives cited in the bibliography.

[41] See the sources for Mende cited in the bibliography, and ms. fr. 17656, 18; ms. fr. 18601, 327, 329.

[42] Charles Porée, *Le Consulat et l'administration municipale de Mende (des origines à la Révolution)* (Paris, 1901), p. lxii.

[43] A.M. Albi BB 10, BB 11, FF 146, FF 147.

compoix.[44] Most likely the defiance of Pierre Gabriel, who 'pissed on a counter in the large consistory of the maison consulaire' in 1646, as well as the enormous election disturbance of 1647 were related to the same grievances.[45]

By 1644 the faction in power in Béziers was fighting to perpetuate its rule against enemies who represented a 'reform' slate focusing on frauds in the municipal butchers' contract. Bolstered by an ordinance of Baltazar, the incumbents extended their term of office in November, 1644. The reformers then obtained a new election by arrêt de conseil in September 1645, ousted their opponents, and set up a board of *policiens* which found evidence of widespread fraud. In December Bosquet arranged a compromise slate, but on January 9, 1646, at a meeting where common women were testifying about the illegal price of pork, the two sides began a shouting match which soon deteriorated into armed bands roaming the streets insulting and attacking their adversaries. Three men were killed including the first consul, and others were wounded.[46] Open trouble also broke out at the elections of 1647, 1650, 1651, 1657, 1658, and 1664.

These conflicts were all happening in the same years, and many more could be cited. They illustrate a serious crisis of authority made up of innumerable petty disputes, each of them distinct and local, but coordinated by a common political climate, common superior officials, and mutual exchange of information. Their cadence was so similar because the participants took advantage of the same moments of royal weakness and responded to the same stimuli of taxes and edicts. The different kinds of threats to authority multiplied simultaneously, each making the other more dangerous. Conjunctural factors (a cycle of plagues, harvests, and mortalities, intensified by higher royal exactions and repeated passages of troops) raised the level of popular discontent and increased the number of beggars, criminals, and spontaneous disturbances. Meanwhile the new intensity of taxation led to protracted disputes in every town over assessments, debts, and provisioning, disputes in which rival authorities fought for greater control over this newly controversial fiscal functioning. Popular effervescence encouraged power rivals to gather a following among the population and raise the intensity of confrontation, but at the same time the blockage of authority caused by power rivalries could leave the way open for unintended and uncontrollable popular revolt. As d'Argenson told the Estates in 1647,

> if individuals who have no part in public affairs fall into disorders, there is little inconvenience for the public interest. But when such disorders pass into the minds

[44] Narbonne, *Inventaire*, Aug. 19–21, 1635, Feb. 2, 1636, Mar. 12, 1636, July 6, 1640, Apr. 30, Nov. 5, 1641, Feb. 8, 1643, Nov. 26, 1643, June 11, 1645, Nov. 7, 1647, Jan. 17, 1644.

[45] Ibid., Oct. 1, 16, 1646, Apr. 28-Sept. 1, 1647.

[46] Ms. fr. 18600, 17; ms. fr. 18830, 240–3.

of the state's greatest figures and of the multitude, then men, grounded in their material condition, no longer heed the spirit [of orderly submission] which they cannot perceive and which they have resisted so many times before.[47]

Meanwhile it was harder to resolve these conflicts because the superiors who should have regulated them were themselves in difficulty. The intendants Bosquet and Baltazar ruled against each other in these disputes. Parlement and Comptes took different sides. The royal council of the minority wavered back and forth.

Authority, the glue that held political society together, was still widely diffused under absolutism and contingent upon a shaky balance of forces. The principle of undivided loyalty to the monarchy was firmly established. But under the absolutist 'umbrella' a 'feudal' diversity of gradations of influence and overlapping spheres still prevailed which presented serious social dangers. Popular unrest was an ever-present threat because the population was highly prone to violent expressions of dissatisfaction which, if not isolated, could easily expand into organized movements. Authority conflicts, though distinct, discredited the forces needed to pacify the people and encouraged factional rabble-rousing which fanned the flames of rebellion.

Having gathered all political power unto itself, royal absolutism had not yet learned to coordinate effectively the interests of those who shared it or to weather the moments when warfare and central weakness eliminated the conditions necessary for the fragile climate of obedience. Faced with these conditions, the rulers of Languedoc seemed only able to defend their power by flailing at each other.

[47] D'Argenson to Estates, April 3, 1647: Roschach, vol. XIV, p. 150.

9

The prospects for provincial solidarity

It is easy to emphasize the conflicts which divided the rulers of Languedoc and the inadequacies of their authority, but it is also important not to lose sight of their fundamental solidarity of interests. Let us examine this other side of the coin. The rulers shared similar social and economic backgrounds. They aspired after the same goals and were enraged by the same 'abuses', most of which seemed to be encroachments on their prerogatives by an overbearing state machine. Given the seriousness of the crisis of relations between 1620 and 1660, we might well ask whether they could not have joined forces in an alliance to protect themselves from royal innovations. This question is especially important because the usual interpretation sees the provinces reacting defensively against an assault by the centralizing state, and the followers of Mousnier argue that the provincial orders and corps fought as units against the encroachments of the crown. What were the prospects for such provincial solidarity?

Consider the elements that were available in Languedoc: a province with long-established historical borders and a tradition of unified action; the rudiments of a constitution in the form of a set of frequently-reiterated privileges and a certain legal tradition; a governing class with no essential economic interests dividing it. Starting with these elements, we can imagine a functional division of labor in which the Estates would set policy, allocate resources, and administer the most effective tax-collecting machinery in France; the Parlement would put its immense moral prestige and social influence at the disposal of the province by issuing supportive arrêts and prosecuting violators; the Cour des Comptes would investigate financial disorders, regulate tax farms, and resolve fiscal disputes with the same authority enjoyed by the Parlement. All three would administer the functioning of the organisms under them – the présidial courts, the treasurer-generals of finance, and the assiettes. Urban oligarchies would manage the towns. Since a regional particularism of this sort was the only viable alternative to the centralized absolutism we are studying, the history of its success or failure is a matter of compelling interest.

The fact is that important attempts at provincial collaboration were made in Languedoc between 1620 and 1660. Their history takes the form of provincial campaigns of self-defense, sporadic in timing but cumulative in the sense that they followed a certain developing logic and that the experience of the participants, most of whom belonged to only two generations of a closely-related circle of families, was cumulative. Each episode explored the balance of power between a triangle of forces: the absolute monarchy, trying to streamline its governmental control over the province in order to meet the crises it faced, but needing the support of provincial leaders to do this effectively; the rulers of Languedoc, desiring to resist but needing ways of uniting among themselves and having to mobilize support among the population in order to do so; 'the people', or more precisely many different groups of common people, whose respect and support was necessary to the rulers' success but whose agitations could easily get out of hand. Each episode also revolved around a basic question: could the provincial authorities extract what they wanted from the monarchy while maintaining their dominant hold over local society and keeping their peace with each other?

RESISTANCE STRATEGY AND THE ÉLUS (1622–32)

Because the rulers of Languedoc based their authority on delegation from the king, the ideal collaboration had to be within the framework of loyalty to the crown, and it had to be Catholic. For these reasons the Huguenot resistance organizations of the 1620s were not appropriate antecedents although they no doubt provided useful lessons for potential organizers.[1] A better place to begin is the defense of the franc alleu, which contained in embryo many of the themes to be developed in the future.

In 1622 the king sold the right to collect lost revenues of the royal domain in Languedoc to two *traitants*, Étienne Goutte and David Falc, who announced a *recherche* to this effect.[2] Their investigation required all those holding seigneurial rights to present written proof of these on pain of confiscation. But the provincial right of franc alleu stipulated that lands were considered free of obligations to a lord (in this case the king) unless the *lord* could produce written evidence to the contrary. Dismay was widespread. In 1623 the Estates protested this violation of provincial privilege. Then the Parlement suspended the royal treaty and issued a warrant for Falc's arrest, which produced a counter-arrêt from the Chambre des Comptes instructing the traitants to proceed with the execution of the treaty (note the conflict of jurisdictions here). Soon the

1 Steven Lowenstein, 'Resistance to Absolutism: Huguenot Organization in Languedoc 1621–1622', Ph.D. dissertation, Princeton University, 1972.

2 This entire episode is analyzed in Jean Bastier, 'Une Résistance fiscale du Languedoc sous Louis XIII: la querelle du franc-alleu', *Annales du Midi*, 86 (1974), 253–73.

Estates, using the Parlement's arrêt as legitimation, sent five of its members with the captain of the guet of Béziers to arrest Falc and throw him in prison (note the attempt at practical enforcement). They repeated the same trick in 1626; then in 1627 they appealed to the king while suing the traitants in the Parlement, the Comptes, and the *bureaux des finances*. Liaison with the Parlement was provided by the syndic-general Lamamie, whose Toulousain family connections gave him the ear of the procureur-general Saint-Félix.[3] The new appeals were printed and distributed to the consuls of all the major towns, and all authorities were enjoined to use them to defend individuals molested by the traitants while the syndic-generals toured their districts lending legal aid to anyone who needed it, at the expense of the province. This movement, which was at least temporarily successful, demonstrates the range of quasi-legal obstruction tactics which could be mobilized with a little coordination among certain of the authorities.

In 1629 a more serious threat required an extension of these tactics. The very existence of the provincial constitution was called into question by the government's plan to impose an alternative tax administration on the province.[4] Twenty-two *bureaux* of élus comprising 490 new venal officers would replace the assiettes in repartitioning and receiving diocesan taxes. The treasurer-generals of finance would handle receipts from each *bureau*, and disputes would pass on appeal from them to the newly-united Cour des Comptes, Aides et Finances. The Estates, though not literally abolished, were left without any function.

Such provocation called for a strong provincial response, and the Estates initiated a two-pronged campaign. While the syndic-general Lamotte worked from November 1629 to April 1630 to negotiate a compromise settlement in Paris, Lamamie began to organize local meetings of municipal authorities in towns having entrance to the Estates, in which notables drew up notarized protests against the élus and named deputies who were officially empowered to appeal on their behalf.[5] The officers of the Estates were in effect engendering local support groups which could continue to agitate in the absence of Estates or assiettes.

In the summer of 1630, when the seriousness of the matter had been driven home by the fact that the Estates had not been called at all in 1630, the Parlement rejected and suspended both the élus and the union of the Comptes which Richelieu had arranged in 1629. The cardinal was so angry that an arrêt de conseil was issued summoning leading parlementaires

[3] Paul Gachon, *Les États de Languedoc et l'édit de Béziers (1632)* (Paris, 1887), pp. 201–19; Dubédat, vol. II, pp. 149–52.

[4] This crisis is analyzed in detail in Gachon, *États*.

[5] Gachon, *États*, pp. 208–9.

to court to explain their actions. Meanwhile there was scattered local resistance to the élus, like the refusal of the consuls of Nîmes, led by the Protestant Vestric who would be a perpetual agitator in years to come, to install them.[6] It is not clear how many other such incidents occurred, but there is no evidence of real disorder. A more decisive round of local agitation took place in the spring of 1632 when these talks were lagging and the government was undermining its promises by instructing the treasurer-generals and the élus to collect taxes for 1632. On May 4 the Estates sent a member into each diocese 'to inform his community of the preoccupations and duties of this assembly and see that no imposition is levied except by our orders'.[7] This move, intensifying the earlier campaign by mandating resistance to tax collections, produced a wave of alarm in Paris. Lamotte and Lamamie toured the province again during June, and in their wake the municipal councils met one after another and denounced the tax rolls drawn up by the élus. This orchestrated municipal resistance was so effective that taxes became uncollectable, and most offices of élus remained unsold.[8]

At this point the Estates were drawn into the foolhardy rebellion led by Montmorency and Gaston d'Orléans which submerged their institutional sabotage in an irrelevant feudal escapade. Such military resistance could only be useful if it was carefully shielded by the pseudo-legitimacy of a great noble patron and if it was militarily successful, thereby forcing the king into more accommodating terms. Otherwise it simply created the conditions for arbitrary change by drawing in the king and his army. Realizing their blunder, the Estates immediately repented and provided no collective support to the rebellion. When the dust had settled, Montmorency and other rebels had been punished and the Edict of Béziers had imposed a more restrictive régime on the province, but the élus were gone and the administration of the Estates continued. This solution had already been in the works and owed nothing to the rebellion.

Thus from the point of view of providing collaboration, the importance of the élus crisis lay in the institutional resistance movement which had made it impossible, or at least too costly, for the élus regime to function and forced the government to redesign its assertion of control to fit the contours of the existing system. The success belonged almost entirely to the Estates, resting on the supple network of relations between bishops, barons, their home dioceses, and the towns – relations which were coordinated by the vigorous 'executive' management of the syndic-generals. The most effective resistance had not entailed fomenting popular riots or joining military rebellions. Rather, its success entailed fomenting the grassroots

6 Ibid., p. 219.
7 A.D. Hér C 8290; letter in Gachon, *États*, p. 282.
8 Gachon, *États*, pp. 234–7, 241.

institutional rejection of a novel administration, the élus, in favor of a familiar one.[9]

THE TAX CRISIS OF 1645–6

The tough atmosphere of Richelieu's wartime regime raised the intensity of conflict, and the decision to regulate rather than abolish the Estates forced the royal government to deal with the existing system in new ways. While no structural reforms were possible, the government had a certain tactical advantage because it was easier to harass existing agencies by imposing arbitrary expedients than to make structural alternatives work, like the élus. Provincial resistance could only go so far, after which each institution had to fend off greater evils by accepting lesser ones. The Estates bought off edicts which threatened their privileges and administration, shifting the expense onto direct taxation. The sovereign courts registered unpopular tax edicts in order to avoid creation of new officers, chambers or companies. These compromises raised anxieties about public support and set one company against another.[10] At the same time such measures were dependent on royal strength. When Louis XIII died, each provincial institution tried to turn back the clock. The Parlement outlawed non-registered *commissions extraordinaires*; the Estates cancelled their recent *subvention* contract;[11] certain dioceses resisted arbitrary tax assessments by the intendants in response to the Estates' repeated calls for rejection of unconsented sums.[12]

Momentum was building for a serious crisis. First there was the reaction to the *joyeux avènement* tax, an assessment for the confirmation of the privileges of corporate groups at the beginning of a new reign which threatened not only higher corporate entities, but by extension artisans, innkeepers, and other groups from the *menu peuple*. In the spring of 1644 the Parlement made a fuss over its collection with the encouragement of the Estates' syndic-general, and the deputies of both the Estates and the Parlement negotiated in Paris for its reduction.[13] Then attention turned to the impending quartier d'hiver. It was clear to everyone that there was going

[9] The Parlement had played a surprisingly small role in this effort. Its arrêts of 1631 had no doubt helped the cause, but in a case of direct taxation its legitimation was not needed in order to act. When the Montmorency revolt broke out the parlementaires would have no part of it. A.D. H.-G. B 1879, 91, 97, 100.

[10] P-V Dec. 13, 1639.

[11] A.D. H-G. B 1879, 383; Malenfant, II, 330–8; Bertier to Séguier, May 4, 1644: Lubl., p. 62; P-V Oct. 30, Nov. 10–11, 1643; Bosquet to Séguier, Oct. 2, 1643; Lubl., p. 41 (letter misdated – must be Nov. 2); Schomberg to Séguier, Nov. 5, 1643: Lubl., p. 45.

[12] Baltazar to Mazarin, May 4, 1644: A.A.E. France 1634, 38; Schomberg to Séguier, *c.* June 18, 1644: ms. fr. 17379, 123.

[13] A.D. H-G. B 1879, 415; Maniban to Séguier, July 25, 1644: ms. fr. 17380, 23; Bertier to Séguier, Aug. 4, 1644: ms. fr. 17380, 63; Baltazar to La Vrillière, Sept. 20, 1644: A.A.E. France 1634, 50.

to be a showdown in the Estates over this heavy burden which provincial leaders were determined to refuse as a way of relieving the province and invoking their much-abused right of consent. What they probably had in mind was the sort of institutional rejection, coupled with popular support, which had worked so well with the élus. But conditions were not ideal for collaboration. Already the Parlement was feuding with the capitouls in the streets of Toulouse, troop embarcations were causing popular unrest, and factional battles were brewing in many of the towns. The royal intendants, Bosquet and Baltazar, were themselves fighting, but they were prepared to levy the quartier d'hiver by force if necessary. Bosquet stressed that such an operation would have to be carefully planned because the people would resist stubbornly 'by order of the Estates, whose instructions they have a habit of embracing obstinately'.[14] When councillors from the Comptes organized a public humiliation of one of Baltazar's agents in their conflict over the Montpellier tax records, they shouted 'no quartier d'hiver!' to arouse the sympathies of the bystanders. It was rumored that certain bishops of Haut-Languedoc had met to plot against the quartier d'hiver before they went to the Estates.[15]

When the Estates finally opened in Narbonne in January 1645, the deputies arrived full of indignation at the atrocities already committed by passing troops. They immediately resolved that 'since the most important of their privileges and the one most essential for the welfare and relief of this province is to maintain the right that nothing can be imposed without consent', all authorities were to *resist* the repartition of unconsented sums on dioceses and communities.[16] The session was stormy and unproductive. The deputies rejected the quartier d'hiver over and over, despite long negotiations. As for the joyeux avènement tax, they declared impudently that its collection was to be suspended until the king's commissioners had chastized the traitants 'by impounding in their offices enough money to cover the fees they have collected [for illicit reasons]'.[17] But the echoes of the 1620s were now more serious. When the deputies went home, the scene had been set for widespread resistance to the quartier d'hiver. Local agents had been instructed to resist its imposition, and popularity had been generated by casting aspersions on the legitimacy of the joyeux avènement tax. The intendants and Schomberg proceeded cautiously with the repartition of the unconsented quartier d'hiver money, making a point of starting with dioceses where they anticipated compliance. This effort at good public relations was counteracted, however, by the Estates' instructions

14 Bosquet to Mazarin, Oct. 10, 1644: A.A.E. France 1643, 52.

15 Baltazar to Séguier, Nov. 20, 1644: Lubl., p. 99. Baltazar also said that seditious handbills were being distributed to the same effect. Bosquet to Séguier, Jan. 23, 1645: Lubl., p. 114.

16 P-V Feb. 3, 1645.

17 P-V Feb. 7, 1645.

that local authorities were to resist. Many assiettes planned to meet on schedule despite Schomberg's command to wait until they received his orders, and some actually did so.[18]

It was in the midst of this battle of wills, just as the royal authorities were poised to begin quartier d'hiver collection and at the very moment when Mazarin was sending Schomberg permission to move more troops into the province, that the plans of both sides were shattered by the unexpected popular uprising of June 29 to July 2, 1645, in Montpellier.[19] This was precisely the sort of event which had *not* been called for. It was a serious wave of rioting in which crowds of women, artisans, and unemployed Cévenols sacked the houses of tax agents, murdering several of their relatives. It intimidated and discredited the authorities, embarrassed the province, and brought closer the possibility of military reprisals. It was directed against the *partisans* of the joyeux avènement tax which rumor had transformed into a terrible scourge on artisans and the poor, and which was hardly at the center of the rulers' preoccupations, though they had prepared the way for these rumors in earlier pronouncements.[20] Most importantly, the revolt did nothing to reinforce the power of assiettes and municipalities against the quartier d'hiver. The crowd reacted in classic form, violently attacking *partisans* and anyone associated with their administration, but never once mentioning the quartier d'hiver which had been so carefully put forward as the thing to resist and which was not collected by *partisans*. Unlike the resistance in 1629, which was choreographed by the Estates and contained no serious threat of popular insurrection, the rioting in 1645 did nothing to reinforce Estates or assiettes as institutions. Instead, this unexpected *popular* uprising was a setback in their mastery of the situation.

The reports of the royal agents afterwards transmitted a compelling sense of the resulting social danger: 'So far the inhabitants of the towns and countryside have not taken up arms, but they will not tolerate anyone with the name *traitant* anywhere, and they praise the Montpellierains' action publicly.' If soldiers were sent, it was predicted, provincial roads would be blocked, hungry Cévenols would descend on Montpellier, the Montpellierains would seize the citadel and the gates, and the Huguenots would use this pretext for an uprising.[21] Women reassembled several times in mid-July, and in August artisans were still guarding the gates of Montpellier. Bosquet lamented this deterioration of authority: 'this impunity [of the

[18] Bosquet to Séguier, Mar. 3, Apr. 17, May 1, 1645: Lubl., pp. 129–30, 132–3.

[19] Mazarin to Schomberg, June 30, 1645: A.A.E. France 1632, 249.

[20] On the uprising, see the references in William Beik, 'Two Intendants Face a Popular Revolt: Social Unrest and the Structure of Absolutism in 1645', *Canadian Journal of History*, 9 (1974), 243–62. Basic descriptions in Alexandre Germain, 'Les Commencements du règne de Louis XIV et la Fronde à Montpellier', *Mémoires de L'Académie des Sciences de Montpellier*, 3 (1859–63), 579–602; and Emmanuel Le Roy Ladurie, *Les Paysans de Languedoc*, 2 vols. (Paris, 1966), vol. 1, pp. 496–8.

[21] A.A.E. France 1634, 147, 151; Porch., pp. 649–52; ms. fr. 18432, 330–3v.

rioters] is a strange precedent which, joined to the sense of their poverty, leads the people into extraordinary determination to pay the king as little as possible, and they even take the liberty of rejecting taxes granted by the Estates'. Across the province in Toulouse, Bertier was saying the same thing: 'the *menu peuple* are crying that the king no longer wants them to pay the taille or any other impositions'.[22]

In this atmosphere the attempt of the Estates to organize a disciplined institutional resistance to certain illicit impositions collapsed in the general reaction against taxes. But the popular unrest did paradoxically aid provincial resistance in a cruder manner by causing a suspension of all the detested special taxes. Schomberg postponed the quartier d'hiver and other edicts until the next Estates, and there was a scramble by each local agency to take advantage of the situation. By the time of the Estates, in late November 1645, the determination of the deputies to resist further grants had grown rather than diminished. Étienne d'Aligre, who was sent from Paris to reinforce the king's bargaining team, was noticeably shocked at the way things had deteriorated: 'the hardness of these people is unimaginable', he reported, advising that conciliation was essential 'unless you undertake to free yourselves from this annual subjugation to the Estates, where the authority of the king is weak and held in very low regard'.[23]

But the Estates' advantage was only temporary. Just when the provincial rulers might have been expected to draw together, consolidate their gains, and forge a more effective control of regional interests, their basic conflicts began to surface, complicating the tax resistance with a counterpoint of selfish in-fighting. In Montpellier the attacks by councillors of the Comptes on Baltazar had made the court a prime suspect in the search for scapegoats for the uprising, and although the company was probably only indirectly responsible, if at all, the wheels began to turn for its disunion, which was eventually carried out in early 1647. This blow at a major provincial institution was protested only weakly by its jealous rivals. In late 1645 and 1646 the Comptes continued to feud with the Estates, the consuls of Montpellier, and the treasurer-generals. In March 1646 it even threw the treasurer of the bourse Le Secq into prison for refusing to pay the Comptes' alleged fees for quartier d'hiver collections of the previous years.[24] In Toulouse the question of the city's obligation to pay 'extraordinary' taxes set it against the Estates. A triangular conflict of capitouls–Parlement–Estates developed which precluded any genuine provincial unity.[25]

The crisis of 1645–6 had tested the ability of provincial groups to take

[22] Bosquet to Séguier, Aug. 1, 1645: Lubl., p. 150; Bertier to Séguier, Aug. 13, 1645: Lubl., p. 153.

[23] D'Aligre to Mazarin, Jan. 8, 1646: A.A.E. France 1634, 194.

[24] A.M. Mp Joffre 10, 240; Baltazar to La Vrillière, May 29, 1646: Lubl., pp. 192–3; Baltazar to Mazarin, Jan. 16, 1647: A.A.E. France 1634, 367.

[25] Bertier to Séguier, Mar. 28, 1646: Lubl., p. 182.

advantage of various related forms of agitation by forming a power bloc strong enough to bargain with a weakened monarchy. The results indicate how far they were from succeeding either to defend the province or to respond consistently to the threat of popular unrest, which was palpably real. The bishops and higher authorities had tried to use rising dissatisfaction to structure an organized resistance which would strengthen provincial institutions. But the unexpected uprising in Montpellier and its echoes elsewhere had inflamed the province to the point where both local and royal authorities were threatened and regular tax collections were jeopardized. Authority had been shaken on every level of administration, and the whole climate of government had been seriously eroded.

THE POSSIBILITIES OF THE FRONDE

This trouble might have subsided if the Parisian Fronde had not suddenly given agitation a new lease on life and opened the possibility of a more ambitious counter-offensive. Now real negotiation was suddenly fashionable. The issues on the agenda could be nothing less than the repeal of the changes of the last generation: the Estates could demand the revocation of the Edict of Béziers; the Comptes and Aides could get themselves reunited in Montpellier; the city of Toulouse could demand restoration of its full abonnement to the taille; the Parlement could reassert its jurisdiction over special commissions, intendants, and municipal affairs. All of them could fight the oppressive burden of taxes and try to deal with the problem of passages of troops, whose growing numbers caused difficulties of policing and disputes about funding. If there ever was a moment for a regional collaboration in defense of a traditional constitution, this was it. In 1648 conscious efforts were made to draw together. The capitouls tried to mend their fences with the Parlement. The Parlement and the Estates continued their collaborative attacks on fiscal edicts.[26] On one occasion the Estates officially requested the Parlement to suspend and examine an edict, and when it did so, sent a message of thanks to the first president 'for the good justice that he and members of his company render to the inhabitants of this province'.[27] The Parlement and the Chambre des Comptes each agreed, in a gesture of collaboration, to suspend cases involving deputies of the Estates during the period the assembly was meeting.

The parlementaires' program, expressed in a series of arrêts and remonstrances, contained the seeds of both provincial collaboration and future conflict. To be sure, they demanded that all special taxes be regulated by the royal council and verified by the Parlement; that any edicts not so verified be suppressed; that Languedoc enjoy the reduction of one-fourth

[26] P-V Mar. 26, Apr. 6, May 2, 1648.

[27] P-V Apr. 6, 1648.

of taille arrears which had been granted to other provinces; that the Edict of Béziers be revoked as unverified; and that the Estates no longer be commanded to reconsider measures already deliberated. These moves would have pleased the Estates. But they also declared that étape levies (administered by the Estates) should be strictly limited; that évocations générales out of the Parlement should be eliminated; that Toulouse should regain its taille abonnement; and that the Parlement should have jurisdiction over appeals concerning municipal elections.[28] They pointedly registered a national edict declaring that members of the sovereign courts should be named to a *chambre de justice* to investigate taille irregularities and began to fulminate against exports of grain from Narbonne.[29] Perhaps most revealing was the arrêt of July 1, 1648, stating that since 'subordinate officers, maires, jurats, consuls and échevins' had not been treating officers of the Parlement with the proper respect in recent years, these persons were to do so in the future, being especially forbidden 'to render extraordinary honors in the name of their companies and communities to any persons whosoever except by order of the king or the court'.[30] In December when the king, ceding to expediency and the need for support, reunited the Cour des Comptes, Aides, et Finances, the Parlement promptly suspended this move at the request of the syndic of the Estates.[31] In early 1649 it issued a series of important arrêts applying the royal reform of the taille to Languedoc: collection of taille arrears from past years was suspended; the taille for 1648 was reduced by one-fifth; Toulouse was discharged of everything but its traditional abonnement, and the principle was asserted that compensation for foules of passing troops was to be taken out of the king's taille funds.[32]

When the Estates met in June 1649 they too were primed for an offensive. They immediately corresponded with the Parlement of Provence, then in rebellion, in a move no doubt calculated to suggest that the loyalty of Languedoc was a valuable commodity. Then with unusual fervor they exchanged deputations with the treasurer-generals, the Comptes, the Parlement, and the capitouls. Finally they sent deputies to Orléans and the queen to initiate the delicate negotiations for the revocation of the Edict of Béziers. Responding creatively to the possibilities of collaboration inherent in the Parlement's recent pronouncements, they noted on July 1 that the troops of the regiment of Languedoc were committing terrible excesses and sent a deputation to Toulouse to ask the Parlement to

[28] Arrêt of July 18, 1648: A.D. H-G. B 1879, 512; remonstrance of Sept. 10: B. N. Languedoc (Bénédictins) 95, 70.

[29] Arrêt of Sept. 12, Nov. 9, 1648, Jan. 8, 1649: A.D. H-G. B 1879, 523, 528, 533.

[30] Roschach, vol. XIV, p. 203.

[31] See the arrêt of Mar. 11, 1651 against the Comptes, which reiterates earlier arrêts: A.D. H-G. B 1880, 30–6.

[32] A.D. H-G. B 1879, 512, 551, 568, 576.

investigate the situation. On July 7 the delighted Parlement commissioned Councillor Hughes de Vedelly of the Grand Chambre, whom it had already nominated to look into crimes of *commissaires extraordinaires*, to pursue as well the question of military excesses and to try and sentence the guilty parties.[33] The Estates' need for a legislative–judicial striking force was playing to the Parlement's desire to reassert its influence. Both were trying to invent a provincial alternative to the already indispensable intendants.

The Estates expressed pleasure at the work of Vedelly, but their deputies to Toulouse came back with disquieting reports that the Parlement's recent arrêts modifying the tailles would hinder collections and make it impossible 'to use legal constraints in the future and to preserve the authority of the Estates over the people'. It was resolved that a major deputation should return to Toulouse to thrash out these points but, at the same time, that every effort was to be made to aid the Parlement's commissioners in collecting evidence against the *partisans*.[34] This position was awkward. Local authorities were supposed to encourage parlementaire investigators, yet not be affected by their tax reductions. On the very day of the new delegation's triumphant reception in Toulouse, the treasurer of the bourse was suing that city for payment of suspended taxes.[35]

But despite these contradictions, the deputation was considered a success. While it was being cheered by crowds along its return route, the Parlement issued several conciliatory arrêts. One stated that many dioceses and communities were using the earlier arrêts forbidding collection of the étape and one-fifth of the taille as pretext for refusing other provincial taxes and ordered that these latter be promptly paid. Another, responding to a petition of the syndic-general, prohibited the holding of 'general council meetings' of all the inhabitants of towns, a practice 'which is tumultuous and disorganized, in which resolutions are regularly presented which are against the well-being of these communities'.[36] This measure was an attempt to curb the factions of dissidents who were challenging both Estates and Parlement on the local level. Back in the Estates, a resolution of comparable importance was adopted on August 4. The sovereign courts should be asked to consult the Estates before registering edicts, and the Estates in turn would use their administrative and lobbying power to keep anyone from obeying edicts not registered by the sovereign courts.[37] Each side had made a major contribution towards sharing with the other the defense of provincial interests. Later the Parlement sent a deputation to Montpellier to return the courtesy of the Estates, and the Estates asked Vedelly to prosecute an insult which a soldier from the citadel had publicly

[33] P-V July 1, 1649; arrêt of July 7, 1649: A.D. H-G. B 1879, 568; arrêt de conseil, Aug. 23, 1649: Le Pesant, 100.
[34] P-V July 8, 1649.
[35] Account of the deputation, Roschach, vol. XIV, pp. 268–76.
[36] Arrêts of July 27 and 28, 1649: A.D. H-G. B 1879, 567, 576.
[37] P-V Aug. 4, 1649.

administered to their syndic-general Roux, as if the Parlement's role was to place a special prosecutor at the disposal of the provincial assembly.[38]

The year 1650 was quiet because the Estates did not meet again until October, and the government had bought peace by restoring the Comptes, revoking the Edict of Béziers, and, in July, restoring the taille abonnement of Toulouse.[39] Only the parlementaires were left without a major concession. Abandoned to their own devices, the agitators within the Parlement formed a 'steering committee' of representatives from each chamber which organized the direct assertion of their authority in the province by sending out commissioners to execute three aspects of the 'program' they had already defined: attacking and prosecuting the intendants of Guyenne and Languedoc, intervening in Toulousain municipal politics, and requisitioning the municipal accounts needed to pay troop damages out of taille funds. This last aspect, which reflected the parlementaires' search for enforcement 'muscle', threatened the fiscal system of the Estates.[40] Relations between the two agencies deteriorated rapidly. From late autumn of 1650 through the summer and autumn of 1651 the province was treated to an extravaganza of mutual attacks and denunciation which laid bare the rivalries underlying provincial politics.

The Estates fired the first round when they met again from October 1650 to January 1651. Reacting to the Parlement's investigation of the taille, they responded that they had 'covered up and tolerated this enterprise in hopes that the Parlement would repair its own faults', but that, despite the promises of the delegation of 1649, the self-styled 'commissioners' had deceived their hopes. Now the Estates announced that they had a 'right of inspection over all corps and companies of officers' because they had been 'established at their demand and with their consent'.[41] On January 5, 1651, they set up their own 'steering committee' by resolving that between sessions the archbishop of Narbonne, as president of the Estates, was to be empowered to act independently or in conjunction with as many bishops, barons and consuls as he deemed necessary to oppose any attacks on provincial rights, or threats to persons carrying out provincial deliberations.[42] Then, in response to the Parlement's attempts to regulate troop disorders, the Estates instructed the treasurer of the bourse to withhold sums from the current *don* for payment of next year's troop damages.

The Estates had hardly adjourned when the Parlement began its counter-attack. Noting that its rival had 'vainly tried to usurp the marks of sovereignty' in trying to 'limit the jurisdiction of the Parlement and

[38] P-V Aug. 31, Sept. 30, Oct. 1, 1649.

[39] Roschach, vol. XIV, pp. 315–17; ms. fr. 17394, 109.

[40] Archbishop of Narbonne to Mazarin, Nov. 21, 1650: A.A.E. France 1634, 505; A.N. E 1696, 190.

[41] P-V Nov. 15, 1650.

[42] P-V Jan. 5, 1651 (Roschach, vol. XIV, p. 352).

persuade the people that [the Estates] have a right of inspection over such an august and honorable company', the Parlement characterized the members of the Estates as 'more concerned about their amusement than about the relief of the people', and the institution as 'a continued comedy underwritten and salaried by the blood of widows and orphans and the subsistence of the poor'. It then went on to detail the Estates' abuses. In a time when the Parlement was attacking extraordinary taxes, the Estates were devising deputations to court to prolong their sessions and augment their stipends. The sessions were riddled with corruption: bribes abounded; the assembly had rejected the lowest bid for étape contracts and allowed 18,000 livres of false claims to be charged to the province; they had threatened the property of the inhabitants of Toulouse 'like sovereign dispensers of the goods of others' by seizing merchants' goods in lieu of city taxes; in addition, their grant of special power to the archbishop of Narbonne to 'convoke whomever he wishes to deliberate on the affairs of the province' was an illicit usurpation of sovereignty. The Parlement annulled the offending deliberations and decreed that they be barred from the record books. Most important, new commissioners of the Parlement were named to investigate 'frauds which are being perpetrated in the levy of assiette funds beyond the Estates' instructions, and the diversion of étape money for fraudulent purposes; also monopolies, factions, corruption, sale of votes in the Estates, and other excesses committed in the province'.[43]

The Parlement issued a similarly critical attack on the Cour des Comptes as soon as it came to the rescue of the Estates by annulling the Parlement's attack. Arguing that the original Chambre des Comptes and the Cour des Aides had performed entirely different functions and should never have been united, the Parlement claimed that since their union the councillors of the Comptes had thought only of 'demolishing the privileges of the province in order to construct the foundation of their own private fortunes' by *traités* they undertook and fees they charged for business. The Estates, it was claimed, had arranged a deal whereby the Comptes and the diocesan receivers shared a cut of all sums levied on the province while overlooking each others' abuses. Although the Comptes had no jurisdiction, they had annulled the Parlement's pronouncements and forbidden all authorities to cooperate with parlementaire commissioners, thereby 'stirring up the people against the commissioners of the Parlement and the sovereign justice of the king'. These vices were also to be investigated, and the reunion of the Comptes was suspended until the Parlement had verified it.[44]

Soon itinerant commissioners from the Parlement, at least ten of them by summer, fanned out through the province to assert the court's influence,

[43] This entire statement is in the arrêt of Feb. 16, 1651: Roschach, vol. XIV, pp. 357–61.

[44] Arrêt of Mar. 11, 1651: A.D. H-G. B 1880, 30.

and hopefully popularity, by demanding the records of diocesan receivers so that the condemned deliberations could be crossed out and 'illegal' impositions cancelled. If the Estates had tried to create a permanent directorate parallel to that of the Parlement, the Parlement in turn was trying to invent a system of controlling the provincial administration parallel to the syndics of the Estates.

The commissioners stirred up trouble wherever they went, while the intendant Breteuil followed in their tracks, trying to undo the damage they had done. In Béziers Councillor Carlincas forced the bishop to retire into his fortified palace and tried to commandeer the key to it, summoned the assiette, changed its accounts, held a public bidding for the étape contract, and tried to induce the municipal guard to support him. He told a large crowd that

> we are seeking the relief of the people with greater passion than the payment of our fees, and we intend to investigate and punish the infamous, mercenary, open purchase of votes from some of those in the Estates, the extortion of provincial taxes, and the support that their leading members gave to this infamous commerce.[45]

Later in Narbonne he distributed printed bills containing a similar message which 'so aroused the inhabitants that many of them took up arms and assembled in hopes of obtaining the reduction mentioned in his [posters]', while cries of 'Vive le Roy, le Parlement et la Liberté' were heard in the streets,[46] Similar incidents were recorded in Albi, Carcassonne, Saint-Papoul, Uzès, Mende, Bagnols, Castres, and Mirepoix. In Montpellier a succession of agents from the Parlement and its adjunct, the Chambre de l'Édit, infiltrated the city in order to execute parlementaire orders, occasioning near riots as the followers of the Comptes rallied and expelled them from the city.[47]

Meanwhile in Toulouse, the radical parlementaires had been fomenting a veritable crusade against the Estates. The cathedral chapter, responding to the Parlement's urging and its rivalry with the archbishop of Toulouse, praised the court's 'use of its authority to elevate the glory of God and the dignity of ecclesiastics as well as to promote the king's service and the relief of his subjects', and protested the fact that bishops or their appointed vicar-generals could attend the Estates without giving the 'second order' of the clergy its rightful place. Because the vicar generals, who often substituted for the bishops, 'consent readily to all sorts of innovative taxes which the rest of the deputies of the second order would never accept

[45] Dubédat, vol. II, p. 248.

[46] These episodes in ms. fr. 18830, 141, 148; A.N. E 1696, 406, 432, 442.

[47] A.D. Hér B 9831; André Delort, *Mémoires inédits sur la ville de Montpellier au XVIIe siècle (1621–73)*, 2 vols. (Montpellier, 1876–8), vol. I, p. 146.

because of their interest in the preservation of the property of their churches', it was proposed that the cathedral chapters attend and vote jointly with the bishops. This reform would have given them veto power over the bishops' votes and revolutionized the provincial constitution since the bishops were the chief support of the crown in the Estates. This proposal was presented to the Parlement and communicated to all the other chapters of the province and to the general agents of the clergy.[48]

A few months later the Parlement authorized a meeting of fifty 'gentlemen of the province of Languedoc' who made the same demand that they be admitted to the Estates along with the titled barons already represented, and given veto power. As the 'syndic' of these unrepresented lesser nobles asked his following, 'what reasons are there, messieurs, for twenty-two persons whose services, condition, titles gave them no privilege over us to appropriate for themselves what should be the common property of all the nobility?'[49]

Not content with these attacks on the very constitution of the Estates, the Parlement proceeded to undermine the authority of the bishops. Noting on April 8 that the people were in 'misery' because of the poor crops of 1650, the Parlement commanded the bishops to perform, within three days, their historic duty of feeding the poor, or else a 'sixth of the fruits' of their bishoprics would be seized for this purpose. It was the duty of the Parlement, asserted an outrageous arrêt of May 22, 'to take care of the urgent necessities and nourishment of the poor at a time when a delay would be fatal'. Another arrêt attacked the role played in the assiettes by bishops 'who abuse the influence they have over the most corrupt deputies of their dioceses, whom they have conquered with gifts and gratuities pushed through the assiettes each year. [The bishops] induce [the deputies] to ratify every measure inspired by their avarice and their desire to recompense their agents and servants'.[50] Soon, with newly-discovered piety, the Parlement charged that the bishop of Lavaur and the coadjutor of Montauban did not reside in their dioceses, leaving 'souls abandoned and churches in ruin'. They were to mend their ways within a month or face seizure of their temporal goods. Consuls of each community were instructed to seize a sixth of the revenues of the ecclesiastical benefices in their area to feed the poor and, if this year's money was already spent, to borrow an equal amount which would be confiscated from next year's revenues.[51]

Meanwhile the itinerant commissioners were sending back information on the Estates' fiscal records when they could get hold of them, or more regularly on the refusal of local authorities to cooperate. These reports provided the ammunition for even more critiques and denunciations. On

[48] Roschach, vol. XIV, pp. 364, 386.
[49] Roschach, vol. XIV, pp. 380–1, 384.
[50] A.D. H-G. B 1880, 87, 81.
[51] A.D. H-G. B 1880, 92; A.N. E 1696, 432.

April 29 an arrêt published the sums being levied by the Estates for unspecified or suspicious purposes (1,389,000 livres for 'debts and affairs', 244,549 for 'special gratuities', 376,598 for étapes shifted to the province as a whole) and specified which parts of these sums were actually to be paid. This amounted to the Parlement mandating an alternative budget.[52] On June 13, noting that most of its orders remained unexecuted and that crimes remained unpunished for lack of physical force, the Parlement denounced the lieutenant-general Bieules for not providing the enforcement which had frequently been requested of him and relegated him to the status gradually being conferred upon most of the provincial authorities – that of rebel. As a result, an even larger delegation of parlementaires was instructed to tour the province with a general mandate to execute arrêts, regulate all abuses, and try the guilty with sovereign authority. This was tantamount to creating a court of Grands Jours.[53]

These challenges threw the Estates into the arms of the crown. Their next session opened July 31 and lasted, with recesses, until January 1652, but even before July the members in Paris were formulating their counter-attack. Feeling as helpless as the Parlement when it came to enforcement, they requested a firm and vigorous commitment from the royal council to enforce the arrêts de conseil which had been issued against all the Parlement's decrees. Subordinate authorities were to be commanded to register and execute the royal orders and to rip those of the Parlement from their books; all gentlemen were to be told to defend the Estates' orders by force; all consuls were to impose taxes by the Estates' schedule and to reject commissioners of the Parlement 'to the point of attacking them and driving them away'; the king's huissier de la chaîne was to be sent to lend weight to these commands, and the lieutenant-generals were to enforce them. It was even requested that royal maîtres des requêtes be sent to tour the province in place of the Parlement's commissioners and investigate abuses in the assiettes, which should then be judged in the royal council.[54]

This action looked to the future. Threatened by the Parlement, and reassured by the abolition of the Edict of Béziers, the Estates were suddenly eager to invoke the intendants and investigations which they had denounced so many times in the past. The Estates' sensitivity to the erosion of their credibility which might result from the Parlement's critiques is evident in their request for touring royal agents:

> this way the people will see that the persons who attend the Estates do not intend to condone irregularities, if there be any, and that His Majesty wants to provide

52 A.D. H-G. B 1880, 60, 81; also Roschach, vol. XIII, pp. 310–11.

53 Roschach, vol. XIV, p. 376.

54 Estates' appeal to the king against the Parlement, 1651: ms. fr. 18830, 61. The appeal was answered, as the instructions to de Sève and Boucherat, maîtres des requêtes, show: ms. fr. 18830, 73.

them with justice through the true and legitimate authority of the true judges of his affairs, and actually provide them with the relief that the Parlement falsely leads them to expect in order to plunge them into trouble and overextend its authority.[55]

As if to answer the Parlement in kind, they also issued a scathing denunciation of its membership, which reads like the other half of the social self-critique inaugurated by the Parlement's denunciation of the Estates. They condemned in explicit detail the grid of illegal family relationships which crisscrossed the Parlement, its illicit admission of underage sons, its organization of *survivances* by the shuffling of family-held offices between chambers, its practice of allowing a father to vote who had already resigned his office to his son.[56]

Most interesting, the Estates also tried to match the substance of the Parlement's reforms, a move which must have met with considerable favor among the population. The Parlement's roving extremists were commandeering accounts in order to see that the cost of troops' lodgings was paid out of the taille. This was when the Estates began to set 'conditions' for their *don* to the king and instruct the treasurer of the bourse, who, since 1649, was once again their own employee, to withhold from the king as 'security' funds which would be used to reimburse victims directly if the royal promises were not kept. The *don* was not to be collected until every member of the Estates and every consul in office was protected from the Parlement by an *évocation* of his law suits to another court and until all the arrêts de conseil against the Parlement had been executed.[57]

Thus the Estates had embraced the most popular aspects of the Parlement's program, but in order to make good their claims, they had been forced to reject the Parlement's enforcement in favor of the intendants', thereby abandoning all hope of provincial collaboration. On October 13 a deputation was sent to inform the intendant that the Estates were 'deeply grieved' at the arrêts against him issued by the Parlement.[58] This was dangerous ground for the cause of provincial autonomy. The eventful session of 1651 prolonged itself into early 1652 without being able to dominate events. Deputations were exchanged with the Comptes in order to obtain arrêts condemning the acts of the Parlement. An additional grant to the king of 200,000 livres for the war effort was refused, but 100,000 livres were granted for the 'restoration of order' and protection from the 'daily insolences' of the Parlement. The lieutenant-generals had to be requested again to discipline the Parlement and support tax collections in Béziers, Castres, Albi, Lavaur, and Saint-Papoul, all parlementaire strongholds.[59] On November 10 the Estates revealed their real weakness by asking that royal troops which were being moved from Italy to Guyenne

[55] Ms. fr. 18830, 61.

[56] Article 8 of the cahier of 1651: A.N. E 1696, 596.

[57] Roschach, vol. XIV, p. 407.

[58] P-V Oct. 13, 1651.

[59] P-V Sept. 11, Oct. 21, 1651.

be lodged in places which had refused to pay their full taxes. The session ended with reports of 'murders and ransoms' by uncontrollable troops and instructions to the deputies at court to ask the king to settle further differences with the Parlement.[60] The attempt to check the crown had collapsed.

THE 'ECHO' OF 1656–7

After the Fronde the opportunity never again presented itself for such a general offensive, but during the 1650s the belief of the Parlement and the Estates that they had the right to agitate on behalf of their privileges died slowly. The most dramatic confrontation between king and province took place in the winter of 1656–7, when all the old elements combined again in one last flurry of resistance. The new crisis paralleled the one in 1645–6 in that the hard-pressed province pushed resistance to a point verging on popular revolt, and it was like the Fronde in its revival of the 'union' between Estates and sovereign courts. But this time the advantage lay on the royal side since the monarchy was reviving, not collapsing, and troops were available to prove it.

The immediate issue was the quartering of the entire army of Catalonia in Languedoc, which coincided with the opening of the Estates and a demand from the royal commissioners for 2,750,000 livres to pay the troops. A quartier d'hiver already in place, unlike the lodgings of 1645 which were only threatened, would seriously undermine the Estates' fiscal control by inducing desperate local communities to go into debt illicitly and by opening the door to financial fraud. The province had to act to save both its power of consent, threatened by forced levies, and its control over the local communities. For ammunition it could muster only the privileges restored in 1649 and whatever strength could be drawn from provincial solidarity.

Deputations were immediately sent to both the Parlement and the Comptes requesting arrêts commanding the communities to supply the troops only in kind and not in coin. The Parlement was to be thanked for its aid in opposing the Rhône Canal and the fabrication of *liards* (unpopular copper coins), both issues which the Estates had been fighting. The Comptes was to be asked to halt the oppressive general searches being undertaken by the guards of the gabelles.[61] The strategy of the Estates was to mobilize the province against paying any support for the troops other

[60] P-V Dec. 6, 9, 13, 18, 1651, Jan. 3, 1652.

[61] P-V Nov. 28, 1656. Authority conflicts were not easy to avoid. In Toulouse the deputies barely averted a confrontation over the first president's characterization of them as *ressortables*, which was unacceptable since in their view the Estates 'recognize no superior but the king'. The Comptes issued expressions of support but continued to allow its deputies to aid the gabelle searches which the Estates were condemning. P-V Dec. 20, 1656, Jan. 2, Feb. 10, 1657.

than the necessary food and lodging, while insisting that the army be removed from the province in return for a monetary grant. The existing institutional structure would again be used to resist innovation and force the king to respect the principle that *dons gratuits* and troop lodgings did not mix. Both the Parlement and the Comptes issued the necessary regulations concerning the troops, and while the Parlement once again named an itinerant commissioner to investigate local disorders, the Estates voted to have the treasurer of the bourse advance any sums necessary to pay his expenses.[62]

The real issues in this power struggle are illustrated by a fascinating debate between the baron of Lanta, the Estates' negotiator in Paris, and Cardinal Mazarin himself.[63] Lanta began by arguing that the government's plan for lodgings funded by the local communities would never work and that the king would have to supply the cash for their rejuvenation. The directness with which an important baron of the Estates could talk back to Mazarin, and his forthright optimism about the Estates' rather arrogant resistance strategy are striking.[64] Mazarin replied that 'the king would make himself obeyed'.

Lanta then tried a more principled approach, expressing his shock at the insistence of the royal commissioners that if the Estates did not grant the money they could collect it themselves in the dioceses, 'which amounted to attacking and overturning their privileges'. Mazarin's reply was that 'the king was not attacking the privileges of the province as long as he started by asking, but if the province refused, His Majesty would mandate the collections'. This pushed Lanta into a more emphatic version of the province's rights which bordered on a theory of resistance:

> that the letters-patent by virtue of which they assemble every year bear the words 'in order to grant to us freely and liberally', and that every time anything was levied on Languedoc which was not consented to by the Estates, the clergy, the nobility, the sovereign companies, and the third estate would be found completely united [*dans une entière union*] for the preservation of their privileges. That as servant of the king, he was obliged to implore His Excellency very humbly to see that the Estates were not attacked in their most sensitive area.

Mazarin's reply was that

> the Estates of Languedoc were treating the king as if they were sovereigns. Last year they had placed a hundred obstacles in the way of His Majesty's business and

[62] P-V Dec. 4, 23, 1656.

[63] This entire account is from P-V Feb. 8, 1657, and is reproduced in Roschach, vol. XIV, pp. 640–53.

[64] Lanta was well placed to speak for the province since he was a baron of the Estates and also a member of the prestigious Barthélemy de Grammont family which was influential in the Parlement. His brother Gabriel (d. 1654) had been president of the Chambre d'Enquêtes. Lanta himself had close ties with the duc d'Orléans.

ultimately they had attached a thousand conditions to their treaty; that this was insufferable conduct and that the king would no longer tolerate it.

Lanta now went even further. Last year the royal commissioners had broken their word and taken new 'edicts' to the Comptes for registration. For this reason the Estates 'had had to take precautions', and history would show, after all, that the setting of conditions was nothing new. Indeed, 'if we did not have the liberty to attach conditions to our treaty, we would be in a worse state than the Girardins and the Monerots who make treaties every day with His Majesty, and incorporate whatever conditions they deem useful to their interests'. This was insolence indeed, for Girardin and Monerot were nationally-known tax farmers. Drawn foolishly into debate, perhaps because of his sensitivity to the issue of *partisans*, Mazarin retorted that 'the Monerots and Girardins were individuals who lent money to the king and who could refuse to do so'; whereupon Lanta replied that 'the Estates had even more right to do so since they *gave* liberally of their own money'.

This was the end of the interview. Three days later, having taken up a defensive position in his bed, Mazarin summoned Lanta again and counter-attacked:

His excellency said that he could not conceal the king's extreme anger at learning of the deputation the Estates had sent to the Parlement; that these were no longer the times of unions; that it had been said in the Estates that one must prepare for going all out to ruin the troops so that no more would be sent in the future; that the *arrêts* which the Estates had requested of the Parlement forbidding the communities to borrow were proof of this; that the king was almost twenty years old and that with one breath he would destroy all these enterprises.

A better expression of the clash of royal will and provincial resistance could hardly be imagined. It was not really a clash between absolutism and provincial rights, however, for both parties accepted the same assumptions. Lanta was thrown on the defensive by the charge of conspiratorial collaboration and beat a hasty retreat:

as for the union which they were complaining about, the Estates had never thought of forming one, for this word was odious to them, and they had given many signs of this truth in recent times. But there were certain unions which formed naturally... and if liberty inhibited a union by formal declaration, nothing could keep their common interests from uniting their hearts.

His final argument was that 'when the people no longer fear the loss of their privileges, nor the Parlement the creation of a Parlement of Nîmes with which it is threatened, then you will see the province calm and tranquil again'.[65] Lanta seemed to be saying that if the king would guarantee a formal status quo, the provincial rulers would cease their agitations. Such a bargain could never be formally struck, but it is exactly what happened under Louis XIV.

Meanwhile the province was gradually discovering that resistance had become more serious and dangerous. Once again there was talk of parlementaire commissioners touring the province, and there was even mention of forming a committee of nobles in each diocese to support the Parlement's decrees.[66] Regulating troops was not nearly as easy as playing the factional games of the Fronde, and unrest mounted. In late December the Parlement's commissioner Clément de Long was almost killed in the village of Avignonet when he tried to rally the neighboring peasants against the undisciplined d'Estrade regiment. The troops fought back, to the point where houses were burned and three of de Long's supporters were killed. Public opinion was outraged and the Estates immediately granted full compensation, coming to a substantial 5,383 livres, to all injured parties 'so that the province as a whole and its individual inhabitants will follow this example and lend all their force to the execution of the deliberations of this assembly and the resulting arrêts of the Parlement', To 'encourage messieurs of the Parlement', they even voted to guarantee the value of the office of any councillor killed in the line of duty, at a moment when the paulette was not in force.[67]

As the winter wore on, the Estates gradually reached an accommodation with the crown. They granted two million livres provided the foules already suffered were subtracted from it. Then they agreed to several additional advances of funds to cover the last weeks of the winter quarters, provided the intendant and the royal treasury would issue receipts certifying that the entire *don* had been paid in full and consumed. When they finally disbanded in April, the king had received most of his money while the Estates had saved face by establishing conditions and obtaining written guarantees that they would maintain a measure of control over the collection and reimbursement process. The crisis subsided as the troops left the province, and no comparable lodgings were seen for almost twenty years. The province had held its own, but at great cost and with no real gains for the future. This time the initiative had been with the king because even provincial cooperation was not enough to manage troops or guarantee compensations.

65 The Parlement of Nîmes was a project once again under consideration at the time: bishop of Nîmes to Mazarin, Oct. 15, 1656: A.A.E. France 1636, 500, 503.

66 Fieubet to Mazarin, Jan., 1657; Piloy to Mazarin, Jan. 1, 1657; Bieules to Mazarin, Jan. 8, 1657; Bezons to Mazarin, Jan. 15, 1657: A.A.E. France 1637, 6, 15, 19, 28, 145.

67 P-V Jan. 8, 1657. This episode is discussed in a number of letters and in L. de Santi, *Germain de Lafaille, le comte d'Aubijoux et l'affaire d'Avignonet* (*1656*) (Toulouse, 1936). See also Roschach, vol. XIV, p. 665.

These were the most dramatic moments in a continuous history of provincial contacts and alliances. The various agencies of the province did have the capacity to coordinate their efforts temporarily for limited objectives, but each time they did so they revealed the fundamental contradictions underlying their position. Fending off royal innovations meant asserting a common front in defense of provincial 'privileges' which were subject to differing interpretations and which were defined only in reference to the king. To succeed, the authorities also had to maintain their influence with a discontented population which was barely controllable in the face of fiscal innovations. Successful resistance, as in 1631 and 1649, required that the people remain disciplined and reinforce the institutional channels put forth by their officials. Any outbreak of rioting, as in 1645, meant loss of control and inability to negotiate. But maintaining influence meant competing with one another for popularity in a context where all authorities were vulnerable to charges of vested interest.

The more provincial agencies tried to appropriate the authority necessary to stand up to the crown while keeping the population in check, the more their weaknesses were revealed. The Parlement could not modify the taille or play watchdog over the interests of the population without treading on the toes of the Estates and the Comptes. The Estates could not make their policies stick without the commanding power of either the sovereign courts or the royal agents. The Comptes had jurisdictional collisions with both. Pushed to their limits during the Fronde, all revealed their true colors in mutual denunciations: the Parlement was a company of posturing dignitaries unable to realize its irresponsible political ambitions; the Estates were a collection of bishops and barons with vested interest in royal taxes and with no local base of support beyond their own clients; the Comptes was a group of financiers, jealous of their fees.

There was no real possibility of a 'provincial front against the crown' because of the very structure of provincial government and because the social interests of the rulers lay with the national monarchy, not the provincial population. The rulers could not subtract their sphere from the larger polity because their authority was based on a system of shared power and gradated privilege which was presided over by the monarch. Without the king there could be no hierarchy of authorities and no 'division of labor' among them. Yet there was no possibility of a royal 'takeover' either because the king relied on his social allies within the province and had no alternative to their rule. The period 1620 to 1660 demonstrated how badly the system could work, even while fulfilling new imperatives. If particularism was not to be a viable option, then the rulers of Languedoc would have to learn to use the system of royal absolutism to better advantage, and the king would have to learn how to get what he wanted from them without stirring up bitterness and rivalry.

PART FOUR

The province and the crown

10

Channels of personal influence

The broader configurations of provincial politics do not completely explain the splits within companies or the factionalism and rivalry which characterized our period. There was another dimension to political activity – the hidden play of personal connections – which was also important and which needs to be explored further. Authority under absolutism was diffuse and very personal. Family ties, corporate pressure groups, and client systems were all central to the functioning of the early modern state, but exactly what the relationship was between these forces and political action is often difficult to determine. This chapter explores that relationship, using the available genealogical information and the vast number of references to personal ties in the sources. The idea is to start with what can be learned of personal relationships and look from there for connections which may illuminate the political activities already discovered. I should stress that the emphasis here is not on the nature of the patron–client bond, which is a subject in itself, but on the implications of such bonds for provincial politics.[1]

THE IMPORTANCE OF PERSONAL INFLUENCE

One fascinating thing about seventeenth-century government was the way institutional processes and personal networks intermingled and influenced each other. Government was articulated first through royal institutions, but while institutional channels were established firmly enough that they

1 A vast comparative literature exists on clientage and patronage which can be sampled in Kay Lawson, ed., *Political Parties and Linkage: a Comparative Perspective* (New Haven, 1980); and Steffen Schmidt, et al., eds., *Friends, Followers, and Factions: a Reader in Political Clientelism* (Berkeley, 1977). Historical aspects are discussed in Yves Durand, ed., *Hommage à Roland Mousnier: clientèles et fidélités à l'époque moderne* (Paris, 1981). However, most studies by historians emphasize the nature of individual relationships, not the impact of all the relationships in a given region. Suggestions abound in Robert R. Harding, *Anatomy of a Power Elite: the Provincial Governors of Early Modern France* (New Haven, 1978); and there is a helpful discussion in Nicholas B. Fessenden, 'Épernon and Guyenne: Provincial Politics under Louis XIII' (Ph.D. Diss., Columbia University, 1972), ch. 10. Sharon Kettering is expanding an unpublished paper, 'Mazarin's Clients in Provence', into a book-length study of clientage in France. For Languedoc, an especially interesting article is C. E. J. Caldicott, 'Le Gouvernement de Gaston d'Orléans en Languedoc (1644–1660) et la carrière de Molière', *XVIIe siècle*, 116 (1977), 17–42.

deflected and modified the nature of personal influence, personal forms of power, which were themselves evolving, still played a central role in the decision-making process.[2] Those who wanted to act had to be able to make their way through a judicial thicket of contradictory pronouncements, overlapping jurisdictions, and unenforceable directives; but to do so they also had to have friends and informers in each center of power.

The 'patron–client' style of operation provided a way of guaranteeing this support. Its essence was partiality – the taking of sides, the bestowing of favors – not, as in feudal law, because of formal contractual obligations between superior and subordinate, but because of mere inclination or whim. The patron, usually a great noble or a dignitary acting in some official capacity, would make a point of expressing gallantly his affection and desire to serve. The client, often a collective entity, would perform symbolic acts of deference, do the patron favors, and appeal in time of need for protection. The result was a language which flattered everyone with its overtones of aristocratic largesse and which also evoked the arbitrary, though theoretically not irresponsible, nature of authority under absolutism – delegated in degrees from the top to the bottom of society.

Such relationships were common in every area of political life. The Estates and the courts cultivated their relations with great nobles and influential individuals like bishops or intendants. Town consulates did the same, and within each of these bodies family alliances and special ties abounded. Everyone tried to know someone at court, in the royal council, in the entourage of the governor. The name of the game – in a sense the other side of the coin from precedence quarrels and authority conflicts – was attracting an extra bit of attention for yourself, because in a society of competition for unequally-distributed favors, anything that set you apart could make a difference. The ceremonial entries of notables, the salutations, visits, and leave-takings could be decisive in cementing relationships,

[2] This dichotomy of 'institutional processes' and 'personal loyalties' is not identical to others which have been applied to the period. Robert Harding contrasts the 'bureaucratic' regime of intendants directed from the center to a 'patrimonial type of administration' in which the king ruled through the client networks of royal governors. But despite allusions to the Weberian literature on bureaucracy, he never pursues the broader implications of these concepts. John A. Armstrong, whom he cites, provides more rigorous definitions of 'bureaucratic and patrimonial attributes', which cast doubt on whether any seventeenth-century official or institution could be called bureaucratic. These approaches relate everything to the process of statebuilding, leaving provincial organisms and local relations in the background. My term 'institutional' refers to the ongoing procedures used by any institution, provincial or 'national'. 'Institutional' was not equivalent to 'bureaucratic', for institutions could impede as well as further the rise of 'rational' or 'bureaucratic' government. Similarly J. Russell Major's contrast between 'consultative monarchy' and 'absolute monarchy' focuses on constitutional arrangements and bypasses the issue of personal influence exerted through institutions. Harding, *Anatomy*, pp. 1, 6, 171, 179; John A. Armstrong, 'Old-Regime Governors: Bureaucratic and Patrimonial Attributes', *Comparative Studies in Society and History*, 14 (1972), 2–29; J. Russell Major, *Representative Government in Early Modern France* (New Haven, 1980).

especially in times when leadership was shifting. Even small things like acquaintances established with dignitaries housed in your residence when the king and his court were passing through your town, dedicatory prefaces to learned essays, or the placement of a patron's coat of arms on town hall doors could tip the balance of patronage in your favor.

Most of the smaller problems brought up in the Estates were patronage matters introduced by interested bishops. The courts were solicited by dignitaries, and in important matters the judges were rarely impartial. Even in the distant mountains of Gévaudan, a brief drawn up for a law suit brought before the Parlement by a noble named Montrodat against Marcillac, the bishop, began by protesting that Marcillac had personal alliances with most of the judges in the case: the bishop himself was an honorary councillor in the Parlement, his nephew was a councillor, another nephew was allied by marriage to a president, and ten to fifteen other members were connected by marriage or interest to the co-defendants of the bishop. The implication was clear that these relatives would naturally take the bishop's side.[3]

Despite the role of personal interventions by patrons in the process of getting one's way in political matters, it was still necessary to pursue a problem through institutional channels, using 'legal–procedural' tactics and style. In a society where most rights were traditional and where the many levels of the judicial apparatus were far more highly developed than the institutions which created or enforced legislation, it is not surprising that the essence of local government was the pursuit of large numbers of cases in the courts: suits against the non-compliance of individuals, lengthy cases concerning financial accounting, appeals for favorable rulings in jurisdictional conflicts, attempts to clarify the nature and extent of individual powers. Letters were constantly exchanged between the syndic or secretary back home and the local body's agents in Paris, Toulouse, or Montpellier, and the latter were forever demanding more documents and reporting to the former on the progress of the various cases they were overseeing.[4] Meanwhile the syndic-generals of the Estates were pursuing similar matters in the name of the province, as were sovereign and lower courts, religious foundations, guilds, and 'syndicates' of individuals. It cannot be emphasized enough that law suits were the society's principal form of regulation and enforcement and that their successful resolution

[3] A.D. Loz. G 624.

[4] In 1670, for example, the city of Toulouse had ten important cases to watch: three in the Parlement, two concerning the accounts of former treasurers and the third concerning ownership of land where the town wanted to build; and seven before the royal council concerning matters such as a precedence quarrel with the juge mage, the sale of lettres de maîtrise in Toulouse, an illegal péage charge, a claim from the heiress who inherited rights over a tax farm, and a claim by the heirs of a former tax collector. A.M. Tse FF 131.

required personal influence. A collectivity's dossier of cases was a jealously-guarded patrimony to be guided, often for decades, through many courts.

Such cases were predicated on the assumption that a point of law was to be interpreted judicially. But because all courts acted in an executive capacity when regulating public life and because 'executive' authorities like the king, the governor, or a commanding army officer also acted judicially in issuing rulings interpreting their directives, the distinction between a legal *appeal* to a higher court and an administrative *petition* to a higher commanding authority was not very great. In fighting for an important decision in a court, one had to mobilize an array of technical judicial tactics which were the special domain of legal advisors, but one also had to invoke the intervention of the great who, as we have seen, would be favorably or unfavorably inclined in proportion to the skill with which the game of patronage had been played.

For these reasons the deputation of a committee of notables to lobby for a given decision was a second tactic invoked when the simple prosecution of one's case did not promise to be adequate. Such deputations were widely used. A town like Narbonne sent frequent deputations to the archbishop, at home or in Paris, to the governor of Languedoc or his lieutenant, to the treasurer-generals or the Comptes of Montpellier, to the intendant, and occasionally even to the king. The 'royal' missions were especially sought-after for they gave their participants an opportunity to establish ties with public figures and make secret arrangements even against their own companies. If we add to the periodic deputations of the larger towns the parallel missions from the two sovereign courts and the Estates' annual deputation to present the cahier to the king, we can imagine the competition for influence which went on constantly around the monarch.

The process of lobbying was fraught with pitfalls. Because of the rhythm of royal council meetings it was necessary to be able to wait months for a case to be brought up and then, at very short notice, to muster the latest documents and arguments.[5] Once a case was actually under way or a deputation was ready to make its presentation, it was necessary to prepare one's path by mobilizing support and neutralizing adversaries. One such deputy, Councillor Ranchin from the Comptes, writes back to his colleagues in Montpellier in 1657 that since the bishop of Montpellier has just spoken favorably of their suit before the Assembly of Clergy, they must immediately take steps to cultivate his favor while the moment is right.[6] But lobbying was not always that easy. When Rudelle, envoy of the city of Toulouse to push for the restoration of the taille abonnement in 1631, was trying to get

[5] In 1667, the king provoked a flurry of anxiety among the waiting avocats au conseil by unexpectedly sending his council back to Paris from the war front: A.M. Tse BB 181.

[6] A.M. Mp AA 9 (Jan. 19, 1657).

a hearing from the *surintendant des finances*, he had to undertake a chilly vigil at seven in the morning in the freezing cloister of the *jacobins réformés* in Paris while his ally, a certain Father Ranguet, 'left the confessional four times' to try to intercept the visiting surintendant and persuade him to grant Rudelle an interview. When Rudelle was finally introduced, he discovered that two of his legal adversaries were plying the surintendant with arguments against his case even as they paced the premises. After much coaxing, Rudelle finally induced one of them to blurt out that he would never let the case come up for judgment until a certain Jesuit named Jacquinot had been 'satisfied'. Taking this hint, Rudelle then made his way to the Jesuit college where he followed Jacquinot up and down the halls during an inspection of classes until finally the priest muttered that it was inexcusable for the capitouls to be jeopardizing the tax exemption of the Jesuits of Toulouse. With this hidden patronage obstacle finally out in the open and his real opposition unmasked, Rudelle was at least able to lobby more intelligently.[7]

In 1644 and 1645 the appointment of Gaston d'Orléans as governor of Languedoc, just at the time when quarrels between the capitouls and the Parlement were becoming serious, provides a good case study in the workings of patronage. In order to assure support for their causes during this crucial 'changing of the guard', both sides had to send high-level deputations to Paris. As soon as the news arrived of Orléans's appointment the deputation of capitouls rushed to Bordeaux to hire special carriages 'because of the heat', and raced to Paris in nine days, arriving two days before Orléans and one day before the rival deputation from the Parlement, as their spokesman proudly reported later.[8] Lobbying was particularly difficult for provincial townsmen whose inferior status made it hard to gain entrance to the proper drawing rooms. They went to see Froment, Orléans's secretary for Languedoc, and Aubijoux, the newly-appointed governor of the citadel of Montpellier. They saluted Orléans. Then they waited outside his chamber while he dined in the Luxembourg Palace until he was ready to escort them across the river to see the queen in the Tuileries. When Orléans went in, however, he was told that Anne of Austria was not dressed and that the interview would have to be 'for another day'. Despite this setback, Froment assured them that Orléans had every intention of presenting them to the queen in person. The next morning, however, she left for Fontainebleau, and Orléans left for Nemours. When he finally returned, the deputies went to Fontainebleau to see him but were not admitted because he was 'pursuing his entertainments'. In the meantime

7 A.M. Tse BB 30, 110–11.

8 This is the account of capitoul Jean-Georges de Salinié, published by Brégail in *Revue de Gascogne*, 41 (1900), 44–7.

they discovered that they had committed a faux pas by asking that the next Estates be convened in Toulouse when Schomberg, who was also present, had already promised otherwise to the deputies from Carcassonne. They finally saw the queen and king in a room 'filled', they reported admiringly, 'with *les grands* and the ladies of the court'. The next step required by protocol was an appointment with Mazarin, but he was sick in bed, and after several days they returned to Paris, where life was cheaper, to await his recovery. Becoming impatient, they finally decided to settle for assurances from Mazarin's secretary Aubry that the cardinal would consider their honest attempts to see him as sufficient evidence of their good will. But now they had to request Orléans's leave to depart, and he had gone off to Blois for ten days! When they were finally able to bid him farewell, they barely averted a command to stay because of news just arrived that the capitouls and parlementaires back home were feuding again. This voyage had not been a frivolity, for during their long waits the deputies were busily making contacts which set the scene for years of future conflicts back home. These capitouls were the ones who induced Orléans to rig the next municipal election in their favor, setting off new battles for years to come.

PROVINCIAL CONNECTIONS

Suppose we compare identifiable family ties and discernible factional affinities. How were the rulers of Languedoc connected to one another personally, and did such connections form a system?[9] The most obvious characteristic of Languedoc was the multiplicity and dispersal of its centers of influence. The bipolarization of authority in two widely-separated

[9] The information which follows is drawn from the genealogical charts of approximately 125 families of notables. These charts are based on information from published genealogies plus all the additional facts I have gleaned from the sources. The most useful collections for Languedoc were Louis de Laroque, *Armorial de la noblesse de Languedoc*, 3 vols. (1860–3; repr. Marseilles, 1972); Alphonse Bremond, *Nobiliaire toulousain: inventaire général des titres probants de noblesse et de dignités nobiliaires*, 2 vols. (Toulouse, 1863); Alexandre Du Mège, *Biographie toulousaine, ou dictionnaire historique* (Paris, 1823); Henry de Caux, *Catalogue général des gentils-hommes de la province de Languedoc* (Pézenas, 1676); Jacques Beaudeau, *Armorial des Estats du Languedoc enrichi des elemens de l'art du blason* (Montpellier, 1686); Bejard, *Recueil des tiltres, qualites, blazons et armes des seigneurs barons des estats generaux de la province de Languedoc*, rev. edn. (Lyons, 1657). For national figures information was also drawn from the *Nouvelle biographie générale*, 25 vols. (Paris, 1857–66) and from the *Dictionnaire de biographie française*, 12 vols. to date (Paris, 1933–72). In addition, certain manuscript sources were used, including B.N. Languedoc (Bénédictins) 100–1, 103–8; B.N. Dossiers bleus and Pièces originales, various articles; B.N. ms. fr. 32549; and A.D. H-G. ms. 193 (for the membership in the Parlement). The members of the Comptes are listed, with family details, in Pierre Vialles, *Études historiques sur la Cour des Comptes, Aides et Finances de Montpellier, d'après ses archives privées* (Montpellier, 1921), pp. 115–229. There are, of course, many additional surveys of sub-regions and individual families, some of which were consulted. An especially admirable example is Prosper Falgairolle, *Une famille de l'ancienne France: les Baudan à Nîmes et à Montpellier pendant quatre siècles* (Cavaillon, 1926).

capitals was a factor in the dispersal, as was the fragmentation of influence deriving from the role of the twenty-two prelates in the Estates. Could traditional noble families have provided a linkage among these diverse centers? It is hard to see how. Presiding over their clusters of estates, these families were usually neither wealthy nor distinguished. Their hope of political prominence had to rest on acquisition of various posts of command: titles and commissions in the army, governorships of permanent forts and garrisons, positions of seneschal and bailli, or baronies in the Estates. The road to influence lay in accumulating a geographically and functionally diversified set of such positions, but there are few examples of success. The best case might be the Lévis-Mirepoix, who dominated the barony of Mirepoix and the nearby post of seneschal of Castres while marrying into a constellation of lesser families of Foix and Guyenne and establishing some ties with parlementaire families (Bertier, Caulet).[10]

What about families from the Parlement? Their influence was extraordinarily concentrated in Haut-Languedoc. They managed to produce twelve bishops in our period, but almost all of these served before 1650, and all but one were in sees immediately surrounding Toulouse. The only really important ties with the church were the Bertier family's hold over the bishoprics of Rieux (1602–1705) and Montauban (1635–74) and the Lestang family's sojourn in Carcassonne (1603–1705). Certain parlementaire families had branches in the landed nobility, or through them, baronies in the Estates. The Baderon de Maussacs had military cousins in Bigorre; First President Bertier married a daughter to Jean-Roger de Foix-Rabat, baron of La Gardiolle, and another to the Lévis-Mirepoix. The barony of Lanta was controlled first by a branch of the Caumels family, then by the 'sword' branch of the Barthélemys. By far the most interesting family was that of Jean Potier de la Terrasse, president from 1596 to 1611, whose son and grandson also served as presidents from 1635 to 1684. The Potiers were allied with the powerful financial–judicial Roux family of Carcassonne, with the Lordats, governors of Carcassonne, with the Puisserguiers, governors of Béziers, and with Hector d'Ouvrier, bishop of Nîmes, whose mother was a Potier. Such contacts take on significance when we realize that these very people played negative and uncooperative roles during the Fronde, leading us to suspect a connection between political and family ties.

Within Toulouse parlementaire alliances were very tight. Of the thirty-nine invididuals who held the ten most important posts of first president, président à mortier, procureur-general, and advocate-general between 1600 and 1683, twenty-six can be easily linked to others in the group through marriage ties in their immediate families. No doubt less visible ties also existed. More interesting, though, is the fact that several distinct networks

[10] *Archives du chateau de Léran*, 5 vols. (Toulouse, 1903–27).

emerge from these linkages. Fifteen key individuals can readily be allied in a single interlocking kinship diagram. Smaller diagrams group three additional individuals around the Bertier family and eight around the Fieubet family, while certain recent 'immigrants' like the Pugets de Gau from Aix, the Calvières from Nîmes, and the Riquets from Béziers, who had reputations as financial or social parvenus, remain isolated. It appears on the surface as if the first presidents, with their close ties to the crown, were kept aloof from the rest of the leading families.

Factions in the Parlement cannot be definitively labelled. However, if lists are constructed of all the names connected with excesses of assertiveness and violent actions from the protests of the 1630s through the Fronde and up to the 'loyalty report' written for Colbert in 1663, a group does emerge of individuals who seem to have been most deeply involved in acts of 'rebellion'. A similar list can be constructed of 'loyalists' who fairly consistently spoke out on behalf of the crown and opposed the trouble stirred up by these 'agitators'.[11] The resulting lists suggest two quite distinct groups separated by a widening gulf. The 'loyalists' often had marriage ties among themselves and links to the Bertiers or certain *gens du roi*, but they were hardly ever linked through marriage to the principal 'agitators', at least after 1640. Most of the 'agitators' appeared to be lesser figures or younger members from the lower chambers. However, these hotheads were supported and patronized by a small core of eminent figures with enough wealth and pedigree to afford to take risks. These included President Étienne Potier de la Terrasse, who published maxims against Mazarin in 1652; Potier's grandfather President François-Étienne de Garaud de Donneville, who had been accused by Bosquet of leading the Parlement's attack on the intendants in 1643; Jean-Antoine Dumai, summoned to appear before the royal council in 1646 for supporting the same events; President Grammont of the turbulent second Enquêtes; Christophe Maynard de l'Estang; and Advocate-General Jacques de Marmiesse.[12] These leaders were closely related; in fact three of the principal agitators seem to have married their children to the children of President Garaud, and another was his grandson.[13] They formed the nucleus of the larger kinship network described above. Thus the factional lists, drawn up from independent sources, bring us back to the circle of families discovered from genealogical evidence.

[11] I use the term 'loyalist' instead of 'royalist' to emphasize that both 'dissidents' and 'loyalists' believed in absolutism. None were genuine traitors or rebels, their differences being only over the degree to which they believed they should be subservient to royal directives and agents.

[12] See especially the memoir, probably by Maugiron, of May 1652: A.A.E. France 1636, 66; and Colbert's list, reproduced in Depping, vol. II, pp. 111–14, 131–2.

[13] These three were President Philippe de Caminade, Councillor Christophe Maynard de l'Estang, and Councillor Jean-Antoine Dumai, along with President Étienne Potier de la Terrasse, whose mother appears to have been a daughter of President Garaud de Donneville.

Another interesting factor is the connection that emerges between aggressive 'loyalism' and royal tax farming. In 1636, during a stormy discussion of whether to accept new offices in the Parlement, certain members of the company were expelled from the meeting because their relatives were already buying up or peddling the offices in question. Chief among them was Jacques de Maussac, son of the ambitious president in the Comptes who was to play an unpopular loyalist role during the Fronde and who left the room muttering 'that we have a king', along with a group of other councillors, all of whom appear on the 'loyalist' list, but none of whom ever played the role of 'agitators'. In 1644 a similar attack by 'agitators' on Jean-Georges de Caulet, the local concessionnaire of the controversial joyeux avènement tax, led to the expulsion of his brothers-in-law Presidents Gragnague and Caminade from the discussion on grounds that they too had an interest in the tax farms.[14] The Caminades and Gragnagues were both related to the Bertiers, and the Maussacs later allied themselves with the Fieubets. These names seem to have represented a particular social type: the rising family associated with the purchase of newly-created offices and with involvement in novel, 'exploitative' tax farms.

The Cour des Comptes suffered the same kind of internal division between entrenched 'regionalists' and aspiring 'loyalists' during the same years; however, in certain respects its circumstances were different. Being a newer, less prestigious court which was more oriented towards financial affairs, it was in some ways less and in some ways more cosmopolitan than the Parlement. Less, because its members lacked the prestigious contacts of its rival. There were no bishops at all from Comptes families in our period, and very few alliances with nobles of regional significance. Only one family, that of Pierre Dauteville, who purchased the barony of Vauvert amidst great controversy in 1642, had any claim to entrance to the Estates.[15] A few claimed links to ancient lines, but the origins of most Comptes councillors were even more geographically restricted than those of the Parlement. Hardly anybody had come recently from outside the province, and there was a concentration of families from nearby Uzès, Nîmes, Béziers, or Narbonne, many of whom had never really abandoned the présidial courts of Montpellier and Nîmes or the bureaux des finances. Comptes families had more cosmopolitan visions in that some of them were Calvinists who had outside ties in the Chambre de l'Édit, like the Ranchins, or connections with other Huguenot centers abroad. Most of them also came from financial circles where broader perspectives were necessary to success.

The history of the Comptes reveals an underlying continuity of political alignments. When a new first president had to be chosen in 1642, one

[14] Malenfant, II, 32–4, 181–185; III, 64–72.

[15] P-V Feb. 3, 1645, Mar. 28, 1661.

faction representing a desire for collegial independence supported President Charles Grasset in order to stop the progress of Jacques-Philippe de Maussac, a loyalist interloper from the Parlement who had purchased an office of president in 1628. The intendants favored Maussac, but a relative nonentity was actually chosen, François Bon, son of a taille receiver of Nîmes who had only entered the company in 1636.[16] Bon was probably the choice of Mazarin himself, and he exemplifies the combination of loyalism and financial connections which characterized the age. The same individuals continued to play the same role in the crisis of the 1640s. After the popular uprising of 1645, it was Maussac who was believed to have denounced the Comptes to the king, along with Dupuy, the *partisan* whose panicky firings on the crown had set off the popular violence in the first place, and Antoine Crouzet, the juge mage and ally of Baltazar who had tried to quell the disturbance.[17] Between 1646 and 1648 the Comptes was split in two, with the 'aides' chamber being exiled to Carcassonne and the 'comptes' chamber being joined in Montpellier by a much-detested 'semester' chamber created by the sale of new offices. None other than Maussac was named first president of this new Comptes of Montpellier while Dupuy became president of the even more controversial 'semester' chamber. Meanwhile it was Grasset who became the leader of the opposition from his exile in Carcassonne. He was even accused along with his ally, Saint-Hillaire, one of the alleged 1645 agitators, of arranging to ambush and murder Dupuy on a road outside of Montpellier.[18] Much later, in Colbert's memoir of 1663, three of those singled out as royal servants were Crouzet, now a president in the Comptes, President Boucaud, and Guillaume Clausel, all of whom had taken Maussac's side in the disputes of 1648.[19]

The permanent officers of the Estates were also linked to local networks. The three syndic-generals were drawn from the urban oligarchies of their respective towns – Toulouse, Carcassonne, and Nîmes – with close ties to the local courts.[20] The most interesting post was treasurer of the bourse,

[16] Baltazar to Séguier, Nov. 22, 1644: Lubl., p. 95; Bosquet to Séguier, June 22, 1643: Lubl., p. 35; memoir on the Comptes from 1642: B.N. ms. fr. 18483, 49.

[17] Pierre Serres, *Histoire de la Cour des Comptes, Aides et Finances de Montpellier* (Montpellier, 1878), p. 52. It is not entirely clear who this President Dupuy was: the *partisan* Jean Dupuy, who was closely related to other members of the Comptes, or Marc-Antoine Dupuy, a treasurer-general of finance of Montpellier. They were probably related.

[18] Memoir against reuniting the Comptes, 1648: B.N. ms. fr. 18483, 66; case of Guillaume Clausel against the Aides of Carcassonne, 1647: ibid., pp. 206–7; Baltazar to Mazarin, Nov. 28, 1646: A.A.E. France 1634, 259.

[19] Elements of family ties among the agitators can be glimpsed in the resistance to Maussac in 1648. President Trinquere de la Greffe took the lead, followed by Ranchin his nephew, Greffeuille his wife's uncle, and Étienne Guilleminet whose relationship to the Lucrèce de Guilleminet whom Trinquere's son married in 1654 is unclear.

[20] In 1662 we find Bezons interceding on behalf of Pierre de Roux-Montbel, syndic-general from Carcassonne, whose connections made him very useful to the crown in the Estates. In 1673 we learn

a position which rose in importance despite the vicissitudes of the period. Bernard de Reich de Pennautier, the treasurer deposed in 1632 for rebellion, belonged to an entrenched dynasty descended from a diocesan receiver of Carcassonne. His mother was a Caulet from Toulouse (the family involved in the tax farms – see above); his wife was Louise de Claret de Saint-Félix (the family of the procurer-general of the Parlement). Pennautier was replaced in 1632 with three royal appointees who served in rotation as part of the settlement in the Edict of Béziers. The most notable of these was François Le Secq, a Parisian banker, and the others were indigenous financial entrepreneurs, friends of Baltazar.[21] Meanwhile Pennautier maintained his presence by exercising his office of treasurer-general of finance in Montpellier. He was related, through his wife, to the influential Toiras and Calvisson families and, through his daughter, to Henri de Puisserguier, governor of Carcassonne. A pro-Pennautier lobby which included these people, the archbishop of Narbonne, and even, on one occasion, Schomberg, was constantly trying to get him reinstated as treasurer of the bourse.[22] This group, which by 1648 was part of the Orléans faction, succeeded in getting Pennautier's son Pierre appointed as one of the two alternating treasurers restored in 1649. After Pierre's death in 1653, his brother, Pierre-Louis de Reich de Pennautier, took over the post (1653–1709). He ultimately became sole treasurer of the bourse and treasurer-general of the clergy of France and married the daughter of Le Secq. In the heyday of Louis XIV he was a figure of national stature, important enough to be implicated in the 'affair of the poisons'. Back in Languedoc he was closely associated with the Roux family in Carcasonne, which was tied to the 'dissident' Potiers of Toulouse as well as to the présidial of Carcassonne and the post of syndic-general of the Estates, which was held by Pierre de Roux, seigneur de Montbel from 1648 to 1704. A Roux–Pennautier–Potier axis might thus have provided a unique judicial–financial orientation for provincial resistance if the restored Pennautiers had not been totally committed to the king's and province's common financial interests after the revocation of the Edict of Béziers.

This brief summary underscores several points. Family and personal connections did underlie or reinforce political factions. They help explain the bitterness of the splits within both the Parlement and the Comptes, and they give continuity to a series of otherwise disconnected flareups. They show links between various power centers – courts, Estates, bishoprics, sénéchaussées, financial posts. Many of the allegiances of the Fronde make

that Jean de Boyer, syndic-general from Toulouse, did not get along with Bezons but was an ally of Verneuil, who recommended him to the new intendant d'Aguesseau. Bezons to Colbert, Mar. 28, 1662: Mel. Col. 107, 91; Verneuil to d'Aguesseau, Aug. 5, 1673: A.N. H 1692.

[21] For more on these figures, see chapter 11.

[22] Archbishop of Narbonne to Chavigny and Mazarin, Nov. 26, 1642: A.A.E. France 1632, 140, 142.

sense in terms of these links, and it is possible to see resistance coalescing around key figures whose ties in various arenas gave hints of potential for dangerous opposition.

The logic of the political changes of the time was that some leaders chose resistance in the name of tradition while others advocated strong support for the royal program. These choices were not made along socio-economic lines although there was a tendency for some of the new 'loyalists' to be aspiring individuals with connections to finance and new offices. Both the factions of 'agitators' and 'loyalists' were parallel groupings of officers tied by marriage or service to a few patriarchs. It is hard to say which came first, the political tendency or the family alliance. But since the same figures reappeared in the same camps through the years, it is clear that there was a strong component of 'clan' which heightened factionalism in moments of tension, regardless of the issue.

The most important characteristic of these networks was their fragmentation. No family, group or corporate entity, not even the noble commanders, had contacts stretching across the whole province. By their very nature family or corporate ties originating locally could provide only elements of client networks because there was no common source of patronage within the province to which they could all look. Personal influence created interlocking fragments of networks, but leadership had to come from without, and in the seventeenth century this meant from the crown. Only royal networks could provide the positions and pull needed by regional potentates to maintain their influence.

ROYAL CLIENT NETWORKS

Ties with the royal agents and, through them, with the king or his ministers, were common, and information on them is plentiful because of the nature of the sources. This material is difficult to interpret, however, because of the fluidity of the data. Ties of influence were constantly shifting in response to a continuous series of deaths, appointments, marriages, and changes in political fortune. The best way to think of this evolving sum of petty facts and biographical trivia is to organize it into five consecutive but overlapping client systems, each conceived as a unit (their sequence is portrayed in figure 8). This method exaggerates the stability of the networks and ignores the different kinds of relationships contained within them, but it brings out an important reality as well. These five networks, revolving around the personalities of Montmorency, Richelieu–Schomberg, Orléans, Mazarin, and Colbert had two interesting characteristics. First, they were reflections of the structure of power at the center, and their timing followed the shifts of regime at the royal court. Second, they were personal

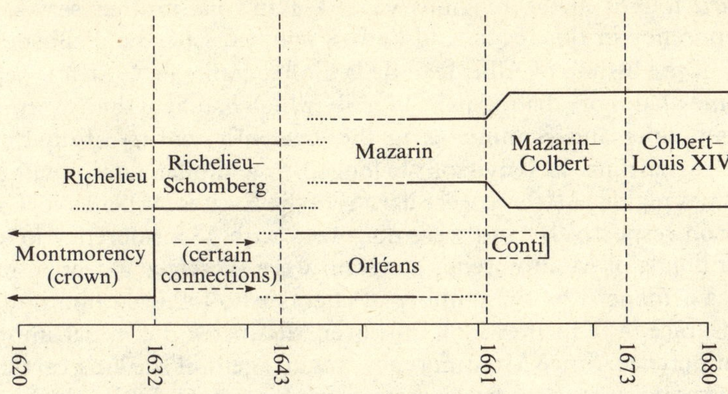

Figure 8. Chronology of royal client networks.

systems which eroded rapidly with the aging of their members. A change at court always required the construction of a new system in the province although the old one might hobble along for the months and years necessary to effect such a shift. For this reason the phenomenon of transition periods was particularly interesting. Turning points like the crisis of the Catholic League, the overthrow of Montmorency, the death of Louis XIII, and the death of Mazarin resulted in free scrambles for power which were critical in the fortunes of families, for the choices made then established alliances which conditioned the political environment for as much as a generation.[23]

A. *Montmorency*. The system over which Henri II, duc de Montmorency, presided before 1632 was extraordinarily powerful and more provincially based than its successors.[24] Montmorency himself symbolized a unique fusion of the regionalist loyalties of the religious wars with the royalism of the politique support for Henry IV and Louis XIII, and this potent mixture had been recharged by the compaigns he commanded against the Protestants in 1621–2, 1627 and 1629. The governor did not own extensive property in Languedoc, but his alliances were based on close marriage ties with most of the prominent local families, and were reinforced by common battlefield experiences.

Among the alliances with mediocre families of local importance, three are worth singling out because of their brilliant futures. Louis de Cardailhac, comte de Bieules, was the son of a royalist noble from the region of Castres

[23] Note the parallel remarks in Denis Richet's suggestive essay, 'La Formation des grands serviteurs de l'état (fin XVIe-début XVIIe siècle)', *L'Arc*, 65 (1976), 54–61.

[24] Montmorency's relationships are well detailed in Paul Gachon, *Les États de Languedoc et l'édit de Béziers (1632)* (Paris, 1887), especially pp. 84–92.

who had fought in the religious wars. He and his brother served under Montmorency in the 1620s, and he had married Lucrèce d'Elbène of the family of the bishop of Albi. Jean de la Croix, comte de Castries, belonged to a somewhat more distinguished family which had held the governorships of Montpellier and Sommières in the sixteenth century. Jean-Louis de Nogaret, marquis de Calvisson, belonged to a similar family with ties to the Nîmes region. All three were barons of the Estates (Villeneuve, Castries, Calvisson respectively) and were disgraced with Montmorency in 1632.

The bonds of Montmorency's system were therefore personal, military ones, as evidenced by the number of clients who followed him into revolt and disgrace.[25] A further look, however, dissipates the initial impression of omnipotence. Since Montmorency was an agent of the king carrying out popular policies, it was hard to distinguish his personal following from the king's or to predict which clients would, like the Ventadours, choose king over governor at the moment of rebellion. Furthermore, his system was strikingly concentrated in Bas-Languedoc and the Cévennes, leaving the region around Toulouse in the hands of less closely allied parlementaire families and certain loyalist nobles like Cornusson and Ambres, seneschals of Toulouse and Lauragais. Montmorency's hegemony was already being undermined in the 1620s by the beginnings of Richelieu's system. The cardinal had built the citadel in Montpellier after 1622 to contain the Protestants and had placed it under his ally the marquis de Fosséz. Three key episcopal appointments in 1628 laid the foundations for royal support: Claude de Rebé in Narbonne, Silvestre de Crusy de Marcillac in Mende, and Clément de Bonzi in Béziers. Finally, during the élus crisis when the loyalty of Montmorency became suspect, Richelieu's own agents, led by Miron and Le Camus, began to infiltrate the province with various assignments.

B. *Richelieu–Schomberg.* Thus when Montmorency fell in 1632 and most of his supporters were removed from their positions, the Richelieu–Schomberg system was already partly in place. The new governor, Charles duc d'Hallwin (later maréchal de Schomberg), played a different sort of role from his predecessor. He had no local roots, but, as a loyal ally of

[25] This analysis of the five networks is based on tables showing who held all the important posts in given years. Some of the principal lists of office holders are Bejard, *Recueil* and Beaudeau, *Armorial* for the barons of the Estates; along with Pierre Louvet, *Remarques sur l'histoire de Languedoc* (Toulouse, 1657); 'Description de la province de Languedoc': Bibl. Mun. Tse ms. 603; and many items from the procès-verbaux themselves. Lists of sovereign court councillors are in Vialles, *Études* and A.D. H-G. ms. 193, as cited above; municipal officers are enumerated in Léon Ménard, *Histoire civile ecclésiastique et littéraire de la ville de Nîmes*, 7 vols. (Nîmes, 1873–5), vol. VI; Charles d'Aigrefeuille, *Histoire de la ville de Montpellier*, ed. Pijardière, 4 vols. (Montpellier, 1875–82); and Barnabé Farmian de Rozoi, *Annales de la ville de Toulouse*, 4 vols. (Paris, 1771–6), vol. IV. Prelates are adequately listed in *Dictionnaire d'histoire et de géographie ecclésiastique* (Paris, 1912). Chronologies of all sorts are in B.N. Languedoc (Bénédictins), 71.

Richelieu, he could rely not only on the cardinal's creatures in the province but also on his own friends who were installed in key positions, left conveniently vacant by the recent rebellion. The bishopric of Albi went to Hallwin's cousin, Daillon du Lude, and the posts of seneschal and governor of Montpellier were given to his intimates, along with the other military governorships along the coast. At the same time Richelieu raised the Bertiers, whose faction of parlementaires began to coalesce in Haut-Languedoc, as a counterbalance to the unfriendly Archbishop Montchal of Toulouse.

The Richelieu–Schomberg system was therefore based more on ties of personal loyalty between individuals implanted in the province than on dynastic alliances between locally-based families. But it would be a mistake to assume that the crown had 'taken over' the province from the 'independent' Montmorency. Schomberg was a gallant and popular leader, 'infinitely loved' in Languedoc, who had close emotional ties with many local leaders and who, though always loyal to royal policy, intervened frequently in support of traditional authorities and privileges.[26] Furthermore, it was not locally-based families, as such, who were removed from power in 1632, but only those families which had made the wrong decisions. In fact, when Ventadour's post of lieutenant-general under Montmorency was divided into three, it was given back to locally-based nobles whose districts now coincided with and reinforced their zones of influence.[27]

Schomberg's function was increasingly military, as the Catalonian war front became critical and resistance to innovations mounted in the province. His network of allies held firm and was reinforced by the constant presence of two intendants serving near him, one more directly concerned with financial and provisioning matters (Miron) and one more skilled at placating the province (Le Camus), while, back in Paris, Schomberg's secretary Baltazar was continually intervening with Richelieu's secretary Charpentier to implement the necessary rulings.[28] This system was nevertheless fragile, resting on loyalty to Richelieu and patriotic acceptance of wartime necessities. Not all of Montmorency's bishops had been deposed, and the hatred of Richelieu later expressed in Archbishop Montchal's memoirs was secretly felt by many.[29]

[26] Senecterre to Chavigny, Jan. 21, 1642: A.A.E. France 1632, 55.

[27] Just-Henri, comte de Tournon, who received the Cévennes, was already baron of the Estates, seneschal of Auvergne, and bailli of Vivarais, and had been married in succession to a Ventadour and a Montmorency-Bouteville! Louis, duc d'Arpajon in Bas-Languedoc, was the son of Henry IV's governor of Rouergue and of a daughter from the local house of Clermont-Lodève. In Haut-Languedoc the marquis d'Ambres, also a baron of the Estates, was seneschal of Lauragais. What these men had in common was not their independence of local influences but rather their loyalty in 1632.

[28] See chapter 5.

[29] Charles Montchal, *Mémoires de Mr. de Montchal archevêque de Toulouse* (Rotterdam, 1718).

C. *Gaston d'Orléans and the Fronde.* The vulnerability of Schomberg's position was illustrated by the confusion of lines of influence which followed the deaths of Richelieu and Louis XIII. Gaston d'Orléans was appointed governor for political reasons in early 1644, but since he had no intention of residing in the province, Schomberg was retained under him as lieutenant-general until the latter's exasperated resignation in 1647. Schomberg's dilemma was that, lacking a firm local power base, his position depended on favor at court, but this favor was fragile because his status was inferior to that of the princes of the blood. Even before 1644 the dilemma was apparent in the duality of lines of authority which developed between Séguier and Mazarin. When Bosquet was named intendant in 1642, it was as a protégé of Séguier while his colleague Baltazar, who arrived some nineteen months later, was Schomberg's right-hand man, obtained through direct intervention of Mazarin and the queen. We have already seen how Bosquet and Baltazar weakened the royal program with their precedence quarrels and contradictory rulings.

Orléans's appointment permitted both frivolous nominations from his immediate coterie and the return to influence of those expelled or discontented under the previous regime.[30] The resurgence of local families was no accident, it being in the nature of things that disgraced notables be allowed to resume their 'natural' roles, provided they had purged their disgrace by appropriate loyalty and service in the meantime. All three of the local leaders mentioned above were promptly restored. Bieules was the first to return, perhaps because of his long association with Schomberg and Montmorency and his heroic performance at the Battle of Leucate. In 1637 his barony was restored to the Estates, and in 1638 he became seneschal of Castres. Calvisson returned to the Estates in 1642, and the son of Castries was restored in 1643. Soon (1644–5) all three of them had their lands raised to marquisates.[31] Meanwhile Orléans named Louis de Saint-Bonnet de Toiras, son of the rebel Toiras, as seneschal of Montpellier, and Orléans's old fellow conspirator, the comte d'Aubijoux, as governor of the citadel of Montpellier. Aubijoux (whose brother had died at Leucate) was brother-in-law of Toiras, and he was also part of the circle of *libertins* surrounding Orléans which included the marquis de Fontrailles (who agitated in Toulouse during the Fronde) and Jean de Lordat, baron de Bram (who was soon named governor of Carcassonne).[32] Sensing the shift in the winds,

[30] In 'Le Gouvernement' Caldicott offers useful new evidence on Orléans's coterie and perceptive comments about his importance. However, some of Caldicott's statements about the situation in the province, especially those concerning the uniformity of client ties, are misleading.

[31] 'Erections to marquisates' in A.D. H-G. ms. 193.

[32] On the complex connections between these parties, L. de Santi, 'Le Château de Montmaur' and 'La Maison de Lévis-Montmaur', in *Mémoires de l'Académie des Sciences, Inscriptions et Belles-Lettres de Toulouse*, 10th series 2 (1902), 295–320, 351–76.

more and more parties jumped on the Orléans bandwagon, celebrating their influence publicly by pulling off minor coups of authority. We have seen the scramble for favor in the deputations to court of 1643–4, leading to the imposition of Orléans candidates on the capitoulat of Toulouse. There was a cabal of bishops and deputies which blocked the Estates of 1645–6 on behalf of Orléans, and in Albi and Béziers, both of which had loyalist bishops, the Orléanist allies took the other side in factional quarrels. By the end of 1646, Baltazar was lamenting that these people wanted to 'use power like Montmorency' and recommended the suppression of the posts of lieutenant general before they were filled with Orléanist nominees whose presence would enhance the influence of Toiras and Aubijoux. Sure enough, Aubijoux himself was soon named lieutenant-general of Haut-Languedoc, Bieules of Bas-Languedoc, and Scipion de Grimoard de Beauvoir, comte du Roure, Orléans's first chamberlain, lieutenant-general of the Cévennes.[33] In the Parlement it was harder and harder to suppress the Potier–Garaud faction which had many links to Orléans allies.

The episodes of the Fronde consolidated and developed these same trends, though the situation was muted by Orléans's role in the Mazarin government, a position which placed him officially on the side of the crown, not the rebels. When he finally did join the princes in rebellion in December 1651, his clients were quick to respond. Aubijoux paraded his illegally-raised troops through Toulouse and made a show of arresting the intendant Foullé, who entered Montpellier bearing royal orders. The Parlement decreed against Mazarin by a narrow margin. Orléanist agents Saint-Luc and Choisy toured around mobilizing the opposition, and the governor of Aiguesmortes seized the salt stores while Roure, Castries and a string of other commanders fortified their strongholds. Those loyal to Mazarin lay low.

The crisis of the minority demonstrates the complexity of the relationship between national client systems and locally-based power centers. Orléans's system represented the opportunity for groups like the Toiras–Calvisson circle to reassert themselves at the expense of those whose fortunes had been tied to Richelieu. It also provided a pole of attraction for the newly-forming groups of 'agitators' which were coalescing in the Parlement and the Estates. Yet, it was not merely a setback in the march forward of royal control because it engendered regroupings, marriages, and resurgences of authority which swung the pendulum of influence toward indigenous ruling families after the swing towards outsiders of the Richelieu–Schomberg system.

D. *Mazarin.* In the very midst of this confusion the client system of

[33] Baltazar to Mazarin, Dec. 19, 1646 and his memoir following this letter, which must date from early in 1647: A.A.E. France 1634, 262, 264.

Cardinal Mazarin was quietly developing, providing a case study in the generation of such a network.[34] Unlike Richelieu, Mazarin did not benefit from a wholesale turnover of officials after a rebellion; in fact, his real adversaries, the clients of Orléans, remained in power. Many of the former Richelieu–Schomberg loyalists also remained, but they no longer proved very useful – a perfect illustration of the deterioration of a predecessor's system. True, Mazarin depended at first on these faltering and beleaguered loyalists, but their crotchety pleas for support, their discredited authority, and their isolation from events limited their usefulness.

The most loyal voices came from new, relatively unknown figures who began reporting to Mazarin as early as 1646. There were local nobles with relatives in the Parlement like the chevaliers de Trelon and Pibrac in Toulouse; churchmen with contacts like the abbé Calvières, brother of the controversial baron of Couffoulens, who held a post in the bishop's household in Nîmes, and the abbé Caumels, also from a distinguished family of parlementaires, who was vicar-general of Toulouse and manager of the bishopric after the death of Archbishop Montchal in 1651; La Baume and Mondevergues, both figures from the judicial circles in Nîmes, and the maître des requêtes Montchal, relative of the late archbishop. Among military men there were François de Moustiers, comte de Merinville, who was beginning to rise to prominence after marrying the heiress to the barony of Rieux; the marquis de Chouppes, one of Mazarin's loyal followers, and the seigneur d'Argencour, a Richelieu–Schomberg nominee as governor of Narbonne.[35] I do not know how these particular men came to Mazarin's attention, but the prominence of lesser clerics suggests ecclesiastical channels, and their concentration in Nîmes and Toulouse might provide a clue.

Mazarin's early contacts continued to work diligently during the bad moments of the Fronde when Orléans's agents were totally unreliable.[36] When the crisis was over, Mazarin's necessarily cautious and gradual policy became clearer. In the Parlement he followed the policy of naming new, personally loyal people, even against the advice of his agents. He had already used the same policy in choosing François Bon for the first presidency of the Comptes a decade earlier. When First President Jean de Bertier died in 1653, the Cardinal refused to name either the candidate of the former frondeur group, Donneville, or that of his own agent Trelon, who recommended Jean-François Gineste, Bertier's son-in-law, as a logical

[34] A summary of all the correspondence, especially A.A.E. France 1634 and 1636.

[35] Pierre de Conty, seigneur d'Argencour, was, however, a respected old-timer who had advised the king on fortifications and participated in many famous battles since the 1620s.

[36] De La Baume and Calvière to Mazarin, Apr. 30, 1652; Mondevergues to Mazarin, July 17, 1652; various letters from Maugiron to Mazarin, March, 1652: A.A.E. France 1636, 42, 44, 89; A.A.E. France 1634, 571, 575, 581.

successor who would put a 'large cabal' at the disposal of the crown.[37] Instead he chose to elevate the procureur-general Gaspard de Fieubet to the post, a man perfectly exemplary of Mazarinist inclinations since he belonged to the Toulouse branch of a loyalist family which was solidly and respectably rooted in the Parlement at the same time that its Parisian branch was intimately tied to the financial circles so familiar to Mazarin's rule.[38] Gradually Fieubet developed a circle of family allies comparable to, but separate from, Bertier's, including his son-in-law, the new advocate-general Jean-Guy de Maniban, and a group of other loyalists including Frezals, Trelon, Villepassans, and Cironis.

Mazarin's other appointments had the same effect of shifting power towards his own support group. Most of his episcopal choices became loyal correspondents and voters in the Estates. Of particular significance was the arrival of the team of agents who had worked together in Catalonia, the intendant Bezons, who was a protégé of Michel LeTellier (1653), and Pierre de Marca, the diplomatic and absolutist jurist who succeeded Montchal as archbishop of Toulouse (1652). It is worth noting how many of Mazarin's choices arrived, like Fieubet, with Parisian financial connections. The Fouquets, François (bishop of Agde, 1643, archbishop of Narbonne, 1659) and Louis (bishop of Agde, 1656), were brothers of the surintendant des finances; Michel Tubeuf (bishop of Saint-Pons, 1654) was brother of the intendant des finances; Bezons himself belonged to a Parisian family which was later to become a financial dynasty.

E. *Colbert.* Colbert's system, which developed in two stages before and after the turning point of 1673, was based on the foundations laid by Mazarin, with important elaborations and a dramatic change in tone. This time the same team of supporters continued to function: Fieubet and his followers in the Parlement, who were able increasingly to dominate the capitouls; the bishops of Lavaur, Montpellier, Saint-Papoul, and Saint-Pons, all of them Mazarin appointees; the comte de Mérinville, named governor of Narbonne in 1664. But more important in these formative years was the mediating influence of another of Mazarin's creatures, Pierre de Bonzi, who was to become the lynchpin of Louis XIV's control over Languedoc.[39] Bonzi was the son of a Florentine senator and heir to a long line of grandiose bishops of Béziers who had been clients of the crown since the days of Catherine de Medicis. He had been raised by his uncle Clément

[37] Donneville to Mazarin, May 4, 1653; Trelon to Mazarin, Sept. 15, 1653: A.A.E. France 1636, 157, 203.

[38] On Fieubet, B.N. Dossiers bleus, 270: Henry Amilhau, *Nos premiers présidents* (Toulouse, 1882), pp. 339–51; Dubédat, vol. II, pp. 260–1.

[39] On Bonzi, E. Sabatier, *Histoire de la ville et des évêques de Béziers* (Béziers, 1854), pp. 374–77; Henri Monin, *Essai sur l'histoire administrative du Languedoc pendant l'intendance de Basville (1685–1719)* (Paris, 1884), pp. 8–12; Roschach, vol. XIII, pp. 494–8.

de Bonzi (bishop of Béziers, 1628–59) and then served Mazarin personally as ambassador to Venice, Tuscany, and Poland. In 1644 (again we see the importance of the minority as crucible of change) a fateful marriage had taken place between Bonzi's sister Elizabeth and René-Gaspard, marquis de Castries, who was just restoring his reputation after the disgrace of his father in the Montmorency debacle. What prompted this opportune alliance between one of the prominent 'regional' figures and a very royalist foreign dynasty is unknown, but the consequences were striking. Bonzi, who was serving as intermediary at court for Mazarin's episcopal allies in Languedoc even before his appointment as bishop, was rapidly raised from bishop of Béziers (1659) to archbishop of Toulouse (1669), cardinal (1672) and archbishop of Narbonne (1673). Castries, who had played a very minor political role as baron of the Estates (reinstated 1643) and governor of Sommières (1646), became governor of Montpellier in 1660 (which was taken from Roure upon the death of Orléans) and lieutenant-general of Bas-Languedoc in 1668 (when Bieules died). Bonzi interceded frequently for Castries, and the latter gradually became the spokesman for interests in Montpellier and the Cour des Comptes. Meanwhile an unprecedented game of musical chairs in which loyal prelates were shifted from one see to another within Languedoc assured the king of continuity of support in the Estates.

The accession of Bonzi to the archbishopric of Narbonne, and thus to the presidency of the Estates in 1673, coincided with the arrival of Henri d'Aguesseau as intendant and the capitulation of the Estates to the 'royal wishes' concerning the *don gratuit*. It also marked the apogee of Colbert's system and a perfect marriage between the interests of the provincial leaders and the courtly aristocracy. Bezons had not gotten along well with the duc de Verneuil, the new figurehead governor (1666–82), and he had not seen eye to eye with Bonzi on important regional issues. In the end, his credit with Colbert had even diminished. D'Aguesseau, on the other hand, was closely allied with Verneuil before even arriving in Languedoc.[40] He was a fiscal and administrative expert in the new Colbertian style and had the social stature to accommodate provincial egos.

Colbert's system, which was built upon the foundations of the Mazarin–Bezons–Fieubet alliance and perfected, after 1672, with the installation of Bonzi and d'Aguesseau, was comparable to the previous four systems, but with certain qualitative improvements. One was the degree to which better communications and organization had made it a 'national' network, directed from Versailles but only in close coordination with d'Aguesseau and other dignitaries in the province.

A second improvement was the way the patronage system expanded

[40] Verneuil to d'Aguesseau, Aug. 5, 1673: A.N. H 1692.

laterally within Languedoc. In addition to his chief clients, Colbert's 'team' now included a host of other notables who not only took the royal side in disputes as their loyalist predecessors had, but actively volunteered to serve as Colbert's eyes and ears, looking after his projects and proposing innovations for his consideration. Not only were several allies in the Parlement (Fieubet, Torreil) and the Comptes (Crouzet, Solas, de Ratte) working in this manner, but there were bishops (Albi, Castres), a number of financier–entrepreneurs (Riquet, Pennautier), some ambitious nobles (Castries), and a flow of engineers and technicians of various sorts. Bonzi managed the Estates and coordinated the syndic-generals, who in turn had relatives and allies in the towns. At the same time, this great set of connections was still an informal client network dependent on individuals. Like its predecessors, it would crumble after the death of Colbert and be replaced with a new system constructed by Lamoignon de Basville; one which entailed the disgrace of Bonzi and the creation of a new set of provincial alliances.[41]

Personal ties were central to the functioning of seventeenth-century absolutism on every level of government and remained so throughout the period. They provided contacts between institutions as well as the means to assure that petitions would be favorably received, law suits would be brought to a satisfactory conclusion, and expressions of support would be generated in the proper places at the proper times. They also provided the framework for factional conflicts by establishing preexistent divisions within companies which served as a catalyst to side-taking as soon as an issue of authority or politics appeared. Networks of contacts were formed by the intersection of local systems 'from below' with national systems 'from above'. Within the province individuals who had considerable wealth and appropriate positions of authority could use marriage or personal allegiance to extend their contacts, but nobody could get very far without royal appointments. These regional fragments were therefore rapidly tied in with larger networks involving the governor, the intendant, or a contact at court.

The succession of royal regimes played a discordant counterpoint to the factional life of the province. Since local factions never included everybody, there was a tendency for those who were left out to rally to any alternative provided by a shift of allegiances at court. Montmorency's system had been the last in which notables who revered the crown and saw it as the buttress against disorder could simultaneously be loyal to the king and follow a congenial independent patron. Already the tough measures associated with Richelieu were straining these ties, as loyalists who supported them began

[41] Monin, *Essai*, pp. 9–12.

to look more and more like opportunists, even traitors, to their compatriots. When Montmorency went into rebellion, he created a crisis for his followers, many of whom were deposed when he was executed. An opening had been created for Richelieu–Schomberg-style loyalists like Bertier, who saw themselves as pursuing no less a 'politique' policy than their predecessors, but who were increasingly embarrassed by the unpleasantness of the measures they had to support and the provincial patriotism of those who opposed them. Before 1643 these loyalists had the advantage, but then the advent of Orléans brought their opponents back into prominence.

His appointment as governor, though caused by the weakness of the royal minority, provided a safety valve for growing dissatisfaction. The spreading networks of 'dissidents', who represented various combinations of loyalty to Montmorency, reaction against royal policies under Richelieu, and factional opposition to the groups in power, coalesced around Orléans. Intense rivalries between the Richelieu 'loyalists' and the Orléanist 'dissidents' wrought havoc with local politics between 1643 and 1660, but the fact that Montmorency's old allies were back in favor and that Orléans was on the side of the king most of the time may have held off a serious rebellion during the Fronde. Paradoxically, the dissolute Orléans helped reunite the courtly and provincial systems by reintegrating the provincial dissidents into the mainstream of politics at court. Meanwhile Mazarin, like Richelieu, had to build a support system from the ground up, but instead of disintegrating on the death of its founder, his network was given new life by the advent of a king whose prestige suddenly made membership profitable, respectable, and attractive.

For the first time under Colbert, the dominant client network was really a *royal* network, centering on the king himself and tied directly to the central administration, with no possibility of divergent signals emanating from rival figureheads. Such a system could deliver effective support far more consistently than its predecessors; thus it is no wonder that Languedocian leaders flocked to join it. The king and the rulers had been linked in one larger unit which guaranteed the king support and lent the rulers glamor and favor as never before, provided they played by its rules. Descendants of 'dissidents' and descendants of 'loyalists' alike basked in preeminence. Even under Louis XIV, however, they were still part of a system built on intensely personal relationships.

11

Tax flows and society

The exchange of taxes was another transaction which established relationships between king and rulers, rulers and population. Too often taxation has been conceptualized as extraction, the chief question being how much the king could draw from the province and how much the province could hold back. What was really at stake, however, was distribution, for Languedocian taxes represented one of the largest, most regular flows of liquid wealth in the province – one which could be tapped by those with influence or privilege. Taille collection siphoned off a substantial amount of the surplus produced by peasants and artisans and channelled it upwards towards the Estates and the king. Along the way it passed through the hands of a multitude of financier–collectors who profited from their possession of it in a variety of ways. When it reached its destination it was redistributed, often within the province. This system of collection and distribution affected the political stance taken by the various provincial institutions and the changing relations of certain individuals and groups to the crown. It was one of the major sources of new wealth for those on the rise, and it explains some of the anger against *partisans* which characterized the first half of the century. Most important, it provides another dimension in explaining the change in royal–provincial relations which took place after 1660.

This chapter traces several interwoven issues. There is first the basic question of where the annual taille funds went – how much of them reached the king and what effect the distribution of the rest had on provincial relationships. We must also consider whether this tax flow shifted during our period. Second, there is the related phenomenon of capital accumulation. One of the most distinctive characteristics of the collection process was its capacity for generating wealth along the way. This took two forms, both important. On the one hand there was the role of financiers-proper in exploiting the system for their own benefit. Here a change took place from an earlier phase when investors from outside the province seemed to be preying on the Languedocian taxpayers to a later phase when local families took control of tax farms and integrated themselves into a more manageable partnership with Parisian finance. On the other hand there was the investment in the provincial debt itself. Here participation spread beyond a few inside leaders to wider circles of elite participants. Both phenomena – the rise of indigenous financiers and the spread of aristocratic investment in the public debt – culminated under Louis XIV in a more profitable form of participation for the rulers of Languedoc, one which helps to explain both the shifts in the pattern of tax flow and the rulers' satisfaction in the system of the Sun King.

To understand these issues we must examine a series of related aspects. First, the special nature of the collection system itself; second, the relationship of financiers, internal and external, to this system; third, the general distribution pattern, seen in two representative years, 1677 and 1647; finally, the significance of the public debt in the new ambiance of Louis XIV's reign.

THE SYSTEM

At the end of a session of the Estates a *mande*, or formal command to pay, was drawn up for each diocese, to be presented by the commissioner from the Estates to the diocesan assiette.[1] These *mandes* were formulated as a series of separate articles, starting with traditionally fixed sums, then moving to new grants and special appropriations. The list of sums became a litany to be recited on each level of taxation: a given town owed so much for its share of the sums granted to the king for the *aide*, *préciput*, *octroi* and *crue*, so much for its share of the *taillon*, so much for the cost of the Estates, and so forth. One thought of taxes not as a lump sum but as a series of distinct sums always allocated for specific purposes and attached to specific authorizing decrees. The itemizing was necessary not only because of the traditional impulse to repeat the customary and separate it from the novel, but also because different items were paid to different treasurers and occasioned different kinds of collection fees. The assiette added on its own expenses in the form of additional articles; then the expanded list was apportioned among the towns and rural communities, each of which received a mande similar in form to its diocesan counterpart, but with the new expenses included, and signed by the principal commissioner of the assiette. These local communities went through the same process, adding on their local costs and then drawing up a roll of the sums owed by each individual taxpayer.

The collection process was more complicated. Most taxes were payable in installments (*termes*) geared to fit the rhythm of the agricultural harvests. It was the duty of the local collectors to pay their share of these installments

[1] Arrangements at the Estates are discussed in the procès-verbaux, including each year's list of the *commissaires principaux des assiettes*, who were sent to preside over the assiettes.

on the customary date to the appropriate receivers (*receveurs*). These diocesan receivers were in turn required to pay their superiors on the provincial level. In theory, therefore, taxes would have flowed from the local collectors up to their provincial or royal recipients in regular installments of one-third each June 1, September 1, and December 1. Two circumstances complicated this picture. The first was that taxes did not come in regularly because the amounts demanded bore no relation to the ability of the population to pay. Many payments were late; some taxpayers simply defaulted. The receivers were office-holding financiers who had contracted to supply the money in return for a percentage of the proceeds. They were therefore expected to make up any deficit out of their own funds. Receivers frequently tried to build extra collection expenses into their accounts or charge off uncollectable arrears as expenses, but such claims were often disavowed. On the other hand, the receivers were well placed to profit from loans to the collectivity and, more important, they had the use of the funds coming in until the day when they could no longer delay meeting their obligations. The whole financial system was in effect a competition for the effective possession and use of rare liquid capital.

The second complication was that receivers were expected to disburse part of their receipts to parties designated in *états* drawn up by the responsible authorities. This procedure by which the costs of government were 'assigned' to particular local revenue sources was necessary in a society where facilities for transfer were primitive and ready cash was scarce. But since the receivers had a variety of payees to consider and their funds came in sporadically or incompletely, their opportunities for withholding, shifting, and manipulating payments were almost unlimited. Rules were established giving preferential treatment to funds destined for the king or the province, but even so the possibility for diversion of funds was enormous. 'It is certain that they [the receivers] take possession of the bourse funds for their private affairs and delay paying what is legitimately owed to the offices and inhabitants of the province, on pretext that the money is owed to the king', complained one memorandum of the Estates.[2]

The backbone of the financial system was this network of financier–receivers.[3] Money passed from the local collectors to the diocesan receivers (*receveurs particuliers*) of the twenty-two dioceses or to the treasurer of the city of Toulouse, except that by a curious anachronism the proceeds of the *taillon*, one of the components of the provincial 'taille', went to distinct *receveurs du taillon*. The diocesan receivers were royal officers accountable before the Cour des Comptes, who received as fees 6 *deniers* per livre of

[2] A.N. H 748[198], 346.

[3] A description of this system is in Henri Monin, *Essai sur l'histoire administrative du Languedoc pendant l'intendance de Basville (1685–1719)* (Paris, 1884), pp. 49–72.

the funds they collected ($2\frac{1}{2}$ percent).[4] From the dioceses the money remaining after articles 'assigned' on these funds had been subtracted was transmitted to several treasurers on the provincial level. Taillon funds went to the receiver-general of the taillon (*receveur-général du taillon*) in the appropriate généralité (Toulouse or Montpellier). The 'taille' component went to the receiver-generals in Toulouse or Montpellier. The rest of the money (a large share of it) went to the treasurer of the bourse, who was responsible for paying it into the appropriate royal treasuries or disbursing it according to the orders of the officers of the Estates. The receiver-generals were royal officers like the diocesan receivers, but the treasurer of the bourse was responsible to the Estates. He was paid 2 deniers per livre (.833 percent) of the money he handled for his services, and, as the custodian of most of the province's funds, he was a banker of immense power.

It is already evident that twenty-two diocesan receivers (really sixty-six if the tripartite nature of the office is considered), two (or more) receiver-generals, and the treasurer of the bourse were important individuals, partly because their cut of the proceeds of taxation, though reasonable in size, afforded them a comfortable income which rose proportionate to the level of provincial taxation; but, more importantly, because their temporary possession of the provincial funds gave them the liquidity to engage in all sorts of other financial operations. A host of lesser financial agents also captured small trickles of the provincial tax flow: the taillon receivers, the *étapiers* who contracted to furnish the étape in each diocese, the *payeurs des gages* attached to each judicial company who disbursed the members' stipends out of funds paid to them by one of the receivers, the treasurers of garrison money, and so forth. We must also remember that the system of Estates dominated by local notables encouraged the restructuring of tax burdens so that originally indirect taxes were transformed into direct ones. We have seen how expensive 'edicts' and tax farms were 'bought out' by the Estates and thus transferred from special interest groups to the taxpaying population at large. The same was true of military étapes redistributed province-wide, of the provincial quartier d'hiver, and of the cost of public works like the canal. For every 10,000 livres of new taxes, at least 333 were added on in fees which passed from the hands of the taxpayers into those of the financiers, and 500 went to the costs of local collection.[5]

4 As a result of multiple creations of offices, each *recette* (receiving office) was composed of three receivers serving in rotation and a group of controllers (*contrôleurs particuliers*) who audited the accounts. The same was true of the taillon receivers and their controllers. For practical purposes, however, a single diocesan receiver and a single taillon receiver functioned in each diocese during each calendar year.

5 The local collectors received 5 percent, the diocesan receivers 2.5 percent, and the treasurer of the bourse .833 percent.

Other credit problems provided further opportunities for financiers to interpose themselves between taxpayers and the recipients of tax monies. Every new loan floated by the Estates channelled tax funds back into the hands of creditors (as interest) and financiers (as service fees for receiving the sums imposed for interest). Thus, for every 10,000 livres *borrowed* by the Estates rather than being immediately imposed, 677 livres were levied annually, almost all of which went to creditors or financiers.[6] The insistence of Louis XIV that his *don gratuit* be paid in Paris in monthly installments led to further expenses. If money had to be advanced monthly by the treasurer of the bourse to meet the royal payments before it came in from the taxpayers, he charged for this service, and the cost of transporting these sums to Paris then had to be added in. In 1684, on a *don* of 2,326,293 livres to be levied, the cost of advances was 64,262 livres or 2.76 percent of the sums levied. The cost of paying in Paris instead of Languedoc was 48,000 livres, or another 2 percent. The charges for collecting these additional sums would have been another 9,351 livres. The taxpayers thus paid 121,613 livres handling costs, or 5.23 percent of the *don in addition to* the 8.33 percent collection costs of the original principal sum.[7]

Clearly those who managed the provincial tax flow at each of these collection and distribution points require special attention. Other provincial agencies were also tied into particular sectors of the distribution mechanism. In fact, their differing ties to the various revenue sources helped reinforce the rivalries between authorities described in chapter 7 (see figure 9). Local courts and local authorities were most directly interested in the 'traditional taille', the relatively fixed sums called aide, préciput, octroi and crue, and the taxes added on by dioceses and sénéchaussées. From these sources came the stipends and fees of the bailliage, présidial and sénéchaussée courts, of certain professors in the Universities of Toulouse and Montpellier, and of local diocesan officers, not to mention interest payments to local rentiers and certain maintenance fees for local services like bridge repair and prévôté forces. Thus most of the money from the core of traditional taxes stayed right in the dioceses, with some of the surplus being channelled to the treasurer-general and the Comptes for fees. The presiding judges in the royal courts, however – the juges mages, the seneschals and juges royaux – were paid out of the royal domain funds, and thus were independent of the interests of their subordinate officers. A second level of taxes went out

[6] If the 10,000 livres were imposed, the burden on the province would be 10,833. If the same sum were borrowed, the cost would be 542 livres per year, or 500 livres for interest and 42 livres for the handlers' fees, assuming an interest rate of denier 20 (5 percent). Imposition channelled 833 livres to financiers and collectors *once*, whereas borrowing channeled 542 livres to them *each year*. This can be broken down into 517 livres for financiers and creditors and 25 livres for local collectors. If the interest rate was denier 16 (6·25 percent), which was common, then the annual cost to the province rose to 677 livres.

[7] A.N. H 748[210], 94.

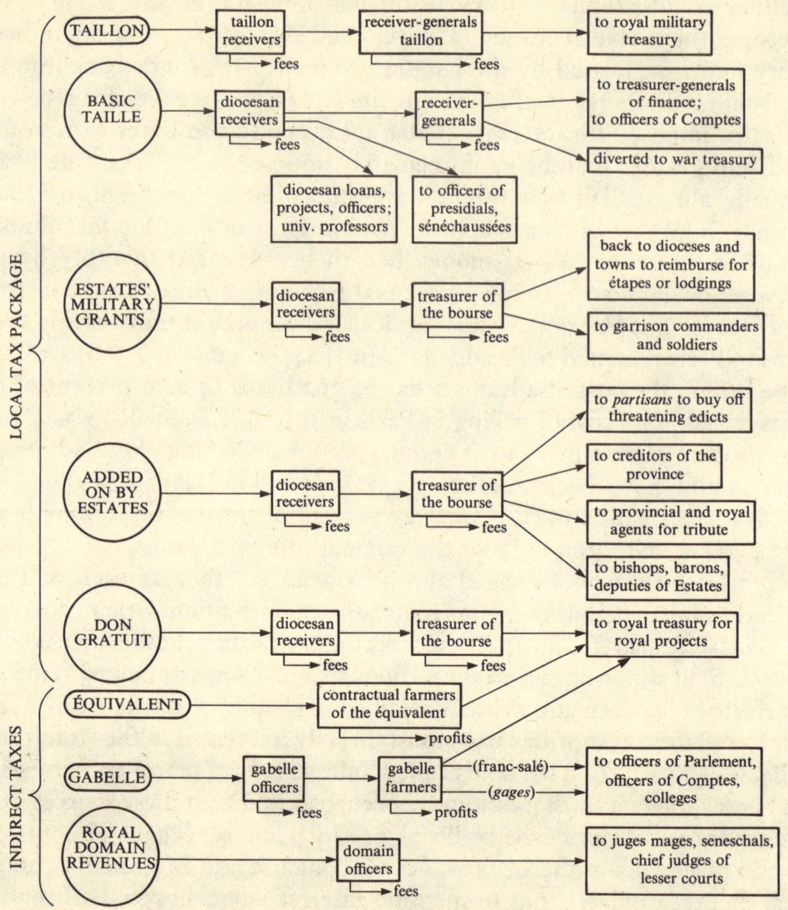

Figure 9. The pattern of tax flow.

of the diocese to the treasurer of the bourse for the Estates' own appropriations, which were redistributed to the governor and lieutenants of the province, the royal agents, the members of the Estates, the officers of the province, and the treasurer of the bourse himself. These sums represented the provincial-level cost of maintaining the dignity of military commanders and bishops and of buying influence in high places. They were divorced from local control and tended to look excessive from below.

The sovereign courts, especially the Parlement, stood aloof. Their officers were paid out of gabelle funds collected indirectly by the gabelle administration. Thus they had no stake whatever in the regular tax collection process and became natural leaders of movements against the Estates. The Comptes and the treasurer-generals, however, had revenues from both tailles and gabelles, and also a regulatory interest in the financial operations of the Estates, though most of their funds also derived from gabelle sources. In this respect the high courts had something in common with the king, who drew a great deal of revenue from a gabelle farm which was entirely independent of the Estates. We may also surmise that, although the parlementaires might quarrel with the gabelle farmers over payment of their stipends, they were not as likely as the Estates to question the principle of salt taxes. Moreover, every royal officer in Languedoc received a free salt allowance (*franc-salé*), but none of the dignitaries associated with the Estates did. Thus inequality and compartmentalization were built right into the tax system. All the rulers of Languedoc had a stake in collections along with the king, but their allegiance to different levels of the process divided them from one another and hindered a common front against the state.

FINANCIERS AND POLITICS

Financiers were the most obvious beneficiaries of the system, and their rise to prominence was one of the most distinctive developments of the seventeenth-century state. The tax system offered an accessible source of enrichment at a time when land produced comfortable but generally stagnant revenues, especially after 1660, and commerce and manufacturing were restricted to a few favored sectors. Taxes, by contrast, offered a growing source of wealth already extracted from the countryside by 'feudal' coercion and already transformed into valuable liquid currency. In addition, the system of management by the Estates offered a greater variety of ways to attach oneself to this wealth than existed in most provinces. There were two ways Languedocian financiers could profit from the system: by farming out indirect taxes and buying into special financial treaties (as *partisans*); or by purchasing financial offices and managing funds and loans (as receivers or treasurers). Both methods were used, but the first was especially characteristic of the troubled period 1630–60 and tended to appear exploitative; the second came into full prominence after 1660. The latter represented a less visible, but in the end more influential way of accumulating capital. It led in the long run to a more perfect integration of regional and Parisian financial interests.

Languedoc's role in this process of capital accumulation was particularly important, for as we learn from an impressive monograph on the eighteenth century, it was Languedoc which provided the seedbed for the great fortunes underwriting the monarchy after 1700. Chaussinand-Nogaret, seeking the origins of the pools of capital which lay behind great bankers like Samuel Bernard, found an international credit network with its roots in places like Lavaur, Castres, or Lodève, where family fortunes served as nodes for a growing network of credit relationships.[8] He attributed this phenomenon to the province's relative backwardness, hence lack of alternative outlets for investment, to its considerable natural resources, and to the curiously useful relationship between Catholic financiers in positions of authority at home and Protestants established all over Europe after the diaspora of 1685.

We can add the Languedocian tax system to this list of reasons. Chaussinand-Nogaret's research reveals the genesis of the great fortunes back as far as the 1670s – the age of Pennautier (treasurer of the bourse) and Riquet (entrepreneur of the Canal du Midi). Before that time his picture of origins becomes indistinct. But if we look back with hindsight, we can discern the process of capital accumulation unfolding from at least the 1620s, and its characteristics emerge in our sources with increasing clarity. It was a collective endeavor involving many separate parties in many places. They gathered surpluses through local enterprises, by lending at interest, and especially through the handling of public funds. Fortunes were made and lost, relayed from one group to another, passed down in families. The parties involved had a variety of dealings, but there was always a connection to public finance. They are most easily spotted in the role of diocesan receiver, where most of the important names crop up sooner or later – Roux, Deydier, Solages, Massia, Pouget, Lafont, Gineste.[9] These offices were 'tripartite', allowing each incumbent to handle revenues for one year out of three, but it was possible for an individual to accumulate several of the posts, and the appearance of such an accumulation was a sure sign of rising importance. Bernard d'Espagne, who exercised two of the three offices in Bas-Montauban from 1638 to 1671, was from a prominent family of Toulouse capitouls which was closely related to a dynasty of syndics and secretaries of the Estates (the d'Espagnes and Mariottes). Philibert Bon, who received for the diocese of Nîmes every year from 1620 to 1636, was the father of the controversial first president of the Comptes.

Taille receivers had to provide solvent backers to underwrite their investment. There was usually a group of investors behind a given individual, and the same cartel might in fact lie behind several distinct office holders. Receivers substituted for one another, backed each other, passed

[8] Guy Chaussinand-Nogaret, *Les Financiers de Languedoc au XVIIIe siècle* (Paris, 1970), pp. 11–81. See also Louis Dermigny, 'La Banque à Montpellier au XVIIIe siècle', *Annales du Midi*, 93 (1981), 17–49.

[9] Names and information on the diocesan receivers can be found in Oudot de Dainville, ed., *Répertoire numérique des archives départementales de l'Hérault: série B, Cour des Comptes, Aides et Finances de Languedoc: Comptabilités soumises à la chambre ou au bureau des comptes*, vol. V (Montpellier, 1945) which summarizes the information for each diocese for every year.

their offices around in the family. A law suit against Guyon de Fleyres, diocesan receiver of Albi in 1642, reveals that his associates were Jean-Jacques de Fleyres, bishop of Saint-Pons (1633–52), and Marie de Fleyres the wife of Antoine Gailhardi, his predecessor in the same post.[10] How many similar arrangements lie buried in the notarial archives? The result was a flexible mode of accumulation far more coordinated than appears on the surface. In fact, as the century progressed, it was clear that more receivers were becoming tied to a provincial network of relationships and that fewer posts were the domain of isolated local families.

We can probe the tangled relationships within an emerging credit nexus by pursuing various families cited by Chaussinand-Nogaret as being influential at the end of the century. The Sartres, who were high officers in the Comptes, ended the century in alliance with the treasurer of the bourse Pennautier as investors in the general receiverships of the province and the general étape farm. The Boscs were parlementaires by origin with money in the port of Sète, the salt flats of Peccais, and the *octroi* taxes of Languedoc. Pierre Crozat was a cashier of Pennautier. Pierre d'Alibert, treasurer-general in Montauban, was one of the chief financial allies of Colbert's enterprises and another friend of Pennautier and Riquet. Keeping these names from the last third of the century in mind, we can seek out origins back in its first half. The Sartres appear as receivers in the diocese of Béziers between 1601 and 1633 while, in Lavaur, Jean Sartre served in 1656 and 1659. But we notice that he and a group of others exercising the same office from 1653 to 1671 were all affiliates of Laurent Bosc, who arranged the closing of their accounts in 1671 on behalf of Pennautier. Jacques de Sartre was in fact married to a Marguerite de Bosc. At the same time another receiver in the same diocese (in 1646) was Antoine d'Alibert, the father of Pierre. Antoine's office soon passed (in 1651) to Pierre Crozat. Somewhat later we find that the third office of receiver in the diocese of Lavaur is owned (1682–9), though not exercised, by Antoine Crozat, receiver-general of the généralité of Bordeaux, the brother of Pierre. The ties which came to fruition in the 1680s and 1690s had been developing since the 1640s and 1650s.[11]

Of course receiverships were not the only connections used by these families. The more successful took on tax farms like the gabelles (Sartre, Riquet) or became receiver-generals (Trinquere, Ranchin, d'Aldiguier). Others undertook a variety of ventures, always associated with the state.

[10] Oudot de Dainville, ed., *Inventaire sommaire des archives départementales de l'Hérault: série B, Cour des Comptes, Aides et Finances: Productions devant la cour des Comptes*, vol. IV, part 2 (Montpellier, 1940), p. 336.

[11] Information from Chaussinand-Nogaret, *Financiers*, pp. 11–56; de Dainville, *Répertoire*, V; and genealogical materials. Pierre d'Alibert appears in Daniel Dessert and Jean-Louis Journet, 'Le Lobby Colbert: un royaume, ou une affaire de famille?', *Annales E.S.C.*, 30 (1975), 1303–36.

We can trace the Creissels family, another participant in the post-1700 banking network, back to Gabriel Creissels, whose social rise can be deduced from the tidbits known about him. In 1639 he supplied the army in Languedoc with a loan of 100,000 livres which the province was later required to repay. In 1643 he was part of a cartel of merchants negotiating with Baltazar to provision the army of Catalonia. The next year he was able to purchase the royal office of treasurer of the bourse, which he exercised once in 1647. In 1653 he was receiver-general of Montpellier. Meanwhile in 1641 a Jeanne Creissels had married Charles Ranchin, receiver-general of Montpellier, who was himself munitioneer of Catalonia in 1648.[12] Ties like these illustrate the role of the financial system in generating the slow, partially concealed rise of a widely-dispersed network of petty accumulators of capital whose fortunes were tied to the royal taxing process.

A second role of the financial system was more clearly connected to the political struggles of the first half of our period. If receiving and administering the various tax agencies provided a slow, safe source of profits, another more visibly exploitative form of finance was involvement in special tax farms – the 'edicts', 'treaties', and investigations associated with *traitants* or *partisans*. Interestingly enough, a close examination of the personalities behind these operations lends new meaning to the conflicts of the 1640s and confirms the impressions gained in chapter 10 concerning the connection between loyalists, royal policies, and finance.

The central fact from 1628 to 1649 was the assault on the province by outsider financiers. They acquired and resold the new élus offices in 1628, arranged the financial indemnities in 1632, handled the new royal offices of treasurer of the bourse after the Edict of Béziers, bought up the revenues of the province's équivalent tax, later sold them back for a profit, and inundated the province with fiscal edicts allowing *partisans* to harass the taxpayers. The majority of these operations were owned and managed by Parisians over whom the province had little control and whose names were sometimes denounced as *partisans* in Estates or Parlement. However, distant investors required local agents, and here ambitious local men of middling stature were ready to take up the banner. These local opportunists are already familiar to us. The focus of the Parlement's attacks in 1644 was Jean-Georges de Caulet, juge mage of Toulouse, who was serving as collection agent for the joyeux avènement tax.[13] In Montpellier Caulet's counterpart was the juge mage François Crouzet, a close ally of Baltazar who fought against the 1645 uprising, and whose father was reputed to be 'a great traitant involved in the joyeux avènement tax'. Crouzet's predecessor as juge mage was André Trinquere, an agent of the detested

[12] A.M. Tse BB 31, July 9, 1639; Baltazar to Le Tellier, Dec. 11, 1643: Lubl., p. 53; A.D. Hér. C 7901; Chaussinand-Nogaret, *Financiers*, p. 39; A.N. H 748[208], 239.

[13] B.N. Languedoc (Bénédictins) 153, 22–5.

franc fief investigation of 1641.[14] All the major victims of the 1645 popular uprising were subcontractors of Parisian–royal financial interests: the merchant Maduron and the *partisan* Dupuy who were attacked in Montpellier were local agents of the amortissement as well as the joyeux avènement.[15] Maduron appears to be the same man who had been granted an office of élus in 1629 by Richelieu. Caulet was similarly the farmer of the élus offices in Toulouse in 1630 and the executor of unpopular fines in 1633. President Maussac of the Comptes, noted in the 1650s for his 'loyalist' first presidency of the 'separated' Chambre des Comptes, was denounced in 1635 for aggressive execution of the interests of the gabelle farmers.[16]

The intendants and military commanders, who were themselves investors in these operations, provided the coordination between Parisian finance and local opportunists. Miron and Le Camus were charged with piloting the interests of *partisans* through the dangerous waters of provincial politics. Schomberg's reputation was used, both with the Estates and with local merchants, to borrow constitutionally illegal funds which the Estates then had to pay back. Three of the purchasers of the royal offices of treasurer of the bourse were lesser provincial financiers: Jacques Peyrat, connected to the gabelle farm; Gabriel Creissels, the merchant we encountered above; and Guillaume Massia, member of an influential family of merchants from Narbonne. Massia's son was murdered by the crowd in Montpellier in 1645. The other treasurer of the bourse was a man of a different order: François Le Secq, a Parisian banker who moved in the best financial circles, the only one of the four treasurers who spanned the entire period of the Edict of Béziers.[17]

The very symbol of exploitative finance was Baltazar himself. We have already seem him at work behind the scenes as Schomberg's secretary and Parisian agent from 1632 until his appointment as intendant of Languedoc in 1643, and he was personally profiting from his position all the while. In 1633, when the property of the deposed bishop of Albi, Alphonse d'Elbène, was being liquidated, the king gave d'Elbène's bishopric to Schomberg's cousin and d'Elbène's furniture to Baltazar![18] The latter was one of Le Secq's financial backers in the 1630s and served as his Parisian representative for business concerning Languedoc. He also lent money personally to the province when the deputies at court ran short: 8,000 livres

14 Bosquet to La Vrillière, Aug. 1, 1645: Porchner, p. 651. A.D. Hér. C. 8291.

15 Dupuy continued to harass the merchants of Montpellier for years over indemnities for his pillaged residence. P-V Nov. 12, 1650, Oct. 25, 1651.

16 Charles d'Aigrefeuille, *Histoire de la ville de Montpellier*, ed. de la Pijardière, 4 vols. (Montpellier, 1875–82), vol. II, p. 105; Paul Gachon, *Les États de Languedoc et l'édit de Béziers (1632)* (Paris, 1887), pp. 214–15; Rozoi, vol. IV, p. 361; A.M. Tse AA 22, 232.

17 A.D. Hér. C 7901; P-V Nov. 27, 1637, Dec. 4, 5, 11, 15, 1638.

18 A.M. Albi BB 29, 686.

in 1636, 8,643 in 1637.[19] Thus his arrival in the province meant that Parisian investments would be protected and extended.[20] Baltazar also took a hard line against provincial attempts to impede the other tax farms, and he spent much of his time raising money for the troops. In 1643 he pledged his own and Schomberg's credit in order to secure advances from companies of merchants in Béziers and Narbonne. These included a certain Cesare in Narbonne, a Gineste in Béziers, Creissels and Massia in Montpellier – most likely the treasurers of the bourse or their close relatives – and a Verchant of Montpellier who was probably the same Daniel Verchant who underwrote the équivalent tax farm in 1659.[21] In 1644 funds for the embarcation of troops were advanced by 'Fabre' of Narbonne, who quarreled with 'Massia' over this, at a time when Guillaume Massia and Guillaume Fabre were the chief diocesan receivers of Narbonne. In 1645 Baltazar was cited by Bosquet as a business associate of Saulger and Beaulac, both treasurer-generals in Montpellier. In 1646 Baltazar, Schomberg's lieutenant Villepassier, and a group of merchants again advanced money to pay for the lodging of Spanish prisoners.[22]

The alienation of the équivalent farm, which was arranged by the Estates in 1634 to repay money lent by the *partisan* Vanel to buy off the élus illustrates further connections among the same group of individuals.[23] The final deal was negotiated in Paris, where the deputies of the Estates sold the entire farm to a cartel of 'engagistes' under the name of Laurent Ardon for 2,300,000 livres. The names of these thirty investors read like a roll call of the Paris–Languedocian financial community.[24] Nine of them are Parisians, including Claude Vanel, the creditor of the élus, and four members of the family of Claude Le Ragois, sieur de Bretonvilliers, secretary of the royal council. Then comes Baltazar himself, along with Pierre Saulger, his associate of 1645, both of whom were still lobbying to recover control of the équivalent in 1656, and François de Beaulac, the other Baltazar associate mentioned above.[25] We see Pierre Crouzet, son of Baltazar's ally of 1645, along with Marc Antoine Dupuy and Guillaume Falguerolles, members of the families attacked by the rioters of 1645. There is Pierre de Greffeuille, treasurer-general of finance, the brother-in-law of

19 P-V Dec. 20, 1635, Dec. 14, 1636; A.N. H 748^{198}, 328.

20 Bosquet to Séguier, May 17, 1644: Lubl., p. 63; Baltazar to La Vrillière, October 4, 1644: Lubl., p. 81. We learn without surprise that in 1643 the *traitant* of the rogneurs investigation requested that President Maussac of the Comptes be named as commissioner to aid the intendant (Baltazar) in this investigation. Ms. fr. 15833, 238.

21 Baltazar to Le Tellier, Dec. 11, 1643: Lubl., pp. 52–4.

22 Schomberg to Séguier, June 18 or 20, 1644: ms. fr. 17379, 123; Bosquet to Séguier, Apr. 17, 1645: Lubl., p. 132; Baltazar to La Vrillière, May 29, 1646: Lubl., p. 194.

23 Jacques Vidal, *L'Équivalent des aides en Languedoc* (Montpellier, 1963), pp. 421–36.

24 Vidal, *L'Équivalent*, pp. 423–5. This list was drawn up in 1648 and might have been altered since 1634.

25 Deputies of the Estates to Mazarin, June 17, 1656: A.A.E. France 1636, 489.

André Trinquere; and Jean Peyrat, controller-general of the gabelles of Languedoc, undoubtedly a relative of the treasurer of the bourse. Finally, there are a certain Gallieres and a Sartre from the Comptes, seven others from the bureau of treasurer-generals of Montpellier, the widow of a juge mage of Limoux, and an unidentifiable Raymond Barthe.

This alliance of intendants, governors, Parisian bankers, and local financiers, many of whom were loyal enforcers of unpopular royal policies, seemed like a divisive wedge driven into the province's ability to manage its own affairs. A group of ambitious profiteers seemed to be using money and unquestioning adherence to absolutist strategies to appropriate profit and influence at the expense of provincial solidarity. This private form of royal–provincial collaboration profited only selected individuals while undermining the more traditional ability of the rest to monitor and influence the king's affairs in the province. It is no wonder that the sides drawn in financial affairs parallel so closely the lines drawn in the political conflicts of the 1640s. The Estates fought against edicts and unauthorized assessments while attacking Baltazar in particular; the Comptes battled their separation and the newly-appointed presidents; the Parlement expelled members related to *partisans*; the populace burned and murdered scapegoats in Montpellier. As we have seen, these protests were not part of a single, concerted movement, but it was no accident that the targets of every one of them were members of related financial cartels. Tax farming seemed incompatible with provincial loyalty, and investment in it seemed like treasonous activity.

After 1649 this situation began to change, as the province gradually regained control of its financial agents and the financiers themselves forged new relationships which integrated them into outside networks without seeming to stand against the province. The revocation of the Edict of Béziers in 1649 was the first step in this process because it returned ostensible financial control to the Estates. A loan of 200,000 livres was floated to buy back the royal offices of treasurer of the bourse, which were then returned to Le Secq and the Pennautier family to serve as officers of the province, not the king.[26] In 1670, when Pierre Louis de Pennautier obtained the post of treasurer of the clergy of France, he used as underwriters his brother, Reich de Reissac, and d'Alibert, the treasurer-general of Montauban whom we encountered above.[27] In the same year he married the daughter of Le Secq, who died shortly afterwards. Thus, while the Estates regained legal control over their treasurer, they did not turn financially inward; rather they were brought closer in touch with a national financial cartel in the process of formation, of which their facilities constituted part of the core.

[26] P-V Nov. 17, 1649.

[27] Chaussinand-Nogaret, *Financiers*, pp. 30–2.

Another element of restoration was the recovery of the équivalent farm.[28] The settlement reached in 1648 was another typical case of transfer of wealth among tax farmers at the expense of the taxpayers. The engagistes were to sell back the farm for 3,675,000 livres plus 500,000 more in various indemnities and gifts. This money was to be raised by allowing them the revenues of the farm for eight years, during which additional sums would be imposed on the province. In 1656 the farm came back under provincial control after an enormous windfall profit had been transferred in this manner from the taxpayers to the engagistes, including Baltazar and his coterie of ally-investors. From then on, the équivalent was farmed out by the Estates for three-year periods and the money used to pay part of the *don gratuit*. The farming and subfarming of the triennial contracts now became another investment opportunity for diocesan receivers and other local financiers. For example, the Daniel Verchant mentioned above, probably the same merchant who aided Baltazar in 1644, underwrote the contract in 1659, as did Tristan Pastourel, receiver of the diocese of Béziers, and Jean Astruc, receiver of Saint-Papoul in 1677. Astruc had also been the principal underwriter in 1668. The appearance of names like Astruc, Galdy, and Pennautier in the 1660s and 1670s indicates that these positions were also becoming integrated into the grid of interconnected financial interests.[29]

Under Louis XIV the separate strands of 'parasitic' finance – équivalent, gabelle, étapes, diocesan receiving, public projects, treasury of the bourse – became so many interlocking opportunities for investment, all controlled locally yet all tied to larger financial circuits. By the death of Colbert one might almost have claimed that Languedocian finance was taking over Paris.

SOCIAL DISTRIBUTION

Let us now return to the tax flow itself and try to determine where the taxpayer's money actually went. There was no such thing as a formal budget, but it is possible to measure the flow of resources through the system by analyzing and combining various records. Certain diocesan and city accounts specify the purpose of the sums demanded by the Estates and what was to be added on at the local level. Certain papers of the syndic-generals give more details about the uses to which the sums that went to the Estates were put and the way these items were to be financed. The *états des finances* drawn up by the king's ministers indicate what the diocesan receivers and the receiver-generals were to do with the part they received. Using the excellent series of accounts from the diocese of

[28] Vidal, *L'Équivalent*, pp. 431–6.

[29] The names of the provincial équivalent farmers are in ibid., pp. 327–9.

Toulouse and additional information from these other sources and from the minutes of the Estates, I have attempted to do a complete breakdown for the years 1677 and 1647, years which were chosen because of the fortunate availability of information from all the sources.

This breakdown should be treated with caution. It is well known that the états des finances were artificially balanced and contained their share of legal fictions. They were also notoriously faulty in simple arithmetic.[30] I have made adjustments where necessary, frequently assuming that the correct total expenditure was the sum of the individual expenditures rather than the incorrect total stated in the documents. I have also had to make some arbitrary choices in classifying the destination of the funds. Still, the figures are based on working documents from three independent archives, and they correspond closely in areas where they overlap. They do not necessarily tell us exactly what was done in 1677 and 1647, but they provide a clear model of the general tendencies of the system.[31]

It is necessary to explain a further complication. My initial breakdown, called 'direct taxes', represents the 5,250,933 livres which were granted by the Estates and levied on the province in 1677, including the sums added on at the level of the three sénéchaussées and the twenty-two dioceses (see table 8).[32] This breakdown has the merit of showing who received the money actually paid by the taxpayers in direct taxes. It has several disadvantages, however. It leaves out the important indirect taxes which also burdened the population, notably the gabelle and the équivalent. These are important not only because of their magnitude but also because some of their revenues were transferred to the Estates' treasury in 1677 to alleviate the direct tax burden, thereby intermingling direct and indirect sums. Furthermore, certain recipients of tax revenues, notably the king and

30 Useful discussions of these problems are Alain Guéry, 'Les Finances de la monarchie française sous l'ancien régime', *Annales E.S.C.*, 33 (1978), 216–39; James B. Collins, 'Sur l'histoire fiscale du XVIIe siècle: les impôts directs en Champagne entre 1595 et 1635', *Annales E.S.C.*, 34 (1979), 325–47; and Richard Bonney, *The King's Debts: Finance and Politics in France 1589–1661* (Oxford, 1981), pp. 1–21.

31 These results have been tabulated from the 'État des finances' of 1677 (Mel. Col. 243), the 'État de la Gabelle' of 1677 and 1678 (A.N. H 748[252], 79; Mel. Col. 252); the 'État du Domaine' for Languedoc, 1675 and 1677 (Mel. Col. 248, 316–336; A.N. H 748[252], 135): and the Taillon, 1677 (A.N. H 748[252], 71). The papers of Joubert for 1677 contain added particulars (A.N. 748[208], 237–238), as does the état of the diocese of Toulouse (A.D. H-G. C 990). *Augmentations des gages*, 1677, are listed in Mel. Col. 250, 301. In addition the budget of 1686 is analyzed in detail in Monin, *Essai*, pp. 58–63.

32 To these provincial sums a hypothetical 385,137 livres have been added to cover the money imposed at the diocesan level, and 30,000 livres have been added for the sénéchaussées. The first sum is a hypothetical projection based on the actual total for the diocese of Toulouse. It is what the other dioceses would have imposed if they had added on an amount proportionate to their share of the provincial tax burden and if this sum had been distributed exactly the way it was in the diocese of Toulouse. The second sum has been allocated entirely to 'public works' on the theory that it was used for roads and bridges.

Table 8. *Total taxes to be distributed in 1677 (in livres)*

1. '*Direct taxes*'	
4,835,796	imposed by Estates (adjusted figure including transfers from gabelle farm)
385,137	added on by assiettes (hypothetical figure)
30,000	added on by sénéchaussées
5,250,933	Total 'direct' taxes
2. '*Combined taxes*'	
5,250,933	direct taxes from above
2,635,127	revenues of gabelle farm (not including sums already transferred to 'direct taxes')
315,000	revenues of équivalent farm
26,106	revenues from royal domain farm in Languedoc
8,227,166	Total 'combined' taxes

the sovereign court judges, derived a large share of their receipts from these indirect taxes. If direct taxes alone were studied, these recipients would seem to benefit less from the tax system than they actually did. I have therefore done a second breakdown, this time called 'combined taxes', which totals 8,227,166 livres of direct and indirect taxes.[33] In the pages that follow these two breakdowns, 'direct' and 'combined' are both cited. Their results are similar, but with significant variations. 'Combined' taxes do justice to the receipts of the Parlement and the Comptes, but increase the royal proportion by adding in vast gabelle revenues. 'Direct' taxes give a better idea of the royal and provincial shares of the taille, but undervalue the advantages of certain recipients.[34]

Let us turn now to the distributions for 1677 which are presented in table 9. Their most salient feature was the division between royal money and provincial money. The king received 62.2 percent of 'direct taxes' or 65.6 percent of 'combined taxes'. All the rest of the money went to provincial (and a few Parisian) notables except for the minuscule percentage I have attributed to 'public welfare', which was mostly made up of exemptions for victims of misfortune, alms, and gifts to religious foundations. We can say, then, that a third or a little more went to the rulers of Languedoc while two-thirds went to the crown.

[33] Of course not all indirect taxes are included in the 'combined' distribution. A comprehensive picture of provincial–royal tax distribution would have to include the proceeds of taxes like the *papier-timbré* which might have hit the elite more heavily than the general population. However, this information is not available. I am indebted to Bernard Barbiche for this point.

[34] Either method of accounting leaves out the principal on sums borrowed (another 340,000 livres for the royal *don*, for example) since this is money which the taxpayers did not pay during the year in question.

The form of this royal 65.6 percent is interesting. Out of this royal share only 47.9 percent was free and unrestricted income, that is, money that was actually supposed to be transferred to the royal coffers in the north. This money came almost entirely from two sources: the *don gratuit* and the gabelle receipts. The negotiations over the *don* in the Estates were thus critical to the king's interests since they provided the only cash income which would be directly managed – the only tax revenues in the modern sense of the term. The rest of the royal share was acquired in a more 'feudal' manner by making a case for a specific necessity, usually military. This was royal money for it was spent on expenditures determined by the king, but it came back to the province, indirectly at least, in the form of supplies purchased or compensation paid for services or damages. Some of this money (2.9 percent) was spent directly by agents of the state on military expenses. Most of it (8.0 percent) represented an intermediate category which the king commanded but the Estates managed. Taxes for étapes, locally-raised regiments, or equipment supplied in kind by the province were royal in the sense that the king could raise or lodge as many troops as he saw fit in the province, but they were locally managed in the sense that their costs were established according to agreed procedures and audited by a joint commission of the Estates and the royal agents. The king established what services he was demanding but not the total cost to be levied or the distribution of the funds. Such expenditures, though royal, brought direct benefit to provincial leaders by giving them regulatory power over who would be compensated. The same was true of a newer phenomenon, the 4.7 percent destined for 'public works' in Languedoc, most notably the Canal des Deux Mers. Here too the money was spent in the province for a designated purpose and regulated by the Estates.

Let us now look at the other third of the tax revenues which went to provincial notables. The list in table 9 reads like a roll call of important personages: 2.7 percent to the governor and the royal agents; 4.5 percent to the Cour des Comptes; 2.3 percent to the Parlement and the Chambre de l'Édit; another 2.3 percent to the treasurer-generals of finance; 4.5 percent to the diocesan and provincial receivers and controllers; 1.6 percent to the treasurer of the bourse; .5 percent to the officers of the Estates; 1.3 percent to the officers and costs of the assiettes. These sums alone total 19.7 percent of the entire 'combined' tax burden, or roughly 60 percent of the funds going 'to the notables'. Most of the rest went to debt service or gabelle officers. It appears, then, that the rulers of Languedoc had a strong vested interest in the provincial tax revenues, and that in most cases the income they shared with the king at the expense of the taxpayers came to them by virtue of their position, not as recompense for services rendered.

But this important question should be pursued further. Just what was the justification for the sums channelled automatically to the various

Table 9. *Distribution of tax revenues in 1677*

	'Direct taxes'		'Combined taxes'	
	livres	%	livres	%
A. To crown	*3,263,226*	*62.2*	*5,395,382*	*65.6*
a. Unrestricted cash payments	2,142,449	40.8	3,939,939	47.9
b. Military in Languedoc	239,640	4.6	239,640	2.9
c. Military in Languedoc, monitored by Estates	661,137	12.6	661,137	8.0
d. Royal public works in Languedoc	220,000	4.2	386,666	4.7
e. Royal pensions	—	—	168,000	2.1
B. Public welfare and misc.	*73,114*	*1.4*	*116,011*	*1.4*
C. To the notables (by office)	*1,914,593*	*36.4*	*2,715,773*	*33.0*
1. Financiers and financial officers	479,469	9.5	597,807	7.3
a. Treasurer of the bourse	127,303	2.4	127,303	1.6
b. Receiver-generals of taille/taillon	47,841	0.9	47,841	0.6
c. Diocesan receivers taille/taillon	321,225	6.1	321,225	3.9
d. General receivers of gabelle	—	—	94,458	1.1
e. Other	1,100	0.02	6,980	0.08
2. Estates: gifts and expenses	578,609	11.0	578,609	7.0
a. To agents of central government	37,900	0.7	37,900	0.5
b. To governor, lieuts., royal agents	224,070	4.3	224,070	2.7
c. To president, officers of Estates	40,833	0.8	40,833	0.5
d. To members of Estates for services	141,371	2.7	141,371	1.7
e. To Estates' employees and expenses	22,360	0.4	22,360	0.3
f. To officers and costs of assiettes	112,075	2.1	112,075	1.3
3. To creditors as interest	542,576	10.3	542,576	6.6

Table 9 (*cont.*)

	'Direct taxes'		'Combined taxes'	
	livres	%	livres	%
4. *Major royal officers*	241,412	4.6	931,704	11.3
a. Cour des Comptes, Aides et Finances	44,652	0.9	368,314	4.5
b. Parlement and Chambre de l'Édit	2,810	0.05	192,816	2.3
c. Treasurer-generals of finance	159,859	3.0	191,237	2.3
d. Sénéchaussées and présidials	34,091	0.6	49,971	0.6
e. Officers of the gabelle	—	—	129,366	1.6
5. *Petty royal officers*	54,527	1.0	65,077	0.8
Totals	5,250,933	100.0	8,227,166	100.0

categories of notables? Was the province simply borrowing money, hiring contractors, and paying functionaries in the manner of a modern administration, or was wealth being distributed for traditional, 'feudal' reasons on the basis of extra-economic coercion – that is, by force of rank or ownership of public authority? Suppose we take the same 36.4 percent of 'direct' taxes which went to the notables and redistribute it according to new categories representing the nature of the claim that the recipient had on the funds (see table 10).

We must define new categories. *Interest on loans* is simply interest in the modern sense, a public debt consisting of short-term loans at 5 percent or 6 percent. *Tribute* is the honorific sum expected by important personages because of their status. It was a modified form of 'feudal' payment in that it translated into monetary terms the claims of precedence so dear to 'feudal' leaders. It was paid by custom, not contract, and its amount varied, but not to have paid it was inconceivable. Although some of it can be written off as bribe money needed to maintain political influence in high places, this tribute was a socially necessary sign of deference which was paid out of all proportion to its political usefulness. *Receiving fees* were collected by financial officers as a percentage share of the money they handled. These officers, whose advantages were discussed above, did provide a genuine service by taking in and disbursing funds, keeping books and effecting transport of specie. Their jobs were contractual and they were held accountable for any mishandling. Nevertheless their function was more an

Table 10. *Taxes 'to the notables' in 1677 by nature of their claim*

	'Direct taxes'		'Combined taxes'	
	% of total taxes	% of notables' share	% of total taxes	% of notables' share
C. *To the notables (by nature of their claim)*	*36.4*	—	*33.0*	—
1. Interest on loans	10.3	28.3	6.6	20.0
2. Tribute to outsiders	1.0	2.7	0.6	1.8
3. Tribute in Languedoc	5.3	14.6	4.2	12.7
4. Receiving fees	6.7	18.4	5.6	17.0
5. Returns on offices	8.4	23.1	12.9	39.1
6. Operating costs	4.7	12.9	3.1	9.4
Total	36.4	100.0	33.0	100.0

expression of the weakness of credit facilities than a recompense for services rendered. These middlemen were parasites whose numbers were hardly dictated by logical necessity and who used their position as a way of tapping provincial revenue flows. One could almost argue that they should have paid the province for the opportunity to collect and manipulate public funds, rather than vice versa.

Returns on offices were the stipends (*gages*) paid by the king to all venal officeholders. They were expressions of the distinctive relationship between the king and his officers which involved shared ownership of public power. Because the officeholder had invested his fortune in an office in order to acquire status, personal influence, and a share of royal authority, he expected a tangible return. It was not a salary, for it was due regardless of the work performed, yet it was not equivalent to interest on an investment because the payments were more arbitrary and less reliable. If *gages* had been totally abrogated by the king, his officers would have protested vehemently. Nevertheless, he could delay payment, reduce the percentage paid, or require additional investment of principal in return for *gage* increments (*augmentations de gages*). Returns on offices were the monetary expression of the decentralization of royal authority and its retention by local notables who shared in it without controlling it.

Operating costs are the items which can be determined to have gone mostly for genuine salaries, travel expenses, and supply costs. I have included in this category the fees paid to the officers of the Estates and the assiettes, the *per diem* grant paid to deputies of the Estates for attending, and the fees of servants and artisans.

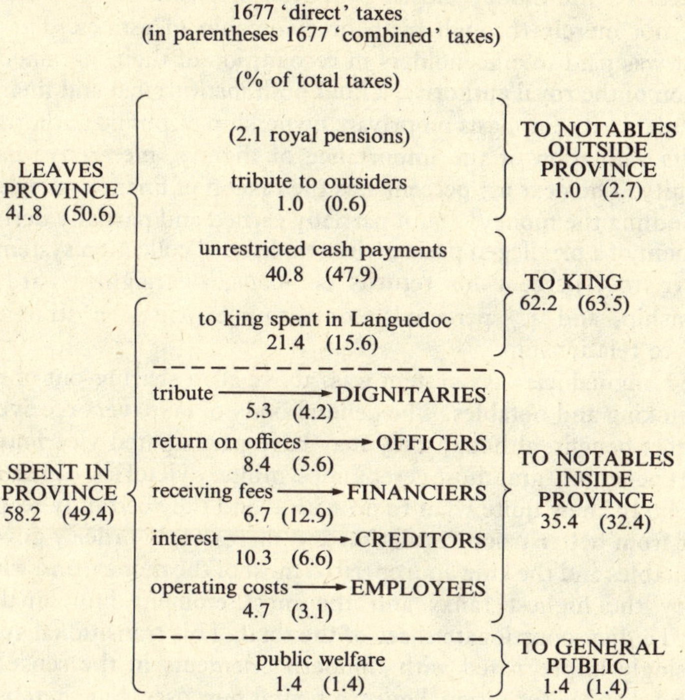

Figure 10. Functional distribution of tax revenues.

These categories provide us with a profile of the relative weight of different kinds of claims on the tax revenues of 1677. We can now put our findings together into a general picture of the taille distribution and ask what sort of social picture it conveys (see figure 10). What emerges is a clear partnership between the king and the provincial ruling class which can be looked at in several ways. We have already noted the crude division of funds between crown (62.2 percent) and notables (36.4 percent). Another way of analyzing the purpose to which tax revenues were put is to distinguish between funds carried away from the province and presumably spent elsewhere (41.8 percent) and funds distributed in Languedoc (58.2 percent). Within this latter category of 58.2 percent are discernible the different elements of the provincial leaders' relationships to the crown and the state. The first 5.3 percent of the total revenues were paid in tribute to the dignity and rank of the most prestigious leaders. This sort of recognition reflected the very essence of a 'feudal' society's mode of distributing resources, but it should be noted that even this most traditional component of the tax structure was deflected through the state, in that the nobles and prelates who received the money did so by virtue of positions appointed by the crown, not merely through birth or ownership of estates. The next 8.4 percent was paid to officeholders in recognition of their ingrained hold on a portion of the royal authority, a hold both institutional and financial, and also feudal in its emphasis on private ownership of public authority as well as in its validation of the importance of dignity, hierarchy, and family continuity. The next 6.7 percent was the rakeoff of financiers for collecting and handling the money, a sum partially earned and partially derived from enjoyment of a privileged position in a traditional collection system. Finally we have 10.3 percent for returns on loans, a straightforward creditor relationship, and 4.7 percent in operating expenses, a straightforward employee relationship.

The Languedocian tax system was, above all, a sharing-out of resources between king and notables. The general body of taxpayers received hardly any direct benefit, although they may have participated vicariously in the indirect benefits – grandiose ceremonies, military victories, canals and ports that nobody knew quite what to do with – and they certainly reaped some benefit from better troop regulation and increasingly orderly government. The notables and the king appropriated most of the money, and within each category the highest ranks and the most eminent individuals always received a disproportionate share of the total. This transitional system was increasingly impregnated with 'modern' elements in the sense of funds allocated directly for rational governmental purposes, but there was much that was 'feudal' about it in the way special advantages were constantly being perpetuated or created.

Were these proportions from 1677 typical, or had there been a dramatic change under Louis XIV? It would be useful to know how the distribution of taxes changed each year, but until the archives of the Estates are fully classified, no such analysis is possible. We can, however, compare 1677 with 1647, a year for which comparable information exists, and we can use cruder measures of the other years to get an idea of whether the trends suggested by the comparison hold up over the longer term.[35]

The two years 1647 and 1677 each represent peaks in the tax curve, 1647 being the return to 'normal' after the turbulent refusals of 1644–6, and 1677 being the culmination of the Dutch War and the efforts to build the Canal des Deux Mers. Both were war years, and both had comparable tax levels, with 1677's higher by 6.8 percent. However, the 1647 figures are not as complete as those for 1677, only its 'direct' taxes being available, therefore no comparison is possible with the 'combined' taxes of 1677.

A look at the distribution of the two years' revenues (table 11) produces

[35] The 1647 figures are tabulated from the 'État des finances' of 1647 (ms. fr. nouv. acq. 173), the assiette of Toulouse for the same year (A.D. H-G. C 989), and other miscellaneous mentions.

Table 11. *Comparative distribution, 1647 and 1677*

	1647 'direct' %	1677 'direct' %
A. To crown	*69.7*	*62.2*
a. Unrestricted cash payments	42.7	40.8
b. Military in Languedoc	6.9	4.6
c. Military in Languedoc, monitored by Estates	19.3	12.6
d. Royal public works in Languedoc	0.8	4.2
B. Public welfare and misc.	*0.7*	*1.4*
C. To the notables (by office)	*29.6*	*36.4*
1. Financiers and financial officers	7.3	9.5
a. Treasurers of the bourse	0.8	2.4
b. Receiver-generals of taille/taillon	1.3	0.9
c. Diocesan receivers taille/taillon	5.2	6.1
d. Other		0.02
2. Estates: gifts and expenses	14.0	11.0
a. To agents of central government	0.6	0.7
b. To governor, lieuts., royal agents	6.1	4.3
c. To president, officers of Estates	0.5	0.8
d. To members of Estates for services	2.7	2.7
e. To Estates' employees and expenses	0.2	0.4
f. Estates, use unknown	2.2	—
g. To officers and costs of assiettes	1.7	2.1
3. To creditors as interest	5.4	10.3
4. Major royal officers	2.1	4.6
a. Cour des Comptes, Aides et Finances	0.2	0.9
b. Parlement and Chambre de l'Édit	—	0.05
c. Treasurer-generals of finance	1.5	3.0
d. Sénéchaussées and présidials	0.4	0.6
5. Petty royal officers	0.8	1.0
Totals	100.0	100.0

surprise. It appears that a smaller share of the taxes went to the king in 1677 than in 1647. Every category of royal receipt – even unrestricted cash payments – is down in 1677, with the exception of royal public works which have risen because of the canal but not enough to offset the others. By contrast, most of the categories favoring provincial notables have risen. Financial officers have made slight gains, and the treasurer of the bourse had tripled his share. All other categories of royal officers have increased their receipts, most notably the treasurer-generals, even though the

Table 12. *Taxes 'to the notables' by nature of their claim, 1647 and 1677*

	'Direct taxes'	
	1647 %	1677 %
C. *To the notables* (*by nature of their claim*)	*29.6*	*36.4*
1. Interest on loans	5.4	10.3
2. Tribute to outsiders	0.7	1.0
3. Tribute in Languedoc	6.5	5.3
4. Receiving fees	4.9	6.7
5. Returns on offices	5.4	8.4
6. Operating costs	4.5	4.7
7. Unknown	2.2	—

sovereign courts are under-represented by the absence of a 'combined' distribution which would allot them their gabelle revenues. The Estates have lost some ground, but the only significant change is the decline in gifts to the royal agents which reflects the absence in 1677 of the bloated payoffs characteristic of the governorship of Gaston d'Orléans in 1647. The largest and most spectacular change, however, was the share of provincial taxes going to creditors of the province – from 5.4 percent in 1647 to 10.3 percent in 1677.

In terms of the kinds of claims provincial notables had on the funds, the same trends are confirmed (table 12). While the crown has lost 7.5 percent of its share between 1647 and 1677, the 'notables', broadly conceived, have gained 6.8 percent. Within their share it is striking to note the progression of the various kinds of exactions. Direct tribute, the most traditional category, has declined slightly. Modern interest payments have doubled their share, indicating the rising weight of the creditor–public debt relationship. The profits of receiving fees have also risen significantly, but since most of this gain went to the treasurer of the bourse whose new fiscal operations were closer to loans than to receiving operations, we may conclude that this important change reflected the rise of financial innovations more than the extension of the traditional receiving system.

The 3.0 percent rise in returns on offices is a reminder that 'traditional' relationships were still operative. Even without the gabelle revenues, which raised returns on offices in the 1677 figures from 8.4 percent ('direct' taxes) to 12.9 percent ('combined' taxes), the share of the venal officers – their claim on the system – was increasing under Louis XIV. This phenomenon requires further explanation. During the Thirty Years War the crown made severe inroads on the *gages* of the officers by cancelling more than half of each officer's share and impounding the difference – in cash – to pay for the war effort. In 1677 the officers were still only receiving half of the face value of what was due them. Relatively more money was going for *gages* collectively, but individuals were receiving the same amount. The higher totals were generated by the creation of new officers in each body and by the sale of *augmentations* to selected parties who then received more in return. Thus the system of venality was being perpetuated and even extended without individual officers necessarily seeing the benefits.

It appears, then, that the traditional aspects of the system which we identified in 1677 were increasing their share of the tax revenues compared to 1647, not decreasing them, despite the apparent state centralization associated with Louis XIV. The notables got more money back from the king, and they had greater control over what he spent in the province. 'Tribute' and 'returns on offices' held their own; financial operations benefiting local investors became relatively more lucrative. The tax picture, in fact, was anything but bleak even though 1677 was a year of military exigency and not one of the happier 'recovery' years of the 1660s.

There is no comparable distribution of funds for the rest of the century, but a rough way of assessing the relative burden of the various kinds of expenses is to plot the basic components of the provincial levy year by year, as in figure 11. Here it is immediately evident that the distinguishing features of the period 1633 to 1661 were military costs and payoffs to *partisans* for 'edicts', two extraordinary forces which increased the royal income at tremendous cost to the province. This was the era of exploitative finance discussed above, when profiteering meant allying with unpopular outsiders at the expense of local control. The 1660s were a time of recovery. Then, when the province-wide tax burden began to rise again after 1671, the impetus came not as much from military expenses as from two new sources. One was the *don gratuit* which, however, was partly covered by loans and équivalent revenues. The other was the rising public debt, an enormously important phenomenon. Not only did the professional financiers begin to extend their grips on a growing body of interconnected tax farms and receiving operations which, as we have seen, the province could now control locally, but the Estates themselves went into the credit business, drawing with them most of the leading families of the province. The curve of estimated indebtedness in figure 11 illustrates this phenomenon, and helps explain why interest on loans was rapidly becoming an important component of the tax distribution. The king was receiving greater revenues without raising taxes proportionately, thanks to the rapidly expanding credit system which appeared in the 1650s and developed dramatically between 1672 and 1685. The richest and best placed creditors

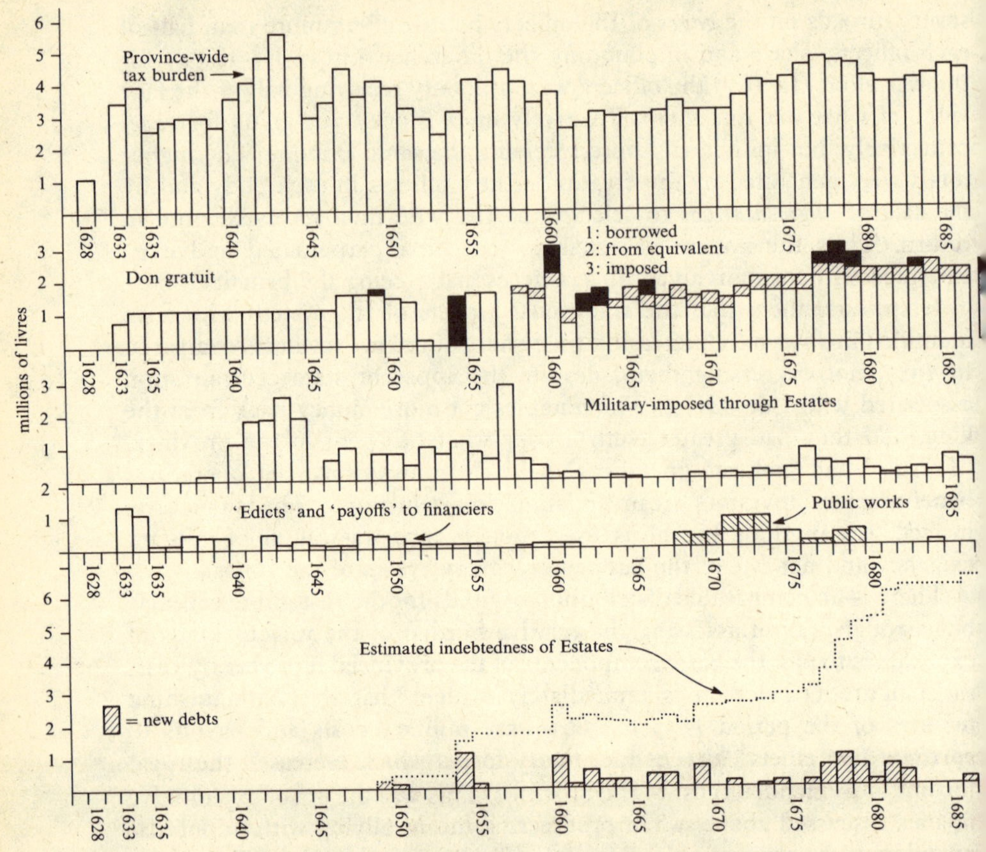

Figure 11. Components of the annual tax burden.

were thus afforded a new source of investment which in a sense compensated them when taxes rose. Loans were a tradeoff: the elite lent surplus money to the king and collected interest from the peasants.

PUBLIC DEBT, PRIVATE INVESTMENT

There had always been some public debt on both the provincial and local levels, the latter including both diocesan and municipal assemblies. But the earlier local debt had been a tremendous headache. Municipal finances fell into disarray as a result of the expenses of the 1630s and 1640s and caused bitter controversies. A list of audited municipal debts, mostly stemming from the first half of the century, comes to 4,064,818 livres in 1684 at a time when the provincial debt was over 5,900,000 livres and direct taxes

·rought in 3,800,000 per year.[36] This figure may be conservative. Loans ɔ the city of Toulouse alone between 1637 and 1654 add up to 1,417,677 ivres, and a register of Toulousain debts drawn up in 1670 lists *outstanding* lebts of 1,294,980 livres from 1622 to 1670. Accounts from Nîmes list nterest payments which would suggest a debt there by mid-century of 00,000 to 200,000 livres.[37]

This sort of massive, decentralized indebtedness was a source of concern o both the Estates and the crown. From 1632 to 1635 the king froze local ebts until the intendants Miron and Le Camus could look into them. In 638 a new arrêt de conseil suspended all interest payments for eight years, luring which communities were to impose the principal. But this was really pretext for the sale of new offices, and in 1639 another arrêt seized the nterest on the frozen debts on behalf of the crown. The 'extraordinary nalice' of such measures was resisted by the Estates as an attack on 'an nfinity of families, mostly composed of widows, and orphans, who had cted in good faith in aiding the poor people of this province with their vealth'. Still, they continued to endorse the principle of genuine erification by the royal commissioners and, in 1642, even sanctioned the mposition of the principal over an eight-year period.[38] The Estates were aking the side of the creditors. They defended interest payments and upported repayment, provided it was voluntary, but took issue with bligatory payoffs and arbitrary seizures which would threaten investments.

This position makes sense if we consider who the municipal creditors vere by looking at the city and diocese of Toulouse. I have analyzed the ew loans undertaken during fourteen peak years from 1637 to 1654.[39] They anged from 36,000 to 234,000 livres annually, averaging 101,263 per year nd totalling 1,417,677. Around twenty to thirty creditors a year invested rom one to several thousand livres apiece. Their names read like an honor oll of Toulousain society: we find major parlementaires like First resident Bertier and his wife Marie le Comte, Advocate-General Maniban, residents Barthélemy de Grammont and Caminade; a great many ouncillors, bourgeois, and avocats from the best families; Roguier, secreary of the Estates, and Lamamie its syndic-general; rich politicians like ean-Georges de Caulet, the hated *partisan*, who invested 10,600 livres as uge mage in 1647 and 2,000 more as president in the Parlement in 1653; inancial dynasties like the Pugets and d'Aldiguiers. Table 13 gives a listribution. Once again the aristocratic nature of the participation is

6 A.N. H 748^{211}, 283.

7 A.M. Tse CC 2071, 2073, 2075, 2077, 2080, 2084, 2088, 2090, 2092, 2093, 2095, 2098, 2100, 2102, 1540; A.M. Nm NN 11–17.

8 P-V Dec. 24, 1638; P-V Nov. 1639 (A.D. Hér. C 7087, 30); P-V Dec. 15, 1642, Feb. 11, 21, 1645.

9 The years are 1637–40, 1642, 1644, 1646–50, 1652–4. References in note 37.

Table 13. *Creditors of the city of Toulouse*

(in selected years, 1637–54. Women are counted under the status of their husbands when this is known.)

	No. of investors	Total investment	% of investors	% of investment
Nobles (including those identified only as 'sieur')	*28*	*169,600*	*7.5*	*12.0*
Religious	*54*	*186,185*	*14.4*	*13.1*
Religious foundations	35	61,460	9.3	4.3
Individual ecclesiastics	14	31,425	3.7	2.2
Bishop of Valence	5	93,300	1.3	6.6
Presidents, gens du roi, councillors sov. courts	*76*	*327,037*	*20.3*	*23.1*
Lesser robe officers	*17*	*72,800*	*4.5*	*5.1*
Financial agents and officers	*23*	*97,600*	*6.1*	*6.9*
Treasurer-generals of finance	4	24,300	1.1	1.7
Treasurers, bankers	4	11,000	1.1	0.8
Diocesan or provincial receivers or controllers	15	62,300	4.0	4.4
Urban 'bourgeoisie'	*144*	*471,705*	*38.4*	*33.3*
'Avocats' or 'procureurs'	77	234,193	20.5	16.5
'Bourgeois'	29	89,150	7.7	6.3
'Secrétaires', 'secrétaires du roi'	11	48,437	2.9	3.4
Professors, doctors	7	31,625	1.9	2.2
Officers of the Estates	4	22,100	1.1	1.6
Officers of the city or diocese	2	3,300	0.5	0.2
Merchants	14	42,900	3.7	3.0
Artisans	*2*	*5,100*	*0.5*	*0.4*
Other				
Inhabitant	*1*	*2,100*	*0.3*	*0.2*
Unidentified	27	67,650	7.2	4.8
Public funds	1	13,000	0.3	0.9
Unidentified woman	2	4,900	0.5	0.3
Total	375	1,417,677	100.0	100.0
Included in the above are:				
[illegible]	[illegible]	[illegible]	[illegible]	[illegible]

striking. The top ranks of society are heavily represented, especially the officers of the Parlement, who alone invested 23.1 percent of the money. The procureurs and avocats, most of whom were attached to the Parlement and many of whom came from parlementaire families, put in another 16.5 percent and the 'nobles' contributed 12 percent. The clergy and the 'bourgeois', broadly conceived, are also well placed. Financial officers are less well represented, and 'ordinary citizens' – artisans and below – are almost completely absent. The constantly reiterated appeals about 'widows and orphans' have some validity in that 21 percent of the funds were invested by widows. In addition 4.3 percent came from religious foundations, many of them confraternities or charitable organizations. The presence of groups of individuals from the same families and of certain heavy investors with evident local ties suggests that personal contacts were helpful in taking advantage of this kind of opportunity. The Carrière family of financial officers jointly contributed 67,300 livres while the bishop of Valence, who happened to be the brother of the lieutenant-general of Haut-Languedoc, put in 93,300 livres. The debts of the Toulouse diocese have a similar complexion, though on a much smaller scale.[40]

These people represented the local branch of the ruling groups we are studying. They had an interest in the system of the Estates, and they needed protection from attacks on their investment. This is exactly what Louis XIV provided. The earlier regulations had collapsed under the new weight of debts in the 1640s. In 1662 the matter was revived. While the Estates were initiating discussions of the funding of municipal debt repayments, the king established a debt commission which, unlike its predecessor of 1635, included members of the three orders of the Estates as well as the royal commissioners. Noting that for the first time their own deputies had a deliberative and judicial voice on the commission 'which would aid the communities considerably', the assembly passed a motion of unqualified support and thanks.[41] In 1675, when a new commission was set up, the Estates demanded – and got – the same conditions.[42] Not only were they participating in the regulation of local debts, but they were paying their creditor-peers back in deflated currency for debts incurred in periods of easier money.

Meanwhile province-wide debts had been developing in a new direction. Before 1649 loans to the province had been short-term affairs. The real borrowing 'habit' began in that year when 200,000 livres were raised,

[40] The most notable investors were associated with the diocese: Pierre de Prat of Miremont, former syndic; Anne, Suzanne, and Guillaume de Puget, the latter a former receiver of the diocese; various Roguiers and Fieubets, relatives of the secretary-general of the Estates.

[41] P-V Jan. 13, Mar. 6, 10, 1662; Bezons to Colbert, Sept. 25, 1662: Mel. Col. 111, 432; P-V Dec. 5, 1662.

[42] P-V Jan. 12, 18, 1674, Feb. 7, 1676.

appropriately enough, to buy back the offices of treasurer of the bourse from the king. Thereafter the floating debt grew, especially after the decision in 1654 to borrow all of that year's 1,500,000 livres *don gratuit*.[43] What distinguished the new debt was its regular growth, its cumulative nature and the way it was raised. The money was borrowed in the name of the province by the syndic-generals and accounted for in the assembly. It could be borrowed from any combination of lenders large or small, local or Parisian. Management by the Estates and their access to funds through the ability to expand the 'debts and affairs' section of the tax burden (with royal permission) guaranteed the lenders a certain accountability. This was enhanced by the fact that the funds were in the hands of Pennautier, a familiar provincial figure, and administered by bishops and lawyers with exactly the right local connections.

The system's flexibility in borrowing was matched by its usefulness to investors. This was an age when land rents were in decline and the rates paid by the Estates were superior to the returns many were getting from their estates.[44] Since loans were made on a yearly basis, funds could be retrieved readily or renewed for another term. This refunding operation was assured by the annual sessions of the Estates and the terms of the debt. On the other hand, if a long-term placement was desired, the debts soon became convertible into annual and perpetual *rentes*.[45] While the obligations were not technically negotiable, it was easy to take over a debt already in effect, like the 40,564 of the loan of 1654 which the sieur de la Baume purchased from the creditors of the diocese of Carcassonne in 1656; and obligations could be used to pay one's own debts, as when President Sartre transferred his 56,000 livres investment in the same loan to the dame de Montlaur as part of a family settlement for raising his children.[46]

The identity of the investors, when it can be determined in the 1670s, demonstrates the flexibility of the system in linking different sources of capital. Sums needed were raised in the capitals of Languedoc, in Paris during the annual deputations, or in the dioceses and communities. For example, a loan of 60,000 livres in 1674 was raised among fourteen investors who averaged 3,286 livres apiece, with the remaining 12,000 livres supplied by Pierre de la Gorce, former capitoul of Toulouse. The fourteen subscribers were mostly persons of middling importance: the widow of a Toulouse merchant, a widow from Pézenas, several nobles, a convent in Pézenas, the lieutenant-principal of the sénéchaussée of Lauragais, a professor and a baker from Montpellier, for example. Also noteworthy were

43 P-V Nov. 17, 1649, Mar. 23, 31, 1654, Jan. 9, 1655, Apr. 21, 1657.

44 Georges Frêche, *Toulouse et la région Midi-Pyrénées au siècle des lumières* (*vers 1670–1789*) (Paris, 1974), pp. 568–71, 581; Emmanuel Le Roy Ladurie, *Les Paysans de Languedoc*, 2 vols. (Paris, 1966), vol. 1, pp. 594–601.

45 P-V Mar. 5, 8, 1655.

46 P-V Feb. 14, 1656, Mar. 5, 1655.

the secretary of the archbishop of Toulouse and the 'governor' of the children of the marquis de Castries.[47] Such servants of the great, who were obviously stand-ins for their masters, appear frequently, indicating that the decision-makers on both sides of the provincial–royal fence were acquiring their own stake in the financial process. Many subscriptions never left the immediate circle of the Estates. In 1662 the syndic-generals borrowed 100,000 livres from the marquis de Castries. In January 1675, 96,000 livres were raised for the 'affairs of the province' from the bishop of Albi, Cardinal Bonzi, d'Aguesseau the intendant, the king's valet de chambre, and two other parties.[48] In 1680, 150,000 livres were raised in Languedoc from seventeen parties headed by the wife of President Mariotte of the Comptes (27,000 livres) and a list of familiar financial names like Belleval, de Ratte, Madronnet, Pouget, and Caulet.[49]

As the public debt skyrocketed, the leading investors became intertwined in a network of relationships connecting them to each other and to Parisian finance. In 1672 we find Étienne Matry, diocesan receiver of Albi, living in Paris and acting as the agent of the syndic-general Montbel for the raising of large sums. Lenders are François Le Maire, seigneur de Villeromarel, trésorier-général de l'extraordinaire des guerres (270,000 livres), a *commis* of Louvois, and various others. Meanwhile, in Pézenas, Montbel himself is arranging other loans with Parisians whose payments will be made in Paris through Matry or through another agent, Laurent Bosc, controller of rentes in Montpellier. Included on the list are the duc de Verneuil, governor, and Verneuil's secretary, whose funds will be made payable in Paris by Pennautier.[50]

A different act drawn up in Paris on August 20, 1675, shows us another web of relationships. A debt of 32,000 livres is to be repaid to André de Jougla, councillor in the Parlement of Toulouse, son of a diocesan receiver of Béziers. The replacement money has been lent by d'Aguesseau, the intendant of Languedoc. In the office of a Parisian notary 32,000 livres *in coin* is presented to Isaac Douzier, Jougla's agent, by Étienne Matry, this time Pennautier's agent (acting in the name of the province). At the same time Douzier transfers the provincial 'IOU' to madame d'Aguesseau, representing her husband, with promises that all the appropriate papers will be drawn up within a fortnight. Also present is André Pouget, greffier of the Comptes of Montpellier, the ally of Riquet and Colbert who later financed the manufactory at Carcassonne. Pouget joins with Douzier (for Jougla) in underwriting the obligation to d'Aguesseau.[51] What a contrast from the 1640s and the age of *partisans*! The distinction between Paris and

47 A.N. H 748[205], 1.

48 P-V Mar. 8, 1662; A.N. H 748[207], 41.

49 A.N. H 748[211], 273, 275.

50 A.N. H 748[208], 90.

51 A.N. H 748[207], 139.

Languedoc had become as financially meaningless as that between 'outside' and 'provincial' financiers.

At the same time the Estates were becoming more sophisticated in their financial technique as experience demonstrated the range of options available to a well-managed administration with working funds and credit at its disposal. In 1657, when troop lodgings had exhausted all the Estates' resources and the king was demanding 300,000 livres more to prepare the royal army for departure, long conferences with the royal commissioners produced a new kind of financial compromise. The money would be borrowed from Pierre Montmoulen, a financier associated with the taillon administration, and paid in subsequent years by an annual allotment of part of the taillon receipts. Since Montmoulen feared that he would not have the authority to resist other claims on these taillon funds, the Estates were to guarantee the loan, and money would be transferred annually to their treasury for payment to Montmoulen. In effect the king was mortgaging part of his taillon receipts to a financier while the Estates used their credit and facilities to guarantee the loan.[52] The same technique of sharing a loan between king and province was adopted in 1658 to pay for an edict selling land ennoblements and in 1673 when a loan of 1,600,000 livres was floated for the Canal des Deux Mers. On the latter occasion the province borrowed the money under its own name, but the king guaranteed the annual interest payments by transferring 100,000 livres each year from the 'basic taille' received by the receiver-generals to the treasury of the Estates.[53]

Consciousness of the politics of credit developed along with these techniques. In 1669 the Estates issued a plea for the renewal of the paulette on behalf of the officers of the Comptes not, as in an earlier age, out of provincial solidarity, but because the insecurity of the Comptes officers had dried up credit in Montpellier, where the syndics had been unable to locate 500,000 livres for the canal.[54] There was similar talk of credit shortages in 1675 when Toulouse creditors wanted to be guaranteed longer-term loans and in 1676 when Pennautier complained that his interest rate would have to be raised because of the high cost of credit.[55] Meanwhile, with such a large outstanding debt the province was faced with problems of regulation and administration. The king's aid was solicited in obtaining legislation favoring the claims of municipal taille collectors over other creditors and

[52] P-V Feb. 24, 27, Apr. 18, 19, 21, 1657.

[53] P-V Jan. 31, 1658, Dec. 21, 1673; arrêt de conseil July 1, 1673: A.N. H 748[204], 207. The province also began developing its own internal sources of credit. In 1662 and 1663 part of the 20 deniers per livre that local communities had the capacity to impose to pay local collectors was impounded to pay the interest on new loans. In 1678 the province called on the dioceses to borrow 226,000 livres towards the *don* of 3,000,000 livres. In 1679 the province chose borrowing money itself over guaranteeing loans taken out by Riquet, entrepreneur of the canal. P-V Mar. 7, 1662, Feb. 1, 1663; A.N. H 748[208], 415; *Inventaire Haute-Garonne*, série C, 1, p. 404.

[54] *Inventaire Haute-Garonne*, série C, 1, p. 374.

[55] P-V Jan. 2, 1675, Jan. 10, 1676.

establishing other credit mechanisms.[56] By the early 1680s comprehensive discussions were taking place concerning the province's total indebtedness and how to manage it.

A picture of Languedocian taxation which emphasizes the arbitrary extraction of a rising burden of taxes from an increasingly prostrate province would be dangerously misleading. Not only would it distort the balance of forces between king and province, but it would ignore the social question of distribution which turns out to be crucial. After 1633 the tendency was not towards further royal encroachments but rather towards the working out of an accommodation between king and provincial notables. There was some pressure upwards from the gradually increasing size of the king's *dons gratuits* and from the rising magnitude of funds managed by the Estates, especially in the second half of the period, but the prevailing theme was adjustment, not increase. Before 1660 the violent fluctuations were due almost entirely to emergency levies imposed under pressure. Military exactions profited commanders and soldiers, many of them outsiders, and contractors to some extent. Fiscal edicts made the fortunes of the *partisans* who farmed them and possibly of individuals who purchased offices. Only the financial receivers who handled all tax monies drew profit consistently from such arbitrary and irregular burdens. The king did indeed receive large additional revenues from these wartime expedients, but they were revenues extracted at enormous political and financial cost and mortgaged in advance for specific purposes. Such methods were traditional for a feudal-minded monarch, but, in the long run, unrestricted, regular payments in cash would be infinitely more useful.

The real issue, especially after 1660, was the sharing-out of a relatively stable, though slowly growing body of provincial revenue. We have seen that as time went on the royal share decreased slightly while the provincial share increased. In fact, Louis XIV was receiving more money from Languedoc through the Estates' borrowing power but less from direct taxation. The result was a collaboration in which both parties gained. The king was assured a greater and much more regular flow of liquid funds while the province grabbed a greater share of the direct taxes. Meanwhile, the traditional beneficiaries of the tax system continued to hold their own or even make slight gains. The leaders in the Estates continued to bestow grants and favors upon themselves and their friends; honorific commanders continued to receive enormous grants. Royal officers continued to prosper.

Absolutism went hand in hand with finance. In the first half of the period there were close links between Parisian tax farmers, resident royal agents, and the more aggressive provincial 'loyalists' who antagonized their

[56] A.N. H 748[215], 564 ('economic' cahier, articles 1, 8).

counterparts by peddling contracts and purchasing exploitative new offices. Baltazar was the symbol of such links. In the second half the province was integrated back into a more genial financial partnership, first because the earlier opportunists had made their way, with time, into more respectable and orthodox positions; second, because the province had regained control over much of its financial apparatus, and the opportunity to profit from it was now opened up to the entire circle of rulers. Meanwhile, behind the scenes, the profits derived from handling the province's revenues were being hoarded, nurtured, passed down in families. These growing pools of resources would come together in the eighteenth century to form the great fortunes that would shore up the monarchy itself.

12

Collaborating with the king: positive results and fulfilled ambitions

By the 1670s a new mood of jubilant collaboration seemed to have taken over the governing bodies of Languedoc. The glories of Louis XIV were evoked more and more frequently in the most glowing of terms: 'can one ever marvel enough at the wonderful order of his finances, at the advantageous reestablishment of commerce and his maritime forces; can one ever admire sufficiently the defenses of his conquered fortifications, the warring genius of his people, their prompt obedience...'[1] Obsequious conformity seemed to be the order of the day. In late 1671, when the first vote of the *don gratuit* in the single deliberation without any bargaining by the Estates was achieved, Colbert was showered with self-congratulatory epistles from the responsible parties: 'I consider myself at once very glorious and very happy to be at the head of this assembly the first time that it accepted the *don gratuit* unanimously.' 'It was the most delicate pleasure imaginable...to support the view most agreeable and useful to His Majesty.' 'The assembly wants to remain in the king's good graces and to do his bidding in a submissive fashion.' 'The vote was unanimous once the royal commissioners gave their word that the king would be satisfied.'[2]

From expressions like these it is easy to draw an exaggerated picture of provincial passivity and institutional subservience, especially since there is considerable truth in the contention that the entire governmental system worked more smoothly under Louis XIV. Dissidence and obstruction did not disappear, but they certainly became less virulent. The Estates began to look like an organism for carrying out the wishes of the crown. The Parlement registered the royal commands promptly and even thanked Colbert afterwards for the privilege of having its *ex post facto* objections mentioned to the king.[3] The Comptes settled into a bureaucratic routine. Although the province would soon face new wartime suffering, there would be none of the obstructionism which had become a way of life before 1660,

[1] Archbishop of Toulouse to Estates, P-V Dec. 9, 1671.

[2] Cardinal Bonzi, Dec. 22, 1671: Depping, vol. 1, p. 270; bishop of Lodève, Dec. 23, 1671: ibid., p. 275; bishop of Rieux, Dec. 22, 1671: Mel. Col. 150 bis, 874; bishop of Mende, Dec. 23, 1671: ibid., 880; bishop of Castres, Dec. 22, 1671: ibid., 860.

[3] Fieubet to Colbert, Mar. 6, 1669: Mel. Col. 150 bis, 756.

at least until later in the eighteenth century under drastically changed conditions. The whole system seemed hypnotized by the glitter of Versailles, and a querulous province seemed content to bask complacently in the glorious rays of the Sun King.

This new atmosphere raises the central issue of why and in what ways Louis XIV's regime was more effective than its predecessors, which in turn raises the more fundamental question of what the contrast between the reigns of Louis XIII and Louis XIV can tell us about the essential nature of absolutism. For despite the attempts of royal propagandists to have us believe otherwise, Louis XIV's success was not a foregone conclusion. Although Languedocian leaders were devoted to the formal principle of absolutism, they had spent the forty years before 1660 struggling – often against the king – to refashion it in their own image. Attempts were sometimes made to collaborate on a province-wide basis, but separate, mutually contradictory struggles were more often the rule, as each provincial power center fought to protect its place within a rapidly evolving system.

Indeed, what needs explaining is the swiftness with which the king's new style was not only accepted but enthusiastically embraced by the provincial notables even though they had to give up positions and strategies for which they and their fathers had struggled long and hard. Traditional answers are inadequate in explaining this complex change of governing mood. Most common is the 'repression' view which looks at the process from the center: royal troops and prompt punishments made it clear that dissidence would no longer be tolerated; courtiers were appointed to key positions; local leaders were enticed to Versailles where they learned to jump at the king's commands; procedures were manipulated, customs violated, laws rewritten. One can alternatively stress the 'creative statebuilding' view: information was systematically collected by agents with a broader vision of how to use it; new procedures were regularized; chains of command were perfected; rational planning was introduced at all levels. One can note as well the favorable conditions of the Colbertian period: the 'breathing-spell' of peacetime, the reduction of taxes, the pacification of the kingdom.

All of these factors played their part, but none is entirely satisfactory in explaining Louis XIV's deep-seated success in the provinces. Coercive threats and vigorous leadership could certainly lead to better compliance with royal directives but not to such widespread eagerness to emulate and extend the new regime. After all, previous rulers had also used strong-hand measures. Richelieu was noted for them, and the previous forty years had been filled with moves like the execution of Montmorency, the repeated suspensions of parlementaires, the disunion of the Comptes, the Edict of Béziers. Many of the bureaucratic tools had already existed, and the royal grandeur had already begun to be used as an ideological weapon. Yet when the change began to be felt in 1659, only three years had elapsed since the Fronde-like crisis of 1656–7.

A more satisfying hypothesis concerning the success of Louis XIV is that his regime must have served the needs of the rulers of Languedoc and met their expectations. The forgotten dimension in accounts which stress repression or superior organization is the potential bond of common interest linking king and provincial leaders. To be sure, a more domineering monarch and a better organized administration were necessary for success, as were improved conditions; but the king would certainly have met with more opposition if his policies had seriously threatened Languedocian leaders who had the demonstrated ability to resist them. In fact, Louis XIV strengthened the provincial ruling class, enhancing its domination and making its life more pleasant at the expense of the rest of society, despite the 'centralizing' and 'levelling' tendencies which are so often stressed by historians. This chapter and the next analyze that process. The question to keep in mind is how Louis XIV's relations with provincial leaders were different from those of the previous forty years.

Part of the answer lies in the resolution of problems which had plagued the province for a generation and which now were alleviated by more effective, collaborative programs. In many cases the royal plans fulfilled ambitions which had been hanging in abeyance for a generation. In others, provincial leaders had to be taught to appreciate activities which they would never have initiated, even some which directly contradicted their interests. But the genius of Louis XIV (or his ministers) did not lie in the ability to ram through innovations which sapped the province of its vitality. On the contrary, his success lay in a special ability to translate royal aspirations towards greater and more centralized power into terms which appealed to the provincial ruling class and which enhanced their class position even while strengthening the state and the monarchy.

Three areas are especially noteworthy. The first of these, the regulation of military burdens, was only the culmination of developments begun under Richelieu, but for the first time they were made to work effectively. The second, Colbert's ambitious program of economic development, was the most original program and the one most alien to provincial thinking. Here the rulers were agnostic, but they rapidly became converted. The third, the repression of the Huguenots, was by contrast the fulfillment of a long-standing Languedocian dream.

TROOPS REGULATED

As we saw in chapter 7, the passage of gens de guerre was always accompanied by disorder and injustice. Military excesses were a fact of life which did not particularly shock provincial leaders, some of whom had close personal ties with the army, and few of whom were really concerned about the inevitable sufferings of common peasants or soldiers, especially in other places. Still, the rulers' traditional role of protector of subordinates required them to consider the welfare of the local population, and in some cases they were genuinely concerned about it. The presence of troops meant discontent in local communities where most Languedocian leaders had close contacts, and even more important, loss of control over the situation. Here Louis XIV's rule brought significant advances. What could be better than a monarch who maintained a bellicose reputation and protected his borders adequately without imposing costly troop lodgings on his subjects at home? Of course the calm of the 1660s was more the result of Mazarin's peace with the Habsburgs than of anything the king had personally done. But by the time troop burdens began to grow again in the 1670s, the unruly elements were better regulated and their costs much better financed. Louis XIV did not remove the burden of troops, but he did improve the aspects of lodgings which were most annoying to the rulers of the province.

Figure 12 illustrates the distribution of various military burdens throughout our period. The crescendo of enforcement problems which obviously faced both the Estates and the royal agents at the end of the 1630s had made the quartier d'hiver and the étapes indispensable, despite the resistance of the Estates. When the intendant Miron proposed the quartier d'hiver in 1639, he stressed its advantages for the province:

> in arranging lodgings and payments supplied by the province yourselves, you can make sure that expenses are not duplicated in a multiplicity of [separate] levies and collections... By appropriating what is needed for the entire year, you can name deputies to confer with us... and to arrange everything necessary... In this way you will completely reestablish the dignity and elevate the authority of the Estates.[4]

What a good description of the merits of collaboration! This was the system established in 1640. Instead of winter quarters being imposed by force, deputies and royal commissioners together drew up precise regulations concerning how much the soldiers were to be paid by the communities and where they were to go. At the end of the year a committee of the Estates studied the accounts submitted by the syndic of each diocese, eliminated unauthorized expenditures, and then granted each community credit equal

[4] Miron to Estates, P–V Nov. 21, 1639.

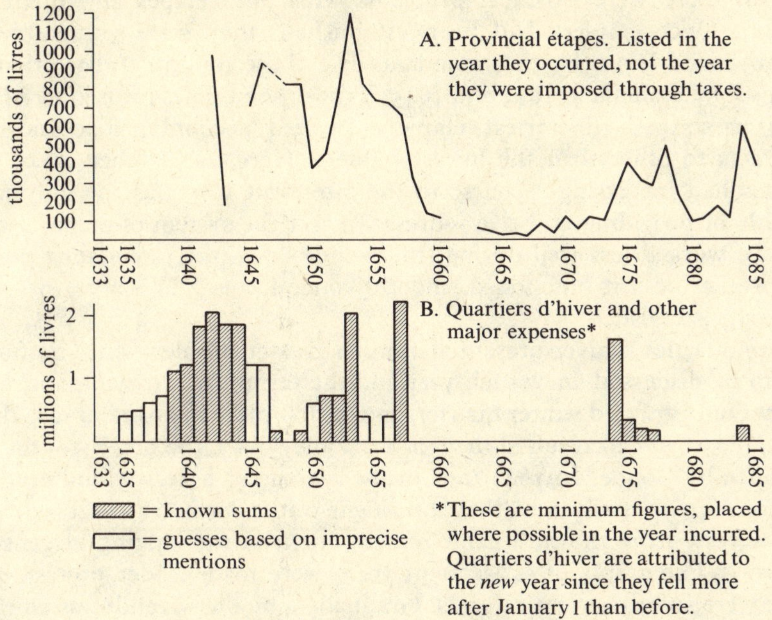

Figure 12. The burden of troops.

to the advances it had made.[5] For similar reasons the assembly capitulated in 1641 and agreed to establish the étape, which continued every year thereafter.

There were considerable advantages in these reforms. First, the Estates participated actively in the process of making the rules, which they discussed in the minutest detail. They debated from which day troops entering the province should be paid, who should bear the cost of loans by dioceses, how the certificates of lodgings were to be signed and counter-signed, how to deal with local measures of wine and grain, what to do about local variations in prices.[6] They also audited and regulated the accounts. They could be much more thorough about surveying abuses since their syndics were more solicitous of local populations than royal agents, and there were more of them (twenty-two diocesan syndics as against one or two intendants). Perhaps best of all for the rulers was the fact that, even while the burden was being shifted from the afflicted communities to the province, it was also being channelled through the provincial repartition system. This perpetuated the usual social and regional inequities and siphoned off profits to the various handlers of money on the various levels.

[5] P-V Dec. 1, 1640. [6] P-V Sept. 30, 1641, Dec. 13, 1642, Nov. 24, 1643.

Still, there were practical problems with both étapes and quartiers d'hiver. Once étapiers had been established, they were vulnerable to unauthorized levies by the intendants like those for the embarcation of troops for Catalonia in 1644 and 1645. Troops sometimes refused to follow their prescribed itineraries; étapiers falsified accounts; dioceses sold contracts to other than the lowest bidder.[7] Here, as in other areas, the Estates had increasing recourse to the intendant who was the only man capable of providing effective redress. In fact the system of étapes seems to have worked less well during the Fronde when the intendant's power was weaker, and it functioned smoothly once Louis XIV's authority was properly established.

The quartier d'hiver presented a much greater problem since its funds had to be discussed anew each year and the terrain was treacherous. The Estates only granted winter quarters in the first place in 1640 because their refusal in 1639 had resulted in an arbitrary levy of 1,100,000 livres on the province by Condé. In 1641 they made a virtue of necessity and granted a second quartier since, as their president put it, 'it is true that we have seen a very great and noticeable improvement in the lodging of gens de guerre'.[8] The grants of subsequent years were made under protest, and there were some outright refusals. Gradually a modus vivendi was worked out where the Estates agreed to pay the troops and the king agreed to let them use his *don* for this purpose. But each occasion required long and acrimonious negotiations in which the advantage always lay with the king because he could send troops to live off the land until the Estates came to some sort of arrangement.

These are the experiences against which the period of Louis XIV must be judged. While the étapes continued to run smoothly, the advent of peacetime provided a period to forget the unpleasant desperation of the quartier d'hiver negotiations of the 1650s. By the time the issue of winter quarters arose again in 1674, there was little chance of evading Louis XIV's demands, which were to grow heavy again by the end of his reign. But, at the same time, the new burdens were administered so flawlessly that the pain which was felt was purely fiscal – and that meant that it was shifted off the shoulders of the rulers, whose concern had always been focused on disorder, not on paying the bills.

After granting a *don* of 2,000,000 livres, the Estates of 1674 were informed that a quartier d'hiver would also be necessary and that the troops would have to live off the province. This was a serious precedent because

7 Examples of étape accounts and lists of étapiers are in A.D. Hér. C 8511 (for 1657) and in A.D. H-G. C 720, 721 (1648–50, 1655–56). There were many disputes with étapiers, for example A.D. H-G. C 2131, 1650 bundle: a lawsuit of the diocese against Jean Flandres, étapier, merchant of Villemur in the diocese of Bas-Montauban.

8 P-V Sept. 6, 1641.

never before had the province granted a large sum *and* had to pay for the troops in addition. The deputies immediately protested to the royal commissioners that they had been given 'positive assurance' that the troops would not be a burden to the province and that 'for several days until the seventeenth of this month they had believed in good faith in a treaty which they had accepted and which His Majesty had since confirmed in his letters'. The commissioners' reply was typical of the age: 'They could not deny that they had signed a treaty and that His Majesty himself had approved it in letters... but since the pure necessity of his affairs had caused His Majesty to desire that certain troops... be lodged in the province... it was necessary that the province be exposed to lodgings.'[9] This was the end of any illusions about principles of exemption. The royal will would prevail, even against royal promises.

But the new effectiveness of execution made the process more painless than ever before. Not having experienced a quartier in so long, the Estates worked out a new system of inspection from scratch: a provincial agent was sent out immediately with very specific instructions to inspect every community where there were lodgings, instruct the local consuls on how they were to handle the affair, and see that the soldiers were in good order. He was to continue his rounds during the entire period of lodgings and report periodically to the syndic-generals.[10] This was an echo of the earlier attempts made in 1649 and 1657 to use a parlementaire as a travelling authority figure to regulate the troops, but now the envoy's task was completely legitimate and supported by both Estates and royal agents.

Meanwhile, as the assembly refined its technique to the point where the minutest problems were legalistically worked out, the process was being streamlined from afar by the stern hand of Louvois who, like Colbert, had such excellent sources of information that he seemed almost to be on the scene. His letters to d'Aguesseau display an apparent mastery of every detail of the local situation. The commander of the regiment of Sault in Narbonne is to be suspended in order to 'give satisfaction' to the people of the town. Militia soldiers in hospitals are to be paid from the étape funds. The king endorses the intendants' arrest of a commander of dragoons until he has returned property stolen from natives. D'Aguesseau is instructed to investigate disorders by a Captain Cabasson of the regiment of Picardy and make an example of him. The king wants the commander of a company of the regiment of Champagne thrown into the citadel of Montpellier because of damages his men caused in the village of Olonzac even though he has paid restitution, 'to show the province the care which His Majesty takes in punishing officers who annoy his people'. Soldiers condemned to

[9] Roschach, vol. XIV, p. 1151.

[10] Ibid., p. 1158.

the galleys for thefts in Limoux are not to be released despite the appeals of the marquis de Malause.[11]

But if protection of civilians was better enforced, Louvois was even more concerned that his troops be properly treated. The consuls of Castres, he writes, are to be punished for bad treatment of soldiers; the consuls of Castelnaudary are to be thrown in prison immediately for leaving the battalion of Bouchet 'on the pavement' when they passed through on étape. Numerous étapiers are to be investigated for refusing to provide services or for not supplying prompt lists of troops. In 1682 the syndic of the diocese of Saint-Pons, who was also its étapier, is denounced because he 'did not fail to be absent whenever troops were due to arrive, leaving his magazines filled with everything awful from six leagues around'.[12]

For Languedocian contemporaries of Louvois, the regulation of troops had become a different kind of operation from what it had been for contemporaries of Richelieu. The financial burden was the same, and the inconvenience for private citizens was still there, but troop discipline and the administration of compensation were improved. Gone were the 'blackmail' threats of approaching forces, the desperate bargaining over dates and numbers, the arbitrary channelling of funds to *partisans* and special purposes. In their place were negotiated regulations and more effective enforcement.

There is something depressingly logical about the final lodging of our period – the troops which were sent in 1685 to convert the Huguenots. There were too many soldiers to lodge only in Protestant households, and most Huguenots had been converted anyway as the troops approached. The Estates went through the same steps as in 1674, studying their archives for precedents and discovering the facts about 1653, 1657, and 1675. What was new was the willingness with which they undertook the accommodation of the troops, after deciding cheerfully that the province, and not the king, should support the expense – the opposite conclusion from their predecessors of 1674. They eagerly thanked the royal agents for their help, named a deputy to tour the province, and drew up elaborate schedules of payments for infantry and cavalry. The other novel element was the use of credit. To meet the need for cash the province planned to borrow money and distribute it where needed, pending later reimbursement through taxes.[13]

[11] Louvois to d'Aguesseau, Nov. 3, Dec. 26, 1674: A.N. H 1695; Feb. 16, 1676: A.N. H 1696; Dec. 6, 1678, Oct. 6, 1680: A.N. H 1700; June 17, 1685: A.N. H 1711.

[12] Louvois to d'Aguesseau, May 5, July 1, Oct. 26, 1677: A.N. H 1700; Oct. 21, 1684: A.N. H 1711; Dec. 31, 1676: A.N. H 1696; Nov. 8, Nov. 15, 1682: A.N. H 1704.

[13] P-V Oct. 31, Nov. 3, 13, Dec. 7, 1685.

MANUFACTURES AND PUBLIC WORKS

One of the most celebrated aspects of Louis XIV's best years was the Colbertian concern for economic development. In Languedoc this effort was represented by a number of new companies, a mass of edicts and regulations, and most important, the construction of the Canal des Deux Mers and the port of Sète. These mercantilistic enterprises were a striking departure from the usual expectations of Languedocian leaders, and thus provide an interesting perspective on the new relationship between the crown and the provincial rulers.

The economy of Languedoc is hard to conceptualize for lack of detailed studies.[14] Haut-Languedoc, especially the region around Toulouse, was a producer of surplus grain with a need to export it eastward toward the complementary shortages of the Mediterranean Bas-Languedoc, and also westward down the Garonne to Bordeaux where there was more competition from the grains of Guyenne. From Carcassonne eastward, the dry climate made grain surpluses rare, and the emphasis was more on olives and wine, along with a variety of town-based manufacturing industries. Nîmes was the center of a growing silk industry. Montpellier sent its drugs, liqueurs, gloves, wool, and various types of woven cloth to a wide market through the fairs of Beaucaire and Pézenas. In the rocky hills of Gévaudan an important rural industry provided 'serges' and 'cadis' for export to southern Europe through the merchants of Nîmes. Most interesting was the network of smaller cloth-producing towns concentrated in the northern crescent circling the Massif Central. There an enormous variety of woolens was produced, each tied to its own traditional outlets and customers by local merchant-distributors. Most of these cloths were low-grade varieties, but certain towns, like Castres, Lodève, Clermont, and especially Carcassonne, had a tradition of specialization in fine woolens for export and had even experimented with some of the new Dutch techniques in the earlier seventeenth century. These towns generated their own mercantile social structures, now prospering and blossoming into a more sophisticated

14 On the economy, Philippe Wolff, ed., *Histoire du Languedoc* (Toulouse, 1967), pp. 337–41, 372–6; Georges Frêche, *Toulouse et la région Midi-Pyrénées au siècle des Lumières (vers 1670–1789)* (Paris, 1974), pp. 749–85; Louis-J. Thomas, *Montpellier ville marchande: histoire économique et sociale de Montpellier des origines à 1870* (Montpellier, 1936), pp. 133–55; Robert Descimon, 'Structures d'un marché de draperie dans le Languedoc au milieu du XVIe siècle', *Annales E.S.C.*, 30 (1975), 1414–46; O. Granat, 'L'Industrie de la draperie à Castres au dix-septième siècle et les "Ordonnances" de Colbert', *Annales du Midi*, 10 (1898), 446–57, 11 (1899), 56–67; Prosper Boissonnade, 'L'Essai de restauration des ports et de la vie maritime en Languedoc de 1593 à 1661 et son échec', *Annales du Midi*, 46 (1934), 98–121; 'Colbert, son système et les entreprises industrielles d'état en Languedoc (1661–1683)', *Annales du Midi*, 14 (1902), 5–49; 'La Restauration et le développement de l'industrie en Languedoc au temps de Colbert', *Annales du Midi*, 18 (1906), 441–72. The best recent study is J. K. J. Thomson, *Clermont-de-Lodève 1633–1789: Fluctuations in the Prosperity of a Languedocian Cloth-Making Town* (Cambridge, 1982).

division of labor, now collapsing back into all-purpose family workshops depending on the economy. A considerable prosperity before 1650 had given way to depression under Louis XIV, and they were therefore in a state of decadence until the new boom of the 1690s.[15]

It is striking how little impact this mercantile activity had on the power brokers of Languedoc. A map depicting industrial activity would form almost the negative image of a map showing political power centers, and where the two coincided in towns like Castres, Lodève, or Nîmes, it was not the mercantile elements which dominated the political positions, but rather the bishop or the royal officers. If there was a 'rising bourgeoisie' in Languedoc, it made its presence felt indirectly by producing taxable wealth, animating fairs and ports, and supplying families with the wherewithal to begin their climb towards church posts, judicial offices, and financial ventures.

The economic concerns of these political authorities were decidedly traditional. They understood the need to generate wealth, but they had no sense of the dynamics of economic growth and no interest in or appreciation of new products, new markets, or new forms of labor organization. When it came to actual improvements, they were more likely to see the threat innovations posed to existing interests than to appreciate the advantages offered.

Colbert had a broader vision and a bolder strategy of reform.[16] He saw the province as part of a larger system of national and international exchange in which Languedoc would lead France's assault on the Levant trade. Quality draperies in the Dutch and English manner were to be produced which could compete in the Mediterranean markets. Natural resources such as timber for ship masts and minerals produced by a royal mining company would be exploited. The Canal des Deux Mers and the port of Sète would facilitate communications and provide a Mediterranean outlet for Languedocian manufactures which was accessible, defensible, and free of the ingrained habits of the merchants of Marseilles. But Colbert's vision was also limited, for he failed to perceive the potential of Languedoc's indigenous industries. His perspective was that of the outsider imposing new structures from above and reacting with impatience to the protests of local merchants. His entrepreneurs were financiers of the traditional sort, not manufacturers whose experience lay in the management of privileged revenue flows.

Thus the provincial rulers and the national minister actually had more in common than might appear at first glance. Both looked down on the

[15] Ibid. pp. 89–131.

[16] On Colbert's mercantilism see the articles by Boissonnade cited above and Charles Wolsey Cole, *Colbert and a Century of French Mercantilism*, 2 vols. (New York, 1939). A somewhat revisionist view is Thomson, *Clermont*, pp. 132–71.

economy from a position of authority and viewed it as a matter for regulation at the highest levels of power. Both had the same objective of generating taxable wealth. Neither had any close familiarity with industrial milieux in Languedoc or any real insight into the dynamics of their international competitors. Given these common elements and differences, the mixed fate of Colbert's projects is readily understandable. To some extent the two sides could develop the common ground provided by their mutual interest in the production of taxable wealth, provided the Languedocians could be taught to distinguish their broader from their narrower interests. But this lesson would be hard to get across to them. Of Colbert's various projects, the more likely to win the begrudging acquiescence of provincial leaders were the public works which they could appreciate and monitor, not the manufacturing innovations which were totally outside their experience.

Although some of Colbert's companies ultimately took hold, one is struck with the number of failures and with the degree to which the great boom of the end of the century was independent of his efforts. The royal manufactory of gunpowder (1667) and the Royal manufactory of tobacco (1674), both set up against protest in Toulouse, were fiscal monopolies little related to economic growth. An attempt to compete with the Italian lace and bonnet trade by producing fine goods in Velay (1668) failed through the resistance of the traditional producers in Le Puy. Between 1666 and 1671 a Royal Company of Mines and Foundries was established under the typical directorship of Clerville, Colbert's engineering expert, Pennautier, Riquet, and Roux, syndic-general of the Estates. Most of the other investors were also familiar names from financial and ruling circles: Dalibert, Le Secq, De la Croix, Bavyn. Despite the importation of Swedish experts and an ambitious program of site-searching and digging, the plan came to nothing, partly because of an inadequacy of resources and partly because of conflicts among the elite directors.[17]

Most significant was the plan to produce luxury draperies for the Levant. Colbert aided and endorsed three companies to this effect: a first *manufacture royale* in Carcassonne grouping twenty-six of the traditional manufacturers (1666), a second at Sapte near Carcassonne (1666) and a third at Villenouvette near Clermont l'Hérault (1674).[18] The combination of local and outside involvement in these enterprises is interesting. Sapte was a long-standing manufactory which was revived by the investment of Pierre de Varennes, a Parisian figure who apparently had local roots and who was aided by Colbert in recruiting Dutch workers to teach the natives their superior methods. Villenouvette was established by a cartel of financiers

[17] Boissonnade, 'Colbert', pp. 28–34; Cole, *Colbert*, p. 460.

[18] On the three companies, Boissonnade, 'Colbert', pp. 9–28; Cole, *Colbert*, pp. 156–71; Thomson, *Clermont*, pp. 132–71.

who had already formed a Compagnie de Sète for exporting wine and eau-de-vie from the new Languedocian port and who wanted to take advantage of a sudden rise in the demand for cloth in the Levant. These people were led by none other than the treasurer of the bourse Pennautier and André Pouget, the chief greffier from the Cour des Comptes and a familiar investor in Languedocian affairs. Others included Laurent Bosc, Gabriel Creyssels, various members of the Roux family, and the diocesan receivers of Nîmes, Mirepoix, Viviers, Le Puy, Albi, Limoux, and Toulouse – in other words most of the members of the indigenous financial networks discussed in chapter 11.[19] Once again, provincial figures were tied into national developments.

All three companies made serious attempts to imitate Dutch methods and began turning out quality products for Turkey, Armenia and Persia, as well as cheaper goods for Spain and Italy. The difficulty was producing them at competitive prices and finding markets. Colbert issued regulations for the industry in 1666, placed a tariff on imports of foreign cloth in 1667, and bought up samples which he sold at a loss in Paris and elsewhere. Finally a system of bounties on each piece exported had to be established to make the prices competitive. Nevertheless, trade limped along because the Dutch simply lowered their prices to undersell the French. They had better representives in the Levant, more experience, and superior credit facilities. Despite Colbert's administrative genius and the employment of a considerable body of other talent, it is hard to see how the likes of Pennautier, Pouget, or Varennes, all primarily bankers and tax farmers, could compete effectively with Dutch merchants whose energies and native economies were devoted to nothing but competitive merchandising. There is general agreement among historians that Colbert's attempts were unsuccessful, although Thomson has recently argued that the controller-general did provide an indispensable service by forcing the province to learn the new techniques which would make it possible for them to seize the opportunity of the boom in demand which began in the 1690s.[20]

By 1681, in spite of all these subsidies, the cloth manufacturers were close to collapse, and Pouget was virtually bankrupt.[21] The result was an interesting dialogue with the Estates. Asked to shore up the manufacturers, they named a committee to study the matter. It consulted with d'Aguesseau at great length and reviewed the entire balance sheet of the enterprise. Its verdict was surprisingly frank for 1681: 'that the advantages that might accrue from this new company would not be worth what the king and the province would put into it, especially since there was no lack of manufactures in the province of Languedoc which were long established

[19] Thomson, *Clermont*, pp. 150–1. [20] Ibid., p. 457.
[21] Cole, *Colbert*, pp. 161–71; Thomson, *Clermont*, pp. 163–71.

and better than the one at Clermont'.[22] The diagnosis was so discouraging that even Colbert was about to give up, until he suddenly changed his mind and demanded that the Estates provide a loan of 100,000 livres, buy up the tools from Villenouvette, pay rent for the buildings, and supply a bounty of 10 livres for each piece of cloth produced over and above what the king was paying. This change of heart was apparently the result of lobbying by Pennautier and Bonzi on behalf of their allies, the financier-investors who did not want to lose their money. The Estates found themselves in a paradoxical position. They were being forced to underwrite a dubious enterprise in order to save the investments of financiers, many of whom were just as Languedocian as they were, and who had close ties with the leading provincial agencies. Once they had reluctantly ratified Colbert's demands, they found themselves overseeing a 'semi-public' operation, which they monitored in the same way as the roads or the troop expenses. Meanwhile the annual rents they paid for taxes for the buildings at Villenouvette provided Pouget with capital for his enterprises. As Thomson put it, 'the industrial failure of Languedocian finance could hardly have been symbolized better than by this act of liquidation'.[23]

When it came to public works projects, the prospects for mutual understanding between king and province were greater, but the immediate prospects were nevertheless discouraging. The Estates had a long history of opposition to such enterprises. They had refused to contribute to Henry IV's project of building a port at Sète in 1596, and even after it had been built by an entrepreneur in 1602, they had denied the king the funds to perfect it since they considered it 'a purely royal enterprise which the province neither could nor should support'.[24] By 1605 the port was in ruin for lack of funds. Money was only reluctantly voted in 1603, 1607, and 1620 to keep open a channel linking Narbonne (and the grain of Haut-Languedoc) to the sea.[25] The only major public works project undertaken from 1632 to 1663 was the improvement of the port of Agde, and that was forced through by Richelieu and regarded by the Estates with the greatest suspicion.

Typical was the Estates' response to the 'Beaucaire' or 'Peccais' canal which was to link the Rhône at Beaucaire with the salt flats of Peccais in order to improve transport and drain a swampy area infested with fever. This project, also proposed originally under Henry IV, was granted to an entrepreneur in May 1644 by royal edict. In 1645 the Estates protested that the king had been 'surprised' by this edict; that Rhône transport was not really difficult; that the marshes did not cause fevers at all; and that the canal was just a pretext for greedy entrepreneurs to acquire cheaply the

22 Quoted in Cole, *Colbert*, pp. 162–3.

23 Thomson, *Clermont*, p. 171.

24 Boissonnade, 'Ports', pp. 108–15.

25 Ibid., p. 104.

lands of legitimate owners and the justice rights of local seigneurs. Later the Estates had the entire canal filled in, and they were still protesting in 1663 when Louis XIV commanded them to consent to its reconstruction. As Bezons reported, 'the project is useful to the royal service and it is in the provincial interest [to build it] but selfish concerns have won out in a region where the advantages of commerce are not understood'.[26]

When the deputies did warm to a public project, it was not because of the utilitarian appeal of a canal or a port but because they could appreciate its decorative and artistic merits, and they enjoyed the management of its many details. Thus amidst the ruins of their roads and bridges, they voted to repair the Roman arena in Nîmes, 'one of the oldest and most beautiful antiquities in the province', and the equally historic but useless Pont du Gard.[27] After the Edict of Béziers was revoked in 1649, they began once again discussing roads and bridges but took care to see that the local communities bore most of the cost and that projects were not funded until the urge for inspection by commissions of dignitaries had been fully satisfied.[28]

This was the atmosphere in which the famous Canal des Deux Mers was proposed, which would link the Atlantic and the Mediterranean by connecting the Garonne at Toulouse with the lagoons near Agde and Montpellier.[29] From the royal point of view, the Canal represented the centerpiece of a comprehensive plan to stimulate the southern economy and rejuvenate trade. But to the Estates it looked like just another dubious scheme. Its promoter, Pierre-Paul Riquet, was a typically ambitious financier, the son of a notary from Béziers with a shady record of fraudulent dealings. Riquet himself had built a vast fortune as sub-farmer of the gabelle of Haut-Languedoc, munitioneer for the royal armies in Roussillon and Cerdagne, and finally director of the gabelle of Languedoc and Roussillon.[30] When such a classic gabeleur proposed a project involving vast outlays of money and immense transfers of property rights, it was no wonder the province drew back in alarm. It had no way of knowing that Riquet was a visionary who really meant what he said and no consciousness of the similar engineering projects being undertaken all over Europe. Riquet had approached Colbert in 1662 through the mediation of the new archbishop of Toulouse and the bishop of Saint-Papoul, both Colbertian allies and power brokers in the Estates, who personally visited the sites and studied

[26] P-V Jan. 28, 1645, Oct. 13, 1651, Jan. 31, 1663; Bezons to Colbert, Jan. 29, 1663: Depping, vol. I, p. 120; Brun to Colbert, Feb. 1664: Depping, vol. I, p. 153; king to Estates: A. D. Hér. A 45, no. 13. See also Roschach, vol. XIII, pp. 383–8.

[27] P-A Apr. 26, 1647, Mar. 19, 1648.

[28] P-V Nov. 9, 1650.

[29] On the Canal, André Maistre, *Le Canal des deux mers: canal royal du Languedoc 1666–1810* (Toulouse, 1968); and Henri Blaquière and Anne de Font-Reaulx, *Documents sur le canal des deux mers et la politique de Colbert en Languedoc* (Toulouse, 1967).

[30] Maistre, *Canal*, pp. 39–47; Blaquière, *Documents*, pp. 25–33.

his project before encouraging its pursuance. His local topographical and financial expertise was thus linked to Colbert's formidable power of direction through the emerging client system which was then reaching fruition. The question was how these mercantilist prophets could induce the reactionary bishops to participate in a scheme which would cost the province millions.

The involvement came in stages. First, an arrêt de conseil instructed the Estates to examine the project. In the fall of 1664 a large commission consisting of the intendant, the experts named by the king, and twenty-five deputies from the Estates set out with surveyors, porters, masons, and twenty soldiers to study the proposed terrain at first hand.[31] This was Colbert's official survey and not an artificial formality designed to woo the Estates. It exposed the assembly's leaders to the technological daring and businesslike precision of the royal experts. Perhaps they caught the bug, for they signed the report which stated that the project was both feasible and desirable.[32] An attempt was then made to impress the Estates of 1664–5. The archbishop of Toulouse noted that the king 'has conceived of a plan which is the greatest and most glorious, but also the most useful for this province of any ever nurtured in the soul of a monarch'; and Bezons added that 'this plan which amazed all of antiquity' would benefit 'all the large towns which are located on the shores of this canal'.[33] But arguments were useless. The assembly again rejected the Beaucaire canal as 'just another toll on the Rhône which will ruin commerce'; and refused all participation in the Canal des Deux Mers and the new port of Sète. Even the idea of dredging shipping channels along the coast was regarded with such extreme suspicion that the deputies only agreed to name commissioners to examine the project after an acrimonious debate which ended in insults and blows.[34] In the 1665–6 sessions the Estates again declared that 'they could not contribute to the expense of the canal in the present or in the future'.[35] However, even as they were refusing the funds for construction, the deputies of 1664–5 revealed their weak spot by appropriating over 19,000 livres in fees to the members who had served on the investigatory commission, scaled according to rank. They thus endorsed the formalities of inspection, participation and remuneration even as they rejected the idea of investment.

The next step for the crown was the construction of a small experimental canal in the summer of 1665 and then the issuance of edicts and letters patent which established the legal basis of the canal and granted the franchise to Riquet. Finally in 1666–7 the Estates could no longer evade

31 Bezons to Colbert, Nov. 10, 1664: Mel. Col. 125, 262.

32 Blaquière, *Documents*, pp. 38–42.

33 Quoted in Roschach, vol. XIII, p. 462.

34 Bezons to Colbert, Jan. 30, 1665: Mel. Col. 127, 356; Bezons to Colbert, Feb. 12, 1665: Mel. Col. 127 bis, 742; royal commissioners to Colbert, Feb. 14, 1665: Mel. Col. 127 bis, 793; Roschach, vol. XIII, pp. 430–7.

35 Maistre, *Canal*, p. 96.

the pressure to contribute to a project which was already under way, which touched their vital interests, and which their own commission had declared to be glorious and beneficial. That year they granted 2,400,000 livres payable over eight years, and further involvement inevitably followed. It is difficult to determine the ultimate cost of the project or the distribution of the burden, but rough calculations based on the figures worked out by André Maistre suggest that of the 17,285,388 livres total cost, Riquet contributed 15 percent out of his own pocket, the crown provided 19 percent, and the province supplied 66 percent, of which 47 percent came from direct taxes and 19 percent from gabelle revenues, indirect taxes or levies on selected groups.[36]

Several innovations made the canal an interesting manifestation of royal–provincial relations. In the first place, it was a joint financial venture to which the king, the entrepreneur and the Estates all contributed, though, as we have seen, the latter covered most of the bill, directly or indirectly. Previous canals had taken the form of concessions granted to private entrepreneurs to build at their own expense. The Beaucaire canal had been a graphic example of the sort of concession whose very existence raised the spectre of loss of control, fiscal extortion, and failure to compensate property owners for their rights. By contrast, the edict of 1666 and the subsequent contracts gave Riquet the right to annex all lands and rights necessary for the canal, but the king assumed full responsibility for paying just compensation to individual and collective owners for lost property, seigneurial rights, dîmes, tolls and taille revenues. This meant that legal responsibility was not foisted off on a potentially bankrupt entrepreneur. Even better, the king made it clear that he intended the process of indemnification to be handled jointly by his agents and by commissioners from the Estates.[37]

We should also note the terms of Riquet's agreement. His rights were guaranteed in the characteristically archaic form of the granting of a fief comprising the canal and all its dependencies. It was to be held directly and hereditarily from the crown, with the obligation of paying one louis d'or at the time of each mutation. Riquet was granted letters of nobility which maintained the fiction that he was resuming a noble status which his family had lost through derogation. His fief was to include a chateau, mills to grind his grain, exclusive hunting and fishing rights, exemption from the taille, exercise of high, middle, and low justice (with the corresponding gallows), enjoyment of twelve guards in royal livery, courts, judicial officers, police powers, the right to issue ordinances, and the right

[36] Maistre, *Canal*, pp. 113–16. Maistre's calculations have several errors of addition, and I have redefined some of the categories. The revised figures are Riquet, 2,580,109 livres; crown, 3,285,631 livres; direct taxation, 8,070,202 livres; indirect taxation, 3,215,186 livres.

[37] Maistre, *Canal*, pp. 64–74.

to collect tolls and fees on the canal. These perquisites thus made him a bona fide seigneur, but they also guaranteed his authority and protected him from the claims of rival seigneurs. As André Maistre points out, moreover, this fief was not just a feudal anachronism for it had built into it certain 'modern' responsibilities for upkeep and service which were to be overseen in a thoroughly non-feudal way by the monarch and the Estates. Judicial appeals were to go to the Parlement and the Comptes, not, as had often been the case elsewhere, to royal courts outside the province.[38]

As the project advanced, the attitude of the Estates gradually turned from negative to positive, not for the reasons Colbert would have liked but certainly as a result of the experiences he had put them through. The deputies' tolerance for manufacturing was limited, and when they conceptualized the role of the canal, it was always as an outlet for their grain or as a generator of taxable income to acquire from their peasants. Even the merits of less restricted regional trade eluded them, for as soon as the canal was completed, they complained bitterly to Colbert that it was flooding the province with grain from Guyenne while the city of Bordeaux would not accept Languedocian wine in return. Their idea of 'equity' in these circumstances was for the canal to be permanently closed to this outside grain.[39]

Two aspects did, however, begin to intrigue them. The first was the question of indemnities which had enticed them almost from the beginning. Their initial grant of 2,400,000 livres contained the stipulation that they be allowed to oversee the work and that priority be given to reimbursing the expropriated.[40] Their later grants often took the form of credit destined for reimbursement which they paid out directly from their treasury. They also underwrote large loans for the project and developed many of the credit mechanisms we have examined above in response to the activity generated by the canal. Commissioners studied the claims for indemnity in the smallest detail and regulated each with loving care, as the minutes attest with their long lists of lands taken, dîmes and tailles lost, streams dried up, mills rendered inoperative, justice rights diminished, and interest due on all of these until compensation was paid.[41] Their solicitude for notables, especially members of the assembly, was particularly noteworthy, and they singled out for special attention problems like the seigneurial rights of Cardinal Bonzi and compensation to the bishop of Rieux for the loss of the fountains in his gardens at Le Petit Montrabe.[42]

The second attraction for the deputies came with the gradual realization that they were participating in a great engineering feat, one of the wonders

38 Ibid., pp. 122–34. 39 Memoir for Colbert on finances, 1684: A.N. H 748²¹⁵, 564.

40 Maistre, *Canal*, p. 99; P-V Dec. 13, 1673, Jan. 12, 1674.

41 P-V Dec. 23, 1671, Jan. 27, 1672, Jan. 30, 1673, Feb. 6, 1676, Jan. 28, 1677, Nov. 29, 1685, etc.

42 P-V Nov. 29, 1685, Dec. 31, 1671, Nov. 24, 1672.

of the modern world. As the work progressed they became increasingly fascinated with its technical and artistic craftsmanship and began to think of it as an embellishment to their province, a monument which reflected their own importance:

The bishop of Saint-Papoul then described the great reservoir of Saint-Ferreol, the construction of which is the admiration of foreigners, both for the boldness of its enterprise and the solidity of its execution; and he described for the company the means used to collect and distribute the water, something unknown in past centuries which appears in one's experience even before it can be formulated in one's imagination.[43]

Once the work was well advanced, they took greater interest in the subsidiary projects needed to complete it: smaller canals linked to the main one, bridges and aqueducts. In 1673 it was noted that something had to be done about the bridges over the canal 'because the province has such zeal for contributing to public works which can give satisfaction to the king and add something to his glory'; and that funds had to be found to complete the port of Sète because the merchants were eager to use it and 'curiosity about this enterprise is attracting the whole world'.[44]

Clearly the deputies had learned Louis XIV's message about glory very well, but Colbert's message had escaped them. In return for their grants, they were being permitted to bask in the rays of the Sun King's glory, sharing his achievements and watching him embellish their province like a giant estate with its fountains and alleys, aqueducts and pumps. At the grand opening of the Canal in 1681 the intendant d'Aguesseau, Cardinal Bonzi, and the representatives of the three orders in the Estates rode ceremonially *together* down the Canal in a decorated barge, followed by other boats of servants and accompanied by violins, oboes, and trumpets to provide a Languedocian 'water-music'. At each town they were greeted with cheers of 'Vive le Roy' and military salutes. Periodically they stopped at the locks for a 'magnificent dinner'. In the midst of all this, d'Aguesseau, the eyes and ears of Colbert, was taking measurements of the depth of the water and examining the construction.[45]

When Arthur Young toured Languedoc on the eve of the French Revolution, he was amazed at the excellence of the roads which spanned the province and the scarcity of traffic on them.[46] By then the Estates had acquired an addiction to magnificent, though not always functional, public works, which dated from the age of Colbert. They had never learned to admire production, however reluctantly they monitored the royal manu-

[43] P-V Dec. 31, 1671.

[44] P-V Dec. 13, 1673.

[45] Blaquière, *Documents*, pp. 61–4.

[46] Arthur Young, *Young's Travels in France during the Years 1787, 1788, 1789*, ed. M. Betham-Edwards (London, 1913).

factories, but they *had* mastered the art of Estate management, and this was the legacy of the Canal, an enforced lesson in the merits of collaboration. Despite its utilitarian purpose, it stands as a monument to the nature of the implicit royal–provincial alliance. It was a project conceived by a *partisan* for traditional reasons – social advancement and profit – which was adapted by Colbert for his own purposes. The province was forced to participate against its will, but, once involved, the benefits were real. Vast sums were generated, in large part from the rural taxpayers of the province, and these sums passed through the hands of all the receivers and bankers in the collection system, over which the bishops and barons had considerable control. A sizeable sum – Maistre cites over 1,100,000 livres – was channelled to local people in the form of indemnities.[47] Most important, the luminaries of the assembly learned a more positive form of activity. Instead of preserving the province from royal projects, they could help with them and share in the prestige of using public monies for monuments to their joint glory.

HUGUENOTS REPRESSED

The keystone of royal-provincial collaboration was, of course, the joint campaign against the Huguenots.[48] Not only were the two sides in complete agreement over this matter, but it was the Languedocian aristocrats who had led the way to the national policy of repression with their petitions, lawsuits, and appeals stretching all the way back to the 1620s. Here the problem was not the coordination of differing interests as much as the elimination of obstacles which stood in the way of common interests. After the military defeats of 1622 and 1629 had ended Protestant claims to military and political independence, a new era of enforced collaboration had been inaugurated, characterized by partition of consulates between Protestants and Catholics, new restrictions on worship, and rising pressure on the Protestants, for the advantage was now on the Catholic side. Petitions poured in to the king and his agents concerning the regulation of every sort of symbolic prerogative: use of places of worship and cemeteries; residence of ministers; upkeep of hospitals and schools; right to maintain church towers or bells; nature of representation; questions of precedence. From 1632 to 1642 the agents of Richelieu – Miron, Le Camus, Jean Chapuy from the présidial of Valence in Dauphiné, and others – were sent on missions to investigate Protestant worship and to regulate all these claims, especially in the Cévennes.[49]

[47] Maistre, *Canal*, p. 114.

[48] See references in chapter 7. The repression in Languedoc is exhaustively analyzed in Paul Gachon, *Quelques préliminaires de la révocation de l'édit de Nantes en Languedoc* (*1661–1685*) (Toulouse, 1899), which also contains numerous documents.

[49] Ms. fr. 15833, 282–499.

The tables were abruptly turned after 1643. Mazarin's policies were technically no different from those of Richelieu, but the circumstances of minority, rebellion, and the worst pressures of the Thirty Years War made it necessary for the cardinal to tolerate excesses of Protestants and even, at times, to court the heretics. Taking advantage of these circumstances like every other group, the Huguenots of Languedoc launched a counter-offensive of agitation – not only appeals and exchanges designed to raise their morale, but at times open confrontation. This agitation made a greater impact on Catholic opinion than its seriousness would seem to warrant because too little time had elapsed since the 1620s for the new religious balance of power to seem permanent, and in the context of the general deterioration of authority, it looked as if Huguenot insurrection was rearing its ugly head again.

During the 1650s, even while the worst Protestant conflicts were still unfolding, the Catholic response was being prepared in Languedoc. As early as 1653 the cahier of the Estates devoted five of its fourteen articles to denouncing the Huguenot revival and calling for royal commissioners to crack down on it.[50] After 1648 the Estates passed a series of resolutions which gradually excluded Protestants from their own meetings and from the assiettes. This new belligerence was growing everywhere. The current intendant, Bezons, was meanwhile preparing the way by developing legal pretexts for restricting Protestant activities. In this, his role was similar to Baltazar's except that he worked behind the scenes, and his name was not associated with the unpopular edicts and fiscal contracts of the 1640s.

After 1661 the king began to take serious notice of this groundswell of opinion, spurred on by the Assembly of Clergy of 1660. From that point on, royal agents and provincial leaders seemed engaged in a repressive relay race where demands from the cahiers or the Parlement were rapidly worked out by the intendant and reissued by the royal council. Bezons and Peyremals, a Protestant *lieutenant particular* in the sénéchaussée of Nîmes, were named *commissaires pour l'exécution de l'édit de Nantes* in Languedoc and Foix and proceeded to issue hundreds of rulings, mostly in favor of Catholics, in response to petitions from all over the province. The immediate result was the prohibition of Protestant worship in 135 communities.[51] This new wave of regulation was a continuation of the work of Miron and Le Camus, but after the long hiatus of the Mazarin period, it was welcomed as a new Catholic offensive, and this time no circumstantial restraints on the crown hindered its effectiveness. In 1663 the Estates thanked Bezons publicly for 'the services he rendered daily to religion'.[52] In 1666 and 1669 royal declarations confirmed the exclusion of Protestants

[50] Ms. fr. 23354, 133.
[51] Ms. fr. 15832, 1–202; Gachon, *Préliminaires*, p. 99.
[52] *Inventaire Haute-Garonne*, série C, I, p. 358.

from Estates and assiettes. At the same time the commission to audit communal debts, again headed by Bezons and members of the Estates, provided an opportunity to regulate the old quarrels over municipal accounts in favor of Catholics.[53]

Gradually, to the general satisfaction of the Catholic population, Protestant rights were whittled down. Edicts were issued restricting Protestant membership in guilds and companies of royal officers, disadvantaging Protestant creditors, forbidding conversions to heresy and relapses from Catholicism, favoring Catholic priests in hospitals and at deathbeds, eliminating divided consulates, and ultimately closing down Huguenot worship in the major towns. The milestones in this depressing journey were the demolition of a Protestant temple in Nîmes (1664) and of the 'little temple' in Montpellier (1670), the transfer of the Chambre de l'Édit to Castelnaudary (1670) and its reunion with the Parlement (1679), and the demolition of the 'great temple' in Montpellier in 1682. These formal blows were accompanied by smaller ceremonial slights. The Catholic notary Borrelly of Nîmes recorded with pleasure in his private journal the 'consternation' of the Protestant consuls in 1673 when they were forbidden to wear their chaperon in the temple; the destruction of the raised benches in the temple which set Protestant notables off from the rest in 1679; and his own accession to a formerly Protestant post in the municipal council in 1679.[54] In 1683 Borrelly described d'Aguesseau's appearance before the Nîmes consistory to read a royal endorsement of an admonition from the Assembly of Clergy for Protestants to 'return to the church' or face dire consequences, followed by an obligatory Catholic sermon on 'God's intention that all his lost peoples should return to the bosom of the church'.[55]

The impending doom of the Protestants, orchestrated by a powerful alliance of provincial instigators and royal accomplices, was evident to both sides for some time. The revocation of 1685 cannot have come as a surprise. In 1678 an angry Protestant crowd in Saint-Hippolyte was quoted as having claimed 'that if the king forced them on the matter of their religion they would go off to England and join with the others, forming an army of more than 50,000 men'.[56] Huguenot leaders continued to assert their rights through legal appeals, but their attempts became increasingly pathetic. They complained to the lieutenant-general Montanègre that Calvinist ministers were being molested on the streets by cries of 'there goes the minister', and that groups on the way to baptize infants were being

[53] Gachon, *Préliminaires*, 21; A.N. TT 260, 697.

[54] Albert Puech, 'La Vie de nos ancêtres', *Mémoires de l'Académie de Nîmes*, 7th series 8 (1885), 248, 271, 264.

[55] Cited in Robert Sauzet, *Contre-réforme et réforme catholique en Bas-Languedoc: le diocèse de Nîmes au XVIIe siècle* (Brussels, 1979), p. 397.

[56] A.D. Gard G. 448.

aggressively solicited to convert by Catholic priests, with the tacit complicity of the authorities. Montanègre's reply was that he would tell the Catholics to restrain themselves, but that the Protestants 'did not have to go to church or spread their teachings'.[57] Far from adjudicating such appeals, as required by law since the suppression of the Chambre de l'Édit, the Parlement actively solicited new repressive edicts from the king. In 1682 Protestant leaders declared a general fast and swore to stand firm and not be converted. Demonstrations and violent incidents broke out in Vivarais and Velay in 1683 which were brutally put down by force.[58] The spectre of popular insurrection lent more urgency to the Protestant 'problem' for Catholic observers.

If the Protestants could guess what was coming, the royal agents were hardly innocent either. In September 1682 d'Aguesseau, who has often been portrayed as a compassionate moderate by contrast to his successor Basville, was already alluding in letters to a possible revocation: 'given the general intention which His Majesty may have of reuniting all his subjects in the same religion, these first steps seemed to us to be extremely delicate'.[59] In July 1683 d'Aguesseau's analysis of a small 'unpremeditated' riot in Nîmes reveals his attitude clearly. The city's dangerous volatility had been demonstrated, he argued, by 'the prodigious rush towards the temple from every part of town on a working day when everyone was preoccupied with his job'; by the number of rumors 'each more false than the last' which had spread through town; and by the way Protestants had suddenly attacked Catholics indiscriminately. This mood, he argued, was the result, first, of the nature of Calvinism itself: 'its temperament is naturally rough and gross'; second, of the artisans' bad habit of bearing arms; third, of the fact that trading contacts brought in 'wild and brutal' mountain men from the Cévennes who were dependent on the merchants of Nîmes for work and who still remembered the 1657 riot against Bezons and the bishop; finally, he noted, the consistory of Nîmes led the rest of the province with 'an air of pride and arrogance' not met elsewhere. D'Aguesseau's solution – one worthy of Baltazar – was to suppress Protestant worship in Nîmes by force. A charge should be trumped up in a case (admittedly a weak one) against a woman accused of relapsing after conversion to Catholicism; this should be used as a pretext for bringing in troops and lodging them more or less permanently in Protestant households; the temple and the consistory could then be outlawed.[60]

Thus, the dragonnades had been solicited by a man who later was

[57] A.N. TT 256^B, 56–77.

[58] A.N. TT 260, 84, 761; Roschach, vol. XIII, pp. 529–35.

[59] A.N. TT 260, 65; see also the memoirs by d'Aguesseau in Gachon, *Préliminaires*, pp. lxxix–lxxv, cx–cxiii.

[60] A.N. TT 260, 99.

pictured as fleeing the province in despair at their approach. In October 1683 Louvois ordered the royal troops sent to quell the disorders in Vivarais 'to create such desolation that the example will contain the other Protestants and teach them how dangerous it is to rise up against the king'.[61] Two years later the job was completed by the new intendant Basville, fresh from the dragonnade atrocities in Poitou, who arrived at the head of troops commanded by the duc de Noailles. Their reputation spread such terror that mass conversions preceded them wherever they went. In a matter of days between September 28 and October 15, 1685, virtually every Protestant in the province had abjured or fled.[62]

Seen in the light of this history, the revocation takes on a symbolic significance. Basville was to become the most powerful intendant Languedoc had ever known: he inaugurated a new stage in the transfer of real authority from independently-based notables to royal clients serving the national monarchy. Yet his arrival was applauded because he came to fulfill the aspirations of the Catholic notables who, for ideological as well as political reasons, found it desirable to eliminate alternative hierarchies and reinforce a single chain of command between themselves, the king, and God. At the same time Basville's troops promised the repression of popular unruliness – the 'wild and brutal' mountaineers who had been associated with the Montpellier uprising of 1645, the Roure revolt of 1670 and the Protestant disturbances of 1683, as well as the arms-bearing artisans and shopkeepers feared by d'Aguesseau. The advent of Basville in 1685 represented the first time that an intendant had arrived *with* repressive troops and one of the only times that troops were welcomed in the province – a far cry from the days of Baltazar when intendants had been suspect and troops had symbolized oppressive expenses and illegal exactions. If the authorities now applauded the arrival of a powerful intendant at the head of intimidating companies of *dragons*, it was because the king and the provincial elite were now collaborating to accomplish common goals which the province was unable to achieve on its own and because the former oppressive connotations of troops and intendants had been removed. As Cardinal Bonzi, whose own power would soon be challenged by Basville, told the Estates on October 31, 1685:

> If this company has shown submission and eagerness to please the king in the past, it must today surpass itself in expressing its zeal and obedience to His Majesty. This assembly's appreciation must be boundless, and if His Majesty did not have the goodness to set limits to his demands, then it would be just for his subjects

[61] Ernest Lavisse, *Histoire de France depuis les origines jusqu'à la Révolution* (Paris, 1906), vol. VII, part 2, p. 70.

[62] Philippe Wolff, ed., *Histoire du Languedoc* (Toulouse, 1967), pp. 359–63.

of Languedoc to open their purses like their hearts and show him by offering everything they have left to what extent they are grateful for the advantage His Majesty has just procured for religion by the general conversion of all the Calvinists in the province . . . This assembly, always Catholic, has long desired and unceasingly solicited in its cahiers all that might weaken heresy; but we never dared to hope that we would see it totally annihilated. This miracle was reserved for Louis le Grand, whom none can resist.[63]

[63] P-V Oct. 31, 1685.

13

Basking in the sun: the triumph of authority and hierarchy

We have seen that one aspect of Louis XIV's success in winning the loyalty of the rulers of Languedoc was the popularity of the programs he carried out. The various agencies, especially the Estates, were swept up in activities which satisfied deep-felt needs and fulfilled many ambitions. There were advantages to participating in the successful regulation of troops, the measuring and embellishing of waterways, the suppression of Protestants. The provincial authorities were also becoming integrated into a larger, more unified network of personal contacts leading to the king, and their opportunities for taking advantage of the profits of state finance were greatly expanded. But these elements of a larger, more effective government do not tell the whole story. The reason for the adulation and conformity lay deeper than particular administrative achievements which, after all, had their disadvantages as well as their attractions. They lay in the very nature of absolutism as a system which protected the rank and hierarchy of a class of advantageously placed landowner-officers and in Louis's ability to reinforce these relationships.

The king's particular genius lay in his capacity for personifying traditional relationships while making them work through improved coordination. More specifically, his success can be analyzed in terms of three techniques, each of which was a skillful new utilization of age-old resources. First was the transmission through newly-expanded bureaucratic channels of the classic absolutist message that obedience to a personal sovereign should be unlimited. The administrative system associated with intendants, secretaries of state, and royal councils was a 'statist' reality, but it was effective only because of this ideological energy which activated all its parts. Second was the policy of restoring to provincial agencies an effective role in public life which gave them a more satisfying share of public power while curbing their excesses – of working 'through' not 'against' the provincial system. Third was the policy of shoring up class rule by a conscious reinforcement of hierarchy, personal and corporate, and by the regulation of authority conflicts which had so undermined authority in the previous generation.

THE ROYAL PRESENCE THROUGH BUREAUCRATIC CHANNELS

Let us begin the argument with the most manipulative aspect of the new regime, for this is what historians have traditionally perceived most clearly. Its organizational components are well known. The king's improved information network, organized around the intendants and the secretaries of state, was used to enforce a more rigorous system of rewards and punishments. The intendant worked with a wider range of local authorities, and many more provincials corresponded directly with the royal ministers. The change went farther than these formal developments, however, for it was the new ideological tone of relations between the king and provincial leaders which was most genuinely new. From the first days of the personal reign a political message was transmitted through all the personal–institutional channels: that the king expected his demands to be met promptly, but that a proper attitude of submission was even more important to him than the content of the demands. Those who pleased the king would benefit from his benevolence. Those who did not would immediately feel the effects of his disfavor. There was more to this message than the dangling of carrots and sticks because the emphasis was placed so strongly on the creation of a proper relationship of dominance–voluntary submission between king and subjects. This was its genius. Proper political conduct was conceptualized in terms of a personal loyalty which seventeenth-century aristocrats could understand and embrace more readily than the abstract ideas of state expediency which might have sounded crass to them. Satisfying the monarch could only be a meaningful goal if the king seemed worthy of being satisfied and capable of rewarding proper conduct, but this was precisely Louis XIV's strongest asset – the capacity to personify an updated version of the noble prince. Here the Sun King had a tremendous advantage over even as masterful a politician as Richelieu, for where the cardinal's position made it necessary for him to demand humiliating sacrifices in the name of a cold raison d'état, a grandiose monarch like Louis XIV acting personally could require the same sacrifice in the name of *personal* loyalty and recompense the subject's loss of private initiative with the prestige of associating oneself with the grandeur of the royal enterprises. Paradoxically, Louis XIV's government advanced the institutionalization of the state machinery more by making personal, '*feudal*' appeals than by advocating 'progressive' attitudes and procedures.

This new style emerged rapidly. It is hard to discern whether the king, Colbert, or Colbert's correspondents originated it. The veteran intendant Bezons seems to be giving lessons to Colbert before the latter's first session of the Estates in November 1661, when he advises that the way to put through the royal program is 'for His Majesty to make a distinction between those who serve well and the rest' on the basis of a list of bishops and barons which Bezons would send to court.[1] But the more ideological concept of 'satisfaction', which was entirely new and which Bezons had already assimilated by the time he spoke to the Estates three months later, probably originated with the king:

The respect and submission with which you have received His Majesty's orders, your complete deference to his wishes, have procured you new favors. In other years you often offered more considerable sums, but your grants were not accompanied with such perfect submission or such complete deference, thus they did not earn the same satisfaction from our sovereign....[2]

Thereafter, the same points were hammered home to the Estates year after year. They were reminded that 'the principal subtlety of your negotiations must be in not negotiating'; and told that the king was avoiding new fiscal edicts because 'it would be unworthy of his grandeur to propose them to you as a method for eliciting negotiations'.[3] Bezons's letters show that, tactically, he now paid more attention to orchestrating a smooth, predictable vote in the assembly without unruly dissent than to maximizing the size of the grant.[4]

The same approach was used in correspondence with individuals. In 1662 Colbert wrote to Lieutenant-General Arpajon that he expected an immediate remedy for the refusal of Arpajon's parishes to pay their taille, 'otherwise it will not be in my power to keep these complaints from reaching the king, a prospect which I know you want to avoid'.[5] This style of speaking as if the king were looking over the minister's shoulder, which was almost unknown in earlier correspondence, gradually took on mystical overtones. It was made clear that 'all graces must come from the king' and that, being fully informed of the degree to which he had been 'satisfied', the monarch would distribute his favors accordingly.[6] Bezons and the other royal agents began reporting regularly on the loyalty of the members of the Estates, and Colbert would then see that the king made a clear distinction between the faithful and the troublesome. Loyal bishops followed a similar policy. They would specifically request that the minister express his gratitude to cooperative consuls in writing so that the letter could be shown to the individuals in question who would then redouble their zeal upon learning that it was recognized at court.[7]

The royal will began to be used regularly as both a rhetorical device and

1 Bezons to Colbert, Nov. 21, 1661: Mel. Col. 105, 148 or Depping, vol. I, p. 50.
2 P-V Mar. 1, 1662.
3 Conti to Estates, P-V Nov. 24, 1662; Bezons to Estates, P-V Dec. 17, 1663.
4 Bezons to Colbert, Dec. 19, 1664: Mel. Col. 126, 449 or Depping, vol. I, p. 161.
5 Colbert to duc d'Arpajon, July 8, 1662: Clément, vol. II, p. 226.
6 Bezons to Colbert, Dec. 31, 1663: Depping, vol. I, p. 136.
7 Bishop of Mende to Colbert, Jan. 16, 1662: Depping, vol. I, p. 136.

an invisible force. In 1662 the bishop of Castres wrote that the Estates were amazed to have granted as large a sum as they had, 'and they have no other explanation than that they had been told so many times they were dealing with the king himself that they went right ahead and granted everything their mandate permitted and more'.[8] Such hyperbole should not be taken too seriously, but it does capture the new rhetoric. The old provincial tactics of delay and compromise also fell on hard times. In 1675, when the king asked the superior courts to contribute 14 million livres for the continuation of the droit annuel, the Cour des Comptes sent a deputation to negotiate, offering to pay in installments. In the 1640s this would have been taken as an encouraging overture. In 1675 the deputies encountered an angry monarch who indicated that he never negotiated his demands; that they were free to pay or not to pay; and that they had seven days to raise their 450,000 livres.[9] When the Estates proposed to suspend their sessions and send a courier to court for negotiations in 1669, their president retorted in a similar vein that 'this had been done during the disorders of the minority but that it was no longer in fashion nowadays'.[10]

This imperious style emphasizing the glory of obedience spread from king to ministers, to provincial agents, then to their subordinates. The marquis de Castries, appealing to Colbert to renew the droit annuel for the Cour des Comptes in 1669, recounts in his letter that the Comptes had appealed to him for support and he had told them they would have trouble obtaining the king's grace 'since they had not taken advantage as they should of occasions to please him, but that since the clemency of His Majesty has no limits, they should never despair, providing they adopted better conduct'. Castries then goes on to explain that, while he hadn't dared to promise to intercede on the Comptes' behalf, he did want to suggest to Colbert that granting their request would be a good idea and that he would be glad to undertake any necessary negotiations: 'I beg you humbly, monsieur, that if there are any negotiations to be carried out, I be included so that I can satisfy my zeal for royal service in this matter and obtain some peace and advantage for Montpellier which is the principal town in my district'.[11] The lieutenant-general and governor of Montpellier is begging the king's minister to give him the chance to build a following in his own center of power!

Disloyalty was also treated with increased effectiveness. It became the practice to exclude uncooperative members quietly from the Estates by indicating in a letter to the intendant that a certain man's presence was

[8] Bishop of Castres to Colbert, Jan. 16, 1662: Depping, vol. 1, p. 66.

[9] André Delort, *Mémoires inédits sur la ville de Montpellier au XVII siècle (1621–1673)*, 2 vols. (Montpellier 1876–8), vol. 1, pp. 285–7.

[10] Archbishop of Toulouse to Colbert, Apr. 12, 1669: Depping, vol. 1, p. 243.

[11] Castries to Colbert, Apr. 5, 1669: Mel. Col. 151, 211.

undesirable. Usually carefully-planted rumors of the letter's existence were enough to prompt the man to stay away so that he could avoid the humiliation of a formal *lettre de cachet*.[12]

There were, of course, dangers inherent in the system of deference and service. Once the 'royal interest' became reified, it rapidly turned into a cliché invoked by all aspiring petitioners – thus the bishop of Montauban asking for protection for his nephew in an insignificant private dispute by arguing that intervention was essential 'because the royal name is involved'.[13] There was also the possibility that the powerful information network might be destroyed by frivolous misuse, especially once Colbert was gone. In 1684 Châteauneuf wrote d'Aguesseau that, due to the shortage of partridges around Chambord, the king wanted gray and red specimens collected from all over the province. 'He was sure', the minister wrote, 'that there will not be a single gentleman who will not take pleasure in sending you one for the satisfaction of His Majesty' and promised to supply the king with the names of the contributors.[14]

Louis XIV's famous style did permeate Languedoc, where it was used to achieve better conformity to royal goals while discouraging independent provincial action. We should remember, though, how far this phenomenon was from impartial institutional control. It promoted the ethic of loyalty to a monarch who personified innate preeminence; it glorified personal favoritism; and it promised rewards to 'friends' for 'satisfaction', not to talent for successful administration. We should also remember that because the most salient element of this method was ideological – the manipulation of the image of the monarch – it was especially well transmitted in the letters and speeches which have come down to us in the archives but which may present far too simplistic a picture of royal commanding and provincial grovelling. This is the story the king and his ministers wanted us to hear. To understand its context we must delve deeper into the political relationships of the day.

WORKING THROUGH PROVINCIAL AGENCIES

The history of the relations of each of the province's major institutions with the crown reveals the same contrast between the period before 1660 and the age of Louis XIV. Before, attempts to supersede or threaten established bodies had led them to respond with exaggerated gestures of defiance and desperate escapades. After, the king made it clear that he would no longer tolerate independent assertions of authority but that, in return for obedience,

[12] Bezons to Colbert, Feb. 8, 1669: Depping, vol. 1, p. 238; bishop of Saint Papoul to Colbert, Jan. 6, 1662: ibid., p. 58. [13] Bishop of Montauban to Colbert, Mar. 11, 1665: Mel. Col. 128, 305.

[14] Châteauneuf to d'Aguesseau, Oct. 6, Nov. 13, 1684: A.N. H 1710, 161, 221.

he would work through the traditional provincial bodies, giving them back a role in governance that was regulated but effective. The rulers of Languedoc were to trade the glamor of a rather hollow local prestige derived from the ability to throw one's weight around for the glory of dispensing regulated authority as part of a grander system.

A. *The Parlement.* The developments of 1620 to 1660 had seriously undermined the political role of the Parlement and wounded its collective ego. Its regulatory and coercive authority had been threatened by intendants, resident military commanders, armies on the march, and many kinds of semi-official *partisans.* At a time when the turnover of members was unusually great and the security of officeholding was being threatened in disturbing new ways, the external situation led to violent internal disagreements about tactics. The strain of these feuds, exacerbated by personal rivalries and resentment against opportunists within the company, led to turbulent assemblies of chambers, confrontations between presidents and the *parquet*, and defiant response to lettres de jussion. It is noteworthy that hardly any royal edicts of the period had been supportive of the Parlement or its policies.

After 1659 the acts of resistance in the Parlement gradually tapered off under the influence of new conditions, although there were still a few echoes of the earlier militancy.[15] A typically restrained response to royal orders was the registration of franc fief edicts in 1659 'without approval' of clauses which threatened the Parlement's jurisdiction, thereby recording an objection without suspending the edict.[16] The royal declaration of 1667 removing the right of remonstrance until edicts had been registered was duly observed, but informal consultations, often with deputies sent to Paris for the purpose, continued. A sign of the times was the fact that when the Parlement named commissioners to investigate abandoned lands, seizures of back taxes, and local election procedures in 1669, it carefully avoided issuing any final decision in these matters until word had arrived of how the king wanted them handled.[17]

Various factors explain this new tone of cooperation. The legal reforms instituted by Colbert, which were drawn up in close consultation with parlementaire leaders, eliminated many of the 'democratic' procedures which had permitted the lower chambers to dominate the company.

[15] In 1659 Councillors Commere and De Long, both agitators during the Fronde, arrested an unpopular gabelle agent and escorted him through the countryside tied up in a cart, proclaiming wherever they went 'that they were going to hang all the gabeleurs and that none should be tolerated in the province'. In 1662 several parlementaires were sent into exile after interfering with taille collections in Guyenne. Yves-Marie Bercé, *Histoire des Croquants: étude des soulèvements populaires au XVIIe siècle dans le sud-ouest de la France*, 2 vols. (Geneva, 1974), vol. II, p. 584; A.D. H-G. B 1881, 176, 181; De la Rue to Colbert, Apr. 5, 8, 12, 19, May 3, 1662: Mel. Col. 108, 52, 73, 119, 184, 371.

[16] A.D. H-G. B 1881, 91.

[17] Fieubet to Colbert, Feb. 13, 1669: Mel. Col. 150, 423.

Already in 1662 a report in the royal council singled out for reform most of the abuses which Bertier had complained of as far back as the 1630s, and proposed rules about the distribution of cases and fees, procedures for calling plenary sessions, and measures designed to concentrate power in the hands of the first president and the procureur-general.[18] The absolutist style was thus reinforced within the court, to the advantage of Fieubet and his many allies. These men began working like intendants and reaping the benefits in prestige and favors. Fieubet carried out even the most unpleasant tasks with apparent zest, as in 1665, when he had to browbeat the parlementaires and capitouls into putting up large sums for shares in Colbert's East India Company.[19] Meanwhile his colleagues were scrambling to please Colbert by proposing and executing royal projects. Procureur-General Torreil wrote dutifully about the transport of prisoners to the galleys, while the former frondeurs Dumai and Donneville spent their time studying potential profits from mines and the dredging of rivers. Fieubet himself enjoyed a commission from the king to furnish ship masts from the Pyrenees. And in 1681 Louis XIV created marquisates for his procureur-general Le Masuyer and his advocate-general Maniban.[20]

But the most striking change was the way Louis assigned the Parlement a legitimate and satisfying role to play in the managing of the province.[21] After the general evocations which had decimated the court's jurisdictions had been revoked in 1656, the parlementaires were once again able to become the arbiters of the interests of capitouls, members of the Estates, and consuls of towns.[22] Another source of jurisdictional impotence had been the recourse of Protestants to the Chambre de l'Édit, which had exasperated the Parlement every time some Huguenot affair had arisen. Now, to the delight of the Parlement, the Chambre de l'Édit was first exiled to Castelnaudary (1670), where there were no facilities or Protestants, then merged with the Parlement in 1679, answering a prayer that had been heard for generations.[23]

Another insistent demand had been that the Parlement be allowed to hold a Chambre de Justice or Grands Jours to repress abuses in the province. In 1666 the king decided to set up just such a special court to clean up

[18] Ms. fr. 17343, 293, 295.

[19] Fieubet to Colbert, Feb. 4, Mar. 4, 1665: Mel. Col. 127, 532; Mel. Col. 128, 142; capitouls to Colbert, Mar. 4, 1665: Mel. Col. 128, 152.

[20] Letters to Colbert of Torreil, Feb. 4, 1665: Mel. Col. 127, 534; Donneville, Sept. 9, 1665: Mel. Col. 131 bis, 993; Dumé, Nov. 18, 1665: Mel. Col. 133, 430; Fieubet, Aug. 10, 1672: Mel. Col. 161, 75; A.D. H-G. B 1047 (cited in *Inventaire Haute-Garonne*, série B, III, 110).

[21] A similar argument for the Parlement of Paris is made in Albert N. Hamscher, *The Parlement of Paris after the Fronde, 1653–1673* (Pittsburgh, Pa., 1976).

[22] A.N. E 1706, 106 (arrêt de conseil of May 18, 1656).

[23] Jules Cambon de Lavalette, *La Chambre de l'Édit de Languedoc* (Paris, 1872), pp. 130–46. See also Madeleine Brenac, 'Toulouse, centre de lutte contre le protestantisme au XVIIe siècle', *Annales du Midi*, 77 (1965), 31–45.

disorder and brigandage in the Cévennes. The Grands Jours at Puy, then Nîmes, were an ideal alliance of king and Parlement. A large deputation consisting of Fieubet himself, the procureur-general Torreil, thirteen councillors, and the intendant Tubeuf were sent into the extremities of the mountains with a powerful mandate to repress disobedience.[24] This was the greatest reassertion of parlementaire jurisdiction since the intendants had started usurping so many functions back in the 1630s. The pleasure of having court orders enforced by royal troops instead of being countermanded by royal arrêts must have been considerable. Furthermore, a great many of the defendants were Protestant, and the parlementaires had successfully blocked Colbert's plan to include deputies from the Chambre de l'Édit alongside themselves.[25] From this point on, councillors from the Parlement were again named as deputies to execute royal edicts in the province.

The most valuable gain for the Parlement, however, may have been the fact that under Louis XIV the other authorities were kept in their place. No longer did the capitouls defy the Parlement, nor the Estates send out rival investigatory teams. It was symptomatic that in 1684 and 1685 while Le Pelletier was working to arrange the smooth payment of the parlementaires' *gages*, they were busily sending agents out to direct the suppression of Protestant worship and the demolition of Protestant temples all over the province. On November 28, 1684, an arrêt du parlement prohibited Protestant worship altogether in Castres, the Huguenot stronghold, and on December 7 Fieubet was commanded by Chateauneuf to use the soldiers of the maréchaussée to execute this repression, in collaboration with the intendant.[26] Through the king, exercise of authority was possible again.

B. *The Comptes*. For the Cour des Comptes the period from 1629 to 1660 had been even rougher. It had begun with the union of the Aides and Comptes which had markedly increased the stature of the company at the expense of a costly *crue* of two presidents, eight counseillers, and fourteen other officers. In 1641 the *gages* of the officers were reduced by one fourth.[27] In 1642 the creation of the Cour des Aides of Cahors, which carved a sizeable chunk from the Montpellier court's district, could not be averted despite a substantial lobbying effort in Paris.[28] These changes were reversed with

24 Dubédat, vol. II, p. 282; Bezons to Colbert, Dec. 7, 1665: Mel. Col. 134, 220; Fieubet to Colbert, Sept. 15, 1666: Mel. Col. 140, 408; Tubeuf to Colbert, Sept. 22, 1666; Mel. Col. 140, 471; J. Baudouin, *Journal de J. Baudouin sur les grands-jours de Languedoc (1666–1667)*, ed. Paul Le Blanc (Le Puy, 1870).

25 Tubeuf to Colbert, Oct. 12, 1666: Mel. Col. 141, 263.

26 Châteauneuf to d'Aguesseau, Dec. 7, 1684: A.N. H 1710, 299.

27 The information which follows on the offices and revenues of the Comptes councillors is drawn from Pierre Vialles, *Études historiques sur la Cour des Comptes, Aides et Finances de Montpellier d'après ses archives privées* (Montpellier, 1921), pp. 72–114.

28 Ms. fr. 18483, 53–5.

the reunion of 1648, but only at the expense of 1,206,360 livres for the suppression of the new officers and an *augmentation de gages*. The 1650s saw more factional competition in the city. Then in 1657 their attempts to harass the franc fief levy led the royal council to suspend three presidents and four councillors. In 1658 the whole company was sent into exile again because of its resistance to the sale of land ennoblements. Its restoration in 1659 was accompanied by another *crue* of officers and another costly *augmentation*.[29]

The personal rule of Louis XIV meant an end to these growing pains and a much-needed stabilization of the company. Between 1659 and 1690 there were no more *crues* of officers, and when a new president and five conseillers were finally added in 1690, the company was compensated by the acquisition of a new jurisdiction over the revenues of the royal domain. There is also some evidence that the *gages* and épices of the councillors were at least stable in this period.[30] In addition, the Comptes fought and won a major battle with the Estates in 1665 over the épices it could collect from the province for hearing tax cases. A sum of 8,529 livres per year had been collected since 1624 which the Comptes claimed was insufficient. The king ruled in their favor, and the annual payment was raised to a new high of 12,465 livres, which continued in force until 1759.[31]

Business as usual under Louis XIV meant, for many officeholders in the Comptes, the opportunity to profit from the great financial transactions of the new era. As in the Parlement, the royalist leaders supported by Mazarin moved into positions of predominance and became focal points for the dispensation of influence while the rest – even former dissidents – fell into line. Ties with the intendant and the tax farms which formerly had appeared illicit now became routine. Most of the king's allies acceded to positions of eminence and were joined by others. Antoine Crouzet, the friend of Baltazar during the 1645 revolt, became president in 1662 and passed his office to his son in 1687. François Bon, the beleaguered son of a tax receiver whom Mazarin had named first president in 1643, became so prosperous that, when the company moved into a new palace (which the king had helped them finance), Bon took over the old one for his private residence. In 1680 his son Philibert gloriously succeeded him as first

29 A.N. E 1706, 561, 619, 665.

30 Vialles, *Études*, pp. 94–9. John J. Hurt, who is studying the fiscal status of the sovereign court judges under Louis XIV, has mustered impressive evidence showing that these officers were heavily burdened with special contributions. The picture of the total impact of these burdens on their fortunes and positions is not yet clear, however. John J. Hurt, 'Forced Loans and the Sale of Offices under Louis XIV: the Ordeal of the Parlementaires' (unpublished paper delivered to the American Historical Association, Dec. 28, 1979); idem, 'Les Offices au parlement de Bretagne sous le règne de Louis XIV: aspects financiers', *Revue d'histoire moderne et contemporaine*, 23 (1976), 3–31.

31 Archbishop of Toulouse to Colbert, Feb. 5, 1665: Depping, vol. 1, p. 177 and Mel. Col. 127, 567; Vialles, *Études*, pp. 100–7.

president, a sure sign of royal favor. The Solas family, which had not always been loyal during the Fronde, made a deal over the construction of the canal of Lattes, which crossed some family lands, and acquired the title of marquis in 1675.[32] And in 1680, when Colbert decided to study the system of taille assessment in the pays d'états in a systematic way, the intendant d'Aguesseau chose two presidents and two councillors from the Comptes to meet with himself and the intendants of Provence and Guyenne in a major reform commission. They drew up a proposal which was discussed at several points with Colbert in Paris, again in collaboration with officers from the Comptes.[33] This sort of joint enterprise, which lasted for two years, would have been unthinkable in 1629 or 1659. The families of the Comptes had become so important that in 1669 the Estates appealed in their cahier of grievances for the renewal of the Comptes' paulette because its members were indispensable to the Estates as providers of credit.[34]

C. *The consulates.* The municipal governments were not as successful in maintaining their authority. Individual urban economies and oligarchies did indeed prosper, but, in terms of power, the consulates were at the bottom of the provincial pecking order, and everyone else's gain was their loss. As the settings for plagues, troop lodgings, tax exactions, and riots, the cities had borne the brunt of the troubles before 1660. Their jealously-guarded municipal constitutions were poorly constructed to bear such a burden because annual elections by intricately-interlocking interest groups, not to mention the division of many consulates between Protestants and Catholics, encouraged factionalism and intrigue. A succession of extraordinary expenses led inevitably to suspicion of those who managed the funds and conspiracies to dethrone them; the resulting election conflicts led to excesses which brought in higher authorities. The cumulative result was twofold: the inability of the local consulates to function without outside intervention, and the development of extravagant municipal debts in the midst of a bewildering confusion of fiscal irregularities.

Both of these problems were resolved under Louis XIV but from the outside. The accumulated debts of the towns were gradually audited and liquidated by commissions of the Estates under the close scrutiny of the intendant and the direction from afar of Colbert. In 1678 d'Aguesseau arrived in Toulouse, requisitioned the municipal accounts, demanded and received a 'free gift' for the king of 30,000 livres, commissioned a new cadastre, and spent four months reorganizing the city's finances, leaving

32 Delort, *Mémoires*, vol. II, p. 7; Louis-J. Thomas, *Montpellier ville marchande: histoire économique et sociale de Montpellier des origines à 1870* (Montpellier, 1936), pp. 142–8.

33 Charles d'Aigrefeuille, *Histoire de la ville de Montpellier*, ed. de la Pijardière, 4 vols. (Montpellier, 1875–82), vol. II, pp. 181–3.

34 Archbishop of Toulouse to Colbert, Aug. 20, 1666: Mel. Col. 139, 286; Estates of 1669 (cited in *Inventaire Haute-Garonne*, série C, II, p. 374).

behind a series of arrêts de conseil regulating future fiscal operations.[35] Meanwhile Colbert made it abundantly clear that 'in no manner, for any reason, under any pretext whatever are any taxes on the communities to be permitted without royal authorization in letters sealed with the great seal'.[36] In fiscal matters the intendant was now the sole authority.

The turbulent elections were more difficult to eliminate because they stemmed from long-standing splits within the local elites. Here the question of authority was controversial because each agency was clamoring for the use of it to further particular interests. When Bezons tried to pacify Nîmes in 1658, he had to withdraw from the city because the accommodation he had reached with all the factions was not acceptable to the bishop, and he lacked the troops to force the prelate's unpopular solution on the majority of the population. The bishop wanted 'authority at all costs', Bezons reported to Mazarin, but added that 'I do not see how his consulates established by pure authority serve the king better than those which are set up with the consent of the factions; on the contrary, factions which are challenged turn to an opposing faction in order to reinforce their position.'[37] This was the problem of the 1640s and 1650s in a nutshell. What was needed was authority acknowledged by all parties, not the propping up of one faction at the expense of another. The solution lay in replacing the system of polarized factions with a system in which one royal ally became the invincible broker of power and influence in each community – and as a rule it could not be someone formerly associated with a divisive faction. This replacement gradually took place. Fieubet, in conjunction with the Parlement, came to dominate the capitouls; the intendant managed the consuls of Montpellier; Cardinal Bonzi dominated Narbonne. In other towns patronage fell to the bishop or one of the military commanders who maintained control by obtaining rulings from the intendant which favored his candidates. In the event of any trouble the king was swift to intervene by imposing candidates approved by the intendant.

The change was significant. By the 1680s the ministerial correspondence was cluttered with requests for the nomination of favored consuls, especially in smaller villages, and about that time the policy of abolishing divided (Protestant–Catholic) consulates offered the pretext for innumerable interventions. In 1680–1, for example, instructions to d'Aguesseau include the catholicization of three consulates in the diocese of Montauban at the request of the bishop; intervention in the elections of Lunel, Gaillac, Auterive, Saint-Hippolyte, and many other smaller towns; naming of the first two consuls in Béziers because of disputes; issuance of new election

35 Rozoi, vol. IV, 532–3.
36 Colbert to d'Aguesseau, Oct. 17, Dec. 27, 1680: A.N. H 1702, 355, 468.
37 Bezons to Mazarin, Aug. 6, 1658: A.A.E. France 1637, 227.

regulations for Castres and Montpellier; and permission for Bonzi to end a two-year-old suspension of two consuls in Narbonne.[38] We can see from these examples how highly developed the information and patronage system had become. Each town had a different situation and a different patron, but all were coordinated to the point that a single outcome could be arranged by the royal agents with little fear of being challenged.

Life in the cities was more placid for those in favor, and municipal government was undoubtedly better managed. But the days of local autonomy were gone forever, leaving consuls and capitouls in the hands of higher client systems. The sale of the offices of *maire* in 1692 was simply a logical extension of a change which had already occurred.

D. *The Estates.* The organization and functioning of the Estates changed after 1660 in two seemingly contradictory but, in fact, complementary ways. On the one hand, the assembly was more effectively manipulated by the king, but, on the other, it had more serious and consequential work to do. Had the Estates simply become a subservient tool for administering royal projects?[39] Such a view would overlook the subtleties of a complex relationship, for it was not so much a loss of power as a change in the nature of their power which the leading deputies experienced, and while they were not always happy about it, they gradually learned to appreciate the advantages of their new situation. Far from being reduced to rubber-stamp status, the sessions of the Estates became the place where accommodations were worked out, regulations were drawn up, and policies were implemented. The annual minutes contained less controversy and more technical detail: complete audits of the accounts of each diocesan assiette every year, minutes of the meetings of the three sénéchaussée assemblies, long discussions of public works projects and financial arrangements, interminable committee reports. This activity was not 'independent', for the intendant and the president had a firm control over everything that was done, but it was a significant and effective way of having a say in the application of unavoidable royal programs – especially in areas where implementation could be a source of local power. Regulation is, after all, an important source of authority. We must imagine these committees of several bishops, several barons, and a double 'third' scrutinizing, hour after hour, the budgets of dioceses or the claims of whole rosters of individuals for compensation and consider the influence it gave them, especially the bishops.

The big change for the Estates was the enjoyment of an unchallenged monopoly over the regulation of taxes and financial operations. Here the contrast between the period 1632–60 and 1660–85 is striking. Faced with

38 A.N. H 1702, 338, 360, 366, 372, 373; H 1703, 4.

39 See, for example, the account of Roland Mousnier in *Les institutions de la France sous la monarchie absolue, 1598–1789*, 2 vols (Paris, 1974–80), vol. 1, pp. 483–4.

a fundamental conflict between the crown and the Estates over money, Richelieu had imposed the Edict of Béziers on the province by force. In response the Estates became combative, resisting new demands all the more in that there were not supposed to be any. Under Louis XIV all of this irregularity ceased. The king now supported the Estates' tax collectors and regulated conflicts clearly and definitively. Requisitions and special taxes by third parties ended, as did most contracts with *partisans* which were outside the Estates' ken or jurisdiction. Gone also were annoying interventions by the Parlement or the Comptes, as well as the devastating municipal feuds which had retarded collections and caused seating fights within the assembly.

The Estates' own administration reflects the change. Whereas in the 1630s the three syndic-generals had spent their time drumming up local support for the Estates' resistance to new royal demands and making desperate attempts to ward off worse misfortunes by presenting petitions to royal agents, in the 1670s we find them placidly regulating and administering the same matters in conjunction with the king's agents. Abuses were no longer external threats arriving without warning; they had become administrative problems to handle through channels. The syndics were now influential bureaucrats in their own right, drawing up budgets, gathering data, corresponding with the great about the regulation of outstanding problems. The province still had interests distinct from those of the king, and Colbert still distrusted the Estates. But the new situation nevertheless provided an effective marriage of convenience in which the Estates enjoyed an enhanced effectiveness, and the king enjoyed more regular financing, if not the absolute control which he theoretically would have liked.

In the quintessential area of taille collection the rise in effectiveness was especially noticeable. We saw in chapter 7 what a difficult problem this had become, given the confusions of impoverished peasants, rampaging troops, devious receivers, spendthrift assiettes, recalcitrant seigneurs, and demanding intendants. The question of who was to pay what, in which order, by whose authority had become acute. In the face of all this trouble, Louis XIV's regime must have felt like a breath of fresh air. The authority which the Estates had been implicitly craving was now provided by the intendant's supervision and Colbert's administrative command. Accommodation was arranged with the city of Toulouse, municipal and diocesan accounts were strictly watched, urban power conflicts were greatly reduced. When communities or districts were overburdened, like the diocese of Narbonne in the 1680s, provisions could be made for remitting their taille, but always *through* the Estates and, most particularly, through Cardinal Bonzi. The king would accept a certain sum from the Estates and then, with 'satisfaction', cancel part of the grant, stipulating that this returned credit was to be applied to exempting the affected areas from the taille that year. This tactic cost the king nothing, gave the Estates (and especially their president) the opportunity to distribute favors as they saw fit, and provided a method whereby the 'non-payments' were clearly accounted for in the fiscal records.

Collections from the powerful continued to be a problem, but they were handled more effectively. In the early 1660s experience had shown that, even when the diocesan syndic led the prévôt and archers to the scene of tax resistance, it was impossible to obtain satisfaction. So in virtually every case the Estates were forced to ask the governor to lend the province his guards for the enforcement of the Estates' orders, and when this practice was successful, it spread rapidly. Permission was soon being granted to assiettes to charge the cost of hiring the guards to the taxpayers, and regulations with increasing emphasis on this gubernatorial enforcement were repeated in 1664, 1668, and 1669. Although scandalous cases continued to arise, there was a new orderliness to their handling. Each case was presented and discussed in the Estates, if necessary for several years in a row, and the appropriate measures were then prescribed. Eventually the use of the governor's guards to foreclose on tax debts was organized to the point where they became a kind of executive police force for special occasions.[40]

THE REINFORCEMENT OF HIERARCHY

Louis XIV's regime conferred an even greater benefit on the rulers of Languedoc than revitalized institutions. He elevated the principle of hierarchical authority, and thus the rank and stature of those on top, to new heights of magnificence, infusing a traditional system of dominance with new life, even as the uses to which it was put were evolving.

Under Richelieu and Mazarin the rulers of Languedoc had faced a crisis of authority. Try as they might to exert independent influence or to collaborate among themselves, they were always coming up against the fact that their power was incomplete without that of the king. To function effectively an agency required four favorable circumstances. First, it had to command the respect of the parties it was trying to influence; thus it

[40] On Collection, P-V Jan. 20, 23, Feb. 14, 28, Mar. 8, Dec. 12, 1662, Jan. 10, 22, 30, 1663; Roschach, vol. XIV, pp. 1017, 1097; p-V Jan. 18, 1674, Jan. 26, 1675; Feb. 6, 1676; Dec. 1, 1685; A.N. H 748[207], 359, 384; Henri Monin, *Essai sur l'histoire administrative du Languedoc pendant l'intendance de Basville (1685–1719)* (Paris, 1884), pp. 90–1. For a particularly notorious case of lawless arrogance on the part of the great, Bercé, *Croquants*, vol. I, pp. 182–3 and Mel. Col. 115, 153. Monin claims that the Estates were lenient in prosecuting their fellow notables. This is possible in individual cases, but on the whole they seem to have taken considerable pains to resolve a troublesome problem.

needed a traditional, accepted claim to legitimacy. Second, it needed to assert its claim by means of an immediate physical presence: a deputy, an envoy, a process-server, who might be vulnerable to insult, had to be there. Third, it needed support up and down the chain of command to head off the inevitable appeals to jurisdictional rivals which could cause interminable delays. Finally, for the same reason, it needed undivided command at the center of royal power. In other words, political authority was incomplete without the coordination at all levels which only a strong monarch could provide. Absolutism required a regulated hierarchy and an ideological legitimacy which could only come from a strong, personal king.

This unified coordination is precisely the element which had been lacking under Richelieu and Mazarin and which was magnificently restored under Louis XIV. Every one of the necessary conditions had been called into question before 1660. Richelieu's policies had advanced rival dispensers of sovereignty – intendants and special agents; the social rise of venal officeholders had upset local power equilibriums; the minority of Louis XIV had caused division within the central government; the scramble to fend off wartime tax burdens had further intensified all these pre-existent authority conflicts. Then when the popular masses began to grumble and riot in response to the terrible conditions caused by taxes and military contingencies, this popular offensive made more headway because the stalemated authorities had left the door open to challenge from below.

In order to understand the contrast between this period and the regime of Louis XIV, it is helpful to imagine how the 1660s must have looked to a regional leader who had lived through the earlier era. In Toulouse, in the troubled spring of 1652, disorder had seemed chronic:

> [seditious] plans are being openly discussed and conferences are being held in the very houses of the officers of the Parlement. Everyone is plotting, down to the lowest artisans; the streets are covered with bills saying 'kill the mazarins;' people are called together in groups which go around town at night by torchlight threatening to burn and assault our creatures.

The effect was dismaying for the speaker, who came from a respectable parlementaire family: 'all these events cause apprehension for the *gens de bien*, who find themselves without a leader and who hardly dare confer among themselves about what to do for fear of arousing the jealousy of their enemies'.[41] The same lament, that there was 'no one with authority from the king' in the province, was heard in more than one quarter.

Only eight years later, in 1660, the situation was dramatically different. When the municipal council of Toulouse decided to punish one of the capitouls who had voted at the Estates in favor of a larger *don* than their

[41] Fresalz to Mazarin, Mar. 13, 1652: A.A.E. France 1636, 51. See also ibid., 40, 89.

instructions warranted, First President Fieubet, who by that time was getting the municipal council under his influence, told the meeting officiously that by 'satisfying' the king the criticized deputy had helped keep the city in the monarch's necessary good graces. Far from being censored, Fieubet argued, the man should be applauded, whereupon the council dutifully issued him a commendation. Not satisfied with having protected the royal ally, Fieubet wrote to Colbert that the other capitoul-deputy, the one who had fought against the *don* and adhered to the city's original mandate, should be roundly scolded when he came to court with the cahier of the Estates, 'so that it will be known that the king protects and rewards his servants'.[42] The point of this comparison between 1652 and 1660 is the contrast between the pleasure which *gens de bien* like Fieubet must have felt at seeing their subordinates put in their places in 1660, and the alarming loss of control over their inferiors which they must have felt during the 1640s and 1650s. Now, through the king, leaders like Fieubet had the satisfaction of asserting their preeminence effectively. Hidden within obedience to the crown, there was often a greater measure of power for the person who obeyed.

The new unity at the center of power symbolized by Louis XIV himself was an incalculable advantage. Gone was the slightest hope that a prince or minister might overturn an unfavorable opinion once it had been issued, as in the days of conflicting reports between Bosquet and Baltazar, Schomberg and Condé, Gaston d'Orléans and Séguier. Gone too was the feeling that royal success or failure in battle might influence the climate of provincial opinion. In 1646 Baltazar had tried to improve the atmosphere for his negotiations with the Estates by circulating a favorable account of the royal siege of Lerida. By 1673 the roles had been reversed, and every successful royal battle elicited an automatic stream of congratulatory letters *to* Colbert from members of the Estates hoping to stay in the good graces of the king.[43]

In the midst of all this adulation it is important to remember that the royal glory enhanced the status of the whole hierarchy of traditional authorities. The rays of the Sun King reflected off all the lesser planets revolving in his solar system. True, it was now necessary to collaborate with the central monarchy in order to enjoy these blessings, and light generated locally through independent sources of prestige like family name or seigneurial reputation was no longer sufficient. But association with Louis XIV increased the sense of hierarchy and privileged superiority which held

[42] Fieubet to Colbert, Apr. 19, 1660: Depping, vol. 1, p. 46.

[43] For example, Bishop of Lodève to Colbert, July 14, 1673: Mel. Col. 165, 148: 'I do not have the opportunity to express to the king personally my extreme joy at his conquest of Maestrik, but I must express it to you ... (etc.)'.

n absolute monarchy together. It was no accident that in 1662 the king estowed the coveted title of Chevalier du Saint-Esprit on eight anguedocian leaders – all of them loyal followers – including two of the ieutenant-generals (the third, d'Arpajon, already held the honor), Castries, he governor of Montpellier, Vardes, governor of Aiguesmortes, Merinville, aron of the Estates and future governor of Narbonne, and two of the reatest nobles in the Estates, Polignac and Uzès. These recipients joined he company of the ducs of Condé, Conti, Enghien, Verneuil, and Noailles s announced special favorites of the king. They were the first luminaries o receive this honor (except for the king himself and his brother) since 633.[44]

Association with a successful monarch could enhance local pull. We need nly think of Cardinal Bonzi, 'king of Languedoc', as Saint-Simon styled im, presiding with great magnificence over the provincial administration nd polite society. In 1672 he induced the Estates to hire a skilled pholsterer to provide him with 'a better decorated armchair more worthy f their chief'; and in 1675 he obtained a royal arrêt stating that he alone nd no other prelate had the right to enjoy an embroidered cushion under is arms and a carpet under his feet during the daily mass of the Estates.[45] Meanwhile the barons had established the principle that nobles or their nvoys had to demonstrate four generations of nobility on both sides of the amily before being admitted to the assembly.[46] Around the same time onorific prerogatives for all deputies were being multiplied, such as the rinciple that if one died while attending the sessions one was treated to procession, a funeral, and hundreds of masses at the expense of the rovince.[47]

A good example of the reinforcement of hierarchy in the 'new' manner vas the king's investigation of false nobles carried out in 1668 by Bezons n conjunction with various allies from the présidial courts of the province. In a certain sense this measure was a crackdown on the nobility. It codified he rules for membership, established centralized bureaucratic control of he process of investigation, and levied fines on those branded as 'usurpers'. Nobody enjoyed royal meddling in a domain so sensitive to families and raditionally so private. There was initial opposition in the Estates and the Comptes, but since the leaders themselves were secure in their titles and elieved that most of the violators were mere 'coqs de paroisse', their oncern was not with the principle of restricting the nobility, which they pproved. Rather they viewed the *recherche* as another 'investigation' which

44 Père Anselme, *Histoire généalogique et chronologique de la maison royale de France* (Paris, 1712), vol. II, pp. 1689–731.

45 P-V Jan. 30, 1672, Nov. 14, 1675.

46 Nicolas Lamoignon de Basville, *Mémoires pour servir à l'histoire de Languedoc* (Amsterdam, 1736), p. 161; P-V Jan. 7, 1662.

47 P-V Dec. 1, 1674, Jan. 20, 1675.

would subject genuine nobles to harassment and expense and drain the province of taxable funds. As long as the 'true nobles' were accommodated, Bonzi reported, the survey would satisfy everybody.[48] Ultimately it was a great success. It established an indisputable canon of legitimacy which became the basis for family claims of nobility right up to the present day, and it listed 'robe' and 'sword' families side by side, codifying the social evolution of the previous century. As Henry de Caux wrote in 1676 in honor of those upheld,

> you have been ennobled for a second time by this authentic declaration of His Majesty, who has caused the false nobles to tumble like those shooting glimmers which seem to be stars but are only vapors from the earth, even while he makes you appear more fixed and brilliant in the sky of the State.

Here too hierarchy was maintained, but at the same time regulated.[49]

In similar manner the intendant became a conduit for the military ambitions of local families, a sort of surrogate king. It was he who nominated local nobles to raise new companies for the army. In 1682, when Louis XIV began a project to aid needy noble families by forming companies of infantry out of their sons and training them at royal expense, it was the intendant who was to enroll them and check on their credentials (he was told not to be strict about nobility and let those who lived nobly slip through). The program proved so popular that in succeeding years there was a constant demand for more places, and the terms had to be restricted. 'One of the greatest things the king has ever done', observed Delort from Montpellier.[50]

Rank and status became daily preoccupations in Languedoc, as at Versailles. Great precedence quarrels among the leading socialites became momentary causes célèbres, but they were no longer the serious ruptures of an earlier age; rather they had become frivolous episodes to titillate salon gossips: how the wives of the marquis de Toiras, seneschal of Montpellier, and the marquis de Castries, lieutenant-general of Bas-Languedoc, snubbed and insulted each other for over a decade until a royal accommodation was elaborately staged in 1680; how the Estates fought over the relative placement of the coats of arms of the various provincial and royal leaders in 1664 and again in 1681; how the king had to rule on who could first set his torch to any bonfire celebrating a royal victory which followed a *Te*

[48] Archbishop of Toulouse to Colbert, Jan. 15, 1668: Depping, vol. I, pp. 234–7.

[49] Henry de Caux, *Catalogue général des gentils-hommes de la province de Languedoc* (Pezenas, 1676), introduction. A similar analysis for Brittany is Jean Meyer, *La Noblesse bretonne au XVIIe siècle* (Paris, 1972), pp. 58–9.

[50] Louvois to d'Aguesseau, Sept. 12, 1676: A.N. H 1696; Louvois to d'Aguesseau, May 25, 1682, Apr. 11, Dec. 29, 1683, Jan. 5, June 14, 1684: A.N. H 1704, H. 1711; Delort, *Mémoires*, vol. II, pp. 70–1.

Deum service in Toulouse – the lieutenant-general or the first president of the Parlement.[51]

The interesting thing about these hotly-contested episodes is that they were continuations of relationships begun in the salons of Paris or at court. The figures who entertained or quarrelled in Montpellier during the Estates, visited in Narbonne or Albi, and frequented the better hôtels of Toulouse were becoming integrated into a national 'social register', and whether they were in Languedoc or at Versailles, they corresponded with friends in the other place, who laughed or wept with their latest gossip. Thus, when the treasurer of the bourse Pennautier was almost ruined in the scandalous affair of the poisons, Bonzi was able to protect him and even joke at court that 'people who held pensions drawn on [Bonzi's] benefices would not live very long because "his star" [Pennautier] would kill them'.[52] Madame de Sévigné corresponded frequently with de Moulceau, who was a councillor, then president, in the Montpellier Comptes, and, through him, kept in touch with the activities of other aristocrats like the duc de Verneuil, Toiras, Castries, Bonzi and the marquis de Vardes, who had been exiled to Montpellier. Molière, who spent time in Languedoc in the train of the prince de Conti, ridiculed provincial society in *Les Précieuses ridicules* while Somaize defended *Les Véritables Précieuses* by portraying some of the Montpellierain ladies mentioned above.[53] Madame de Sévigné's daughter was at one time considering a marriage with Mérinville, the governor of Narbonne, and the daughter's actual husband, the Comte de Grignan, was lieutenant-general of Haut-Languedoc in the 1660s while his uncle was bishop of Uzès and his brother soon became bishop of Carcassonne. If outside luminaries had simply invaded Languedocian high society, importing fashions from Paris and colonizing the provincial 'wasteland', we might conclude that a vibrant local society had been denatured by the compelling attraction of Versailles. But when we consider that the persons involved were mostly Languedocians – the Bonzis who, though royal clients, had held local bishoprics since 1621; the Castries, in-laws of Cardinal Bonzi, who had recovered from the disgrace of the Montmorency revolt; the Toiras family, intermarried with the Aubijoux, who had similarly returned to favor; Pennautier, from a dynasty of bankers of the Estates, now a national financial potentate; a variety of literati in the Parlement and the Comptes, headed by the Fieubet family with their

[51] Delort, *Mémoires*, vol. I, pp. 228–38, vol. II, pp. 33–5; P-V Jan. 10, 11, 12, 1664; Delort, *Mémoires*, vol. II, p. 56; Roschach, vol. XIV, p. 1180.

[52] Madame de Sévigné, *Lettres*, ed. Gérard-Gailly (Bibliothèque de la Pléiade), vol. II (Paris, 1960), p. 153.

[53] Delort, *Mémoires*, vol. I, pp. 229–34 (notes by the anonymous editor); Sévigné, *Lettres*, vol. II, pp. 904–5, 912–13, 918–20, for example.

Toulouse and Paris branches – then we must conclude that, in a sense, i was the local families who had triumphed. Like the financiers, they ha integrated themselves into a national high society which gave them adde sparkle. and they brought that society home to their province.

A characteristic new phenomenon was the reconstruction and embellish ment of episcopal palaces at public expense and with the full approval o the king. This movement, which had its debut in 1658 with the 24,000 livre granted to the bishop of Montpellier, rapidly expanded in the 1660s an 1670s, just at the period when episcopal budgets were being pinched by th decline of land rents described by Le Roy Ladurie.[54] Major construction were undertaken in Béziers (1662), Uzès (1662), Montauban (1663) Pamiers (1663), Lodève (1666), Castres (1667), Mirepoix (1669), Montauba (1670). In addition 12,000 livres were appropriated in 1667 to repair th château de Balma near Toulouse because it was the 'only safe place wher the Archbishop of Toulouse could keep his grain and wine'.[55] Althoug the intendant and the commissioners of the Estates were scrutinizin budgets more stringently than ever before, there always seemed to be roon to authorize these investments in episcopal pomp either through th Estates or through the assiettes, and they added up to substantial sums Of course, the rationale for this expenditure was that many bishops residences had been demolished by Protestants during the religious war and that their reconstruction was part of the general offensive agains heresy. But earlier phases of the counter-reformation had taken the mor appropriate form of the introduction of new religious orders, seminaries and schools. It was characteristic of the age that the Catholic–royal offensiv now took the form of reinforcements to the prestige of the church's to authorities and that this contribution to their éclat was done at public, no church, expense. From their new palaces and country estates bishop could laugh at the urban notables and diocesan bureaucrats who had give them so much trouble a generation earlier.

On a lesser level, the municipal authorities were also basking in the glor reflected off them from the glitter of Versailles. The consuls of Narbonn began charging the cost of each others' funerals and infant baptisms to th city, in imitation of the practices of the Estates. The consuls of Bézier decided that, since they held the title of governor, they were above othe citizens and that, to raise their esteem in the eyes of the population, the would henceforth always wear the chaperon and be accompanied abou

[54] Emmanuel Le Roy Ladurie, *Les Paysans de Languedoc*, 2 vols. (Paris, 1966), vol. I, pp. 585–6.

[55] *Inventaire Haute-Garonne*, série C, II, pp. 341, 353, 360, 363, 366, 370. List of churches built in Le Roy Ladurie, *Paysans*, vol. II, p. 892. Comments: Delort, *Mémoires*, vol. I, p. 174; letters to Colbert from bishop of Montauban, Oct. 17, 1663: Mel. Col. 117 bis, 710; Bezons, Dec. 25, 1665: Mel. Col. 134 bis, 774; bishop of Mirepoix, Apr. 9, 1669: Mel. Col. 151, 316; bishop of Montauban, Feb. 3, 1672: Mel. Col. 158, 221.

town by one captain and two halberdiers. Consuls of smaller towns followed suit with their own requests to the king to be allowed to wear the chaperon 'to distinguish them from the other inhabitants'. After 1671 the capitouls began commissioning portraits of their most illustrious predecessors; then they planned a new square in front of their Capitole, and, by 1681, they were designing a whole gallery with busts and murals of the local 'illustrious'; they also initiated a funeral service to be put on at the expense of the town for each former capitoul who died.[56]

Enhanced prestige on every level of authority was a considerable asset, but it would have been useless if the various agents had dissipated it in feuding among themselves in the manner of the previous generation. Here, too, Louis XIV restored a healthy political climate by arbitrating provincial quarrels more effectively, using the intendant as an expert investigator and the royal council as an authoritative judge. We noted above the difficulties Bezons had encountered in regulating the factional quarrels of Nîmes in 1658 because the bishop would not recognize his compromise. In 1672, when a conflict between the bishop and his chapter again upset the town, two royal allies, the bishop of Uzès and the president of the présidial of Nîmes, were named by Colbert to arbitrate. Soon Uzès reported that all of Nîmes was praising the king for 'using his authority' and 'giving peace to the city'.[57] Bishops, whose conflicts with defiant urban factions had disrupted local government under Mazarin, now demanded and received not only favorable judgments against local subordinates who acted disrespectfully but – like Fieubet above – the means to 'put them in their place' by assertions of superiority.[58]

The ministerial correspondence illustrates dramatically the degree to which divisive disputes – questions of precedence, abuses of jurisdiction, challenges to authority – were now being informally regulated. Previous intendants had gathered information and mediated disputes, but the cases had been far fewer, and each had taken on the air of a small crisis. Under Louis XIV, the unification of the central government's outlook and its infusion with increased ideological consistency and glamor made it possible for the king's ministers and agents to collaborate with little fear of contradiction. Royal arbitration through letters increasingly facilitated the

[56] Narbonne, *Inventaire*, pp. 679–688; Antonin Soucaille, 'Le Consulat de Béziers', *Bulletin de la Société Archéologique de Béziers*, 3rd series I (1895–6), chapter 5; A.N. H 1702, 420; Rozoi, vol. IV, pp. 519, 559, 573, 579; Robert Mesuret, *Évocation du vieux Toulouse* (Paris, 1960), pp. 303, 323.

[57] Bishop of Uzès to Colbert, Aug. 2, Sept. 1, 1672: Mel. Col. 161, 37, 208, 290. A conflict identical to the quarrel between the consuls of Montpellier and the officers of the Comptes over seating in the cathedral during the Easter service which had threatened public order in 1645 was duly noted and swiftly regulated by the crown in 1684. Châteauneuf to d'Aguesseau, Apr. 19, 1684: A.N. H 1709, 272.

[58] Bishop of Lodève to Colbert, Nov. 19, 1663: Depping, vol. II, p. 21.

rule of local aristocrats influential enough to gain attention. In a few sample months in late 1680, disputes were resolved between two claimants to the chateau of Alais, between rival recipients of the same seigneurial dues from the same village, over payments owed to President Sartre of the Comptes by the inhabitants of two of his villages, between a royal guard and his brother, over duels, between the officers of the présidial of Castelnaudary and its lieutenant-criminel – the list seems endless.[59]

With hierarchy enhanced and quarrels among authorities better regulated, the scene was set for more effective management of the threat of popular insurrection. We noted in chapter 8 that popular unrest was a very serious concern in the seventeenth century because of its capacity to turn nasty, compromising authorities, destroying property, and upsetting the governmental equilibrium. The common people's propensity for grumbling and protesting was in no sense eliminated by the reign of the Sun King, though such incidents may have declined in number. The difference, which was the result of the new governmental climate, lay in the ability of the authorities to cope with such crises.

The contrast between the two most threatening popular episodes of our period, the Montpellier uprising of 1645 and the insurrection of 1670, is instructive. In 1645 a series of crises had undermined and weakened the effectiveness of authorities. Urban factions were fighting; the Parlement and the Comptes were trying to block the actions of *partisans*; the royal agents quarrelled incessantly; the Estates mounted a constitutional battle against the quartier d'hiver. The riots of late June, started by children, desperate mothers, and hungry mountaineers who heard rumors of a tax on heads, children, or trades, were not fomented directly by the authorities, nor did the rioters champion the causes of the Estates or the courts. Angry crowds murdered *partisans*, burned records, and showered Schomberg with rocks in reaction to shots fired on the demonstrators and arrests of popular leaders. They forced the authorities to suspend most of the more flagrant abuses and kept the government in nervous suspense for months as the villages surrounding Montpellier guarded the roads and threatened new violence. The authorities were too weak to dare to send troops, and their lack of unity was revealed by the mutual recriminations which followed.

In 1670, by contrast, one is struck with the serenity of the authorities in the face of a very similar, and ultimately more devastating, event. Popular discontent was again on the rise as a result of terrible weather and high prices, and once again it took the form of complaints about *partisans*' special taxes. On April 15 in Montpellier, a crowd of angry wives of innkeepers

[59] A.N. H 1702, H 1703, 137. It is important to note that, in some of these cases, such as that of President Sartre, Colbert and Louis refused to intervene, indicating that the matter should be handled by the regular authorities while, in others, they arranged a quiet accommodation.

gathered in front of Bezons's house to demand justice from the intendant and the first consul. They complained that they had sold so little wine in the past eight months that they could hardly survive; yet they were being charged a tax on the wine they were still able to dispense. Bezons went downstairs alone to talk to them, saying that they should take their grievances to the commissioners of the Cour des Comptes who would give them justice; that they were to disperse; and that in the future when they had a request they should only send two or three emissaries to see him. Early the next morning the same women reassembled in front of Riquet's house, shouting insults and demanding that he cancel their taxes. They spoke insolently and resisted when the first consul tried to arrest a ringleader, but she escaped, and the crowd dispersed.[60]

It had been similar incidents under almost identical conditions which had set off the rioting in 1645. Angry women uttering threats outside the doors of the king's representative, Bezons, and the province's leading gabeleur, Riquet, in the midst of the worst spring in a decade were not to be taken lightly, and the slightest provocation might have brought the rest of the *menu peuple* out into the streets. But if the popular reaction in 1670 was almost identical to that of 1645, the authorities' response was very different. For one thing, responsibility for special taxes now lay so clearly in the joint hands of the royal and provincial agents (Bezons and Riquet) that there was no possibility of discontent being diverted onto a hapless *partisan* by provincial authorities. For another, the authorities were now united and could afford to respond moderately and sensibly. The intendant could face the crowd without fear of backstabbing; he could actually refer the crowd to the Comptes, a prospect unthinkable in 1645; there were no beleaguered *partisans* to fire impulsively on the crowd.

An old-style rebellion *was* still possible, but only in the hills of Vivarais.[61] There, in the midst of the same conditions and rumors, a movement started in Aubenas on April 30 which rapidly turned into a major peasant insurrection. The spark that lit this unrest was the now-classic arrival in town of a *partisan* to collect a new tax, but typical of the new age was the fact that he was not an 'enemy' outsider but an agent of Samuel Verchant, one of the leading financiers who stood behind the Estates and an investor in the Sète company of 1676.[62] Thus the rebels were attacking the local establishment itself, and no longer a mutually-detested 'foreigner'. Meanwhile all the surrounding villages began raising troops to ward off

60 Account of Charles de Varanda, Apr. 15, 1670; A.M. Mp bundle labelled 'FF Attroupements et Séditions'.

61 Accounts of the revolt are Le Roy Ladurie, *Paysans*, vol. 1, pp. 607–11: and 'Fidèle relation de ce qui s'est passé en la ville d'Aubenas pendant les derniers Mouvemens du pays-bas du Vivarais', in J. L. de Laboissière, ed., *Les Commentaires du soldat du Vivarez* (Privas, 1811), pp. 376–444.

62 Guy Chaussinand-Nogaret, *Financiers de Languedoc au XVIIIe siècle* (Paris, 1970), pp. 40, 103–4.

imagined taxes on children, deaths, hats, and shoes which, interestin enough, were denounced as abuses being perpetrated by the élus – th hated symbols of the new fiscality who had last been denounced by Estates in 1629!

The movement spread rapidly under the leadership of Jacques Rou a relatively prosperous landowner who, according to some reports, forced by the peasants to take up the leadership. Three to four thousa peasants pillaged the houses and farms of those they perceived as th enemies; towns were invaded; and Aubenas was taken over by the reb Prosperous bourgeois fled while unfortunate scapegoats were murdered a dismembered in the streets. The rebels seem to have perceived that authorities were not on their side, for the best contemporary account quo them as reviving age-old slogans of class conflict: 'that their turn had co and it was not just for them always to be blinded'; that it was time ' the earthen pots to break the iron pots'; that the marquis de Castries, bishop of Viviers and all the clergy were 'swindlers'. There was even t of sending an army of twenty thousand to Toulouse to force the Parlem to answer for the edicts it had registered against the interests of province.[63] The movement spread for almost three months.

The peasants' belligerence, yet apparent aimlessness of strate contrasts strikingly with the specific demands of many earlier rebellio Rebels were raising the Estates' old battle cry of 'down with the élus', there were no real élus to expel. It was not surprising, therefore, that th should turn against nobility, clergy, bourgeois moderates, Parlement a financiers, none of whom could be counted on any longer to fight para battles or even to feud among themselves. In this respect, the Ro rebellion was less a successor to the disturbances of the 1640s than harbinger of the Camisard wars of thirty years later. It had the isolati and desperation of the latter but none of the governmental ambivalence a elite conflict which had characterized the former.

In fact, the authorities acted in 1670 as if they had rediscovered th class solidarity. The bourgeois of Aubenas played with appeasement wh waiting for outside aid. At no time did they support any rebel deman Indeed, they attempted secretly to pay the taxes being assessed in or to avoid angering the king *or* the crowd. The nobles of the vicinity simila made false promises about an amnesty which was unthinkable, and wait for the royal troops. Their real attitude was better expressed by Sain Colombe, lieutenant of the duc de Verneuil's guards, who arrived on J 11 with the first official message from outside that, although he would list to the rebels' grievances, they should lay down their arms because 'it w

[63] 'Fidèle relation', pp. 390–2.

never safe to dispute terrain with one's master and it would be an affront to His Majesty to demand that his troops disarm first'.[64] A week later Sainte-Colombe sent word that the intendant had returned from court with a royal amnesty, but, by July 21, it was clear that this was a ruse and that a royal army was descending upon the Vivarais. The king's musketeers led by d'Artagnan himself, plus 1,500 cavalry and 3,000 infantry joined by Verneuil, Castries, the comte de Roure, and 'a large quantity of Languedocian nobles who wanted to participate', rapidly decimated the peasant army, sacked Privas and Aubenas, and butchered the fleeing peasantry. Summary trials conducted by Bezons and Rochemaure, juge mage of Nîmes, issued thirty death sentences and sent a hundred to the galleys while the royal troops razed peasant villages in the vicinity. Roure himself was eventually captured and broken on the wheel in front of the hôtel de ville in Montpellier. His body was displayed on the main road from Montpellier to Nîmes, and his head was posted over one of the gates of Aubenas while royal agents razed his house and his farm to the ground, degraded the wood, and posted a plaque reminding posterity of his crimes.[65]

Under Louis XIV there was no longer any difficulty deciding which side to be on when popular disorder challenged the normal functioning of things. With ambiguities in the chain of command ironed out and prospects for increasing one's private authority by playing off one side against the other eliminated, true class justice was once again possible. Having united behind the indispensable royal troops to wipe out ugly popular insubordination, the various authorities returned to the important business of the day without any of the aftereffects which had plagued the 1640s and 1650s. There was the Canal to complete, loans to be floated, episcopal palaces to renovate. In the next Estates the bishop of Viviers, one of the authorities most hated by the rebels of his diocese, assured Colbert that he would manipulate the deputies into granting everything that was needed for the Canal, using the Roure rebellion as a pretext: 'I will remind the deputies that our happiness depends on the King because our unfortunate disorders in Vivarais have corrupted our spirits.' The bishop was conscious of poor conditions, but they were decidedly secondary in his thinking:

> We will arrange for the assembly itself to demand the suppression [for cash] of these edicts, leaving until later the question of how to finance the suppression satisfactorily on terms approved by His Majesty which place the least possible burden on His subjects from this province. Indeed, they *are* overwhelmed with taxes, not to mention the ruin which those poor wretches of my diocese have brought upon us and the whole region by their rebellion, or the loss of their olive

64 Ibid., p. 416.

65 Ibid., pp. 428–9; Delort, *Mémoires*, vol. 1, pp. 245–6; A.D. Hér. C 162 (damage claims).

trees . . . I hope, Monsieur, that in spite of these problems His Majesty will receiv all the satisfaction he could hope for from a most submissive province and a mo obedient assembly.[66]

In 1645 resistance in the Estates had opened the way for the popula rebellion. In 1670 a popular rebellion was providing a pretext for th obedience of the Estates. It is worth noting that when the king bega constructing new military roads and fortresses, the first since the demolition of the 1630s, they were designed to strengthen, not challenge, provinci rulers by dominating the areas most vulnerable to Protestant and popula rebellions.[67] The wars of the Camisards were ample proof that king an province would now be united against either kind of divisiveness fror below.

[66] Bishop of Viviers to Colbert, Dec. 13, 1670: Depping, vol. I, p. 257 and Mel. Col. 155, 484; De 9, 1670: Mel. Col. 155, 476. See also bishop of Mirepoix to Colbert, Dec. 16, 1670: Mel. Col. 15 494.

[67] Roschach, vol. XIII, pp. 599–602.

Conclusion

I

In his memoirs Charles de Montchal, archbishop of Toulouse from 1628 to 1651, lashed out bitterly at the governmental policies of his day, especially the attack on the clergy which he attributed to the greed and arrogance of Cardinal Richelieu.[1] In Montchal's view Louis XIII was a just and wise monarch, but Richelieu was a usurper who put pride above service and literally wore out the king with his misguided projects. In the interest of his own vanity, the cardinal had abandoned the opportunity to effect a general conversion of the Huguenots at the Siege of Montauban in 1629. He had insulted the pope, manhandled the religious orders, and attacked the Sorbonne. When only the bishops were left to protect the church, he incited the regular orders against them and packed the ranks of the episcopacy with sycophantic 'men of low birth'. Meanwhile clerical elections were fixed, and the bishops' right to assemble was denied although they 'have always had the right to assemble to consider their affairs, like the basest of artisans'.[2]

The crux of the matter was financial privilege. In 1639 the edict on *amortissements* led to seizures of clerical property and harassment of the clergy. Then new offices and *augmentations de gages* were forced on the church, and disputes with the sub-farmers of these disguised taxes led to the imprisonment of various agents of Montchal and his cathedral chapter. Clerical protest culminated in the Assembly of Clergy of 1641 at Mantes, where Montchal unsuccessfully led the opposition to Richelieu and, as a result, was exiled to his diocese, along with six other prelates. 'A less furious man would have respected their *camail* and *rochet* and issued [the banishment] orders to them when they were wearing private clothes in their own chambers, but [Richelieu] wanted to lend authority to his judgments by carrying them out publicly.'[3]

Montchal's pique took a distinctively clerical form, but it was similar to the exasperation which other provincial leaders must have felt; in fact, he himself made the analogy with the parlements whose presidents and

[1] Charles de Montchal, *Mémoires de Mr. de Montchal archevêque de Toulouse contenant des particularitez de la vie et du ministère du Cardinal de Richelieu* (Rotterdam, 1718).

[2] Ibid., pp. 27, 67.

[3] Ibid., p. 216.

councillors were being exiled or their offices attacked 'without bein heard'.[4] Many did express anger and frustration when royal creatures we favored over those with better claims on positions; traditional procedur were ignored; and burdensome fiscal novelties were peddled by 'foreigr investors or local opportunists. Showing through Montchal's priva bitterness is a deeper feeling of uneasiness, a sense that his status an privileged access to power were being threatened and that the moral an social order around him was somehow coming apart:

The opinion which the people have of the king's religion is the principal bond their obedience. This is why kings revere prelates and respect the freedom whic priests have to reprimand and correct them... If the people held other views the king, they would hate him and blame all the inconveniences which befell th kingdom on his bad faith and imperfect religion, and perhaps might accord hi only a forced obedience, which experience shows us is subject to revolt, from whic scandalous episodes might arise.[5]

The government's efforts, meanwhile, come down to us through th unpleasant voice of Baltazar the intendant, whose arrogant distrust everyone, acknowledged ties to profiteers, and disdain for procedures whic got in his way made him a symbol of the sorts of innovations hated b Montchal and his friends. Absolutist *par excellence*, Baltazar's repeate advice was to 'take the main road of royal authority'; to put people in the place by showing them that their secret intentions were known; to use forc and compulsion in place of bargaining and consulting.[6] He called repeated for the disunion of the Comptes, the abolition of the Estates, th humiliation of all opposing groups, the restoration of the Edict of Bézier Yet he was a talented administrator, good at producing results when troo or money had to be raised quickly, and his services were indispensable. H represented the voice of a government in crisis, needing to cut corners an evade privileges in order to get things done.

As we listen to Montchal and Baltazar and their many counterpart it is easy for us to conclude that they epitomized a struggle betwee backward-looking provincial aristocrats and progressive agents of sta centralization. But a closer look reveals that the idea of a rationalizing sta crushing corporate privileges and provincial liberties is crude at bes Baltazar's voice was one of desperation, not domination, uttered during time of royal weakness. He only just managed to do his job in the face antagonism, disruption, and resistance, some of which he caused himse by his intransigent behavior. The problem with men like him was that the were unable to collaborate enough with local forces, unable to get what wa needed quietly and smoothly without causing sensations and riskin

[4] Ibid., p. 215.   [5] Ibid., p. 216.

[6] Baltazar to La Vrillière, Feb. 20, 1645: Lubl., p. 120.

opular disturbances. One might almost say the same of Richelieu and Mazarin. As for the Montchals in the provinces, they were hardly rejecting ne state, but rather demanding that it do its job better. Montchal thought nat the monarchy had lost sight of its true goals. He wanted the king to ule more personally and directly; to convert the Huguenots, not make deals vith them; to reinforce the status of the great, not humiliate them; to ppoint those of stature, not upstarts. Tax farmers should not be allowed) pester the notables for revenues. Authority should be reinforced, not ndermined in the eyes of the people.

These are tasks which Louis XIV performed much more effectively. The olicies so often detested in Richelieu were admired and approved in him.)omination of the clergy, arrogance towards the pope, promotion of loyal ppointees and punishment of those who failed to collaborate, encourage-nent of sycophancy, wasteful extravagance – all these sins of Richelieu eem to have become virtues under Louis XIV. The difference was that he Sun King performed them without the accompanying jolts and ncertainties of his predecessors, and when sacrifices were necessary, they vere amply compensated by other needs fulfilled.

The rulers of Languedoc could not function outside the national system f domination. Montchal may have feuded with Richelieu, but he also euded with the Parlement of Toulouse, and in 1639, at the very time of he *amortissement* crisis, he was successfully using the royal council to obtain rrêts in support of his preeminence over the Parlement. These rulers – a ew hundred politically influential individuals and ten thousand or so others ke them – based their social power on control of both land and offices. They were advantageously placed to dominate the peasantry, and in ddition their access to privileged status – to legal superiority, to mem-ership in municipal, royal, or clerical corps and to the contacts which led o such positions – gave them further unearned revenues and a share of arious forms of political influence. These advantages were not sufficient o assure the rulers of social superiority, however, because their class osition was dependent upon protection from the absolute monarchy. In Europe of rival states with marauding armies of unprecedented size, they eeded military and diplomatic protection which only an organized nonarch could provide. They were also beginning to need the economic irection which would be necessary to compete with the Dutch and the English internationally. The decisions which caused the greatest concern vere controlled by the king, as were fiscal deals negotiated with cartels of Parisian investors. The regime of the Edict of Nantes and the legal status f each Protestant community – matters which affected the jurisdiction of very authority in the province – were in royal hands alone.

Even more crucial was the tax system with which many of the Languedocian rulers had an advantageous connection. We have seen that the taille was a complicated flow of resources refreshing many parties an not just a siphon of funds to Paris. It paid the stipends of many of the roy officers (with the gabelle and the royal domain paying the rest). It funde the influence-trading at the Estates and a number of valuable trips to cour not to mention mammoth tribute payments to the most powerful. It pai for episcopal palaces and honorific ceremonies. It bought off innumerab investigations, feudal levies, threatening offices, and unpopular edicts. I provided a gold mine in profits and handling fees to a variety of investor whose speculations with public funds were the foundation of many of th great eighteenth-century fortunes. Roughly half of it stayed in the province and a third was channeled directly to the notables rather than the king. Th cost of all these activities was then passed on to the province, which mean that it was divided unequally among dioceses and individuals by formula which favored some and damaged others.

Beyond these practical concerns loomed the most fundamental issue o authority. The king symbolized power in a society where domination was a much based on intangible 'magic' as on physical coercion. If the kin found himself in a humiliating or advantageous military position, th corresponding effects were immediately felt up and down the hierarchica chain of command in the form of greater 'license' or 'obedience' fron subordinates. Power was personal; yet it was exercised in the name of th king. The first imperative, of making the social system work by keepin the common people from challenging the workings of government, wa easily jeopardized. Poor conditions and several generations of social turmoi created a living tradition of popular protest. But public demonstrations o influence by agents of government invariably brought clashes with riva agents, which in turn damaged the reputation of each and encourage popular disturbance. The only way to regulate such clashes was to hav recourse to the king. The very system of political rule, which was in essenc a royal system, required close collaboration with the larger monarchy an precluded any real autonomy on the part of the provincial ruling class. Onl the king could maintain hegemony.

This system went through a severe crisis of adjustment between 162 and 1690. During a whole generation regional and national rulers seeme to be working at cross purposes, trying to resolve the contradictions in polity which required centralized direction to defend decentralized privi leges. While the social pretensions of ecclesiastics and royal officers wer rising in the wake of improved land rents and guaranteed heredity of office the corps through which they exerted political influence were all faced wit the shock of new pressures from an insistent royal government. Th Protestant community was defeated in 1629 but not dismantled. Th Comptes were reorganized, and the Estates were subjected to tighte controls. New offices and companies of officers were created. Taxes wer aised to unprecedented heights, and new forms of taxes challenged raditional collection mechanisms. *Partisans*, viewed as alien exploiters, pened offices to do business in the misfortunes of their neighbors. Royal ommissioners usurped functions formerly performed by other parties and ept the central ministers abreast of who was loyal and who was not. Laws vere forcibly registered; recalcitrant judges were exiled. Consular elections vere modified; debts were suspended; supplies were requisitioned.

These rude disruptions did not signal a takeover as much as a crisis of aanagement, for the royal government did not perform these operations ffectively, and the rulers did not ward them off successfully either. The esulting confusion confirmed the underlying weaknesses of the system. Ieavy demands on the subsistence economy led to popular unrest ulminating in waves of contagious violence and near-violence. The uthorities were unable to cope with these popular pressures because they vere paralyzed by their own intense rivalries. Individuals who tried to rotect themselves by lending support to the royal innovations quarrelled vith those who tried to enhance their authority by posing as defenders of ocal liberties. These antagonisms amplified other factional differences. The arlement and the Comptes split into warring parties issuing contradictory irectives. The Estates fought bitterly to stem the tide of military excesses, etting off riots in Montpellier. The intendants and their allies were olarized over what course to take – conciliation or repression – when either promised satisfactory results. The consulates were decimated by actional struggles which were intensified by the animosities of each set of igher authorities all the way up to the king.

In facing these emergencies, the rulers of Languedoc did their best to ooperate. They exchanged deputations, issued complementary directives, nd experimented with ways of jointly sharing authority in order to keep heir subordinates in check while administering the royal program according o their own, more benevolent dictates. But their partial, contradictory uthority was rapidly unmasked. The Estates and the Comptes had a vested nterest in the fiscal system, yet they lacked the coercive power to defend heir collections effectively. The Estates had no legitimate claim to epresent the province and rightly came to be perceived as extorters of taxes or the benefit of a few bishops and financiers. The Parlement had vast olitical pretensions but no effective way to enforce them. The town ouncils were victim to rivalries of all the other powers. Without the king, ollaboration deteriorated into mutual vilification which destroyed the limate of obedience and left the province vulnerable to those outside forces vhich it had no way to control.

Louis XIV's success in Languedoc stemmed from his almost instinctive bility to reinforce class rule. He brought 'order' to his affairs in a way vhich must have been especially satisfying to the high percentage of younger officials who had known only the uncertainties of the 1650s and who were eager to join the grand enterprise. He administered a larger dose of reward and punishment, making it clear that 'negotiations were no longer in season' and that 'satisfying the king' was the only worthy goal. But the reason his policies worked so well was that they took place in an atmosphere of social confidence. Under Louis XIV it was perfectly clear that hierarchy would be reinforced, the claim of the privileged to their share of society's resources would be guaranteed, and collaboration would be properly rewarded. Languedocian society was shored up, not levelled. Many aspirations of the past were fulfilled; many frustrations were eliminated. Each institution felt stronger and more competent within its sphere. The Estates collected taxes with less challenge. The Parlement asserted itself in the mountains, in the towns, against the Protestants. The Comptes' jurisdiction over taxes was confirmed. Towns lost autonomy, but their debts were safe, fiscal disputes were minimized, and their consuls enjoyed unprecedented prestige. Troops were more effectively disciplined. Protestants were restricted and converted. The tax burden became more regular and a slightly larger share of it was channeled to rulers within the province. Languedocians participated in the social life at court, and many felt that through the royal agents, their services were known and rewarded. Banking contacts tied Montpellier and Toulouse closer to Paris and made placement of funds a unified national enterprise. The magnificence of ceremonies gratified even the most demanding of pretensions.

On November 17, 1667, an enormous chapel hung with rich tapestries was erected in a meadow by the Garonne in Toulouse for the ceremony of the laying of the first stone of the lock connecting the Canal des Deux Mers to the river. The archbishop of Toulouse and the bishops of Comminges, Lectoure, and Saint-Papoul, with their complete companies of clergy, assembled in the chapel, along with the entire Parlement, the eight capitouls and eight former capitouls who had arrived in full regalia on horseback, and an army of six thousand canal workers who had marched there in formation. After a solemn mass and the blessing of the stones, the entire company processed to the construction site, where one cornerstone was laid by Gaspard de Fieubet, first president of the Parlement, and the other by the capitouls. Then a large number of medals were distributed to the people showing, on one side, Louis XIV as 'master of the earth' and, on the other, a picture of Toulouse and the canal, 'marketplace of the seas'. Bronze plaques commemorated in a single inscription the names of Louis XIV, Colbert, Fieubet, the first two capitouls, the archbishop of Toulouse, and Riquet the entrepreneur, all collaborators in the same client network. Continuous artillery volleys were fired as the crowd shouted 'long live the king', and Riquet distributed food and wine to his workers. It was reported that God sent a break in the weather 'to show favor for this ction'.[7] Here was the way authority and hierarchy were supposed to work, ith prelates, officials, and financiers ranged obediently around the ionarch and the deity, and the people participating only as laborers and espectful onlookers. I suspect that Archbishop Montchal would have been elighted.

II

he experience of Languedoc can tell us something about the evolution f French society and its relationship to absolutism. Of course the province as in no sense 'typical'. But if the rulers of Languedoc were favored in ome ways by their circumstances, they may have been disadvantaged in thers, such as the lack of the personal tax exemptions they would have ad in areas of *taille personnelle* or their relatively weak seigneurial istitutions. No province was typical under absolutism; rather each had its wn political personality, along with its distinctive field patterns and village tructures. Instead of looking for typicality we should take the circumstances 1 Languedoc as variations on a common theme of aristocratic privilege and istitutional inequality and see whether that theme is helpful in explaining ther situations.

What sort of absolutism is suggested by these findings? A hypothetical icture might look something like this. Absolutism was the political ıanifestation of a system of domination protecting the interests of a rivileged class of officers and landed lords. Strong bonds linked the rovincial nobility, the episcopacy, the various corps of royal officers, and he town oligarchies to the crown and to each other. These bonds were more mportant than the many conflicts which divided corps from corps or king rom province. The 'society of orders' did not exist as a system, but only s one aspect of a distinctive early modern form of a society of classes. The arious 'orders' and 'corps' were part of the structure of authority, which n turn reflected the organization of power necessary to extract wealth from he land in a 'late feudal' society.

Each detailer of authority had a claim on a portion of society's roduction, not by virtue of talent, ingenuity, or productive investment, ut through control of positions gained by inheritance or purchase, or onferred by a superior. In the Middle Ages, such positions of extra-conomic coercion had been largely self-sustaining, based on direct eigneurial domination over land and peasants and protected by local force. n the seventeenth century, after a long evolution involving changing elationships to peasant production, the social reputation which assured lomination was guaranteed by seigneurial authority, *plus* economic dvantage, *plus* privileged status guaranteed by the crown. It was still ossible to maintain social prominence solely through ancestral title or

[7] Roschach, vol. XIV, pp. 957–60.

seigneurial possessions, but it was increasingly difficult. Now dominance on the land was also assured by special status with respect to laws, taxes, and enforcement mechanisms and by control of a share of the 'official' power of command. In other words, social position was increasingly dependent on privileges created and defended by the state and on offices and titles which were defined in relation to the state.

These two sources of authority and prestige – the original seigneurial and the newer royal – were related. Both involved private 'ownership' of a public authority which was held in unequal portions by many different parties whose jurisdictions overlapped. Royal power had been constructed out of, and in reaction to, seigneurial power. But it reproduced the shared degrees of jurisdiction over persons and land which characterized the seigneurial landscape, and in its differentiation into layer upon layer of rival agencies and its unequal treatment of each town, province, corps, and individual, it reflected the historical conditions under which the monarchy had gradually taken over a pre-existing system of fragmented and diversified jurisdictions. Inequality, whether of persons, agencies, or geographical districts, was built into the system, along with considerable 'autonomy' on every level, deriving from the fact that privileges were 'owned' as well as 'conferred'.

The society of the seventeenth century which the monarchy and the privileged class were jointly engaged in defending was thus a hybrid society. Its foundations were still sunk deep in the land, and it was still built around a class of nobles whose fundamental existence was based on the domination of units of peasant production. But it was also a political system in which royal institutions developed the conditions necessary to continue to prosper in the Europe of expanding merchant capitalism while extending the membership of the dominant class to new groups and slowly pulling old and new together. The rising prestige of royal offices provided a point of attraction for provincial aristocrats. The royal officers themselves found ways of becoming privileged landowners and eventually nobles, if they did not already enjoy nobility. Rich merchants took advantage of the monarchy's network of revenue flows and absolute power of command to become parasitic financiers by acquiring special claims over potential or actual sources of revenue. With their profits they, too, bought status and official power by joining the ranks of the privileged class. Meanwhile the king, through his institutions, was regulating and reinforcing the society of privilege by regularizing the tax exemptions of nobles and clergy and the rules of derogation, arranging the differential status of each town, province, corps and company, selling offices and through them nobility, bestowing titles on families and estates, inspecting and regulating all privileges.

This new 'feudal' society was thus one of lords and manors but also of officers with ownership of delegated power. Its state was a 'feudal' state constructed out of the aristocracy's need to assert its right to dominate and designed to maintain privilege and inequality. The authority of the king was predicated on an ideology of personal loyalty, not impersonal service, and power was still mobilized through client systems based on the principle of partiality. Differentiation of rank, with its corresponding public display, was encouraged, even enhanced. Taxes continued to be levied unequally, though they were better managed, and all kinds of private claims on the funds were perpetuated. Special corporate status was retained, like the tax abonnement of the city of Toulouse or the regime of the Estates with its curious entrance privileges, not as relics from the past, but as natural parts of a living system built upon infinite inequality of treatment.

There was always a contradiction within feudalism between the decentralizing tendencies of a situation where power was locally grounded in land and authority was exercised through the innate preeminence of individuals or groups, on the one hand; and the necessity for higher coordination inherent in such a system of personal authority, on the other. Divided, personally-owned power implied a hierarchy of levels to be coordinated from above, and the idea of innate superiority required a higher source of legitimacy. Tension inevitably arose between the desire of a class of dispersed landed aristocrats to own and exercise power themselves and their need for a higher organism which could justify their existence and protect their system of domination, but at the expense of some of their personal initiative. Periods of royal extension, when personal and regional autonomy were threatened, alternated with periods of reaction, when noble rebellions forced a new compromise on the king.

The seventeenth century saw a major adjustment of this type. The assertion of a more centralized absolutism under Richelieu and Mazarin was based on the realization in some circles that the society could not function effectively without a strengthening of the state. Noble revolts, Protestant rebellions, popular uprisings, Spanish conspiracies – the problems are familiar, most of them being an aftereffect of the wars of religion. They suggested a breakdown of hierarchical order and a failure of the king to coordinate the society properly for lack of continuous prestige and adequate resources. They also reflected the unrest of a traditional nobility threatened by venality of office and rising urban–bourgeois influence. The result was a new royal offensive which was rapidly diverted, perhaps unwisely, into an overly ambitious effort to assert the power of the French state in Europe. The effort at greater internal control thus took place under extreme pressures of financial exigency and division of authority. Angry and divided, the rulers were split along factional, political, and corporate lines, unleashing more breakdowns of influence and serious social unrest. Their divisions might look like the natural cleavages in a 'society of orders' except for the fact that a more fundamental class unity held the orders together in the face of challenges from the rest of the population. The 'estates', 'orders', and 'corps' proved incapable of representing anything apart from the royal regime. There could be no 'provincial', 'community', or 'corporate' front, except for temporary, limited objectives, because basic class interests united royal and provincial dignitaries, and only disagreements over relative position divided them.

Louis XIV and his contemporaries were the great beneficiaries of these struggles for, despite the turmoil, two great changes had been effected. First was the unification of the client network at both ends: there was finally a single line of command at the top and a unified network in the provinces, accompanied by the administrative channels to make it function properly. Second was the intensification of taxation and the restructuring of the financial system, with the assistance at every level of financiers whose 'new money' could be traded for influence and exploitative advantage. These changes were related, for both were effected by the intendants in conjunction with the *partisans*. Indeed, exploitative finance almost seems to have been the glue which held together the Mazarinist regime. Both changes had required unpleasant adjustments which were not well understood by threatened provincial leaders. But when the smoke had cleared, the Louisquatorzian system of absolutism was standing on a firmer, more centralized foundation which made the entire social system function more effectively.

Success was achieved at a price. To attain this serenity the ruling class had to abandon its pretensions to autonomy and place its fate more than ever in the hands of the monarch, opening up new vulnerability to weakness at the center. Local power was still important, but it could only be exercised within parameters established at Versailles. Most important, the perpetuation of the system of hierarchy required the rejuvenation of its ranks. Not only was it necessary to accept the venal officers into the ranks of the privileged ruling class, but also the financiers and opportunists whose aggressive royalism during the 1640s had outraged the more tradition-minded regionalists. The king was increasingly the arbiter of privileged status, even among the old nobility. Ancient families might be outraged at the pretensions of upstarts, but as long as the principle of differentiation was maintained, it was no longer appropriate to be squeamish about the identity of particular titularies.

Of course seventeenth-century France also contained forces of change. Some Frenchmen were investing profits in land consolidation or larger-scale production without being caught up in the game of buying hereditary influence through social preeminence. Others were pursuing colonial trade. Some administrative theorists dreamed of genuine reorganization based on rational division of labor and impartial application of uniform rules. But while these activities were important, they were clearly not the motivating forces behind the absolutist state. In fact, the state might almost be seen as a buttress against changes of this sort in the way that it reinforced the opposite tendencies. Moreover, those who were in the forefront of progressive enterprises were rarely among the politically influential.

This picture is a hypothetical projection requiring further exploration. If valid, it would explain the sudden success of Louis XIV, and it would end the problem of why a supposedly anti-aristocratic reign was sandwiched so tightly between the aristocratic Fronde and the aristocratic eighteenth century. It explains the functioning of the state more satisfactorily by seeing it as part of a class alliance, and it suggests a royal government, the characteristics of which were concordant with those of the society it presided over, without necessitating a quest for bourgeois influences strong enough to call into being a 'bourgeois monarchy'.

Most important, it highlights the contrast between the continental monarchies built upon privileged aristocracies and the England of William and Mary. Despite the parallel developments of central institutions and 'aristocratic' styles in France and England, the social structures of the two countries and the principles on which they were based were profoundly different. Whether or not there was a 'growth of political stability' in England, the world we encounter there – the world of oligarchic political parties, electoral popularity contests, modernizing landlords, central bank and joint stock companies – is strange indeed from the perspective of Louisquatorzian society.[8] Far more familiar is the realm of Leopold I where the monarch 'took for granted a hierarchical society built upon ascending orders of social privilege'; and 'the Habsburgs chose to regard privilege as a source of regal power rather than a challenge to it'.[9] Might the same not be true of the Spain of Charles II and even, on a more advanced level, the Prussia of Frederick the Great, who also struck a deal, though a different one, with a privileged aristocracy?

I am arguing for a change of emphasis in discussions of absolutism. Absolute monarchs and their ministers did improve the state apparatus in significant ways, but their modernity has been overemphasized by historians. It is necessary to stress the influence of the traditional social climate in which such innovations took place. Early modern society, so familiar from the regional studies of the Annalistes, also had its own characteristic, regionally-varied politics with corresponding structures and class content. The king's government was constructed in response to this politics. Absolutism must be seen accordingly, not as a modern state grafted onto a pre-modern society, but as the political aspect of the final, highest phase of a venerable, though modified, feudal society – a society in transition, if you like, from feudalism to capitalism.

8 J. H. Plumb, *The Growth of Political Stability in England 1675–1725* (London, 1967). For a more telling perspective on the contrast with France, Marvin Rosen, 'The Dictatorship of the Bourgeoisie: England, 1688–1721', *Science and Society*, 45 (1981), 24–51.

9 John P. Spielman, *Leopold I of Austria* (London, 1977), p. 19.

Appendix: Breakdown of taxes from the diocese of Toulouse, 1677

The social distribution of taxes discussed in chapter 11 is based on an analysis of the accounts of the diocese of Toulouse.[1] Other dioceses would have similar articles with variations for the local items.

Table 14 shows the articles as they were listed in the account, with appropriate explanation. Of the total 317,995 livres imposed, 293,516 livres (92.3 percent) were provincial taxes, while 24,479 livres (7.7 percent) were added on by the diocese in the form of fees or local expenses. If we start with the sums added by the diocese, we can see from table 15 that most of them went directly into the pockets of the local notables. Some items did recompense local officers and notables for services rendered, but most of these services were only marginally useful, especially the 5,480 livres – almost 2 percent of the entire diocesan tax burden – which went for the banquets, refreshments, and stipends of the representatives who attended the annual assiette meeting.

What became of the 'provincial' funds?

1. *The 'traditional taille'* (*aide*, *octroi*, *crue*) was assigned by the crown to cover 'ordinary' expenses at the local level, notably the stipends of royal officers. The diocesan receivers themselves paid their own officers, the présidial and sénéchaussée judges, and certain functionaries of the universities of Toulouse and Montpellier. The rest of the money was forwarded to the receiver-generals of Toulouse or Montpellier who paid the stipends of the officeholders in their bureaux, plus those of the treasurer-generals of finance, interest due on certain royal loans, and various other petty expenses.[2]

2. *The taillon*, a traditional sum very similar to the taille, was handled by a distinct set of receivers. It had originally been a military tax, and the bulk of it still went into the royal military treasury. Its destination in 1677 is indicated in table 16.

3 and 4. *Garrisons and mortes-payes*. These were sums destined to support the troops occupying the various mouldering fortresses in the province, the citadel of Montpellier, and the ramparts of Narbonne. Most of them were

[1] The budgets of the diocese of Toulouse are in A.D. H-G. C 988, C 989, and C 990. Further information is in C 958–9, C 1006–11, etc.

[2] Mel. Col. 243: État des finances, 1677.

sinecures for provincial nobles and their followers. The Estates influenced them indirectly by pushing their own members as appointees for the positions involved.

5. *Étapes* were the sum of the claims of all the local communities for the costs of troop passages during the preceding year. These costs were then imposed on the whole province through the regular channels and reimbursed to the specific communities which had undergone the expenses. The provisioning of the troops was subcontracted at the local or diocesan level to an *étapier* who bid for the contract. These agents, whose status differed from place to place, undoubtedly made a substantial profit, but it is impossible to estimate how much.[3] It is clear that the treasurer of the bourse took 2.5 percent in fees for receiving the money; thus, the 1677 figures would be 300,435 for the étape itself and 7,511 for the treasurer of the bourse.

6. *Special charges* (*deniers extraordinaires*) were the most important since they included all the special grants made by the Estates, often under vague rubrics sure to arouse suspicion on the part of local taxpayers. It was these items which had been explicitly attacked by the Parlement during the Fronde on grounds that they were padded and unnecessary.

(A) The largest item was the *don gratuit*, in 1677 a sum of 2,700,000 livres granted to the king. This sum was not entirely imposed since the Estates had taken up the practice of using the profits of the équivalent tax farm for payment of the *don* and of borrowing part of the rest. Table 17 shows how the 2,700,000 livres became 2,062,041 in actual imposed taxes.

(B, C, and 7A) 'Umbrella' categories. These three categories are best grouped together since their destinations overlapped. The 'salaries, debts and affairs of the province' included a whole range of items not clearly specified in the *mandes*. The 'special gifts and deficits in the accounts' included items which required royal permission to impose because the Estates did not have any automatic jurisdiction over them. These sums were collected and held until the king approved them, which he routinely did. A similar item, though listed separately as article 7A in table 14, was the 75,000 livres routinely imposed for the 'expenses of the Estates'. These three 'umbrella' categories came to 1,534,914 livres imposed on the province. Their destinations are broken down in table 18. It is striking that influential personalities ('dignitaries and operating expenses') managed to corner 31.3 percent of this large sum while the treasurer of the bourse *alone* received another 7 percent. Table 19 shows where this 480,534 went. Most of the money was paid in tribute to the royal agents in Languedoc (46.6 percent) and the Parisian bureaucracy (7.9 percent). The archbishop of Narbonne (Cardinal Bonzi) received 2.5 percent personally, and other

[3] See, for example, the accounts of the étape of 1657 in A.D. Hér. C 8511.

Table 14. *Impositions on the diocese of Toulouse in 1677*

(as established by the diocesan assiette)

	livres
1. Share of 429,517 livres for the 'traditional taille' (*aide*, *octroi*, *crue*)	26,144
Fees of diocesan receiver	653*
Total	26,798†
2. Share of 165,000 livres taillon and augmentation du taillon	10,130
3. Share of garrisons (193,182 livres)	11,861
Fees of diocesan receiver	296*
Total	12,157
4. Share of mortes-payes (27,335 livres)	1,698
Fees of diocesan receiver	41*
Total	1,739
5. Share of étape coming to 307,946 livres (which sum includes the 2 deniers per livre paid to the treasurer of the bourse (.833%) and also the share of the city of Toulouse)	19,600
Fees of diocesan receiver	490*
Total	20,090
6. Special charges (*deniers extraordinaires*)	
A. *Don gratuit* of 2,700,000 livres of which 2,045,000 is imposed. To this is added 17,041 for fees of treasurer of the bourse	126,601
B. Share of salaries, debts and affairs of the province, maintenance of frontier fortresses, plus fees of the treasurer of the bourse, making a total of 1,308,421 livres	80,997
C. Share of 'special gifts and deficits' to be held pending royal approval: 151,493 livres	9,301
D. Share of 10,027 livres imposed on the sénéchaussée	2,574
E. Stipend (*gages*) of the *ancien receveur*	1,500*

Table 14. (*cont.*)

	livres
F. Fees of the officers of the Comptes (793 livres by the articles of 1665) and the treasurer-generals of finance (290 livres by deliberation of 1661)	1,083*
Fees of diocesan receiver	5,551*
Total special charges	227,609†
7. Expenses of Estates and diocesan assiette	
A. Share of 75,000 livres for expenses of the Estates and stipends of their officers	4,604
B. Expenses of the assiette	5,480*
C. Interest due on debts audited in 1628	1,046*
D. Interest due on money borrowed in 1660 by order of the Estates of 1659 to raise 300,000 livres for the *don gratuit*	1,052*
E. Upkeep of prévôt of diocese and four archers	800*
F. Extra days put in by diocesan syndic (by regulation of 1654)	804*
G. For diocesan syndic	800*
H. Increment for bridges near the Oratory of Villefranche and the hôpital in Villefranche	600*
I. Interest to four named individuals on sums borrowed in 1675 for cost of raising militia	962*
J. To clerk of diocese for cost of stamp tax, documents drawn up, minutes of assiettes, mailings, summons	50*
K. To inhabitants of Hauterive for cost of passage of militia of the diocese of Rieux by étape	13*
Fees of diocesan receiver	405*
Total for this category	16,619†
Grand total of all the above	315,142
Fee to diocesan receiver for advancing the first third of the money and not collecting until the second term has passed (this item is unusual)	2,853*
Final total impositions	317,995‡

* Included in distribution in table 15.

† *Note*: these are the correct subtotals when sous and deniers are added in.

‡ This is the correct total. The document states 317,979.

Source: A.D. H-G. C 990.

Table 15. *Distribution of sums added-on by the diocese of Toulouse in 1677*

(The total of 24,479 livres is the sum of the items marked (*) in table 14.)

Destination	livres	percent of diocesan taxes
To diocesan receiver	10,289	3.24
To creditors as interest	3,060	0.96
To treasurer-generals and Comptes councillors for 'fees'	2,583	0.81
To diocesan officers for costs of administration of diocese	7,134	2.24
(meeting of assiette)	(5,480)	(1.80)
For public services including charges of local agents (prévôt, bridge repair, compensation for troop costs)	1,413	0.44
Total	24,479	7.69

Source: A.D. H-G. C 990.

Table 16. *Destination of taillon funds 1677*

(Généralité of Montpellier only)

Receipts: 99,120 livres

Expenditures	livres	% of taillon
For the king (to trésorier de l'extraordinaire des guerres)	57,668	58.2
For highway patrols (to prévôt-général of Languedoc and subordinates)	18,650	18.8
To diocesan receivers of taillon	13,085	13.2
To receiver-generals of taillon	8,237	8.3
Exemption of diocese of Narbonne	1,480	1.5
Totals	99,120	100

Source: A.N. H 748[252], 71.

Table 17. *Imposition of the don gratuit in 1677*

2,700,000 livres granted to the king,
minus 315,000 raised from revenue of équivalent tax farm
minus 340,000 borrowed by the Estates
leaves
2,045,000 to be raised by direct taxation
plus 17,041 for fees of treasurer of the bourse
equals
2,062,041 livres actually imposed on the province

Table 18. '*Umbrella*' *categories further broken down*

(province-wide figures)

Categories in question	
'Salaries, debts and affairs'	1,308,421 livres
'Special gifts and deficits'	151,493
'Expenses of the Estates'	75,000
Total	1,534,914

	livres	% of these funds
Destination of Funds		
1. Special Grants to the king	588,841	38.4
A. For public works	(232,000)	(15.1)
(canal project, 200,000)		
(port of Sète, 20,000)		
(frontier fortresses, 12,000)		
B. For military expenses	(356,841)	(23.3)
(raising special troops)		
2. For debt management	337,799	22.0
3. Fees of Treasurer of the Bourse	107,727	7.0
4. Dignitaries and operating expenses	480,534	31.3
5. Unknown	20,013	1.3
Totals	1,534,914	100.0

Table 19. *Distribution of 480,534 livres for Estates' 'dignitaries and operating expenses' in 1677*

Destination:	livres	% of these funds
1. To obtain influence in Paris	37,900	7.9
To contrôleur-général, 6,000 livres		
To secrétaire d'état and his secretary 13,000		
To province's agent in Paris, 1,600		
To Guénégaud and his secretary, 7,300		
To Châteauneuf, 6,000		
To king's grand audencier, 4,000		
2. To royal agents in Languedoc	224,070	46.6
To governor of Languedoc, 120,000		
To governor's guards, 25,170		
To governor's secretary and secretary's agent, 15,500		
To lieutenant-general and his secretary, 48,600		
To intendant and his secretary, 7,300		
To treasurer-generals serving as royal commissioners in the Estates, 6,000		
To king's greffier in the Estates, 1,500		
3. To members of the Estates	204,564	42.6
To president of the Estates, 12,000		
To officers of the Estates, 28,833		
Per diem of all members, 84,975		
To members of the accounting bureau, 9,000		
Stipends of deputies sent to court, 31,000		
Expenditures of deputation to court, 6,396		
Cost of special commission to study the tax system, 10,000		
Lesser employees and petty expenses, 22,360		
4. Other expenditures	14,000	2.9
Alms, 6,500		
Academy of Montpellier (Jesuit), 1,500		
Officers of military headquarters in Narbonne, 6,000		
Totals	480,534	100.0

bishops who cumulated several functions during the sessions could also have received healthy shares.

(D) *Share of the sénéchaussée.* At each session of the Estates, meetings were held of the traditional three sénéchaussées, or thirds of the province (Toulouse, Carcassonne, Beaucaire–Nîmes) which had existed before its subdivision into smaller judicial units. Each sénéchaussée was served by one of the three syndic-generals and used to administer the maintenance of roads and bridges, which were viewed as regional concerns. Expenditures voted by the sénéchaussée were then repartitioned among the member dioceses. The sums were small: 10,027 for Toulouse and 10,240 for Carcassonne in 1677.

Select bibliography

I. MANUSCRIPT SOURCES

In a study of this kind almost all political sources are potentially relevant, and valuable information can turn up anywhere. Only the most useful documents and the most important series are listed here.

A. Bibliothèque Nationale

1. Manuscrits français

4198, 4199, 4200, 4201, correspondence of Le Tellier
6880, state papers of Le Tellier
7686, correspondence of trésoriers de France with their deputies in Paris
8660, manuscript history of Parlement of Toulouse
8668, consistory of Nîmes
14018, biographies of maîtres des requêtes
15621, 17308, 17340, 17341, 17342, 17343, 17346, 17560, 17566, 18552, 18600, administrative papers, mostly of Séguier
15828, 15832, 15833, Protestant affairs
17367–96, 17404, 17405, correspondence of Séguier
17344, 17345, 17355, 18432, 18830, papers on popular uprisings and disturbances
17296, 23159, Parlement of Toulouse
17326, letters from prelates to Séguier
17656, clerical affairs
18483, Cour des Comptes, Aides et Finances of Montpellier
18158, documents from conseil d'état
18231, prices of offices
18510, finances
18601, urban conflicts
20636, 20637, Henri de Maupas du Tour, bishop of Le Puy
22403, 23354, Estates of Languedoc
25025, 25844, newsletters concerning the Fronde
32549, 32550, recherche de la noblesse by Bezons
32785–6, history of the maîtres des requêtes
n.a. 173, finances
n.a. 1081, the intendant Morant in Guyenne
n.a. 7323, various parlements

2. *Collection Baluze*

121, 123, 124, correspondence of Pierre de Marca
291, collection on the Fronde
339, 340, correspondence of Charpentier

3. *Collection Dupuy*

100, Protestant affairs, 1628
380, the revolt of 1632
590, troubles in Villefranche de Rouergue
546, conflicts in Parlement of Toulouse
558, arrêts of Parlement of Toulouse against the élus

4. *Collection Clairambault*

513, mémoires pour la réformation de la justice, 1665

5. *Collection de Languedoc* (*Bénédictins*)

11–26, notices on parishes
71, list of intendants
100, 101, 103–8, biographical and genealogical notices
133–4, Estates of Languedoc
149, parlementaires
153, memoirs on finances

6. *Mélanges Colbert*

102–76 bis, correspondence of Colbert
173, taille 1647
243, état des finances 1677
248, domaines 1675–7
250, 252, gabelles

B. Archives Nationales

H 748, collection Carrière on Estates of Languedoc
H748^{120}, 'Memoires servants au ceremonial des Estats generaux de la province de Languedoc', by Descudier
H748$^{195, 196, 198, 201, 202}$, papers of the syndic-general Lamotte
H748$^{203-16}$, papers of the syndic-general Joubert
H 1688-H 1713, correspondence of Henri d'Aguesseau
G^7 1, correspondence of controler-generals to Languedoc
G^7 294, correspondence of controler-generals from Languedoc
E 204^B, E 359^C, Conseil d'état et des finances, 1662

E 1684, 1692, 1696, 1700, 1706, Conseil d'état, arrêts en commandement
TT 239, 256[B], 260, consistories of Castres, Montpellier, Nîmes
U 799, cases concerning rebellions in Languedoc

C. Archives du Ministère des Affaires Étrangères

Mémoires et Documents, France, 1505, 1632, 1633, 1634, 1636, 1637, correspondence of Richelieu and Mazarin with Languedoc

D. Archives Départementales de la Haute-Garonne

C 161, 263, various papers of the intendants
C 713, 715, 716, 717, 720, 721, 722, 727, accounts rendered by the diocesan syndics to the assiette of Toulouse
C 816, financial directives from Estates to assiettes
C 846, 959, troop payments, étapes
C 958, minutes of assiettes
C 988–90, impositions of the assiettes
C 1006–1011, distribution of taxes on diocese
C 1362, préambules des rôles des impositions
C 2093, communications concerning Estates
C 2131, 2133, troops, lodgings, expenses
C 2301–2331, minutes of Estates of Languedoc, 1632–86
C 3816, minutes of special session of Estates, 1642
B 1879, 1880, 1881, 'Affaires du roi et du public': collection of important arrêts du Parlement
B 974, arrêts du Parlement, April 1674
B 1914–1922, enregistrements (studied through inventory B IV cited below)
1 G 974, archbishopric of Toulouse: political documents
Mss. 147–9, 'Mémoires, collections et remarques du palais', by Malenfant
Ms. 193, list of officers in the Parlement

E. Bibliothèque Municipale de Toulouse

Ms, 603, 'Description géographique de Languedoc' by or for d'Aguesseau

F. Archives Municipales de Toulouse

AA 16, 20, 21, 22, 24, 25, 26, 27, memoirs for deputies to the Estates, important royal directives, etc.
BB 30–40, deliberations of municipal councils, 1629–1682
BB 154–5, proclamations d'édits
BB 181–5, 188, correspondence to capitouls
BB 266, testaments capitulaires
BB 280, annales manuscrits
CC 1528, loans 1644–8
CC 1532, outstanding interest payments

CC 1540, municipal debts 1670
CC 1632, 1633, 1634, 1636, 2031, 2049, 2060, 2062, 2064, 2066, 2067, 2069, 2071, 2073, 2075, 2077, 2080, 2084, 2086, 2088, 2090, 2092, 2093, 2095, 2098, 2100, 2102, 2105, 2107, 2109, 2111, 2113, 2123, 2130, 2132, 2138, 2145, 2149, municipal taxes 1610–84
FF 68, 131, 133, litigation against other authorities and individuals
FF 260, 276, hearings by the court of the capitouls
FF 499, papers from court of the capitouls
FF 609, directives from higher authorities
FF 668, process-serving by huissiers

G. Archives Départementales de l'Hérault

A 22, A 45, A 53, royal edicts and ordinances concerning Languedoc
B 6306, 8727, 8804, 8805, 8806, 9768, 9831, cases in the Cour des Comptes concerning rébellions and gens de guerre
C 161, 162, 163, Protestant troubles, uprising in Privas
C 4056, fortresses
C 7654–7703, minutes of the Estates (used for reference, the set in Toulouse being my primary resource)
C 7655, 7677, cahiers of Estates
C 7720, attendance at Estates
C 7825, entrance of barons to Estates
C 7901, officers of the province
C 8290–2, 8308, 8312–14, accounts of the syndic-generals
C 8511, accounts of the étape 1656–7

H. Archives Municipales de Montpellier

This collection was originally classified in the seventeenth century by Louvet and Joffre according to 'drawers' (*tiroirs*), and the modern reclassification was still incomplete when I used it. Some numbers ('Arm.' for *Armoire*) are therefore cited in the old system and some in the new (double letters).

Arm. A 10, consular elections 1560–1772
Arm. C 401–2, deliberations of the council of twenty-four
AA 5, Continuation du Grand Thalamus (1680–1789)
AA 9, correspondence
AA 11, Thalamus Historique (1598–1662)
BB 197–8, memoirs of Sabatier
BB 207, elections
BB 239, Quatorze de la Chapelle (taxes)
BB 281–5, 380, business of the consulate
EE 956, passage of troops
FF liasse, 'Attroupements et séditions'
FF liasse, 'à classer sans côtes 2': various litigation
FF 533, Falgairolles case

I. Archives Départementales de la Lozère

1. Archives Municipales de Mende (housed in A.D. Loz.)

AA 5, consulate
BB 4–6, 16–17, 19, deliberations and elections of consuls
CC 244–7, municipal accounts
FF 3, memoir against the bishop
FF 24, arrest of inhabitants of Mende
FF 28, litigation in Montpellier
II 12, uprising 1645

2. A.D. Lozère

C 1837, correspondence
318 B[1], litigation: temporality of Mende
324 B[7], litigation: chapter of Mende
G 282–3, 291, 623–9, elections and administration of the consuls from the bishop's perspective
G 1533, Colomb family

J. Archives Départmentales du Gard

1. Archives Municipales de Nîmes (housed in A.D. Gard)

BB 2, election disputes
DD 1, 4, 5, religious conflicts
II 5, ecclesiastical affairs
LL 21, 49, deliberations of the consuls
OO 58, Protestant–Catholic tax disputes
NN 11–17, annual taxes
RR 41–42, accounts of tax collectors
RR 60, Protestant alms

2. A.D. Gard

B 25, office of lieutenant-particulier assesseur-criminel
G 42, bishop's role in consulate, assiette
G 447–450, bishop's cases against the Protestants

K. Archives Municipales d'Albi
(housed in Archives Départementales du Tarn)

AA 7, list of consuls
AA 50, correspondence to deputies at Estates
BB 10–11, consular elections
BB 29–30, BB 111, deliberations of consuls
FF 146–148, conflict with the bishop

Select bibliography

L. Archives Municipales de Carcassonne (*housed in Archives Départementales de l'Aude*)

BB 5–6, deliberations of consuls

II. PRINTED SOURCES AND WORKS PUBLISHED BEFORE 1800

Aguesseau, Henri d', *Mémoire secret pour Mr le Duc de Roquelaure allant commander en Languedoc*, ed. Gaston Vidal. Montpellier, 1958

Albisson, Jean, *Loix municipales et économiques de Languedoc*, 7 vols. Montpellier, 1780–7

André, Ferdinand, ed., *Procès-verbaux des délibérations des états du Gévaudan*, vols. 4–6. Mende, 1878–80.

Aubéry, Antoine, ed., *Mémoires pour l'histoire du Cardinal duc de Richelieu*, 2 vols. Paris, 1660

Avity, Pierre d', *Description générale de l'Europe*, vol. II, by François Ranchin. Paris, 1643

Baudouin, J., *Journal de J. Baudouin sur les grands-jours de Languedoc (1666–1667)*, ed. Paul Le Blanc. Le Puy, 1870

Beaudeau, Jacques, *Armorial des Estats du Languedoc enrichi des élémens de l'art du blason.* Montpellier, 1686

Bejard, *Recueil des tiltres, qualites blazons et armes des seigneurs barons des estats generaux de la province de Languedoc* ..., rev. edn. Lyons, 1657

Blaquière, Henri and Anne de Font-Reaulx, *Documents sur le canal des deux mers et la politique de Colbert en Languedoc.* Toulouse, 1967

Boislisle, Augustin, ed., *Correspondance des contrôleurs généraux des finances avec les intendants des provinces, 1683–1715*, 3 vols. Paris, 1874–97

Brégail, ed., 'M. de Saliné, syndic des capitouls de Toulouse; épisodes de la Fronde', *Revue de Gascogne*, 41 (1900), 42–7

Catel, Guillaume de, *Mémoires de l'histoire du Languedoc.* Toulouse, 1633

Caux, Henry de, *Catalogue général des gentils-hommes de la province de Languedoc* ... Pézenas, 1676

Chapelle et Bachaumont, *Oeuvres*, ed. J. B. Tenant de Latour. Paris, 1854

Chouppes, marquis de, *Mémoires du marquis de Chouppes ... suivis des mémoires du duc de Navailles et de la Valette*, ed. C. Moreau. Paris, 1861

Colbert, Jean-Baptiste, *Lettres, instructions et mémoires*, ed. Pierre Clément, 7 vols. Paris, 1861–73

Controlle des logemens de nosseigneurs des etats de la province de Languedoc, various years. B.N. Lk[14] 81

Daguesseau, Henri-François, *Oeuvres de M. le chancelier d'Aguesseau*, vol. XIII: *Discours sur la vie et la mort de M. d'Aguesseau, conseiller d'état.* Paris, 1789

Delort, André, *Mémoires inédits sur la ville de Montpellier au XVIIe siècle (1621–1673)*, 2 vols. Montpellier, 1876–8

Depping, Georges Bernard, ed., *Correspondance administrative sous le règne de Louis XIV*, 4 vols. Paris, 1850–5

Du Cros, Simon, *Histoire de la vie de Henry dernier duc de Mont-Morency contenant tout ce qu'il a fait de plus remarquable*... Grenoble, 1665

L'État de la France...2 vols. Paris, 1672

Fermat, Pierre, *Oeuvres de Fermat*, ed. Paul Tannery and Charles Henry, vol. II Paris, 1894

Foucault, Nicolas-Joseph, *Mémoires de Nicolas-Joseph Foucault*, ed. F. Baudry Paris, 1862

Gariel, Pierre, *Les gouverneurs du Languedoc*, ed. P. Sainctyon. Montpellier, 1873

Idée de la ville de Montpelier recherchée et présentée aux honestes gens... Montpellier 1665

Germain, Alexandre, ed., 'Chronique inédite de Manguio', *Mémoires de la Société Archéologique de Montpellier*, 7 (1881), 1–100

Grasset, Charles, *Remonstrance faicte à l'ouverture des audiences après la S. Martin en la Cour des Comtes, Aydes et finances de Montpelier*, N.p., 1634. B.N. Lf² 20

Graverol, François, *Notice ou abrégé historique des vingt-deux villes, chefs des dioceses de la province de Languedoc*. Toulouse, 1696

Griselle, Eugène, ed., *État de la maison du Roi Louis XIII... comprenant les années 1601 à 1655*. Paris, 1912

Isambert, François, et al., *Recueil général des anciennes lois françaises depuis l'an 420 jusqu'à la révolution de 1789*, 29 vols. Paris, 1822–33

Laboissière, J. L. de, ed., *Les Commentaires du soldat du Vivarez... suivis... de la relation de la révolte de Roure en 1670*... Privas, 1811

Lamoignon de Basville, Nicolas, *Mémoires pour servir à l'histoire de Languedoc* Amsterdam, 1736

Le Bret, Henry, *Histoire de Montauban*, ed. abbé Marcellin and Gabriel Ruch, 2 vols. Montauban, 1841

Recit de ce qu'a esté et de ce qu'est presentement à Montauban. Montauban, 1701

Locke, John, *Locke's Travels in France 1675–1679*, ed. John Lough. Cambridge, 1953

Louvet, Pierre, *Remarques sur l'histoire de Languedoc*. Toulouse, 1657

Louvreleul, Reverand Père, *Mémoires historiques sur le pays de Gévaudan et sur la ville de Mende*, new edn. Mende, 1825

Lublinskaya, A. D., ed., *Vnutrennyaya politika Frantzyskovo absolutizma, 1633–1649* (*Lettres et mémoires adressés au Chancelier P. Séguier*). Moscow–Leningrad, 1966

Mazarin, Cardinal, *Lettres du Cardinal Mazarin pendant son ministère*, 9 vols. Paris, 1872–1906

Ménard, Léon, *Histoire civile, ecclésiastique et littéraire de la ville de Nîmes*... 7 vols. Nîmes, 1873–5

Histoire des évêques de Nîmes, 2 vols. The Hague, 1737

Mondonville, Madame de, *Contribution à l'histoire religieuse du XVIIe siècle: lettres inédites de Madame de Mondonville (1655–1697)*, ed. Léon Dutil. Paris, 1911

Montchal, Charles, *Mémoires de Mr. de Montchal archevêque de Toulouse contenant des particularitez de la vie et du ministère du Cardinal de Richelieu*. Rotterdam 1718

Mousnier, Roland, ed., *Lettres et mémoires adressés au Chancelier Séguier (1633–1649)*, 2 vols. Paris, 1964
Noguier, Louis, ed., 'Palais épiscopal de Béziers: mobilier des évêques', *Bulletin de la Société Archéologique de Béziers*, 3rd series 1 (1895), 5–36
Olive Du Mesnil, Simon d', *Les Oeuvres*, rev. edn. Lyons, 1657
Peuch, Albert, 'La Vie de nos ancêtres d'après leurs livres de raison ou les Nimois dans la seconde moitié du XVIIe siècle d'après des documents inédits', *Mémoires de l'Académie de Nîmes*, 7th series 7 (1884), 439–90; 7th series 8 (1885), 143–298; 7th series 9 (1886), 331–433
Richelieu, Cardinal, *Lettres, instructions diplomatiques et papiers d'état du Cardinal de Richelieu*, ed. M. Avenel, 8 vols. Paris, 1853–77
Roschach, Ernest, ed., *Histoire générale de Languedoc par Dom Claude Devic et Dom J. Vaissete*, vol. XIV (documents 1643–1789). Toulouse, 1876
Rozoi, Barnabé Farmian de, *Annales de la ville de Toulouse*, 4 vols. Paris, 1771–6
Serres, Pierre, *Histoire de la Cour des Comptes, Aides et Finances de Montpellier*. Montpellier, 1878
Serroni, Hyacinthe, *Sermon prononcé dans l'église de Notre-Dame des Tables de la ville de Montpelier, à l'ouverture des états généraux de la province de Languedoc* ... Montpellier, 1670
Sévigné, Madame de, *Lettres*, ed. Gérard-Gailly (Bibliothèque de la Pléiade), 3 vols. Paris, 1953–63
La souveraineté des Roys à l'ouverture du parlement de Tolose. N.p., 1646. B.N. Lf[25] 70
Wolff, Philippe, ed., *Documents de l'histoire du Languedoc*. Toulouse, 1969
Young, Arthur, *Young's Travels in France during the Years 1787, 1788, 1789*, ed. M. Betham-Edwards. London, 1913

III. SECONDARY WORKS: GENERAL AND THEORETICAL

Anderson, Perry, *Lineages of the Absolutist State*. London, 1974
Passages from Antiquity to Feudalism. London, 1974
André, Louis, *Michel Le Tellier et l'organisation de l'armée monarchique*. Montpellier, 1906.
Ariazza, Armand, 'Mousnier and Barber: the Theoretical Underpinning of the "Society of Orders" in Early Modern Europe', *Past and Present*, 89 (1980), 39–57
Armstrong, John A., 'Old-Regime Governors: Bureaucratic and Patrimonial Attitudes', *Comparative Studies in Social History*, 14 (1972), 2–29
Asher, Eugene L., *The Resistance to the Maritime Classes: Survival of Feudalism in the France of Louis XIV*. Berkeley, 1960
Aston, Trevor, ed., *Crisis in Europe, 1560–1660*. New York, 1965
Avenel, vicomte d', *Richelieu et la monarchie absolue*, 4 vols., 2nd edn. Paris, 1895
Aymard, Maurice, 'L'Europe moderne: féodalité ou féodalités?', *Annales E.S.C.*, 36 (1981), 426–35
'From Feudalism to Capitalism in Italy: the Case that Doesn't Fit', *Review*, 6 (1982), 131–208

Bastard d'Estang, vicomte de, *Les Parlements de France: essai historique*, 2 vols. Paris, 1857

Baxter, Douglas, *Servants of the Sword: French Intendants of the Army, 1630–1670*. Urbana, 1976

Bercé, Yves-Marie, 'De la Criminalité aux troubles sociaux: la noblesse rurale du sud-ouest de la France sous Louis XIII', *Annales du Midi*, 76 (1964), 41–59

Fête et révolte: des mentalités populaires du XVIe au XVIIIe siècle. Paris, 1976

Histoire des Croquants: étude des soulèvements populaires au XVIIe siècle dans le sud-ouest de la France, 2 vols. Geneva. 1974

Bitton, Davis, *The French Nobility in Crisis, 1560–1640*. Stanford, 1969

Blet, Pierre, *Le Clergé de France et la monarchie: étude sur les assemblées générales du clergé de 1615 à 1666*, 2 vols. Rome, 1959

Bloch, Marc, *Feudal Society*, tr. L. A. Manyon. Chicago, 1961

French Rural History: an Essay on its Basic Characteristics, tr. Janet Sondheimer. Berkeley, 1966

Bois, Guy, *Crise du féodalisme*. Paris, 1976

Bonney, Richard J. 'The Intendants of Richelieu and Mazarin'. Ph.D. diss. Oxford, 1973

The King's Debts: Finance and Politics in France 1589–1661. Oxford, 1981

Political Change in France under Richelieu and Mazarin 1624–1661. Oxford, 1978

Boscher, J. F., ed., *French Government and Society, 1500–1850: Essays in Memory of Alfred Cobban*. London, 1973

Braudel, Fernand, *The Mediterranean and the Mediterranean World in the Age of Philip II*, tr. Siân Reynolds, 2 vols. New York, 1972

Brenner, Robert, 'Agrarian Class Structure and Economic Development in Pre-Industrial Europe', followed by a symposium and the author's reply, *Past and Present*, 70, 78, 79, 80, 85, 97 (1976–82)

Buisseret, David, 'A Stage in the Development of Intendants: the Reign of Henry IV', *Historical Journal*, 9 (1966), 27–38

Sully and the Growth of Centralized Government in France. London, 1968

Castan, Nicole, *Justice et répression en Languedoc à l'époque des lumières*. Paris, 1980

Castan, Yves, *Honnêteté et relations sociales en Languedoc (1715–1780)*. Paris, 1974

Centre d'Études et de Recherches Marxistes, *Sur le féodalisme*. Paris, 1971

Charmeil, Jean-Paul, *Les Trésoriers de France à l'époque de la Fronde: contribution à l'histoire de l'administration financière sous l'ancien régime*. Paris, 1964

Chauleur, Andrée, 'Le rôle des traitants dans l'administration financière de la France de 1643 à 1653', *XVIIe siècle*, 65 (1964), 16–49

Chaunu, Pierre and Richard Gascon, *Histoire économique et sociale de la France*, vol. 1; part 1: *L'État et la ville*. Paris, 1977

Church, William F., *Louis XIV in Historical Thought*. New York, 1976

Clamageran, Jean-Joseph, *Histoire de l'impôt en France*, 3 vols. Paris, 1867–76

Cole, Charles Woolsey, *Colbert and a Century of French Mercantilism*, 2 vols. New York, 1939

Collins, James B., 'Sur l'histoire fiscale du XVIIe siècle: les impôts directs en Champagne entre 1595 et 1635', *Annales E.S.C.*, 34 (1979), 325–47

Corvisier, André, *L'Armée française de la fin du XVIIe siècle au ministère de Choiseul*, 2 vols. Paris, 1964

Critchley, John, *Feudalism*. London, 1978

Cummings, Mark, 'The Social Impact of the Paulette: the Case of the Parlement of Paris', *Canadian Journal of History*, 15 (1980), 329–54

Dent, Julian, 'An Aspect of the Crisis of the Seventeenth Century: the Collapse of the Financial Administration of the French Monarchy (1653–1661)', *Economic History Review*, 20 (1967), 241–56

Crisis in Finance: Crown, Financiers and Society in Seventeenth-Century France. New York, 1973

Dessert, Daniel, 'Pouvoir et finance au XVIIe siècle: la fortune du Cardinal Mazarin', *Revue d'histoire moderne et contemporaine*, 23 (1976), 161–81

Dessert, Daniel and Jean-Louis Journet, 'Le Lobby Colbert: un royaume, ou une affaire de famille?', *Annales E.S.C.*, 30 (1975), 1303–36

Dethan, Georges, *Gaston d'Orléans: conspirateur et prince charmant*. Paris, 1959

Dewald, Jonathan, *The Formation of a Provincial Nobility: the Magistrates of the Parlement of Rouen, 1499–1610*. Princeton, 1980

'Magistracy and Political Opposition at Rouen: a Social Context', *Sixteenth Century Journal*, 5 (1974), 66–78

Deyon, Pierre, *Amiens, capitale provinciale: étude sur la société urbaine au 17e siècle*. Paris, 1967

'Rapports entre la noblesse française et la monarchie absolue', *Revue historique*, 231 (1964), 341–56

Deyon, Solange, *Du loyalisme au refus: les Protestants français et leur député général entre la Fronde et la Révocation*. Villeneuve d'Ascq, 1976

Dictionnaire d'histoire et de géographie ecclésiastique. Paris, 1912–

Dobb, Maurice, *Studies in the Development of Capitalism*, rev. edn. New York, 1963

Doucet, Roger, *Les Institutions de la France au XVIe siècle*, 2 vols. Paris, 1948

Duby, Georges and Armand Wallon, eds., *Histoire de la France rurale*, vol. II: *L'Âge classique des paysans 1340–1789*. Paris, 1975

Duby, Georges, *The Three Orders: Feudal Society Imagined*, tr. Arthur Goldhammer. Chicago, 1980

Du Plessis, Robert S., 'From Demesne to World-System: a Critical Review of the Literature on the Transition from Feudalism to Capitalism', *Radical History Review*, 4 (1977), 3–41

Durand, Yves, ed., *Hommage à Roland Mousnier: clientèles et fidélités en Europe à l'époque moderne*. Paris, 1981

Esmonin, Edmond, *Études sur la France des XVIIe et XVIIIe siècles*. Paris, 1964

La Taille en Normandie au temps de Colbert (1661–1683). Paris, 1913

Feillet, Alphonse, *La Misère au temps de la Fronde et Saint Vincent de Paul*, 5th edn. Paris, 1886

Foisil, Madeleine, *La Révolte des Nu-pieds et les révoltes normandes de 1639*. Paris, 1970

Ford, Franklin, L., *Robe and Sword: the Regrouping of the French Aristocracy after Louis XIV*, rev. edn. Cambridge, Mass., 1962

Gams, P. Pius Bonifacius, ed., *Series episcoporum ecclesiae catholicae quotquot innotuerunt a beato petro apostolo*. Ratisbon, 1873

George, C. H., 'The Making of the English Bourgeoisie, 1500–1750', *Science and Society*, 35 (1971), 385–414

Germain-Martin, Louis and Marcel Bezançon, *Histoire du crédit public sous Louis XIV*. Paris, 1911

Godard, Charles, *Les Pouvoirs des intendants sous Louis XIV particulièrement dans les pays d'élections de 1661 à 1715*. Paris, 1901

Goubert, Pierre, *L'Ancien régime*, 2 vols. Paris, 1969–73

Beauvais et le Beauvaisis de 1600 à 1730: contribution à l'histoire sociale de la France du XVIIe siècle. 2 vols. Paris, 1960

Clio parmi les hommes: recueil d'articles. Paris, 1976

Louis XIV et vingt millions de Français. Paris, 1966

Gresset, Maurice, *Gens de justice à Besançon de la conquête par Louis XIV à la Révolution française 1674–1789*, 2 vols. Paris, 1980

Guerreau, Alain, *Le Féodalisme: un horizon théorique*. Paris, 1980

Guéry, Alain, 'Les Finances de la monarchie française sous l'ancien régime', *Annales E.S.C.*, 33 (1978), 216–39

Haag, Eugène and Emile, *La France Protestante*, 10 vols. Paris, 1846–59

Hamscher, Albert, *The Parlement of Paris after the Fronde, 1653–1673*. Pittsburgh, Pa., 1976

Hanotaux, Gabriel, *Origines de l'institution des intendants des provinces, d'après les documents inédits*. Paris, 1884

Harding, Robert R., *Anatomy of a Power Elite: the Provincial Governors of Early Modern France*. New Haven, 1978

Harsin, Paul, *Crédit public et banque d'état en France du XVIe au XVIIIe siècle*. Paris, 1933

Hartung, Fritz and Roland Mousnier, 'Quelques problèmes concernant la monarchie absolue', *Relazioni X Congresso Internazionale de Scienze Storiche*. Florence, 1955, pp. 3–55

Hatton, Ragnhild, ed., *Louis XIV and Absolutism*. London, 1976

Hindess, Barry and Paul Q. Hirst, *Pre-Capitalist Modes of Production*. London, 1975

L'Histoire sociale, sources et méthodes: colloque de l'École Normale Supérieure de Saint-Cloud, Mai 1965. Paris, 1967

Hobsbawm, E. J., 'Class Consciousness in History', in *Aspects of History and Class Consciousness*, ed. István Mészaros. London, 1971

Hobsbawm, Eric J., ed., *Karl Marx, Pre-Capitalist Economic Formations*. New York, 1965

Holton, Robert J., 'Marxist Theories of Social Change and the Transition from Feudalism to Capitalism', *Theory and Society*, 10 (1981), 833–67

Hurt, John J., 'Les Offices au parlement de Bretagne sous le règne de Louis XIV: aspects financiers', *Revue d'histoire moderne et contemporaine*, 23 (1976), 3–31

'The Parlement of Brittany and the Crown 1665–1675', *French Historical Studies*, 4 (1965–66), 411–33

'La Politique du parlement de Bretagne (1661–1675)', *Annales de Bretagne*, 81 (1974), 105–30.

Jacquart, Jean, *La Crise rurale en Île-de-France 1550–1670*. Paris, 1974

Kettering, Sharon, 'The Causes of the Judicial Frondes', *Canadian Journal of History*, 17 (1982), 275–306

Judicial Politics and Urban Revolt in Seventeenth-Century France: the Parlement of Aix, 1629–1659. Princeton, 1978

Kiernan, V. G., *State and Society in Europe 1550–1650*. Oxford, 1980

Kossmann, Ernst H., *La Fronde*. Leiden, 1954

Kula, Witold, *An Economic Theory of the Feudal System: Towards a Model of the Polish Economy 1500–1800*, tr. Lawrence Garner. London, 1976

Labatut, Jean-Pierre, *Les Ducs et pairs de France au XVIIe siècle: étude sociale*. Paris, 1972

Labrousse, Élisabeth, *Pierre Bayle*, 2 vols. The Hague, 1958

Labrousse, Ernest, et. al., *Histoire économique et sociale de la France*: vol. II: *Des derniers temps de l'âge seigneurial aux préludes de l'âge industriel (1660–1789)*. Paris, 1970

Lassaigne, Jean-Dominique, *Les Assemblées de la noblesse de France aux XVIIe et XVIIIe siècles*. Paris, 1965

Lavisse, Ernest, *Histoire de France depuis les origines jusqu'à la Révolution*, vol. VII, parts 1 and 2. Paris, 1906–11

Lebigre, Arlette, *Les Grands Jours d'Auvergne: désordres et répressions au XVIIe siècle*. Paris, 1976

Lefebvre, Pierre, 'Aspects de la "fidélité" en France au XVIIe siècle: le cas des agents des princes de Condé', *Revue historique*, 250 (1973), 59–106

Le Roy Ladurie, Emmanuel, ed., *Histoire de la France rurale*: vol. II: *L'Âge classique des paysans 1340–1789*. Paris, 1975

Le Roy Ladurie, Emmanuel, *Montaillou, village occitan de 1294 à 1324*. Paris, 1975

Le territoire de l'historien, 2 vols. Paris, 1973–8

Le Roy Ladurie, Emmanuel and Michel Morineau, *Histoire économique et sociale de la France*: vol. I, part 2: *Paysannerie et croissance*. Paris, 1977

Livet, Georges, *L'Intendance d'Alsace sous Louis XIV 1648–1715*. Paris, 1956

Lublinskaya, A. D., 'The Contemporary Bourgeois Conception of Absolute Monarchy', *Economy and Society*, 1 (1972), 65–92

French Absolutism: the Crucial Phase 1620–1629. Cambridge, 1968

'Popular Masses and the Social Relations of the Epoch of Absolutism: Methodology of Research', *Economy and Society*, 2 (1973), 343–75

Lüthy, Herbert, *La Banque protestante en France de la révocation de l'Édit de Nantes à la Révolution*, 2 vols. Paris, 1959–61

Major, J. Russell, 'Henry IV and Guyenne: a Study Concerning the Origins of Royal Absolutism', *French Historical Studies*, 4 (1965–6), 363–83

'Noble Income, Inflation, and the Wars of Religion in France', *American Historical Review*, 86 (1981), 21–48

Representative Government in Early Modern France. New Haven, 1980

Representative Institutions in Renaissance France 1421–1559. Madison, Wisc., 1960

Malettke, Klaus, *Opposition und Konspiration unter Ludwig XIV*. Göttingen, 1976

Mandrou, Robert, *Classes et luttes de classe en France au début du XVIIe siècle*. Messina, 1965

Introduction à la France moderne; essai de psychologie historique 1500–1640. Paris, 1961

Louis XIV en son temps 1661–1715. Paris, 1973

Marion, Marcel, *Dictionnaire des institutions de la France aux XVIIe et XVIIIe siècles*. Paris, 1923, rep. 1968

Meuvret, Jean, *Études d'histoire économique: recueil d'articles*. Paris, 1971

Le problème des subsistances à l'époque de Louis XIV, 2 vols. Paris, 1978

Meyer, Jean, *La Noblesse bretonne au XVIIIe siècle*, 2 vols. Paris, 1966

Moote, A. Lloyd, 'The French Crown versus its Judicial and Financial Officials, 1615–83', *Journal of Modern History*, 34 (1962), 146–60

'The Parlementary Fronde and Seventeenth-Century Robe Solidarity', *French Historical Studies*, 2 (1962), 330–55

The Revolt of the Judges: the Parlement of Paris and the Fronde 1643–1652. Princeton, 1971

Mougel, François-Charles, 'La Fortune des Bourbon-Conty, revenus et gestion 1655–1791', *Revue d'histoire moderne et contemporaine*, 18 (1971), 30–49

Mours, Samuel, *Le Protestantisme en France au XVIIe siècle*. Paris, 1967

Mousnier, Roland, 'Les Concepts d'"Ordres", d'"états", de "fidélité" et de "monarchie absolue" en France de la fin du XVe siècle à la fin du XVIIIe', *Revue historique*, 247 (1972), 289–312

Les XVIe et XVIIe siècles. 4th edn. Paris, 1965

Fureurs paysannes: les paysans dans les révoltes du XVIIe siècle. Paris, 1967

Les Hiérarchies sociales de 1450 à nos jours. Paris, 1969

Les Institutions de la France sous la monarchie absolue, 1598–1789, 2 vols. Paris, 1974–80

'Monarchie contre aristocratie dans la France du XVIIe siècle', *XVIIe siècle*, 31 (1956), pp. 377–81

La Plume, la faucille et le marteau: institutions et société en France du moyen âge à la Révolution. Paris, 1970

Problèmes de stratification sociale: actes du colloque internationale (1966). Paris, 1968

Recherches sur la stratification sociale à Paris aux XVIIe et XVIIIe siècles: l'échantillon de 1634, 1635, 1636. Paris, 1976

'Les Survivances médiévales dans la France du XVIIe siècle', *XVIIe siècle*, 106–7 (1975), 59–76

La Vénalité des offices sous Henri IV et Louis XIII. 2nd edn. Paris, 1971

Navereau, Lieut. André Eugène, *Le Logement et les ustensiles des gens de guerre de 1439 à 1789*. Poitiers, 1924

Pagès, Georges, *La Monarchie d'ancien régime en France (de Henri IV à Louis XIV)*. 4th edn. Paris, 1946

'La Vénalité des offices dans l'ancienne France', *Revue historique*, 169 (1932), 477–95

Pagès, Georges, ed., *Études sur l'histoire administrative et sociale de l'ancien régime*. Paris, 1938

Parker, David, *La Rochelle and the French Monarchy: Conflict and Order in Seventeenth-century France*. London, 1980

'The Social Foundations of French Absolutism, 1610–1630', *Past and Present*, 53 (1971), 67–89

Pillorget, René, *Les Mouvements insurrectionnels de Provence entre 1596 et 1715*. Paris, 1975

Porchnev, Boris, *Les Soulèvements populaires en France de 1623 à 1648*. Paris, 1963

Rabb, Theodore K., *The Struggle for Stability in Early Modern Europe*. New York, 1975

Ranum, Orest A., 'Courtesy, Absolutism, and the Rise of the French State, 1630–1660', *Journal of Modern History*, 52 (1980), 426–51

Richelieu and the Councillors of Louis XIII: a Study of the Secretaries of State and Superintendants of Finance in the Ministry of Richelieu 1635–1642. Oxford, 1963

'Richelieu and the Great Nobility: Some Aspects of Early Modern Political Motives', *French Historical Studies*, 3 (1963–4), 184–204

Richard, Guy, 'Un aspect particulier de la politique économique et sociale de la monarchie au XVIIe siècle: Richelieu, Colbert, La Noblesse et le Commerce', *XVIIe siècle*, 49 (1960), 11–41

Richet, Denis, 'La Formation des grands serviteurs de l'état (fin XVIe–début XVIIe siècle)', *L'Arc*, 65 (1976), 54–61

La France moderne: l'esprit des institutions. Paris, 1973

Robin, Régine, *La Société française en 1789: Semur-en-Auxois*. Paris, 1970.

Roche, Daniel and C. F. Labrousse, eds., *Ordres et classes, colloque d'histoire sociale, Saint-Cloud, 24-25 mai 1967*. Paris, 1973

Rotelli, Ettore, 'La Structure sociale dans l'itinéraire historiographique de Roland Mousnier', *Revue d'histoire économique et sociale*, 51 (1973), 145–82

Rothkrug, Lionel, *Opposition to Louis XIV: the Political and Social Origins of the French Enlightenment*. Princeton, 1965

Roupnel, Gaston, *La Ville et la campagne au XVIIe siècle: étude sur les populations du pays dijonnais*. Paris, 1955

Saint-Jacob, Pierre de, *Les paysans de la Bourgogne du Nord au dernier siècle de l'Ancien Régime*. Dijon, 1960

Salmon, J. H. M., *Society in Crisis: France in the Sixteenth Century*. New York, 1975

'Venal Office and Popular Sedition in Seventeenth-Century France: A Review of a Controversy', *Past and Present*, 37 (1967), 21–43

Scoville, Warren C., *The Persecution of Huguenots and French Economic Development 1680–1720*. Berkeley, 1960

Shennan, J. H., *The Parlement of Paris*. Ithaca, New York, 1968

Stoianovich, Traian, *French Historical Method: the Annales Paradigm*. Ithaca, New York, 1976

Sweezy, Paul, et al., *The Transition from Feudalism to Capitalism*. London, 1976

Temple, Nora, 'The Control and Exploitation of French Towns during the Ancien Régime', *History*, 51 (1966), 16–34

Thompson, E. P., *The Poverty of Theory and Other Essays*. London, 1978

Tilly, Charles, ed., *The Formation of Nation-states in Western Europe*. Princeton, 1975

Tocqueville, Alexis de, *The Old Régime and the French Revolution*, tr. Stuart Gilbert. Garden City, New York., 1955

Vassal-Reig, Charles, *La Guerre en Roussillon sous Louis XIII (1635–1639)*. Paris, 1934

Vindry, Fleury, *Les Parlementaires français au XVIe siècle*, 2 vols. Paris, 1912

Weber, Max, *The Theory of Social and Economic Organization*, tr. A. M. Henderson and Talcott Parsons. New York, 1964

Westrich, Sal Alexander, *The Ormée of Bordeaux: a Revolution during the Fronde*. Baltimore, 1972

Wolf, John B., *Louis XIV*. New York, 1968

Wolfe, Martin, *The Fiscal System of Renaissance France*. New Haven, 1972

Wood, James B., *The Nobility of the Election of Bayeux, 1463–1666: Continuity Through Change*. Princeton, 1980

Zeller, Gaston, 'L'Administration monarchique avant les intendants', *Revue historique*, 197 (1947), 180–215

Les Institutions de la France au XVIe siècle. Paris, 1948

IV. SECONDARY WORKS CONCERNING LANGUEDOC

This list includes only a selection of the more important, useful, or representative works from the multitude of local and regional studies having some bearing on the subject.

Adher, J., 'La "préparation" des séances des États de Languedoc'; *Annales du Midi*, 25 (1913), 453–71

Aigrefeuille, Charles d', *Histoire de la ville de Montpellier*, ed. de la Pijardière. 4 vols., Montpellier, 1875–82

Angelras, Armand, *Le Consulat nîmois: histoire de son organisation*. Nîmes, 1912

Appolis, Emile, 'Les États de Languedoc au XVIIIe siècle: comparaison avec les états de Bretagne', in *L'Organisation corporative du moyen âge à la fin de L'Ancien Régime*. Louvain, 1937

Un pays Languedocien au milieu du XVIIIe siècle: le diocèse civil de Lodève, étude administrative et économique. Albi, 1951

Armengaud, André and Robert Lafont, eds., *Histoire d'Occitanie*. Paris, 1979

Armogathe, Jean-Robert and Philippe Joutaud, 'Bâville et la Guerre des Camisards', *Revue d'histoire moderne et contemporaine*, 19 (1972), 45–72

Arnaud, A., 'Fonctions et juridiction consulaires à Montpellier aux XVIIe et XVIIIe siècles', *Annales du Midi*, 31 (1919), 35–67; 32 (1920), 129–56

Arnaud, E., *Histoire des protestants du Vivarais et du Velay, pays de Languedoc, de la réforme à la Révolution*. Paris, 1888

Astre, Florentin, *De l'administration publique en Languedoc avant 1789*. Toulouse, 1874

'Les Intendants du Languedoc', *Mémoires de l'Académie des Sciences, Inscriptions et Belles-Lettres de Toulouse*, 5th series 3 (1859), 7–36; 5th series 4 (1860), 421–43; 5th series 5 (1861), 102–24; 6th series 6 (1868), 20–55; 7th series 3 (1871), 31–54

Azema, Xavier, *Un Prélat janséniste: Louis Foucquet évêque et comte d'Agde (1656–1702)*. Paris, 1963

Balincourt, Comte E. de, *Un épisode ignoré des troubles de Nîmes en Juin 1657*. Nîmes, 1906

Balmelle, Marius and Suzanne Pouget, *Histoire de Mende*. Mende, 1947

Barrière-Flavy, C., *La Chronique criminelle d'une grande province sous Louis XIV*. Paris, 1926

'Les Prisons de la conciergerie du palais à Toulouse aux XVIIe et XVIIIe siècles', *Revue historique de Toulouse*, 10 (1923), 161–8

Bastard d'Estang, vicomte de, *Du Parlement de Toulouse et de ses jurisconsultes*. Paris, 1854

Bastier, Jean, *La Féodalité au siècle des lumières dans la région de Toulouse (1730–1790)*. Paris, 1975

'Une Résistance fiscale du Languedoc sous Louis XIII: la querelle du franc-alleu', *Annales du Midi*, 86 (1974), 253–73

Baumel, Jean, *Montpellier au cours des XVIe et XVIIe siècles: les guerres de religion (1510–1685)*. Montpellier, 1976

Beik, William, 'Magistrates and Popular Uprisings in France before the Fronde: the Case of Toulouse', *Journal of Modern History*, 46 (1974), 585–608

'Two Intendants Face a Popular Revolt: Social Unrest and the Structure of Absolutism in 1645', *Canadian Journal of History*, 9 (1974), 243–62

Bellaud-Dessalles, Mme, *Histoire de Béziers des origines à la Révolution française*. Béziers, 1929

Berlanstein, Lenard R., *The Barristers of Toulouse in the Eighteenth Century (1740–1793)*. Baltimore, 1975

Bernet, Gabriel, 'Jean Giscard, marchand drapier toulousain sous Louis XIV', *Annales du Midi*, 91 (1979), pp. 53–70

Bisson, Thomas N., *Assemblies and Representation in Languedoc in the Thirteenth Century*. Princeton, 1964

Blanchard, Anne, 'De Pézenas à Montpellier: transfert d'une ville de souveraineté (XVIIe siècle)', *Revue d'histoire moderne et contemporaine*, 12 (1965), 35–49

Blaquière, abbé Constant, *Histoire des évêques de Lodève: Plantavit de la Pause*. Montpellier, 1910

Boissonnade, P., 'Colbert, son système et les entreprises industrielles d'état en Languedoc (1661–1683)', *Annales du Midi*, 14 (1902), 5–49

'L'Essai de restauration des ports et de la vie maritime en Languedoc de 1593 à 1661 et son échec', *Annales du Midi*, 46 (1934), 98–121

'L'État, l'organisation et la crise de l'industrie Languedocienne pendant les soixante premières années du XVIIe siècle', *Annales du Midi*, 21 (1909), 169–97

'La Production et le commerce des céréales des vins et des eaux-de-vie en Languedoc dans la seconde moitié du XVIIe siècle', *Annales du Midi*, 17 (1905), 329–60

'La Restauration et le développement de l'industrie en Languedoc du temps de Colbert', *Annales du Midi*, 18 (1906), 441–72

Boudon, Albert, *La Sénéchaussée présidiale du Puy*. Valence, 1908

Boulenger, Jacques, *Les Protestants à Nîmes au temps de l'édit de Nantes*. Paris, 1903

Bremond, Alphonse, *Nobiliaire toulousain: inventaire général des titres probants de noblesse et de dignités nobiliaires*, 2 vols. Toulouse, 1863

Brenac, Madeleine, 'Toulouse, centre de lutte contre le protestantisme au XVIIe siècle', *Annales du Midi*, 77 (1965), 31–45

Brink, James Eastgate, 'The Estates of Languedoc: 1515–1560'. Ph.D. diss., University of Washington, 1974

Buisseret, David, 'Les Précurseurs des intendants du Languedoc', *Annales du Midi*, 80 (1968), 80–8

Burdin, Gustave de, *Documents historiques sur la province de Gévaudan*, 2 vols. Toulouse, 1846–7

Caldicott, C. E. J., 'Le Gouvernement de Gaston d'Orléans en Languedoc (1644–1660) et la carrière de Molière', *XVIIe siècle*, 116 (1977), 17–42

Cambon de Lavalette, Jules, *La Chambre de l'édit de Languedoc*. Paris, 1872

Carrière, Charles, 'La Draperie Languedocienne dans la seconde moitié du XVIIe siècle: contribution à l'étude de la conjoncture levantine', in *Conjoncture économique, structures sociales: Hommage à Ernest Labrousse*. Paris, 1974

Carrière, vicomte de, *Les Officiers des États de la province de Languedoc*. Paris, 1865

Caster, Gilles, *Le Commerce du pastel et de l'épicerie à Toulouse de 1450 environ à 1561*. Toulouse, 1962

Charpentier, Léon, *Un Évêque de l'ancien régime: Louis-Joseph de Grignan (1650–1722)*. Arras, 1899

Chaussinand-Nogaret, Guy, *Les Financiers de Languedoc au XVIIIe siècle*. Paris, 1970

Clarke, Jack Alden, *Huguenot Warrior: the Life and Times of Henri de Rohan 1579–1638*. The Hague, 1966

Cochin, Augustin, 'Les Églises calvinistes du Midi, le Cardinal Mazarin et Cromwell', *Revue des questions historiques*, 76 (1904), 109–56

Contrasty, Jean, *Histoire de la cité de Rieux-Volvestre et de ses évêques*. Toulouse, 1936

Coppolani, Jean, *Toulouse au XXe siècle*. Toulouse, 1963

Coquelle, 'La Sédition de Montpellier en 1645, d'après des documents inédits des Archives des Affaires Étrangères', *Annales du Midi*, 20 (1908), 66–78

Corbière, Philippe, 'Histoire du siège de Montpellier en 1622 sous Louis XIII', *Académie des Sciences de Montpellier: Mémoires Section des Lettres*, 4 (1864–69), 187–282

'Démolition du Grand Temple des Réformés à Montpellier (1682)', *Bulletin de la Société de l'Histoire du Protestantisme français*, 25 (1876), 21–36

Histoire de l'Église Réformée de Montpellier depuis son origine jusqu'à nos jours. Montpellier, 1861

Crozes, Hippolyte, *Le Diocèse d'Albi: ses évêques et archevêques*. Toulouse, 1878

Delcambre, Étienne, *Contribution à l'histoire des États provinciaux: Les États du Velay des origines à 1642*. St-Etienne, 1938

Dermigny, Louis, 'La Banque à Montpellier au XVIIIe siècle', *Annales du Midi*, 93 (1981), 17–49

Naissance et croissance d'un grand port, Sète de 1666 à 1880. Montpellier, 1955

Descimon, Robert, 'Structures d'un marché de draperie dans le Languedoc au milieu du XVIe siècle', *Annales E.S.C.*, 30 (1975), 1414–46

Devic, Dom Claude and Dom J. Vaissete, *Histoire générale de Languedoc*, new edn, vols. XII–XIV. Toulouse, 1876–89

Dognon, Paul, *Les Institutions politiques et administratives du pays de Languedoc du XIIIe siècle aux guerres de religion*. Toulouse, 1896

Doublet, Georges, *Un ami de Mgr de Caulet: Jean du Ferrier Toulousain d'après ses mémoires inédits*. Toulouse, 1906

Dubédat, Jean-Baptiste, *Histoire du Parlement de Toulouse*, 2 vols. Paris, 1885

Du Mège, Alexandre, *Biographie toulousaine, ou dictionnaire historique*. Paris, 1823

Dutil, Léon, *L'État économique du Languedoc à la fin de l'ancien régime*. Paris, 1911

'La Fabrique de bas à Nîmes au XVIIIe siècle', *Annales du Midi*, 17 (1905), 218–51

'L'Industrie de la soie à Nîmes jusqu'en 1789', *Revue d'histoire moderne*, 10 (1908), 318–43

Estèbe, Janine, 'La Bourgeoisie marchande et la terre à Toulouse au XVIe siècle (1519–1560)', *Annales du Midi*, 76 (1964), 457–67

'Le Marché toulousain des étoffes entre 1519 et 1560', *Annales du Midi*, 75 (1963), 183–94

Eyssette, Alexandre, *Histoire administrative de Beaucaire*. Beaucaire, 1884

Falgairolle, Prosper, *Une famille de l'ancienne France: les Baudan à Nîmes et à Montpellier pendant quatre siècles*. Cavaillon, 1926

Fessenden, Nicholas B., 'Épernon and Guyenne: Provincial Politics under Louis XIII', Ph.D. diss., Columbia, 1972

Forster, Robert, *The Nobility of Toulouse in the Eighteenth Century: a Social and Economic Study*. Baltimore, 1960

Frêche, Georges, 'Compoix, propriété foncière, fiscalité et démographie historique en pays de taille réelle (XVIe–XVIIIe siècles)', *Revue d'histoire moderne et contemporaine*, 18 (1971), 321–53

Toulouse et la région Midi-Pyrénées au siècle des lumières (vers 1670–1789). Paris, 1974

Frêche, Georges and Geneviève, *Les Prix des grains, des vins et des légumes à Toulouse (1486–1868)*. Paris, 1967

Gachon, Paul, *Les États de Languedoc et l'édit de Béziers (1632)*. Paris, 1887

Histoire de Languedoc. Paris, 1921

Quelques préliminaires de la révocation de l'édit de Nantes en Languedoc (1661–1685). Toulouse, 1899

Garrisson-Estèbe, Janine, *Protestants du Midi 1559–1598*. Toulouse, 1980.

Germain, Alexandre, 'Les Commencements du règne de Louis XIV et la Fronde à Montpellier', *Académie des Sciences de Montpellier: Mémoires Section des Lettres*, 3 (1859–63), 579–602

Histoire de l'église de Nîmes, 2 vols. Nîmes, 1838–42

Histoire du commerce de Montpellier antérieurement à l'ouverture du Port de Cette, 2 vols. Montpellier, 1861

Gilles, Henri, *Les États de Languedoc au XVe siècle*. Toulouse, 1965

'Fermat magistrat', *Actes du XXIe Congrès de la Fédération des Sociétés Académiques et Savantes de Languedoc-Pyrénées-Gascogne*. Toulouse, 1966

Gorlier, Pierre, *Le Vigan à travers les siècles*, new edn. Montpellier, 1970

Granat, O., 'L'Industrie de la draperie à Castres au dix-septième siècle et les "Ordonnances" de Colbert', *Annales du Midi*, 10 (1898), 446–57; 11 (1899), 56–67

Grasset-Morel, 'Les Consuls et l'hôtel de ville de Montpellier', *Mémoires de la Société Archéologique de Montpellier*, 2nd series 1 (1894–99), 17–76

Guiraud, Louise, 'La Réforme à Montpellier', *Mémoires de la Société Archéologique de Montpellier*, 2nd series 6–7 (1918)

Henry, l'abbé Paul-Émile, *François Bosquet intendant de Guyenne et de Languedoc, évêque de Lodève et de Montpellier*. Paris, 1889

Hufton, Olwen H., 'Attitudes towards Authority in Eighteenth-Century Languedoc', *Social History*, 3 (1978), 281–302

Jolibois, Émile, 'Troubles dans la ville d'Albi pendant l'épiscopat de Gaspard de Daillon du Lude', *Revue du Tarn*, 9 (1892), 49–61, 135–45

Joret, C., 'Basville et l'épiscopat de Languedoc', *Annales du Midi*, 6 (1894), 420–64; 7 (1895), 5–50

Lamouzèle, Edmond, *Essai sur l'organisation et les fonctions de la compagnie de guet et de la garde bourgeoise de Toulouse*. Paris, 1906

Lapierre, Eugène, *Le Parlement de Toulouse*. Paris, 1875

Laroque, Louis de, *Armorial de la noblesse de Languedoc*, 3 vols. Toulouse and Montpellier, 1860–3; repr. Marseilles, 1972

Le Roy Ladurie, Emmanuel, *Histoire du Languedoc*. 2nd edn. Paris, 1967

Les Paysans de Languedoc, 2 vols. Paris, 1966

The Peasants of Languedoc, tr. John Day. Urbana, Ill., 1974

Lexpert, Albert, *L'Organisation judiciaire de l'ancien pays de Vivarais*. Aubenas, 1921

Lowenstein, Steven, 'Resistance to Absolutism: Huguenot Organization in Languedoc 1621–1622', Ph.D. diss., Princeton, 1972

Maistre, André, *Le Canal des deux mers: canal royal du Languedoc 1666–1810*. Toulouse, 1968

Mesuret, Robert, *Évocation du vieux Toulouse*. Paris, 1960

Michel, Albin, *Nîmes et ses rues*. Nîmes, 1876

Miron de l'Espinay, A., *Robert Miron et l'administration municipale de Paris de 1614 à 1616*. Paris, 1922

Monin, Henri, *Essai sur l'histoire administrative du Languedoc pendant l'intendance de Basville (1685–1719)*. Paris, 1884

Morineau, Michel and Charles Carrière, 'Draps du Languedoc et commerce du Levant au XVIIIe siècle', *Revue d'histoire économique et sociale*, 46 (1968), 108–21

Mours, Samuel, *Le Protestantisme en France au XVIIe siècle (1598–1685)*. Paris, 1967

Palm, Franklin Charles, *Politics and Religion in Sixteenth-Century France: a Study of the Career of Henry of Montmorency-Damville, Uncrowned King of the South*. Boston, 1927

Paris, H. G., *Histoire de la ville de Lodève, de son ancien diocèse et de son arrondissement actuel*..., 2 vols. Montpellier, 1851

Paulhet, Jean-Claude, 'Les Parlementaires toulousains à la fin du XVIIe siècle', *Annales du Midi*, 76 (1964), 189–204

Pegat, Ferdinand, 'Des consuls de Montpellier sous l'autorité des fonctionnaires royaux et notamment pendant les années 1640 à 1657', *Académie des Sciences et Lettres de Montpellier: Mémoires Section des Lettres*, 5 (1870–73), 567–608

Porée, Charles, *Le Consulat et l'administration municipale de Mende (des origines à la Révolution)*. Paris, 1901

Puech, Albert, *Une ville au temps jadis ou Nîmes à la fin du XVIe siècle d'après le compoix de 1592 et des documents inédits*. Nîmes, 1884

Puntous, Th., *Un Diocèse civil de Languedoc: les états particuliers du diocèse de Toulouse aux XVIIe et XVIIIe siècles*. Toulouse, 1909

Ramet, Henri, *Le Capitole et le Parlement de Toulouse*. Toulouse, 1926.

Ramière de Fortanier, Jean, *Chartes de Franchises du Lauragais*. Paris, 1939

Renard, E., 'Les Postes en Languedoc', *Annales du Midi*, 46 (1934), 122–60, 256–74, 360–96

Roques, Henri, *L'Administration municipale à Toulouse de 1693 à 1699*. Toulouse, 1908

Roschach, Ernest, *Les Douze livres de l'histoire de Toulouse*. Toulouse, 1887

'Henri d'Aguesseau, intendant de Languedoc', *Mémoires de l'Académie des Sciences de Toulouse*, 7th series 7 (1875), 576–92

Histoire générale de Languedoc par Dom Claude Devic et Dom J. Vaissete. vol. XIII (continuation to 1790). Toulouse, 1876

Rossignol, Élie A., *Assemblées du diocèse de Castres*. Toulouse, 1878

Petits États d'Albigeois, ou assemblées du diocèse d'Albi. Paris, 1875

Sabatier, E., *Histoire de la ville et des évêques de Béziers*. Béziers, 1854

Sahuc, Joseph, *Un ami de Port-Royal: messire Pierre-Jean-François de Percin de Montgaillard, évêque de Saint-Pons (1633–1665–1713)*. Paris, 1909

Sahuqué de Goty, Louis, 'Une rivalité sous Richelieu: Évêque de Lavaur et mq d'Ambres 1637–1646', *Revue du Tarn*, 25 (1908), 325–38

Santi, L. de, 'Le Combat de Souilhe (3 novembre 1627)'; 'Le Château de Montmaur'; 'La Maison de Lévis-Montmaur', *Mémoires de l'Académie des Sciences de Toulouse*, 10th series 2 (1902), 150–72, 295–320, 351–76

Sauzet, Robert, *Contre-réforme et réforme catholique en Bas-Languedoc: le diocèse de Nîmes au XVIIe siècle*. Brussels, 1979

'Miracles et Contre-Réforme en Bas-Languedoc sous Louis XIV', *Revue d'histoire de la spiritualité*, 48 (1972), 179–92

Sicard, Roger, *L'Administration capitulaire sous l'ancien régime: Toulouse et ses capitouls sous la Régence*. Toulouse, 1953

Sol, Marguerite, *Claude de Rebé, archevêque de Narbonne*. Paris, 1891

Soucaille, Antonin, 'Le Consulat de Béziers', *Bulletin de la Société Archéologique de Béziers*, 3rd series 1 (1895–6), 217–504

Thomas, Louis-J., *Montpellier ville marchande: histoire économique et sociale de Montpellier des origines à 1870*. Montpellier, 1936

Thomson, J. K. J., *Clermont-de-Lodève 1633–1789: Fluctuations in the Prosperity of a Languedocian Cloth-Making Town*. Cambridge, 1982

Thoumas-Schapira, Micheline, 'La Bourgeoisie toulousaine à la fin du XVIIe siècle', *Annales du Midi*, 67 (1955), 313–20
Trouvé, Baron, *Essai historique sur les états-généraux de la province de Languedoc*, 2 vols. Paris, 1818
Viala, André, *Le Parlement de Toulouse et l'administration royale laïque 1420–1525 environ*, 2 vols. Albi, 1953
Vialles, Pierre, *De l'administration du Languedoc avant 1789*. Montpellier, 1889
Études historiques sur la Cour des Comptes, Aides et Finances de Montpellier, d'après ses archives privées. Montpellier, 1921
Vidal, Auguste, 'Un évêque de Lavaur au XVIIe siècle', *Revue du Tarn*, 5 (1884–5), 328–33, 358–64
'Passages de troupes à Lavaur sous les règnes de Louis XIII et de Louis XIV', *Revue du Tarn*, 4 (1882–3), 25–30, 38–44
Vidal, Jacques, *L'Équivalent des aides en Languedoc*. Montpellier, 1963
Virieux, Maurice, 'Une Enquète sur le parlement de Toulouse en 1718', *Annales du Midi*, 87 (1975), 37–51
Vitalis, A., 'Fleury, les origines – la jeunesse', *Annales du Midi*, 18 (1906), 40–62
Wolff, Philippe, *Histoire de Toulouse*, 2nd edn. Toulouse, 1961
Wolff, Philippe, ed., *Histoire du Languedoc*. Toulouse, 1967
Wolff, Philippe, *Regards sur le Midi médiéval*. Toulouse, 1978

Index

Index